CYBERWAR:

SECURITY, STRATEGY, AND CONFLICT IN THE INFORMATION AGE

Contributing editors:

Alan D. Campen
Douglas H. Dearth
R. Thomas Goodden

AFCEA International Press
Fairfax, Virginia

AFCEA International Press is the book publishing arm of AFCEA, publisher of *SIGNAL* Magazine. Acquisitions and General Editorship of AIP books are under the direction of Colonel Alan D. Campen, USAF, (Ret.)

Book and jacket design by Donna Seward and Alan Campen
Illustration of Sun Tzu by Daniel M. Armstrong, *Airpower Journal*

May 1996

Published by AFCEA International Press (AIP)
4400 Fair Lakes C ourt
Fairfax, Virginia 22033-3899 USA
(703) 631-6100 or (800) 336-6100 ISBN 0-916159-26-4

9 8 7 6 5 4 3 2

Library of Congress Cataloging-in-Publication Data

Cyberwar: security, strategy, and conflict in the information age / contributing editors, Alan D. Campen, Douglas H. Dearth, R. Thomas Goodden.

p. 298 cm.

Includes bibliographical references

1. Information warfare. 2. Information superhighway. 1. Campen, Alan D. II. Dearth, Douglas H. III. Goodden, R. Thomas.

U163.C94 1996

355..3'43- -dc20 96-19365

CIP

This book is dedicated to the first line of defense—the system and network administrators.

CONTENTS

Part Three: Organizing for Cyberwar

Part Four: Warfare in the Information Age

Preface

The information Age presages excitement and uncertainty, promise and peril, and risk and opportunity to the valiant who venture out onto the digital superhighway. For we are pilgrims all: private citizens eager to explore the Internet—but fretful that our rights may be abused and our privacy violated; businesses obliged to embrace information technology to remain competitive—yet fearful of exposure to theft of proprietary strategies and designs; even nation-states searching for a new security sanctuary—but in a cyber-realm that offers no comforting geographic buffers.

All of us—citizen, soldier and entrepreneur—are, so to speak, fellow voyagers, and we should be curious about the condition of our vehicle, the skills of its designers and operators, and about any obstacles we may encounter. But where to turn for "truth" about this unprecedented journey into an inchoate *virtual* world?

The functions of human enterprise rapidly are being digitized, interconnected over networks, and stored and processed within information systems having only the most rudimentary safeguards against disruption or manipulation—accidental, intentional, or malicious. Yet our enthusiasm for and burgeoning dependence upon computers and communications is accompanied by a perplexing indifference to the uncertainties and risks of conducting our most private affairs over electronic systems that can so easily be monitored, penetrated, disrupted, altered or terminated: anonymously and with impunity. What are the dependencies and risks? Are there safeguards?

It is the policy of our government that the design, development, ownership and operation of the National Information Infrastructure (NII)—which is the U.S. portion of and our ramp into the Global Information Infrastructure (GII)—be guided and shaped by the *informed choices of educated customers,* as expressed by their purchases in a competitive marketplace. In sum, policy presumes that requirements for the design and operation of the NII will be provided by customers who: 1) appreciate the value of their digitized property to others; 2) comprehend the technical means by which that property can be held at risk; 3) understand the alternatives available to protect that intellectual property from misuse. But are we consumers sufficiently informed to make wise choices?

AFCEA is pleased to offer this anthology on risks, challenges and solutions in the information age: articles and essays prepared by academicians, government and military officials, scientists, philosophers, educators, and commentators—people who's job is to contemplate these complex, unprecedented and controversial matters.

These experts do not always agree: there are far too many uncertainties, and information technology is exploding too rapidly for the prudent to risk prediction. However, we do believe it is time to add balance to the hype and hubris that characterizes so much of the discussion and media coverage of life in the information age.

Alan D. Campen
Manager AFCEA International Press

Introduction

This anthology begins with the insight of the physicist, scholar and lecturer who introduced the phrase "information warfare" to our lexicon in 1976—a time when the nation was preoccupied with the threat of nuclear war. Dr. Thomas Rona reminds us that the principal weakness in military ventures always has been logistics, and that "information" is the *fodder* of modern warfare—with threats aimed not just at warriors in combat, but at the civilian information infrastructure as well. The security of these "infrastructures"—civil as well as military—is the focus of this book.

Part One

The Information Age in Historical Perspective

The Information Age has come under the view of historians who are well-grounded in the agricultural and industrial revolutions, but who seem inattentive to the unique factors that are shaping the Information Revolution. ***Information Age/Information War*** is an historical analysis of the *information quotient* in military and geopolitical affairs; an era of fundamental and global change in intellectual, philosophical, cultural and social terms. This essay, by Douglas Dearth and Charles Williamson, examines the impact on the growing urban masses, huddled in under-developed countries, becoming aware of what they do and do not have, and, who are obliged to traverse the information highway "on foot."

Knowledge becomes the core of military power and the central resource of destructivity, rather than brute force.

The Revolution in Military Affairs: The Information Dimension takes the reader on a sweeping overview of the military role today, and what it might be like under varying interpretations of information warfare. Michael Brown begins with the synergistic effects of information on military operations, describing an Information-based revolution that is producing a new environment from technologies that already exist, and from weapons that have either been built, or are on the drawing board. He examines the impact of information technologies on intelligence (where most targets will be discovered), on logistics (where "just in time" means no expensive and vulnerable baggage train), on command and control (where simulation replaces sand tables and where command arrangements combine hierarchical and non-hierarchical processes); and, where "fire support" becomes precision strike.

A nation without an IW capability will be a nation without a military capability.

Alvin Toffler gave us the theory of the Three Waves, but this essay contends the Information Revolution predated and actually shaped the Agricultural and Industrial Revolutions. While the current literature on information war begins 2500 years ago with Sun Tzu, **War, Information and History: Changing Paradigms,** commences with an information-based culture over ten thousand years ago, where the power of hunter-gatherers was based on "knowing" not "owning," and there was no war. Elin Whitney-Smith writes about the social dynamics of information and war, and a series of Information Revolutions that changed how people defined themselves, and defined what people are willing to fight and die for.

Connecting people to an independent source of information will foster economic, political development, and individual identity.

Part Two

Cyberwar and society

Uncommon Means for the Common Defense is about the search for a new national security sanctuary in cyberspace. The National Information Infrastructure—which transports the bulk of government and military communications—will be built and owned by the private sector; in response to the requirements of poorly-informed customers; and by industries with little financial incentive to buttress what they build against malicious attacks. "It is precisely the standards designers use to make technology efficient that make it easy to attack." This essay argues that only strong federal guidance and funding can adequately secure the NII against the effects of information warfare.

The Federal Government is poorly organized and resourced to ensure adequate security of the NII.

Creating a Smart Nation: Information Strategy, Virtual Intelligence, and Information Warfare is a sweeping indictment of our national security posture. Robert Steele asserts that national security is at risk by confronting current threats with 19th century concepts; for preoccupation with digital technology; and by an intelligence community optimized, less for thoughtful analysis than for "the collecting of secrets." This essay examines structural and policy defects in the processes of intelligence, and calls for a National Information Strategy built upon political, military, economic and cultural objectives, to guide preparation for conflict in the Information Age. A transnational, "virtual intelligence structure" is proposed, employing *voluntary* participation across a broad spectrum of citizenry.

To survive in the 21st Century we must have a National Information Strategy.

Protecting the United States in Cyberspace is an alternative view of risks, threats and solutions by an expert who provides a balanced, objective assessment. Martin Libicki concludes the problem lies more in the "tomorrow" than in the "today," and that solutions lie in shared responsibility, not vesting in a "commander-in-chief" with a console of "buttons that attach to nothing." He calls for more perception and less panic about a very real, but as yet poorly defined threat, and provides a check-list of practical and do-able steps of things to do—and things not to do—to secure our networks, while there is yet time to do so. "Who should guard the NII? If it's yours, then you should."

The situation is desperate but not serious!

The Role of The Media is about a new reality where the media believes that it has not only a duty to report the news, but also has the power to influence events. James Adams is an experienced reporter who provides candid and detailed insights into how the media likely will react when it next goes to war. He portrays a world where "many of the political leaders...have no concept of the political and personal consequences of warfare...No true concept of the horrors of war...and few reporters and editors who have covered conventional conflicts." This essay describes a world where politicians are driven by newspaper headlines and the results of opinion polls which are formed by those very same headlines. This essay contains advice for public, political and military planners who must confront an evermore intrusive media, and opines that it would be foolhardy for any government to plan for the control of information in the event of tension or conflict. Instead, Adams argues, that attention be focused on the exploitation of Cyberspace: the potential for "huge force multiplication by inserting the right information in the right part of the network."

The selective and extraordinarily intense media focus is driving policy.

We live and work in a physical world where safety and well-being heavily depend upon the ability to fix people, things and transactions precisely and accurately in place and in time. Cyberspace knows no such boundaries and the potential for fraud, abuse, misuse in this virtual world are significant when jurisdictions cannot be determined. ***Grounding Cyberspace in the Physical World*** is about the use of the Global Positioning System to aid personal and network security by affixing a secure, precise and continuous location signature to all terminals, fixed or mobile. This could be used to control login access, locate perpetrators of cybercrimes, prevent spoofing, summon emergency services, or serve as an electronic notary. This essay by Dorothy Denning and Peter MacDoran describes technical capabilities, risks and safeguards as well as privacy considerations

An entity in Cyberspace will be unable to pretend to be anywhere other than where it actually is located.

In modern warfare, it is information technology that fuels modern tactics, but our current acquisition system is designed for large products that are stable in design and bought for more than a decade of use—hardly a blueprint for buying off-the-self items that will have a life of a few years at most. **New Approaches to DOD Information-Systems Acquisition** argues that the benefits of information warfare will be foreclosed unless some fundamental changes are made to the way we acquire information technology: a shift from thinking about *building* systems, to *buying* systems. Keys to this new approach are what Michael Loescher calls Pyramidal Programming; Cyclical Acquisition—a notion that AFCEA encouraged two decades ago—and Assembly Line Fielding.

Acquisition has become a tactical issue in the Information Age.

Business Strategies in the Information Age examines the role of government, trade, and industry associations in strengthening the NII; and about the predatory aspects of competition that chill cooperation among the many industries that must work together if the NII is to be safe and secure. How well equipped and motivated are those industries to produce a "system of systems" that will satisfy the disparate demands of the private and public sectors? Author Goodden asks—and provides some practical answers to the question—how can government and industry cooperate in the design and maintenance of a secure NII, without compromising competitive position and jeopardizing survival in the marketplace?

It is easier to writeoff loss than to take the heat for a marginally adequate network.

From InfoWar to Knowledge Warfare: Preparing for the Paradigm Shift is about commercial information warfare, and tells why some companies win and others lose. The information infrastructures of France and the U.S. are contrasted. This essay is about destabilization caused by InfoWar attacks and Professor Philippe Baumard provides real-world experiences to support his theories and recommendations for the paradigm shift from InfoWar to Knowledge Warfare. The author contends that *information* is not *knowledge;*, that we must understand the difference between 'knowledge' (a commodity) and 'knowing' (our sense-making skills);, and he urges creation of a "knowledge infrastructure"—a communal where demands and supplies of tangibles and intangibles would find their matches."

New businesses live on the brink of disaster.

Part Three

Organizing for Cyberwar

Entrepreneurs and warriors face the same problems in applying information systems to any enterprise. This essay is about the design of resilent systems—military and business—that can function under uncertainty, be that from human error, system failure, or malicious attack. The shift from industrial warfare to information-based warfare has brought unrecognized dependencies and risks that are not understood and, therefore, not well managed. But, they could be says Ronald Knecht in ***Thoughts About Information Warfare***. He explains the profound but unrecognized impact upon any enterprise when the computer is introduced into the normal business model, opening that enterprise to interference, and surrendering configuration control to outsiders. A list of defensive and offensive tools and strategies is provided and assessed.

Understanding functional characteristics and dependencies is the best deterrent to attack.

Information Warfare is an appeal to think more broadly about the implications of information warfare, by going beyond the narrow definition of C^2W adopted by the Joint Chiefs of Staff. Professor George Stein writes about a new strategic level of warfare made possible by new technologies and their use to manipulate reality, rather than simply multiplying the power of conventional armed forces in combat. This essay describes the potential for altering reality with a "fictive" universe of altered data: replacing the opponents "known" universe with an "alternative reality." This essay is about defining and developing a strategy for information warfare, against new and dangerous non-state players in cyberspace who can wage attacks on a global basis.

It is the interaction of strategic vision with new technology that will produce the revolution in military affairs and a new warfare form.

Strategic Information Warfare and Comprehensive Situational Awareness also questions the wisdom and utility of the JCS decision to adopt C^2W as the military component of information warfare. Professor Daniel Kuehl contends that information warfare must reach out to encompass national-level political, economic, military and social systems—including diplomatic and economic actions—by destructive or non-lethal military operations. He argues that the narrow definition precludes discussion of the legal, political and interagency issues that are a part of a strategic perspective. A notional target set is postulated for strategic information warfare.

Information Warfare will, almost by its nature, be conducted at the strategic level.

The Information Warfare Campaign provides a concept for planning an information war with a mix of sensors, targets, communications and weapons that are widely distributed, owned by many, and operated by all military services. Commander Mike Loescher asks how diverse assets—many of which are neither owned nor operated by the commander, nor even in-area—can be employed to appear to act as an effective force? He describes the concept of three grids—sensor, communications, weapons—operating across air, land, sea and space, that allow the commander to assign the right mix of resources to the tactical situation.

How to focus "borrowed" parts on the tactical problem? Answer: Grids!

In ***SOFTWAR***, TV reporter Chuck de Caro describes in chilling detail how global television has been used to shape a nation's will, and how vulnerable and defenseless the U.S. is to this new form of information warfare. He describes exactly how the medium of television—which defines events by viewer perception of images and sound, rather than reality—has been used to influence public thinking and behavior. This essay explains how, by instantly creating domestic political pressures, an opponent could preclude our political leadership from acting, thus freezing the U.S. military and rendering policy and military capabilities ineffectual. "Hatred had to be created artificially [to fan the fires of pan-Serbiasm] and the key instrument was television." The author believes that the U.S. has ignored the use of TV to positively influence the course of human events around the globe.

SOFTWAR: hostile use of television to shape another nation's will by changing its vision of reality.

Part Four

Warfare in the Information Age

Information Warfare: The Future is about the cooperation, rather than confrontation and "brute force," as an agent of change in the world of interconnected systems; and how, in the process, we can redefine our notions of security. John Petersen describes himself as a "futurist" and his essay portrays a world where systems must "cooperate" rather than "compete;" where the contest over information is not a "zero-sum" game; and, where our industrial-age experiences and tools will not be effective. It is a world where ideas, messages, and admonitions are focused on individuals and groups, who never figure out that they have been soldiers in a battle: unwitting "victims" of subliminal communications. He asks how one can plan for change when "everything is connected to everything else," and all systems are "out of control?" He says that the process of getting all of the parts of a complex system to work together requires communications—knowledge must be shared—with little concern over cultural or political boundaries.

We may not know that we have been attacked, and that we lost.

Information warfare is a revolutionary strategy that can strengthen our national security apparatus by enhancing the effectiveness of our military forces. But the rush to a new form of conflict is risky because it rests on new, poorly understood, controversial and unproved assumptions and strategies about our ability to dominate the information spectrum. ***Rush to Information-Based Warfare Gambles with National Security*** describes a quest for a strategy that is impeded by the lack of historical precedent, common definitions, doctrine, guiding principles, and a national-level policy to integrate and synchronize military initiatives with complementary actions of non-defense activities. This essay contrasts IW with "resource-based warfare"—a proven strategy that made minimal demands on national intellect or foresight, and was forgiving of an apathetic public and procrastinating political leaders—for one which depends on the agility and decisive firepower of a smaller force that has been empowered and effectively enlarged through superior knowledge.

Converting information technology into military capability risks ceding strategic advantage to low-tech adversaries.

A Theory of Information Warfare: Preparing for 2020, is about epistemological warfare and and the moral and ethical risks of this form on conflict directed, not necessarily against military forces, but against the adversary's knowledge and belief systems. Richard Szafranski argues that the adversary is subdued by IW when he behaves in ways that are coincident with the ways in which we intend for him to behave. This essay describes IW at the *operational* and the *strategic* levels, and suggests that the Congress may conclude that employment at the operational level is useful and necessary, but employment against noncombatants, or their employment at the strategic level is wrong. The essay examines the ethical, moral and legal aspects of conflict that cannot discriminate between combatants and noncombatants, and where the interposition of a false reality ultimately may be wrongful and inhumane

The profession of arms in a democracy is not exempt from oversight or from consideration of just conduct, even in warfare.

Ethical Conundra of Information Warfare. With every grisly detail of our military activities covered by television, and viewed by the family over the dinner hour, the U.S. seeks tools and methods for a "clean war," and it has invented a host of "non-lethal" techniques, among which is Information Warfare. But, Winn Schwartau asks, is IW really non-lethal—disrupting a nations power, transportation and banking system, for example—if these might violate the political, social and ethical consciences of our own nation, as well as our friends. He believes the U.S. should face the ethical consequences of this form of conflict now, and announce to the world our intentions on how we will fight and defend ourselves in the Information Age. This essay

Is Information Warfare a potential step which can lead to an escalation to a military conflict that was meant to be avoided in the first place?

presents several hypothetical scenarios for the employment of Information Warfare, and invites the reader to contemplate the ethical issues.

The U.S. already is arming itself with weapons and tactics that demand more than the serendipitous flow and incidental exploitation of information.

Coming to Terms With Information Warfare, by Alan Campen is an essay about the varying and often contradictory interpretations of the meaning, intent and weapons, targets, and tactics of Information Warfare. It also discusses the assumptions, uncertainties and risks to ourselves—as the most dependent of nations upon vulnerable information systems—if we employ some of these tools and methods in ways that have no doctrinal, ethical, legal, or moral precedents. The varying terms are explained and the underlying assumptions of each tested for dependencies and vulnerabilities. The essay provides a simple test to determine the meaning and implications of the often-conflicting terminology, and provides conclusions and recommendations.

A model for government-industry cooperation to secure the public network.

While the public ponders the unsettling questions about vulnerabilities to the nation's information infrastructure, a little-known agency—born in response to earlier concerns about the health of the nations communications structure—has quietly moved to address the multiple challenges of deregulation of the telecommunications industry, and the nations growing dependence upon a vulnerable *Public Network*. ***Information Assurance: Implications to National Security and Emergency Preparedness***, by James Kerr of the National Communications System staff, describes the work underway, in cooperation with industry, to assess this nations dependencies upon "information assurance," and the actions needed to deter, prevent, or mitigate attacks on the public network. This essay reports on the conclusions of several recent assessments of security weaknesses in the public network, and on changes in the FY1996 National Defense Authorization Act, calling for a national policy and an architecture for an indications and warning center to detect attacks on the National Information Infrastructure.

From Scorched Earth to Information Warfare

THOMAS P. RONA

From prehistoric to modern times, the art and science of strategy was aimed at preventing the adversary from effectively marshaling his forces for use in the actual military engagements. Some of the strategy elements involve political, ideological or perceptual aspects by weakening the enemy's "will to fight," but here the focus of attention is on the connection between the military and economic aspects of strategy.

The onslaught of barbarians on the settled civilizations of Europe and the Far East was made possible by the remarkable evolution of an ancient "weapon platform"—the war horse. Instead of cumbersome chariots, small horses, capable of covering long distances with minimal logistics support, carried lightly armed warriors practically unopposed to victory against agricultural societies and ineffectually protected cities. The medieval civilizations reacted by building massive fortifications, with the territory and populations protected by a new class of armored knights. Gunpowder and siege artillery progressively required increased thickness of fortification walls, but more to the point here, the longbow, musketry and field artillery also rapidly increased the weight of protective armor to be carried by knights and war-horses alike. The powerful destroyers capable of serving as the essential of mobility and offensive momentum were vitally depended on grass or forage, hardly ever available under natural conditions in all seasons to support large-scale protracted military operations.

"Scorched earth" strategy consisted of devastating the countryside, so that the enemy could not find food for men or horses. It required no technological breakthroughs, no specialized training, no massive industrial base; but only the grim determination to overcome the enemy at all cost, including that of inflicting cruel sufferings on local populations. *It became the preferred choice of military strategists not otherwise equipped to resist the momentum of heavily armored cavalry.*

It was widely used for many centuries: By the Moslems opposing the Crusaders (1096 through 1204), by both sides in the Hundred Years War (1342-1450), by Peter the Great of Russia prior to his decisive victory over Charles XII of Sweden at Poltava (1709), by the Spanish guerrillas against the powerful armies of Napoleon's generals (1803-1808), and by the Russians forcing Napoleon's Grand Army to ignominious and disastrous retreat from Moscow (1812).

In all these cases, the logistic support required by horses as well as by men became the limiting factor in military operations. Whoever managed to interrupt or destroy this support could gain important, and often decisive, strategic advantage.

A famous example is offered by the daring descent of Sir Francis Drake on the coast of Spain in 1587. Having entered the Port of Cadiz, he managed to destroy not only large tonnage of shipping, but also the whole stock of seasoned oak staves to the used for the barrels of the Spanish Armada's water supply. The barrels made of unseasoned replacement staves leaked to the point that the Armada's mission was seriously (and it turned out, fatally) impaired.

With the scale of violence rapidly increasing and with the progress in transportation technology, railroads became new targets for strategic offensive action. In the U.S. Civil War and in the Franco-Prussian War the destruction of railroads and of rolling stock were primary strategic objectives, while horses remained still vital for tactical mobility and supply lines.

In the present century, trucks progressively replaced horses, but railroads, bridges and tunnels still remained important strategic targets. With the advent of industrialization, war production facilities began to compete with the massive military transportation needs for attention by planners of strategic missions. Only the lack of long-range means of weapon delivery precluded strategic attacks against industrial facilities in World War I.

With the development of long-range bombers and missiles, destruction of transportation and production facilities deep within enemy territory became the essential strategic objective in World War II. Typical of such strategic missions were the German "blitz" against England, the Allied air attack against Germany, the German pilotless aircraft and rocket attacks against England and the U.S. bombing of Japan. The epitome of this trend was reached in the Cold War period with ballistic missiles of intercontinental range, carrying nuclear warheads, threatening to inflict "unacceptable damage" to military as well as to urban/industrial targets. The legendary U.S. Strategic Air Command with its bombers and ICBMs, jointly with the Navy's SLBMs, have for almost five decades shouldered the responsibility for this mission. Collateral threat to civilian population was recognized as inseparable from deterrence or retaliation, but accepted as part of the military necessity, while publicly and piously deplored as being unavoidable.

For several of the recent past centuries the concept of strategic attack against the supply sources, the logistics and, more recently, against war production facilities has been accepted and endorsed by the exponents of military science as well as by the planners of military missions. The "scorched earth" principle has withstood the test of time, the advances in technology, and the stupendous growth in the scale of military conflicts.

In the lurid imagery of general nuclear warfare, an important, and perhaps vital, further evolution apparently escaped public attention. The national cohesion and the production potential of modern societies depend on the cultural and physical attributes of their industrial base, but also increasingly on the supporting information infrastructure. This term is used to designate the hardware and software of all civilian and military communications links, terminals and networks, decision nodes, data storage/retrieval components, and the participating human operators. The modern version of the *scorched earth principle becomes logically the destruction, incapacitation and corruption of the enemy's information infrastructure*. This aspect of "information warfare" has the side benefit for the attacker to create confusion, panic and irrationality among the civilian target population, further contributing to the weakening of its political "will-to-fight." It can be applied surreptitiously, without massive destruction of cities or other economic assets.

Information warfare aimed at the civilian information infrastructure may be the next major innovation in the domain of strategic warfare. The concepts and techniques for attacking the information infrastructure are well known to the technical community; they are available to potentially hostile groups ranging from private individuals (saboteurs or terrorists) through small nations to regional powers not willing to abide by the principles of peaceful cooperation with their neighbors, or harboring implacable hostility against the wealthy nations such as the U.S. and its Allies. Precisely because of their technical sophistication and the advertised reliance of their military power and civilian activity on the information infrastructure, the Western-style nations are quite vulnerable to information warfare, as compared to more primitive adversaries.

For all we know, strategic application of information warfare may be already part of the thinking of some of our potential adversaries. Those responsible for planning our future national security may do well by accounting for this possibility.

Information Age/Information War

Douglas H. Dearth and Charles A. Williamson

Where Are We in History?

The central thesis of this article and of this book is that we are experiencing fundamental historical change on a global basis. The scope of this change is, in a sense, not historically unprecedented, but it is significant. In retrospect, the change now occurring in the world will easily rank with 1815, 1919, and 1945 in "modern" political and military terms, and perhaps with the Reformation and the Renaissance in intellectual, philosophical, cultural and social terms.

"Post-X" Labels

The opening of the Berlin Wall in November 1989, followed seemingly inevitably by the abortive Soviet coup in August 1990 and then by the relinquishment of Communist Party power in Moscow in December of that year, will be viewed in broad historical perspective as constituting a major watershed in world history. The events we are now witnessing will rank among the defining moments of the modern era. These events—while philosophically and emotionally satisfying to the democratic West—do not automatically herald a bright new day, an "end to history,"[1] or the unalloyed promise connoted by the already shopworn term "New World Order." Rather, the current era is characterized by political, demographic, and economic instability and uncertainty. We are witnessing, perhaps, "the end of *one kind of history*."[2]

One of our contemporary difficulties just now is how to characterize our time. In daily professional interchange and in media and academic discourse, we commonly use such terms as "Post-Cold War Era," "Post-Bipolar World," "Post-Industrial Economy," and "Post-Capitalist Society." Some commentators speak of a "Post-Westphalian Age" in describing the erosion of traditional concepts of the nation-state and sovereignty.

Each of these terms is to a degree descriptive, and they certainly are evocative; but they are not positive evocations of our time. They simply tell us where we think we have been, not where we are, and certainly not where we are going as states, as nations, as societies, or as human beings.

The only term that seems to be reasonably useful and accurate in describing our times and our challenges is: *Information Age*. For it is information—and perhaps more properly *knowledge*—that is the driving imperative of our time.[3] This article will attempt to come to grips with some of the characteristics and implications of this phenomenon and attempt to set the stage for a series of assessments concerning implications for modern societies in the early 21st Century and for the age-old profession of arms.

Traditional Historians

Interestingly enough, the information quotient in military and geopolitical affairs has not until very recent times been a focus of historical analysis. Analysis of change in human affairs and the development of warfare have highlighted all manner of industrial, technological and organizational phenomena, principally having to do with firepower, logistics and supply. The impact of the industrial, production, and management revolutions are duly noted and analyzed. Leadership and command studies abound. But nary a word about the impact of information.

For instance, in his otherwise excellent and ambitious study, *A History of Warfare*, John Keegan highlights the influences in different eras of fortification, organization, logistics and supply, but not a word on information or intelligence.[4] In the likewise comprehensive and perceptive *War and the Rise of the State*, Bruce D. Palmer notes the historical "ratchet effect" of war, taxation, and state growth in analyzing the evolution of the nation-state in its modern and contemporary collectivist, welfare, and totalitarian guises. Technical revolutions are duly noted, but not a word on information.[5] The Israeli scholar Martin Van Creveld has written excellent studies of the roles of technology, command, and supply in war, but his recent *The Transformation of War* contains no mention of the influence of information and its centrality to modern conflict.[6] Similarly, Sir Michael Howard's learned and otherwise excellent survey of war in the modern era, *The Lessons of History*, contains no specific reference to the information revolution in the industrial age.[7]

Historical Eras & Revolutionary Epochs

Academic descriptions of Man's progress over the past 50,000 years essentially have been economic. The terms Stone Age, Iron Age, and Bronze Age describe Man's progress in mastering basic natural elements with increasing sophistication to the end of providing an improved ability to sustain his basic physical needs and those of his family and community. The terms Agricultural Revolution and Industrial Revolution describe Man's further progress and mastery of technology to harness nature and his environment for his increased material well-being. In fact, the Industrial Age, beginning roughly around 1700 A.D., can be further differentiated in terms of the Industrial Revolution, the Productivity Revolution, the Management Revolution, and the Information Revolution. In the process, each successive stage of the Industrial Revolution also fundamentally changed the ongoing Agricultural Revolution through industrialization, productivity, and managerial improvements. Meanwhile, each successive stage of the Industrial Era fundamentally changed the meaning of industrialization. Now, we increasingly speak of a full-fledged Information Age and Information Revolution, which in turn changes all that went before in human development.

The most interesting thing about Man's economic and technological development is the *accelerating rate of change*. Each successive era is significantly shorter than the one before it. Consider just the Industrial Age. In hindsight, we can see that the first phase, that of fundamental Industrial Revolution, lasted from around 1700-1750, during which period *technology* was *invented*, to about 1880, about a century-and-a-half. Its successor, the Productivity Revolution, lasted from 1880 to around 1945, or just sixty-five years. In turn, its successor, the Management Revolution is thought to have lasted until about 1970, or only about twenty-five years. With the advent of the micro-processor, we are in (or might have even already passed through) another significant era, one dominated by Information or Knowledge.[8] From its beginning less than three centuries ago, the rate of technological change was been incredibly swift and frequently wrenching in its impact on society.

Tri-sected Worlds

While Information and Knowledge are the principal drivers in the world economy and culture, in fact we live in a tri-sected world and, indeed, tri-sected national societies. Agricultural, industrial, and information economies (the Tofflers' First, Second, and Third Waves) coexist, just as in the previous era agricultural and industrial economies coexisted. Only now the mix is more complex, and the differentiation is more important in terms of international and intra-national interaction. In the final analysis, there is concern that the differentiation is also potentially more explosive.[9]

The principal discriminator among economic classes of citizens and of nations is information: access to it and the ability to manipulate it. Robert Reich identifies three broad categories of workers in the Information Age: routine production services, in-person services, and symbolic-analytic services.[10] Drucker distinguishes between "service workers" and "knowledge workers."[11] The common concern of these writers is the broadening gaps within societies between these categories of workers in terms of well-being and identification with community. There is also concern on a broader level in terms of inter-national relations among societies.

Information Age

Knowledge Explosion

Many commentators speak of the information explosion. It is the view of the authors that it is, rather, the *interaction* of the information *and* the knowledge explosions, along with attendant developments in telecommunications and micro-processing technology, and basic demographic trends that produce the defining characteristics of the Information Age. More scientists are alive today than have lived collectively in the history of civilization, and all of them are creating knowledge in their respective fields at record rates that ultimately will impact the rest of humankind. More and more fields of specialization are being created, and there are now more fields of cross-specialization. Thus, there is not only more "net" knowledge, but also more complex knowledge. Disparities in access to the global information infrastructure will likely mean that this knowledge will not be equally accessible to all the individuals who are affected by it. *The ability to access and interact is critical.*

Compare the "knowledgeable" person of the late 20th Century with, say, Thomas Jefferson, a true Renaissance Man of the late 18th Century. Jefferson, not atypical of his class and time, was highly knowledgeable in the fields of agronomy, architecture, surveying, the law, politics, modern and classical languages, and science. Yet today, simply by regularly reading cover-to-cover the Sunday *New York Times* and the weekly *Economist* a person could conceivably know more about a greater number of things than could Jefferson. However, it is impossible to reach the level of proficiency in mastering the available knowledge of our time as did Jefferson in his, nor could we have that knowledge readily available in our personal library. The potential ability that we do have is the capacity to selectively access needed—and voluminous—knowledge via the Internet and other automated information retrieval systems.

Population Explosion

To help understand the profound changes that are occurring in the world and in our own society, it is important to look at these changes in terms of certain on-going global demographic trends. The first of these is *asymmetrical population growth.* Using generally accepted population growth estimates, the population of the developed countries of the world will increase by about 12.5% between now and the year 2025. By these same estimates, the population of the less-developed countries will increase by 75%, and by 143% in the least-developed of those countries. Put another way, the total world population is projected to grow from something over 5 billion today to 8.5 billion in the year 2025. During this period, 97% of the total growth in world population will occur in the less developed areas. These figures also portend a lowering of the median age of the population in the less developed world, in some cases to the point where in some countries the number of individuals under the age of 16 could easily exceed the number of individuals over age 30.[12] According to Peter Schwartz, by the year 2001 there will be over 2 billion teenagers in the world, most of them living in Asia and Latin America.[13] Imagine trying to get a telephone call through to someone's home in Mexico City or Beijing when that happens! Of course, the political, social, and economic implications will be far more serious than this mundane example.

Related to this trend is increasing *global urbanization.* Between now and 2025, the urban population of the world will more than double, to some 5.1 billion. Again, the less developed regions of the world will experience the greatest rate of urban growth. By the year 2000, the urban population of Africa will have doubled from what it was in 1985. Absolute growth during this period will be greatest in Asia, where cities will gain some 500 million people. Not only will more people live in cities, the cities in which they live will get bigger. Large urban agglomerations—areas comprising a central city or cities surrounded by a definable urban area—are increasing in number. In 1985, 60% of the urban agglomerations of over two million people were in the less developed world. The U.N. estimates that: in the year 2000, there will be 45 urban agglomerations of over 5 million people, again located primarily in the less developed world. By 2025, Latin America will be 85% urban; Africa 58%; and Asia, 53%.[14] In this sense—and likely in this sense alone—Latin American demographic concentrations will approximate those common in Western Europe, North America, and Japan.

The twin trends of population growth and urbanization in the less developed world are putting great stress on both the environment and on traditional social and administrative infrastructures. In some countries, particularly in Africa, those infrastructures are breaking down altogether. The experiences of Liberia and Sierra Leone are but the most obvious and most extreme examples of this trend. While a causal relationship is difficult to prove, it seems intuitively obvious that the increasing religious, tribal and ethnic conflict worldwide is related to more people competing for increasingly scarce resources in an environment where central authorities are less and less able to impose their will on the populations. Alternatively, of course, these same central authorities may attempt to redraw borders as a means of acquiring scarce resources or redressing perceived inequities. In any case, it is apparent that the world is experiencing increased inter- and intra-national violence, albeit often at levels below that which we normally associate with "war."

The result of this conflict is a growing number of refugees and internally-displaced persons, again primarily (but not exclusively) in the less developed world. In 1951, there were an estimated 1.5 million refugees—defined as "any person who, owing to a well-founded fear of being persecuted for reasons of race, religion, nationality, membership of a particular social group, or political opinion, is outside the country of his nationality and is unable, or owing to such a fear, is unwilling to avail himself of the protection of that country." By 1992, this number had grown to 15 million. If one adds "refugee-like" persons—those who are of ambiguous status residing outside their national borders—persons internally displaced by violence within their own countries, the number jumps to 42.5 million.[15] Such population displacement further strains existing infrastructures and of itself creates new "urban" areas in the form of refugee camps. Rwandan refugee "cities" in Zaire and Tanzania are examples of this new phenomenon. Indeed, as this is written, second only to Dar Es-Salaam, the second largest "city" in Tanzania is not a city at all, but the cluster of Rwandan refugee camps near Ngama. At its height, the refugee camps at Goma constituted the third largest "urban" area in Zaire. The perception of relative deprivation will be inescapable. While many of these refugees may eventually return home, those who do not return typically gravitate to urban areas in their host country.

Of note, the figure of 42.5 million does not include the countless additional millions of "economic migrants" who leave their homes or countries in search of better jobs or living conditions. Almost all such individuals move to urban areas, putting demands on host-nation social services and competing for jobs on the bottom rungs of the national economic ladder. The result frequently is social, ethnic, and racial resentments and strife.

What is important here, in terms of the Information Age, is that each of the growing number of urban areas in the less developed world will increasingly come to function as communication nodes, offering at least some access to the global information infrastructure for their inhabitants. Individuals in such areas will increasingly be "informed" (as opposed to knowledgeable) of events taking place around the globe. Be it propaganda broadcast via radio to ethnic groups, soap opera reruns on television or Internet connectivity, the increased flow of information to and within these urban areas as a result of the growth of information technologies will likely have very profound effects. In short, people in less-developed societies will be increasingly made aware of what they do not have.

Accelerating Rates of Change

Demassification & Profusion of Information Media. Advances in information technology have produced significant changes in the mass communications environment. The authors remember their childhood in Ohio at mid-century, listening to the Lone Ranger on the radio. Later, in the early 1950s, they found out what he and Tonto *really* looked like by watching a snowy, flickering blue image on a small screen housed in a wooden box. By the 1960s, most homes in suburban America had a television that brought in all three networks, providing a choice of three programs at any given time when local stations were on the air—typically between 7 a.m. and 11 p.m. With the advent of UHF broadcasting, the number of available programs increased. But it was in 1980 with the advent of CNN 24-hour news and cable access, that the change in our viewing habits really came about. And not just in the U.S. Ten years ago in Western Europe, the average citizen had one or two television channels available, usually operating under some sort of government sponsorship or control. Today, there are 96 channels available to most Europeans, although the typical European cable company provides "only" a few dozen.

Interestingly, as the electronic media continue to proliferate, print media are declining. Most major cities that fifty years ago had several thriving newspapers are down to one or two; smaller cities and towns still have a local paper, but one that is increasingly devoted primarily to local issues. The reason is that television is dominating the news and entertainment businesses, nationally and internationally. In the U.S., our "national newspaper" *USA Today* uses a television-like format and satellite technology to print the same stories at various locations around the country simultaneously, adding only a little local advertising. Even hard-core news addicts, who once tended to pore over the *New York Times* or the *Washington Post* daily as a source of "in-depth" coverage of particular issues, are turning to the Internet for their access. Although the print news media may be facing hard times, the age of print is not dead. A visit to the magazine section of any bookstore, grocery, or druggist will reveal a plethora of magazines on every imaginable subject and interest. A major source of information, even for the hard-core electronic enthusiast, is an increasing number of hard-copy magazines such as *Wired*, *PC World*, etc. In short, we are rapidly moving away from what we used to think of as "mass" media to an array of more specialized sources of information, including "niche" publications. In both print and electronic formats, we are witnessing the trend toward "narrow-casting" rather than broadcasting. We are experiencing, in fact, a *demassification of the mass media.*

Computing Power & Communications Capacity. Computing power has seen a relatively steady growth since the first days of the vacuum-tube UNIVAC-style main-frame machines. This processor has continued through development of the transistor and of the microprocessor. Just as computing power increased three orders of magnitude between 1940 and 1960 and again between 1960 and 1980, projections of growth by 2030 call for another six orders of magnitude. In fact, computing power doubles about every two years, as those of you who want to run Windows 95 on a 386 PC are painfully aware. According to Moore's Law, this has been happening since 1965.[16] The cost of computing power continues to drop dramatically, yet worldwide chip revenues in recent years have risen even more so. Even without a Cray, vast numbers of bits are crunched every day by millions of individuals around the world using office or home computers, including laptop PCs that they drag around with them. Anyone who has a PC has potential Internet access. Although exact numbers are unknown, it is believed that there are some 40 million Internet users, with literally thousands more being added every month. There are now in excess of 16 million home pages on the World Wide Web, a number that will be considerably out of date between the time these words are written and the time this book goes to press.

Yet in terms of volume of data, individuals using the Internet pale in comparison to software programs that rely on global communications to track delivery of packages, aircraft and automobile parts, airline reservations, stocks and bonds transactions, airline and hotel reservations, and—arguably most critical—money. Money no longer moves; *information about money* does. Global communications and the ATM have made plastic cards the coin of the realm worldwide. "Cyber-cash" might well be the wave of the future.

Global Connectivity. As more and more commercial broadcast satellites go into operation, virtually all areas of the globe will be within some satellite broadcast footprint. In fact, the U.S. has lagged behind somewhat in terms of direct broadcast satellite television simply because we were hard-wired to our cable earlier. Where cable companies did not exist, the expansion of satellite broadcasts grew more quickly. In any case, the result will be the same: more sources of information from which to choose. And despite the efforts of some governments such as China and Iran to control access to these information sources, small satellite dishes continue to sprout on the balconies of apartment buildings in Tehran and Canton. Realizing its inability to prevent homemade fabrication of the requisite 18-inch receive dishes across the south of China, the Chinese government decided to license their manufacture instead, a more farsighted—but fateful—policy than that of Iran.

At the same time television proliferates globally, inter-personal communication capacities will continue to grow. Fiber optic cable is being laid worldwide, providing huge communication capacities linking continents, countries, and most especially urban areas. Wireless technology will also continue to expand, providing connectivity to areas unreachable by twisted copper wires. It is estimated that global communication capacity will increase by six orders of magnitude by the year 2025. The growth in communication capacity has no apparent technical limits—rather it is limited by the economics of *demand*. In fact, the projected increase in communication capacity is based on estimates in the continued growth of computing power, which is also (not coincidentally) estimated to increase by six orders of magnitude in the same time frame. The growth in communication capacity far exceeds that needed for people to communicate with other people, as is confirmed by the fact that roughly one-third of the fiber optic cables laid in the U.S. remain "dark" at present. The capacity that is being built is for computers to "talk" to each other.

Information Superhighway

GII, NIIs and DIIs. The idea of global interconnectivity is still somewhat difficult for most to envision. Historically, "lines-of-communication" were two-dimensional, and thus relatively easily depicted on maps. Telegraph and telephone lines tended to follow roads and railroads; and even rivers, sea lanes and airways could be reduced by cartographers to lines on paper. National borders were similarly depicted. Today, however, in the era of satellites and cyberspace, it can be argued that lines-of-communication are three- or even four-dimensional, with information moving at the speed of light across national and geographic boundaries. We have difficulty understanding—much less graphically depicting—the non-spatial dimensions and attributes of "cyberspace."

It seems that as early as 1970, Ralph Lee Smith coined the term "electronic highway," envisioning a government-sponsored system of communications analogous to the interstate highway program that so changed America. The more recent and familiar term "information superhighway" was popularized by—among others—U.S. Vice President (then-Senator) Albert Gore in the 1980s. The "information superhighway" is, in fact, the Global Information Infrastructure (GII), of which various National Information Infrastructures (NIIs) are subsets. Defense Information Infrastructures (DIIs), in turn, are subsets of various NIIs, although in practical terms the latter two are increasingly difficult to identify separately, as more and more defense information traffic travels on non-military national infrastructures. In the U.S., more than 90% of the DII rides on the NII.

Stretch Limos/Hyundais/Motor-Scooters/Armed Pedestrian Gangs. Since the advent of the term "information superhighway," the analogy has been strained further by references to "potholes," "road-kill," "on- and off-ramps," etc. With awareness of the risks—and with some trepidation, we offer our own further analogies for the phenomenon of the "superhighway."

While traditional nation-state sovereignty may be eroding, it is still useful as a concept for identifying national groups or transnational businesses which, by dint of their corporate organization and revenues, benefit the economic well-being of a particular nation-state or group of states. Using this concept, traffic on the information superhighway is likely to consist of a goodly number of "stretch limousines," a lesser number of "Hyundais," a few "motor-scooters," and an as yet unknown number of hostile "armed pedestrian gangs."

In the "stretch limos" will be national and transnational consortia from Western Europe, North America, and Japan. By this, we mean that these societies will be fully equipped and wired to participate in the Information Revolution, with a sizable portion of their populations economically well-off, broadly literate and capable of exploiting these capabilities. Their ride on the superhighway will be relatively plush, comfortable and satisfying. A well-justified sense of contentment—indeed superiority—will prevail. And these societies will tend to deal financially, politically, and culturally with each other.

"Hyundais" are fully capable and functional machines. They transport their riders in adequate comfort, with comparatively little in the way of fancy accoutrements. In the "Hyundais" will be similar groups from the Pacific Rim (including China, Taiwan, and Singapore); probably only Israel in the Middle East; possibly some of the Eastern

European states such as Hungary, the Czech Republic and Russia; and also possibly a handful from Latin America (e.g., Chile, Brazil, Argentina, and Colombia). While putting Colombia and Russia on the "Hyundai" list might seem to be a reach, we have included them because of the huge amounts of money generated by narco-trafficking and other international criminal activities. Criminal groups in the two countries, like legitimate international businesses, increasingly rely on global telecommunications capabilities to facilitate their activities. In all cases, those who find themselves in "Hyundais" will be looking to "trade-up" to "stretch limos" as soon as possible, and some of them might succeed, particularly Singapore and Israel.

In the rest of the world, those less-developed countries where the bulk of the population growth will be occurring, only a micro-elite will even be able to ride "motor scooters." They will have the barest means of automated transportation, and the ride will not be very comfortable. They, too, will be looking to "trade-up" to four-wheeled transport, but their prospects are not so bright.

The vast majority of the world population will find themselves on foot, perhaps informed but not truly knowledgeable, and thus consigned to watching traffic go by. Because this pedestrian population is also likely to be armed, hostile—and increasingly beyond the control of national or international authorities—the information superhighway leading to the future is likely to be a pretty dangerous place.

Second Renaissance: The PC & the State

We cannot predict how the global information explosion will ultimately shape the world, but we can draw some lessons from the past. Controlling information—and thus knowledge—has always been important to traditional hierarchies. When Gutenberg in Mainz and Coster in Haarlem began printing by employing moveable type around 1445, their intent probably was not to start a revolution in human affairs. Rather, Gutenberg's intent in publishing the Christian Bible in 1457 was to glorify the Church and the Word of God. Within half a century, the result was just the opposite. By about 1500, there were an estimated 30,000 books set by moveable type in print, and they were not by any means all Church screeds. We now understand that the ability of a non-clerical (i.e., non-Roman Church) workforce to possess, understand, and disseminate *knowledge* changed the world forever. In retrospect, we understand that Gutenberg's noodling constituted not simply *invention*, but *discovery*. Technology removed information and knowledge from the determined grip of the Roman Church and delivered it to alternative powers. Ideas flourished, and old regimes went into decline where the new technology was not allowed to develop and proliferate (e.g., Spain and for some time France). New powers arose where the new information technology was embraced and allowed to flourish (e.g., England and Holland).

In our own time, a similar phenomenon is occurring. The electronic computer, the *personal* computer (or PC), is seizing power from the established order or simply establishing new orders of power with hardly a "by-your-leave." As a consequence, human society is experiencing a "step-change" of historic proportions. Just as the Church could no longer control social, philosophical, and scientific *truth* in the face of the printing press, today states can no longer control *ideas*. Spain, the ultimate super-power of the day, went into a long decline from which it never recovered. Technological development (the personal computer) has been joined with an invention of the Cold War "garrison-state" (the Internet) with the result that the State can no longer control social, philosophical, and scientific *truth*.

In the face of the Xerox machine, the cellular phone, and the PC, communism and the Berlin Wall and the Soviet Empire in the end didn't stand a chance. By the time Gorbachev and his "reformers" grasped the problem, it was far too late for limited reform. The related irony of the power of technology, and particularly information, is that the Orwellian fear of their domination by totalitarian regimes has been stood on its head. That is because, as Walter Wriston observes, communications technology has proved to be nearly completely immune to effective national control.[18] The corollary to this is that the fundamental means of production has changed so radically that, as John Lewis Gaddis notes, "repression no longer represses" in the traditional sense.[19] Whereas Stalin could order traditional proletarians and peasants about with great expectation that his orders would yield gross production, however inefficient, Gorbachev could not order "knowledge workers" to write imaginative computer programs or design efficient silicon chips unless they wanted to do so. Ultimately other structures and strictures will be changed as well. State censorship by any government will fall before "the Net" and "the Web." Those states that try (and nominally succeed in the short run) to maintain "control" will simply become irrelevant.

Technology is not value-free. Thus, information technology has the effect of eroding traditional hierarchies which have served as information filters, constraining the actions of the individuals within them. National sovereignty has less and less to do with currency valuation and market regulation in today's world. Greater access to information opens behavioral alternatives to individuals independent of traditional family, business, mass media, government and military strictures—whether the individual chooses to engage in the behavior or not. Transnational activities are greatly facilitated, in terms of markets, trade, production and finance. But because this global interconnectivity has a price, both literally and figuratively, nation-states can no longer successfully isolate themselves from events in other countries, be it the collapse of the Mexican peso or striking athletic shoe workers in Djakarta. State sovereignty as we understand it today will not disappear; it will just become increasingly irrelevant to the events that impact most peoples' lives. National (as opposed to State) identity, on the other hand, may well increase, independent of administrative borders, as global telecommunications provide linkages among geographically separated national groups.

Information War: Rethinking the Application of Power in the 21st Century [20]

Nations make war the way they make wealth. That is the premise of the Tofflers' book *War and Anti-War*. Consequently, there has emerged in recent years among first-rate powers a form of "Third-Wave War" to match the evolution of "Third-Wave Societies." *The hallmark of both is information.* The Tofflers' book is a paean to the work of the U.S. military over the past twenty years essentially to "reinvent" itself in these terms.[21] The evidence and effectiveness of this fundamental change was portrayed to an extent in the Second Persian Gulf War against Iraq.

Just as information is changing society, it is changing concepts of national security, the definitions and parameters of battle-space, and measurements of force. "Force" is becoming less tangible and more dependent upon qualitative factors. Battle-space is expanding greatly in terms of frontage, depth, and altitude (as it has since the Napoleonic Era). Movement rates—for forces, materiel, and ideas—are increasing; therefore, time is shrinking. War increasingly is becoming a conflict of decision processes; success will be determined by the "information differential" between forces and between commanders. "Third Wave War" is "Information War." These "post-industrial war" operations must be not only "joint" and "unified," but "holistic" and "simultaneous."[22]

Characteristics of Information War:

Continuous, Simultaneous, Accelerated, and Non-linear. At the heart of the concept of Information War is the concept of achieving military objectives with an absolute minimum of force application and/or cost. While one would argue that this has always been a warfighting objective, in the past the ability to achieve this objective depended upon a number of variables, many of which were controlled by the potential or real enemy. A duel between two knights to determine the dominance of opposing kings works only as long as both sides agree on the rules; as soon as one side decides to field two knights, the other side must respond in kind or (more likely) escalate.

With the Information Revolution, however, the minimum force/cost objective becomes attainable to the side that has information dominance. If we have continuous real-time surveillance of a potential adversary's military forces we can simultaneously position our forces to achieve and maintain an advantage. By communicating this advantage and our intentions to the adversary—perhaps along with other information through other channels that further complicates his decision process (i.e., deception)—we may deter or preclude his use of military force altogether. But even failing that, by maintaining perfect knowledge of enemy force disposition and by positioning our forces accordingly, while denying the enemy knowledge of our own force disposition, we can maximize the effectiveness of any force application, thus allowing use of only as much force as necessary to achieve objectives. In addition to maintaining the element of surprise, because we are aware immediately of the results of application of force on the enemy, we can accelerate response to changes in enemy activity and tailor our re-application of force to only those critical nodes that require it. By dominating the adversary's information systems, along with the use of smart stand-off weapons, we will be able to impose our will on the enemy without the costs associated with occupying his territory. Rather than moving through a battlefield in a linear fashion, we will be able continuously to select and neutralize critical targets in a non-linear battlespace "just in time," thus obviating the need for a large inventory of backup weaponry, in much the same way that "just in time" delivery from subcontractors relieves automakers from maintaining large warehouse inventories of parts to keep assembly lines running.

Instant Feedback. The ability to take the right action "just in time" depends, of course, on feedback. Since the beginning of human organization, decision-makers have sought information about the results of their decisions as soon as possible, so that if corrective or reinforcing actions are required, they could be taken while it was still possible to influence the course of events set in motion by the initial decision. Until relatively recently in our history, the ability to gain such information was limited by many factors, but most especially by distance. Prior to the advent of electronic communication, an observer might record in great detail events resulting from a decision, but the available lines of communication often put days, weeks, or even months between events and information about the events reaching the decision-maker, rendering it of more historical than practical interest. Electronic communication changes all this, particularly the advent of communication satellites and high-capacity fiber optic cables. Decision-makers can now remain "plugged in," not only receiving instant feedback on the effects of their decisions, but also using these same lines of communication to transmit new decisions based on feedback information. In some cases, the quantity and/or speed of feedback information is such that the decision-maker requires computer assistance to process the information.

Take, for example, the pilot of an F-117 stealth fighter. As he moves the controls, he generates electronic signals that activate the aircraft's control surfaces. However, the F-117 is an inherently unstable platform requiring constant correction to remain airborne. These corrections are made automatically, many times a second, based on information provided by sensors which monitor the aircraft's attitude, airspeed, etc. The human pilot cannot react quickly enough to provide the inputs necessary to keep the aircraft in the air; instead, his inputs provide additional information needed to allow the aircraft to fly where he wants to go. The next step in the evolution of man-machine interface—and one which the USAF is currently pursuing—would be to move beyond the requirements for physical reaction at all, taking electrical impulses directly from the brain and using these impulses as commands for a computer-driven control system.

As discussed above, the concept of instant feedback as it relates to Information War is viewed in the context of a closed system, whether the F-117 or the Army's "digitized battlefield" envisioned in Force XXI. We think of instant feedback in terms of operational- and tactical-level decision-making. But instant feedback, or something close to it, increasingly operates at the strategic level as well. While the media, and particularly television, may not be responsible for the U.S. "losing" the war in Viet Nam, the public reaction to the images of U.S. soldiers in combat being brought into living rooms across the country most assuredly influenced the decisions made by the Johnson and Nixon Administrations on how to prosecute the war. During the Gulf War, Saddam Hussein, during a speech covered live by CNN, called for a debate with President Bush; within thirty minutes, President Bush held a press conference to advise the world (and Saddam) that he had no intention of participating in such a debate. Even in non-democratic societies, both leadership and the general public are simultaneously aware of the results of policy decisions via television news coverage. Boris Yeltsin was without doubt no more pleased than the citizens of St. Petersburg to view the less than sterling performance of the Russian Army in Chechnya. The point here is that, as noted by Professor George Stein of the Air University:

> "...[T]he worldwide infosphere of television and broadcast news ...[will] shape the political context of the conflict. It will define the new 'battlespace.' We face an 'integrated battlefield,' not in the usual sense of having a global positioning system (GPS) receiver in every tank or cockpit, but in the Clausewitzian sense that war is being integrated into the political almost simultaneously with the battle.[23]

Under such conditions, the distinctions between the tactical, operational and strategic tend to blur into insignificance. Like it or not, the actions of a single soldier, if caught by the international media, can potentially affect the outcome of a conflict."

The problem with this, Stein points out, is that this media-created world is a "fictive universe"—not because the images are untrue, but because they do not contain sufficient information to capture the context and totality of the truth. The average "sound bite" (more accurately described as a "video bite") on the evening news today is somewhere between 8 and 12 seconds—very little time to articulate a policy position within a 90 second story consisting of visual images selected for their sensational value, overlaid by commentary from a reporter who, to seem objective, feels compelled to present opposing views. In a perfect world, decision-makers would have perfect instant feedback upon which to base subsequent policy decisions. In the real world, the temptation to rely on timely fictive feedback, as opposed to less timely but more fulsome feedback from intelligence or other official sources, may prove to be overwhelming.

War as Work: Third Wave War. The basic characteristics of the new "war-form" essentially mirror those in the civilian economy. The watch-words are: *information dominance* and *information assurance*. *Knowledge* becomes the core of military power and the central resource of destructivity, rather that pure brute force. *Intangible values* more accurately determine the military balance, rather than hardware. *Demassification* requires increased precision and more selectivity in the application of military power. Military *work* is more often dependent upon education and expertise than traditional machismo and brute force; information will become the nature of war. *Innovation* is increasingly prized; improvisation replaces rote and routine. *Organization* becomes more fluid and less hierarchical. *Integration* of all assets, forces, and services is essential. *Acceleration* characterizes operations at all levels (not necessarily absolute speed, but speed relative to the enemy's pace of decision-making and movement—his "OODA-loop").[24] These characteristics of information warfare will affect combat arms, as well as combat service and combat service support functions, most markedly in terms of intelligence, signals, transportation and logistics.

War as Improvisational Theater.[25] In the future, we will be operating in a media-rich environment, where our military actions will be broadcast instantaneously via worldwide television. Think of the intelligence and operational security implications of private-sector news media operating their own remote-sensing imaging satellites, which certainly will happen within the decade. Consequently, military commanders must be increasingly adept at operating effectively in this environment. If we consider a military

OPLAN as a script, the ensuing events will increasingly resemble improvisational theater on a global stage where reactions of a variety of audiences and critics can ultimately determine the difference between success and failure in a political, if not military, sense.

The SEALs reconnoitering the beach at Mogadishu, Somalia, in the glare of the lights of the assembled video cameras looked more silly than formidable, an inauspicious beginning to what was to become a well-intentioned but ultimately frustrating and futile military exercise.[26] Consider also the image of illiterate thugs on the docks of Port-au-Prince, Haiti, who greeted U.S. and Canadian troops aboard the USS Harlan County, waving their English-language placards and shouting, for CNN, that Haiti would be "another Somalia for America." We then watched as the Harlan County steamed away, much to the consternation of the U.S. military advance party waiting on the wharf. When the U.S. advance elements of the NATO Enabling Force entered Tuzla, Bosnia, they found themselves outnumbered by the media at easily a ten-to-one ratio. And because the global information infrastructure is nothing if not interactive, commanders may find their OPLAN or "script" being rewritten as they go along. As a RAND study suggests, the level of "script" adaptability may be a critical predictor of success for military operations in the Information Age.[27]

What Does It All Mean?

Despite the changes in both the ends and means (but not the purpose) of war, it is highly unlikely that armed conflict will totally disappear into cyberspace. Indeed, if an "armed pedestrian gang" were to start firing figurative RPGs at "stretch limos" belonging to our national groups as they speed along the information superhighway, we would in all likelihood determine such behavior to be a threat and employ combat forces with authorization to use some degree of lethal force in *defense and/or retribution*. As other contributions to this volume will demonstrate, it is possible that we will not be readily able to do so, because of our inability to understand the principles of war in the Information Age.

Proliferation of the Means of Conflict. The rigorous application of information technology to warfare means, first of all, that there will be a proliferation of the *means* of conflict. To the traditional means of firepower and maneuver will be added the means of attacking one's enemy ever more powerfully *electronically*. One can not only attack his command and control systems with destructive firepower, but with other destructive technological techniques. Disinformation, rumor, and propaganda have long been means of attack. These means are now enhanced. Some have speculated that effective deception operations are no longer possible in the age of satellite reconnaissance. The effectiveness of deception depends upon available "channels" of information and the penchant of one's opponent for self-deception. Hence, the possibilities for successful deception operations have never been better.

Lethality vs. Effectiveness. Electronic combat will potentially enable a commander to inflict "effective neutralization" upon his opponent without the necessity of physically destroying infrastructure, forces, or people. Military professionals often overlook the fact that the purpose of warfare is not (in the common jargon) "killing people and breaking things." Those means have been the *mechanics* of war, not its *purpose*. The purpose of war is to inflict your *will* upon the opponent. If one's will can be imposed (i.e., modifying the opponent's behavior or intent) without widespread physical destruction, the post-conflict possibilities for political reconciliation and human progress may actually be enhanced. War in the Information Age holds out at least the prospect of that eventuality.

Devalued Traditional Ends of War. If all of this has validity, we now have the prospects of changing fundamentally the way war is conducted and the perceived ends to be achieved. The traditional ends of war were: to destroy the opponent's forces in the field, in the air, and on the seas; to destroy his productive war capacity; and to occupy his capital. With the destruction or disabling of his command and control capability and the ability to influence the perceptions of his policy elites and population, there is the possibility to work one's will upon the opponent without necessarily wreaking physical havoc upon the infrastructure and population of one's enemy. The concern here need not necessarily be humanitarian in the short run. The calculation can be purely utilitarian in terms of preserving the economic wherewithal to sustain a viable and productive society with altered political aims.

Clausewitz & anti-Clausewitz. Much of this analysis flies in the face of traditional Industrial Age warfare. In the military forces, there is an ingrained "Clausewitzian" value system, and we have all been raised within it. Much of the foregoing contradicts the Clausewitzian approach to warfare as taught in our Staff Colleges and War Colleges. Clausewitz still has much to contribute to military thinking, even in democratic societies (a phenomenon with which he had no experience). The "holy trinity" of State, Army (actually, Armed Forces), and People is crucial, and its continued importance cannot be over-emphasized. But his fixation with physical destruction and annihilation may be outdated. Yet, the possibility of the decisive winning battle (at least in peer-competitor warfare) theoretically could be resurrected. The danger for "Third-Wave" societies is that the potential for success in this regard may rest with niche-competitors in asymmetrical conflict.

Recent attempts to come to grips with the "Revolution in Military Affairs" and "Military-Technical Revolution" have not dealt satisfactorily with such phenomena as "asymmetrical warfare." It is a common conceit of advanced nations and their armed forces that they can impose their will upon lesser powers and relatively primitive forces through application of advanced technological means. Painful historical experience since the late 19th Century indicates just the opposite. Historical experience in recent decades similarly should indicate that "low-intensity" conflict (or the current concept of "operations-other-that-war") is not a lesser-included case of higher-order strategy, doctrine, tactics, techniques, and procedures. Relatively primitive forces will—and do—have access to sophisticated technology, and they will know how to use it. Technology will be increasingly available to them. While such relatively sophisticated concepts as air-battle management and air-land operations might be lost on them, there will be some opponents who *do* understand "perception management" and "information warfare" in its rudimentary sense.

Another conundrum will face sophisticated military forces: the possibility of the passing of what might be called "heroic warfare." If the Tofflers are approximately correct that a hallmark of future combat is "brains over brawn," a change will be required in the selection, retention, development, and promotion of cyber-warriors who attack the enemy and defend the nation by means other than cold steel and hot lead. This possibility might appeal more to a nation that shies from incurring combat casualties; it likely will appeal less to their military sub-cultures that intrinsically value blood sport, distance running, and the machismo self-image.

The Social Impact of Information War

It is difficult for democratic society to discern "good news" from the prospects of war. If there is any good news to infer from the kind of warfare likely to predominate in the 21st Century, it might be the prospects for reduced levels of physical and human destruction. Among Third-Wave peer-competitors at least, perhaps humankind will be spared the carnage of the Somme and Passchendaele and Gallipoli in World War One, the tens of millions of civilian and military deaths in World War Two, and the prospects of thermonuclear annihilation in the Cold War.

It is equally difficult, however, to foresee the end of total war in a world increasingly dominated by technology. In the future, perhaps as never before, it might be possible for technologically sophisticated societies to truly wage war against the very fabric of the opponent's society—and to do so digitally. For generations now, we have witnessed indiscriminate attacks against civilian populations by military forces. The world likely will not be spared the genocide of Rwanda, the senseless waste of Liberia, or the religio-ideological destruction of Afghanistan. In the future, it might be increasingly difficult to detect who is attacking—and indeed perhaps from what quarter and for what purpose. One could envision a politico-military future in which irregular warfare might be possible on an unprecedented scale. The targets (ours or theirs) need not be physical infrastructure, but a nation's financial and automated distribution systems.

A primary characteristic of the nation-state era has been state monopoly of the means of violence. We surely are witnessing—in both Third-Wave/First-World and First-Wave/Third-World societies—a trend away from state monopoly of lethal violence. In a future characterized by cyberwar, technology offers the prospect of non-state possession in abundance of the "non-lethal" means of violence.

Endnotes

[1] Francis Fukuyama, *The End of History and the Last Man*, New York: The Free Press, 1992. Fukuyama first advanced his concept of liberal democracy being the logical "end of history" in human political development in *The National Interest*, No. 16 (Summer) 1989, pp. 3-35.

[2] Peter Drucker, *Post-Captialist Society*, New York: *Harper Collins Publishers*, 1993, p. 7.

[3] For the purposes of this article, the term "information" will be used most often in the collective sense, encompassing a hierarchy consisting of data (facts and figures), information (related packages of data linked in a meaningful manner), and knowledge (information required by individuals to understand and/or perform a given function or task).

[4] John Keegan, *A History of Warfare*, New York: Alfred A. Knopf, 1993.

[5] Bruce D. Palmer, *War and the Rise of the State: The Military Foundations of Modern Politics*, New York: The Free Press, 1994.

[6] Martin Van Crevald, *The Transformation of War*, New York: The Free Press, 1991.

[7] Michael Howard, *The Lessons of History*, New Haven: Yale University Press, 1991.

[8] Indeed, Jerome Clayton Glenn wrote of the "post-Information Age" as early as 1989. See his *Future Mind: Artificial Intelligence*, Washington, DC: Acropolis Books, p. 8.

[9] Alvin Toffler, *The Third Wave*, New York: William Morrow, 1980; and Alvin and Heidi Toffler, *War and Anti-War: Survival at the Dawn of the 21st Century*, Boston: Little, Brown and Co., 1993.
[10] Robert Reich, *The Work of Nations: Preparing Ourselves for 21st Century Capitalism*, New York: Alfred A. Knopf, 1991, pp. 171-184.
[11] Drucker, *op. cit.*
[12] *United Nations Statistical Survey*, 37th Edition, 1988/89.
[13] Peter Schwartz, *The Art of the Long View*, New York: Doubleday, 1991, pp. 124-140.
[14] *UN Statistical Survey, op. cit.*
[15] U.S. Committee for Refugees, *World Refugee Survey 1992*, American Council for Nationalities, Washington, D.C., September 30, 1992.
[16] Even Gordon Moore, himself, thinks that this trend might not be immutable. See: "The End of the Line," *The Economist*, July 15, 1995., pp. 61-62.
[17] Ralph Lee Smith, "The Nation Wired," *The Nation*, May 18, 1970..
[18] Walter B. Wriston, *The Twilight of Sovereignty*, New York: Charles Scribner's Sons, 1992. See also his article of the same title in *The Fletcher Forum of World Affairs*, Vol. 17, No.2, (Summer) 1993, pp. 117-130.
[19] John Lewis Gaddis, "Tectonics, History, and the End of the Cold War." An Occasional Paper from the Mershon Center project *Assessing Alternative Futures for the United States and Post-Soviet Relations*, undated [1992], p. 13. See also: Scott Shane, *Dismantling Utopia: How Information Ended the Soviet Union*, Chicago: Ivan R. Dee, 1994.
[20] Rona, Thomas, "*Weapon Systems and Information War*," Boeing Aerospace Co., July 1976.
[21] Tofflers,*War and Anti-War*, op. cit.
[22] See: Joseph S. Nye, Jr., and William A. Owens, "America's Information Edge," and Eliot A. Cohen, "A Revolution in Warfare," *Foreign Affairs*, Vol. 75, No. 2 (March-April) 1996, pp. 20-36 and 37-54, respectively.
[23] See George J. Stein, "Information War," Chapter xx, below.
[24] Tofflers, op. cit., pp. 64-80.
[25] *Information Technologies and the Future of Land Warfare*, RAND Study DDR-659-A, February 1994 (draft).
[26] This unfortunate (but thankfully non-fatal) incident was the fault of neither the SEAL Team nor of the waiting journalists. The latter had been informed of the landing site by U.S. officials. The SEALs apparently did not know that U.S. forces would be met by no hostile resistance, and they were following "normal" procedures. The oversight in proper coordination lay with senior planners, who failed to grasp the importance of melding purely military concerns and operations with public diplomacy requirements and activities.
[27] RAND DDR-659-A, *ibid.*

The Revolution in Military Affairs: The Information Dimension

Michael L. Brown ©

When military historians look back on the past hundred years, one of the principal characteristics they will note is the constancy of change. With almost continuous improvements in the underlying technologies, tanks, rifles, airplanes and ships have steadily evolved from one generation to the next. Sometimes they have grown larger, sometimes smaller, but always more capable. Doctrine and organization have followed close behind as soldiers, sailors, airman and marines have tried to exploit the characteristics of their new weapons to achieve the maximum effect on the battlefield.

This evolution, however, has been anything but smooth, for periodically through the course of the past century, leaps in technology have led to the development of entirely new military capabilities, or to quantum leaps in the characteristics of existing systems. When only one weapons system is effected, existing doctrine can usually be modified to capitalize on the new technology. When several systems change simultaneously, however, it is the environment itself that begins to transform and revolutionary, rather than evolutionary, change becomes the order of the day.

Over the past two decades, there has clearly been an explosion of technologies, and with those technologies have come radical changes in the nature of military systems. Space-based reconnaissance and surveillance systems, unmanned aerial vehicles, and myriad terrestrially-based sensor systems have led to the development of Intelligence, Surveillance and Reconnaissance (ISR) capabilities undreamed of a decade ago. Digital communications systems that can span the globe and relay wide-bandwidth information in near real-time are changing the very nature of command and control (C^2). "Smart" weaponry—manifested in bombs, missiles, artillery projectiles and even infantry weapons systems—have created a new category of weapons called precision guided munitions (PGMs) and have led to an environment where "everything that can be seen can be hit, and everything that can be hit can be killed." These technologies are laying the foundation for one of the most dramatic changes in military history in the past century. They are laying the foundation for a *Revolution in Military Affairs (RMA)*.

Too many authors talk about the coming revolution in military affairs as THE RMA—as if "The End of Military History," is nigh. Nothing could be further from the truth. Technological developments in fields we, today, barely know exist, are likely to lead to major changes in warfare tomorrow.[1] What is unique about the next RMA is that it will derive from technologies that already exist and from weapons that have either been built or are already on the drawing board. Moreover, it should come as no surprise that these changes in military systems are driven primarily by the explosion in information technologies. It is the increase in data collection capability, storage capacity and processing power, for example, that has led to the development of the emerging ISR system; improvements in digital communications technologies that underlie the near-billion-fold increase in bandwidth which are profoundly changing the way commanders command and control their forces; and improvements in processing power and data storage capability have enhanced the accuracy of precision guided munitions. What we are seeing is the emergence of an Information-Based RMA.

But incorporating new technologies into the military—or any other facet of life—is hardly the basis of revolution. While technologies alone may enhance efficiency, to underlie a revolution they have to be followed by new ways of doing things and changes in organizational structures. When information networks and desk top computers were first introduced into the workplace, for example, they frequently increased efficiency at the margin. Word processors allowed executives and staff officers to write their own letters, eliminating the need for massive retyping by secretaries; e-mail permitted managers to communicate more efficiently with both superiors and subordinates; and networked systems saved various departments time and transaction costs. But, as Arquilla and Ronfeldt note, "improved efficiency is not the only, or even the best possible effect" of technological changes.[2] It was not until companies began to reorganize and redistribute their workload—to reengineer—that businesses began to feel the full impact of the information revolution.

The same is true of the military environment. Simply modifying doctrine to accommodate the technologies does not make a revolution. Rather, an RMA occurs when:

> ... the application of new technologies into a significant number of military systems combines with innovative operational concepts and organizational adaptation in a way that fundamentally alters the character and conduct of conflict. It does so by producing a dramatic increase—often an order of magnitude or greater—in the combat potential and military effectiveness of armed forces.[3]

Thus, underlying a true revolution in military affairs is a radical change in *operational concepts* and *organizational structures*. To cite one illustration: by 1916, the principal World War I Allies all had tanks, airplanes, and radios, and, in fact, used them during the Battle of Cambrai. The tanks, however, were used primarily as "infantry support" weapons, the radios used for high-level command-and-control, and the airplanes given reconnaissance and interdiction missions. It would take 20 years before soldiers and airmen would thoroughly understand the revolutionary potential of these systems, and build operational concepts and organizational structures around them. Today, we call that operational concept *Blitzkrieg*, and the most noteworthy of the organizations it spawned was the *Panzer Division*. The result was "a dramatic increase...in the combat potential and military effectiveness" of an armed force. Similarly, the U.S. Navy had aircraft carriers, destroyers and cruisers prior to our entry into World War I, but everyone knew that carriers were primarily for reconnaissance, and that battleships were the backbone of the fleet. It took twenty years to recognize the importance of aircraft and aircraft carriers to naval forces, to develop new conceptual approaches, to build larger carriers, to organize them into Carrier Battle Groups, and thereby to change the "character and conduct" of war at sea.

To understand the nature and implications of the coming Information-Based RMA, this article will examine the impact of recent and emerging information technologies—and the military systems they have spawned—on military operations. In this context, the first section below describes how information technologies have changed, and are in the process of changing even more radically, the nature of the battlespace. The following section discusses the importance of information systems and information flows on emerging operational concepts. With all these changes in the nature and conduct of warfare, and with modern military forces becoming more and more dependent on information flows, the third section argues that something called the "information space" will become a new domain of military operations, and that information warfare will become a new dimension of interstate conflict with vast implications for the future of military conflict in particular, and national security more generally.

The Changing Battlespace

Changing information technologies are having a profound effect on the nature of the battlespace. One way to look at the battlespace is through the lens of time, of force, and of space. Using this technique, we find that traditional notions of time, space and force have changed forever. *Time has been compressed; space has been distorted and expanded; and our notions of force will have to change.*

Time

Changes in the information environment have had the effect of compressing time in the battlespace. During the Battle of Britain, for example, the RAF worked out procedures to identify incoming enemy aircraft with their new radars. Fighters were then scrambled and vectored to the general enemy location. If all went well, the RAF pilots intercepted the enemy, shot them down and returned to base. Already today, and increasingly in the future, air warfare is moving much too fast for this old-fashioned procedure. Identification, notification and engagement decisions have to be made more quickly than human physiology and decision-making capability will allow. As a result, Aegis cruisers and Patriot missile batteries both have an "automatic" mode, in which the time-consuming human decision-making process is taken entirely out of the loop. The target is automatically located, tracked, identified and engaged without human involvement. In the future, the same will be true in land and sea combat. Sensor-to-shooter links are likely to become increasingly automated, reducing the time lag between identifying a target and launching a weapon to engage it. ISR systems will identify multiple, fleeting targets in near real-time and the information will be relayed to computerized decision systems. There, based on human programming, the decision will be made on whether or not to engage, which systems to use, and whether or not to re-engage. The war will move entirely too fast for humans to be engaged in each and every engagement decision.

The same will be true at the operational level of war. In an article in *Military Review*, former Chief of Staff of the Army General Gordon R. Sullivan included a chart depicting changes in the importance of time on the battlespace. Using John Boyd's model of Observation-Orientation-Decision-Action Cycle (OODA Loop), Sullivan illustrated how methods of observation had changed since the Revolutionary War, and how the time available for orientation, decision and action had been reduced accordingly. Based on his observations of the Gulf War, for example, he believed that the old fashioned notions of a campaign "season" had been reduced to a campaign "day." Extrapolating into the future, he indicated that campaigns would likely be decided in an hour or less from the onset of hostilities. In referring to the chart, he pointed out that on the battlefield, "the concept of time itself [has] changed."

	Revolution	Civil War	WW II	Gulf War	Tomorrow
Orientation	Telescope	Telegraph	Radio/wire	Near real-time	**Real-time**
Observation	Weeks	Days	Hours	Minutes	**Continuous**
Decision	Months	Weeks	Days	Hours	**Immediate**
Action	Season	A month	A week	A day	**Hour or less**

Figure 1: Time and Command

Operations, moreover, will be continuous, running day and night, regardless of visibility. In Desert Storm, for example, during 90 hours of continuous movement and combat, the VII US Corps "... reported destroying more than a dozen Iraqi divisions; an estimated 1300 tanks, 1200 fighting vehicles and APCs; 285 artillery pieces and 100 air defense systems; and captured nearly 22,000 enemy soldiers."[5] Similarly, Allied forces were able to make accurate attacks on the enemy's capital even at night, as cruise missiles and other precision-guided munitions found their targets regardless of visibility. Night vision systems, millimeter-wave radar and a whole host of other technologies make human endurance the principal limiting factor in the constancy of operations.

It is very clear that in an information-rich environment, traditional military notions of time will have to change. What in World War II took days will, in the future, take hours; what used to take hours will take minutes, and what used to take minutes will be accomplished in seconds. The implications for military operational concepts and organizations are enormous.

Space

The battlespace has expanded in all three spatial dimensions. For land combat, General Sullivan documented this change in graphic form in his pamphlet *Land Warfare in the 21st Century*.[6] Since the 1973 October War, for example, the area of the battlespace occupied by a deployed force of 100,000 soldiers has expanded by an order-of-magnitude in both depth and breadth. In part, this extraordinary expansion has been the result—directly or indirectly—of improved information flows. In an age when commanders had to use signaling flags, all subordinate units had to be within sight of the signal hill. As portable radios became reliable, the battlefield expanded as far as a commander could reliably communicate. But with the advent of modern digital communications technology and satellites, a commander can communicate with increasingly dispersed forces. Distance on the battlespace is no longer limited by communications technology. In fact, by focusing on land power, General Sullivan may have grossly underestimated the expansion of the battlespace. Missiles fired from far offshore and aircraft launched from the continental United States also had tactical and operational-level effects.

The battlespace has also increased vertically. Before World War I, of course, the battlefield was essentially two-dimensional. With the introduction of aircraft into the battlespace, however, a third dimension began to emerge. This third dimension has grown significantly in recent years. Today, communications and intelligence satellites have expanded the third dimension into outer space.

The control of the third dimension had significant impact on the Gulf War. It was because of their control of outer space during the Gulf War that U.S. forces were able to see better than the enemy, to navigate better than the enemy, and to communicate better. Through the control of space, Allied forces had satellite information and imagery and a robust command, control and communications system; Saddam Hussein did not. We enjoyed access to our Global Positioning System or GPS; he did not. As such we could locate targets and hit them with timeliness and precision. Saddam could not. Because outer space plays such an important role in warfare today—and will play an even larger role in the future—the volume of the battlespace with which commanders have to be concerned has been increased by thousands of cubic miles. Commanders at all echelons have to be aware of the orbit paths of enemy reconnaissance satellites. Theater commanders have to know about the adversary's communications and navigation capabilities and about his anti-satellite potential. At the same time, of course, commanders must have the same information about their own systems. The battlespace is no longer limited to the reaches of the atmosphere—it extends well into outer space.

Force

In the past, it was possible to count the number of soldiers, cavalry and guns available to either side, and have a reasonable idea who would win a particular war. As technological sophistication and rates of platform modernization became increasingly important, however, complex computer models were used to the same end. We are entering an age, however, when one "smart" munition delivered by a single airplane, ship, or possibly even from the continental United States, is more likely to accomplish certain missions that a squadron of World War II-era bombers could; an era when advancing armor columns can be identified from space, targeted in near real-time by high-speed computers and attacked by a handful of modern missiles carrying hundreds of sub-munitions; when an enemy's command-and-control system can be identified and attacked, with extraordinary impact on his entire force structure. As General Sullivan notes, "a paradigm shift is developing. Many of the old rules of land warfare that concern the calculation of combat power have been shattered already."[7] We are entering an age when old notions of "force" need to be reexamined.

To address this problem, analysts began to talk about "force multipliers." But this concept does not capture the impact of the many new military capabilities and operational techniques. Rather than "multiplying" the value of traditional elements of the force, some of the new technologies increase it in an *exponential* way. Others increase traditional notions of "force" in a fundamentally *non-linear* manner that we do not yet understand. Still others—such as certain kinds of information capabilities—may have value as weapons systems themselves in *alternative operational paradigms*. In such an age, how do we think about force and force relationships? How can we compare one force with another? How do we calculate combat power?

One way to analyze the effects of information and information systems on warfare is to examine how they have changed traditional battlespace functions. While a comprehensive listing of the various functions from all the Services would be useful, each of the armed forces has chosen different mechanisms to analyze their particular segment of the battlespace. The Army has identified seven "Battlefield Operating Systems." Of these, four have been directly and profoundly effected by information and information systems:

- Intelligence
- Logistics
- Command and Control
- Fire Support

The nature of military intelligence is in the process of being changed fundamentally by new collection, processing, storage and disseminating technologies. The extraordinary resolution of modern satellite platforms has changed the way commanders look at the battlespace. Already, the Joint Staff is examining the doctrinal and force structure implications of "Dominant Battlespace Awareness," defined by its most ardent advocate, former Vice Chairman of the Joint Chiefs of Staff Admiral Owens, as knowledge of all observable enemy objects in a 200km x 200km battlespace. With advances in IMINT, SIGINT, ELINT, COMINT, MASINT and a plethora of other "INTs," U.S. forces can already obtain a fairly comprehensive view of an enemy's force structure; with AWACS and JSTARS, friendly troops can develop an accurate radar picture of enemy air and ground-based forces on the move; and, with existing space-based platforms and first-generation UAV's, one can literally "see" hundreds or thousands of miles into the enemy's rear area. Based on systems already in development, however, these capabilities represent only the tip of the iceberg.

Relatively near-term technological developments will yield long-endurance UAV's carrying sophisticated sensor suites. These hard-to-detect systems will hover over the battlespace identifying enemy activities and locations. When used in conjunction with platforms in outer space, along with JSTARS and AWACS, commanders will be able to obtain a comprehensive picture of the battlespace in near real-time. With all the information coming in from these and other sources, the key will be to process the data and present it in a form that does not overwhelm commanders. Here, too, information technologies will help. Digitally processed information using computers that are one or two orders-of-magnitude faster than today's, together with intelligent "search engines"—whose first-generation predecessors are already in wide use on the Internet—are likely to provide at least part of the solution.

As a result of these projected changes, Admiral Owens estimates that,

> "In Desert Storm, we had real-time, all-weather, near-continuous information on no more than 15% of the militarily significant phenomena we wanted to know about. Were we to fight a similar war today (1995), that figure would be somewhere around 20 to 30 percent. In five years, it will be more than double today's capacity."[8]

By the year 2005, U.S. forces should be able to identify 90% of the militarily significant targets on the battlefield.[9] The very nature of military intelligence is in the process of changing profoundly.

Collecting and processing information is not enough; it must be made available to those who need it. To make this information available to the right person at the right time, the Army envisions an information "carousel"[10] with intelligence relevant to his area of operations available to any commander on request. The Air Force intends to deliver updated information from the sensors straight to the pilot in the cockpit. In short, information systems are changing the very nature of military intelligence and yielding to commanders products of extraordinary accuracy.

The technology to change the military logistics system is also at hand. While the peculiarities of military operations may preclude copying the techniques of corporations like Federal Express and Wal-Mart, the principles underlying their operation, as well as the those providing the foundation for techniques like Just-in-Time delivery and Total Asset Visibility are as relevant to the military world as they are to the private sector. Military forces are slowly adapting to the capabilities inherent in information-based logistics systems. As the process develops, they may find that the day of huge in-theater logistics depots, or huge air bases—both of which will be known to the enemy as "targets"—are finally at an end; that battalions, brigades, divisions, corps and even armies can move rapidly without the impediment of hundreds of thousands of tons of supplies.[11] They may find that the down-time of ground combat vehicles, and of ships and airplanes decreases significantly, and that they can perform their mission more efficiently—freeing soldiers, sailors, marines and airmen for other duties. An information-based military logistics system carries the potential to change the nature of military operations just as reengineering has changed the nature of many commercial organizations.

Having near-real-time intelligence and vast storehouses of information will not be useful, unless commanders can influence the action through means and methods of command-and-control. Increasing bandwidth and faster processing speed are providing commanders just this capability. Rather than build sand tables or use hand-held models to describe their plans, commanders will be able to use simulations to communicate their intent and to rehearse operations before they even begin. Moreover, during the planning process they will be able to tap expertise thousands of miles away, reducing the need for large staffs simply to plan and track ongoing operations. As one observer has noted in the wake of the Gulf War:

> "The difference is not just in conducting operations more effectively. Communications and computing capability made it possible to do things very innovatively. For example, resources that were 7,000 miles away from the battlefield were used to assist commanders and staffs."[12]

The emergence of these new capabilities will have far more profound effects in the future, for the nature of command itself may be changing. The implications of near-real-time situational awareness for commanders at all echelons have already led analysts to begin questioning the hierarchical basis of military organizations. As one Army pamphlet puts it:

> "Future technology will require the Army to reassess time-honored means of battle command—to recognize that in the future, military operations will involve the coexistence of both hierarchical and internetted, non-hierarchical processes. Order will be less physically imposed than knowledge-imposed."[13]

When the Gulf War demonstrated—even to the doubters—the value of "smart weapons," the notion of precision fire support was taken off the drawing board and put onto the battlespace. To be sure, some of the systems did not perform as well in the field as they did in the laboratory, but as technicians tweak the existing technologies, they are liable to find that smart weaponry becomes even smarter, and, in the process, that the systems become cheaper and more reliable. Some argue that these weapons, by introducing the notion of precision strike into the arsenal of military planners, have already revolutionized warfare. Even if not quite true, they have demonstrated that warfare will be different in the age of the economical smart weapons than it was before.

Some of the implications of employing precision strike weapons are startling. In the first 24 hours of the Gulf War, for example, Coalition forces struck three times as many strategic targets in Iraq as the entire Eighth Air Force hit in Germany in all of 1943, with very little collateral damage. As a result, entire industries were disabled. At the same time, nearly the entire Iraqi Air Force was destroyed on the ground. At the tactical and operational levels, long-range precision fires allowed the Allies to attack Iraqi forces from the air and from the ground before the enemy even knew that there were Coalition forces in the area. Not only did this attrit the total numbers of Iraqi armored combat vehicles significantly, but, even more importantly, the psychological impact of watching their tanks blow up from out of nowhere was devastating to Baghdad's soldiers. Whole units crumbled without firing a shot or even seeing Allied ground forces.

Information systems have had an important impact on these and many other military functional areas; but even these effects fail to capture the essence of warfare in the information age—*for it is the synergy of all these individual effects that create the potential to revolutionize warfare*. Better intelligence systems will allow the identification of more and better targets for PGMs. Better intelligence will also reduce the need for saturation bombing or attacking area targets with vast amounts of ammunition. The decrease in ammunition requirements will reduce significantly the strain on the logistics system, allowing U.S. forces to deploy into theater much more quickly. Moreover, improvements in the logistics system will allow ground forces to be much smaller and to move much more rapidly. Capitalizing on better intelligence, these ground forces will be able to strike precisely where their capabilities will have the greatest effect.

Emerging Operational Concepts

As noted earlier, however, new technology and new weapons systems do not make a revolution. New operational concepts have to be adopted and new organizations built before an armed force will be fully able to harness the implications of the new technology. Several different operational concepts have already been proposed. While it is impossible to sketch out all of these approaches in any detail, it is possible to identify representative ones. These notions can be arranged into two categories. One, the "Strategic Attack Paradigm" argues that changes in the technological environment obviate the necessity to fight through a nation's armed forces to win wars. Instead, the adversary's most essential systems can be attacked either through the use of smart missiles and bombs, or through the employment of new kinds of "information weapons," such as hacking techniques or malicious code. A second sort of operational support might be called the "Operational Attack Paradigm." Proponents of this approach argue that a nation's armed forces still represent a country's center-of-gravity; and, until the military is defeated, victory cannot be achieved. The issue to advocates of this paradigm is how to develop and use new operational concepts that capitalize on the new technologies to defeat an adversary's armed forces.

Strategic Attack Paradigm

Colonel John Warden, one of the principal planners of the Gulf War air campaign and one of the Air Force's best strategic thinkers, argues that all organizations, including the modern nation-state, consist of five interdependent systems. These, he arranges into a model consisting of concentric rings, with leadership in the innermost circle followed, in order, by "system essentials" (e.g., communications), infrastructure, population and fielded forces. Warden further argues that, in fractal-like fashion, each of these systems has five similar subsystems, and those in turn each have five subsystems. Thus, contained within the ring containing the "fielded forces" are: subordinate leadership, system essentials, infrastructure, population and fielded forces rings.

Historically, the only way to defeat an adversary was to first face the outer ring—his military. Only when this ring was defeated could one attack or threaten to attack the various internal systems. Not only did that mean facing the enemy's strength rather than his weaknesses, it also meant fighting systems in a sequential, or as Warden calls it a "serial," strategy. He goes on to argue that modern airpower—combined with information systems—allows military forces to ignore the enemy's strong outer ring and to attack the more vulnerable internal systems first. Thus, for example, rather than fight through an adversary's military ring an attacker can go straight for the leadership system. Moreover, he holds that these attacks can be conducted almost simultaneously, or in "parallel," rather than serially. The effect of such an attack would be to "paralyze" the enemy.

> The idea of paralysis is quite simple. The enemy is seen as a system, we need to identify those parts of the system we can affect in such a way as to prevent the system from doing something we don't want it to do. The best place to start is normally at the center for if we can prevent the system's leadership from gathering, processing, and using information we don't want him to have, we have effectively paralyzed the system at a strategic level.[14]

It is critical to note that Warden's operational concept is absolutely dependent on the existence of modern information systems. His concentric circle model relies on the flow of information among the various rings. A nation that could not communicate with its fielded forces, for example, would not be much of an adversary. But the operational concept, itself, is also dependent on information. The attacker has to have exact and timely intelligence about the location of targets within the rings; targets have to be designated precisely; attacks can only be carried out with "smart" munitions, etc. Absent the precision that derives from modern information systems, Warden's approach to air warfare in the 21st Century would be impossible to implement.

A second operational concept in support of the Strategic Attack Paradigm is what might be called "strategic information warfare." Proponents argue that all modern nations rely extensively on information flows, and hence on their national information infrastructures. A country's financial, commercial, transportation, industrial, telecommunications, power generation, and its military systems all depend on the timely and efficient flow of information. Moreover, each of these systems are dependent on the others. A collapse of the national power grid, for example, would lead to the failure of transportation networks (petroleum is generally moved along pipelines by electrical pumps), food distribution becomes problematic, banks collapse, industry doesn't produce, cities become uninhabitable, etc. Similarly, an attack on a nation's telecommunications system would prevent the financial, commercial, industrial and military systems from functioning efficiently. It could even affect the power grid, as components of the network would no longer be able to shunt power from areas that have an excess of energy to those that need it. Attacking a nation's information infrastructure, and through it the power grid, could result in untold devastation.

These attacks need not be conducted by bombs, missiles or any other "hard kill" mechanisms. Instead, most advocates of strategic information warfare see the assault as being carried out in the cyberspace with hacking techniques, "chipping" Trojan horses, worms and viruses,[15] together with the odd terrorist attack. Although few believe a strategic information attack could be decisive today, there are those who believe that they have the potential to play a major role in future conflict.

Quite clearly, the success of a strategic information attack will be a direct function of the dependence of an adversary on information flows. An attack on Iraq's financial systems during the Gulf War would not likely have been decisive; a well-planned, well-executed and successful attack on America's financial system might, however, have changed the course of the war. But an adversary's reliance on information is not enough. Friendly forces must have accurate intelligence, access to the system, and the technology necessary to effect the attack.

Operational Attack Paradigm

Advocates of the Operational Attack Paradigm, on the other hand, argue that the destruction of the adversaries' armed force remains the key to strategic victory. If the Allies failed in the Gulf War, they maintain, it was in failing to finish off the Iraqi military. There are at least three emerging operational concepts that support this Operational Attack Paradigm.

The first might be labeled "Precision Attrition." If, through the use of sophisticated information collection and information processing technologies, U.S. military forces can locate and identify all militarily important targets in the battlespace, then the only issue is whether the theater commander would have adequate precision attack systems, and whether he could destroy targets fast enough. If the commander knew the location of every fighter, bomber and logistical support aircraft, if he knew the position of every tank, every infantry fighting vehicle and every artillery piece, and if he could locate every surface, sub-surface and airborne naval platform, then why should the nation not develop the capability to destroy them in one single integrated precision strike? While the notion of "attrition warfare" may not be aesthetically pleasing to military professionals, precision attrition is attractive to those who believe that Americans are much less willing to risk casualties today than they have been in times past. Some historians, moreover, argue that it is in keeping with the United States predilection for attrition warfare.

A contrasting operational perspective could be called "OODA Loop Warfare." Primarily advocated by those who believe that the ability to use *time* effectively is as important in the Information Age as was employing *mass* in the Industrial Age, believers in OODA-Loop Warfare hold that the commander who can observe the situation, orient his thinking and his forces, decide what to do, and act with his available forces more quickly than his adversary will be victorious. He will be able to attack and complete the destruction of each subordinate element before the senior enemy commander can coordinate a response.

Developing this kind of capability would clearly require a shared situational awareness based on timely and accurate information about both friendly and enemy forces, delivered to the right person at the right time. It is here, of course, that modern information systems come into play. Collection mechanisms would allow the commander to observe and to orient more quickly than his adversary; processing power will help him decide on one of several possible courses of action; dissemination systems will ensure that his vision is shared by his subordinates and that he will be ready to act when the time comes. In short, OODA-Loop Warfare is, in many ways, a competition between information systems.

Yet a third operational attack method has been called by its creator, Jeffrey Cooper, "Coherent Operations." Cooper argues that information technologies have made it possible effectively to eliminate the "fog of war" that has long plagued attempts to coordinate military operations, and that they enable commanders to communicate their desires more effectively. In Cooper's words:

> The "Information Revolution" facilitates or enables a "Cognitive Revolution"; the real information revolution is not in the volume of information made available, but in the enabling of the higher order cognitive processes of better knowledge and better understanding...At the same time, the same technical advances across the range of C⁴I technologies also allow significantly improved real-time flows of information which bring situational awareness to all elements of the force and provide the means to communicate with and coordinate all elements of the force. Together the combination of cognition and coordination can provide the coherence that has heretofore been lacking in the conduct of military operations.[16]

Both of these paradigms and all of the emerging operational concepts based on them have a unique set of advantages and disadvantages. More striking, however, is that they all have two things in common. First, they are all *dependent* on information flows. Absent the ability to use information freely, none of the operational concepts described would work. As U.S. forces substitute the flow of information for the flow of troops, they may be creating a "center-of-gravity" for America's armed forces.

In a related sense, all of these operational concepts describe ways in which an Information Age power can defeat a nation still in the Industrial Age. Warden's model is useful in describing an attack against Iraq, but how would it work against an Information Age China, Russia, Japan or even a country like the United States? The Strategic Information War concept not only ignores both the extreme vulnerability of the U.S. to a counteroffensive, but, more importantly, the implications of global connectivity. How could one attack the financial system of an Information Age powerhouse without simultaneously attacking the world's financial system as a whole?

The operational attack paradigm has similar deficiencies. Although Precision Attrition, OODA-Loop Warfare and Coherent Operations might all work well against emerging second-wave armies, what would happen if the U.S. faced an "information peer?" If an adversary had as perfect an awareness of the battlespace as American forces, what would happen to the notion of Precision Attrition? Would victory fall to the side that struck first? To the side that possessed the greater number of weapons? If an information peer of the United States were expert in OODA-Loop Warfare and as determined to slow our decision cycle as we were to attack his, who would win? If an enemy built a force with sufficient cognitive and communications capabilities to fight Coherent Operations which side would have an advantage? If their advocates are correct and Precision Attrition, OODA-Loop Warfare or Coherent Operations are potentially revolutionary, war-winning approaches to military conflict, is it possible the U.S. could lose to a future information peer competitor?

Many who have thought about the answers to this question argue that no nation, in the foreseeable future, could develop as effective a fighting force as the U.S. military has become. Possibly, but with its reliance on commercial-off-the-shelf technology, can the United States be assured that its weapons will be superior to those of an adversary who may be purchasing off the same shelf? Consider specifically:

• The universal access to the Global Positioning System.

• The <1m resolution of commercial satellite imagery.

• The high bandwidth, universal coverage of new communication satellite constellations.

• The increasing availability of supercomputer technology.

• The willingness of Russia, China and a number of other countries to sell very high technology weaponry in the global arms market.

• The few resources it takes to produce biological, chemical and information weapons in the modern age. A computer dealer in Pakistan, after all, constructed the first computer virus released in the "wild."

• The initial work on the potentially revolutionary impact of the new technology on warfare was done in the Soviet Union in the early 1980s—not in the United States.

Some authorities have suggested that combat between Information Age peers—where both sides have equal forces and full knowledge of the battlespace—is likely to have some of the characteristics of a chess match. In chess, it is the better player that normally wins. The implication of this line of thinking is clear: we must train our leaders at all levels to understand Information Age combat better than their opponents. While few would challenge the wisdom of more and better training and education for our military leadership, the chess analogy has a flaw, for in war, "all's fair," and in chess one has to obey the rules. What if it were possible to place a screen between your opponent and the board that effectively hid certain specific squares from his view? If you could, you might be able to win handily and with far fewer pieces. What if it were possible to make the pieces on the chessboard look as if they were in different positions than they actually were, so that your opponent had a flawed understanding of the location and strength of the situation? What if a player could move pieces as fast as possible, without waiting for his opponent's response? While clearly against the rules in chess, these efforts to deny or distort the adversary's view of the battlespace are arrows in the quiver of the Information Age warrior.

Information Warfare

As a result, one of the major foci of combat in the Information Age will be efforts to control, perhaps even to dominate, the information environment. Both sides will aim at reducing an adversary to the equivalent of an Industrial Age power—to eliminate his ability to collect, process, store and disseminate information. They will try to deny the enemy advantages of force, time and space that come with the use of modern information technologies. In so doing they will be trying to contract the battlespace so that the opponent's long-range precision-strike systems cannot be used; they will try to increase the amount of time it takes the enemy to make decisions and execute operations; and they will try to deny him the use of cruise missiles and smart munitions that rely on information flows, forcing him to rely solely on his tanks, ships and planes—all of which are vulnerable to attack.

The fight to obtain an information advantage will take place in the physical space with bombs and bullets, in the cyberspace with hackers and jammers, and in the "mental space" with deception and psychological operations. Both sides will work to refuse their opponents the resources required to implement Precision Attrition, OODA Loop Warfare, Coherent Operations, Warden's inside-out warfare, or even the fruits of strategic information warfare. The conflict in the information space will require friendly forces not only to be able to attack the enemy's information systems, but also to defend their own.

Some maintain that battling for the information high ground has always been important in warfare and that attacking an enemy's information system is nothing new. But such an argument is like suggesting that nuclear weapons are nothing but larger explosives, that guided missiles are simply pilotless airplanes, or that the balloonist of the Civil War grasped the principles and implications of controlling the airspace above the battlefield. While at some level of abstraction these statements may be true, they are also irrelevant. *The use, reliance and subsequent dependence on information and information systems in modern military conflict has created a new environment for competition—the information environment. In this context, Information Warfare is rapidly becoming a new method of conflict in a new medium with revolutionary implications.*

Serious-minded soldiers, sailors and airmen have recognized the critical nature of the new information space. Admiral David E. Jeremiah, former Vice-Chairman of the Joint Chiefs of Staff, has argued that in the future "Global Dominance will be achieved by those that most clearly understand the role of information and the power of knowledge that flows from it."[17] Air Force Colonel James McLendon has written that "Information Warfare adds a fourth dimension of warfare to those of air, land and sea. In this new dimension, we must stay ahead."[18] And General Ronald Fogleman, Chief of Staff of the Air Force, has suggested that:

> "...this information explosion... signals that we're crossing a new frontier. Information has an ascending and transcending influence—for our society and our military forces. As such, I think it is appropriate to call information operations the fifth dimension of warfare. Dominating this information spectrum is going to be critical to military success in the future."[19]

Clearly, then, military forces will depend on information far more in the future than they have in the past. It is also clear that conflict in the information space—what analysts have called "Information Warfare"—will be a critical element of military conflict in the future. But what, exactly, is Information Warfare? What does it include? How ought we think about it?

One of the many problems one faces in understanding Information Warfare is the absence of a widely accepted definition. While some have suggested that a pure definition is not necessary, Martin Libicki from the National Defense University disagrees.

> Clarifying the issues is more than academic quibbling. First,... sloppy thinking promotes false synecdoche. One aspect of information warfare, perhaps championed by a single constituency, assumes the role of the entire concept, thus becomes grossly inflated in importance.

> Second, too broad a definition makes it impossible to discover any conceptual thread other than the obvious (that information warfare involves information and warfare), where a tighter definition might reveal one. Third, the slippery inference derived from loose aggregation points to the conclusion that the United States can and must seek dominance in information warfare it currently enjoys in air warfare, as if these arenas were comparable.[20]

Information Warfare has fallen prey to each of the pitfalls Libicki has identified. There are those in the Defense Department who see Information Warfare as nothing more than what Libicki calls "hacker warfare," and others believe it is little more than "a new form of psychological warfare."[21] In addition, some have argued that because information and perceptions are at the very heart of military conflict, information warfare encompasses everything. As a result, it is almost meaningless.[22] Finally, although there are some useful analogies between air warfare and Information Warfare, there are areas where the analogy breaks down. The cyber and perceptual spaces are not the same as the airspace; where "dominance" may have meaning in one, it may not be an achievable—or even a useful—objective in the other.[23]

Key to understanding Information Warfare is realizing that people think about the term "information" differently. To a commander, information is what his staff gives him; to a systems engineer, information is what flows within information systems; to an intelligence analyst information is the input to the intelligence process. Without a common understanding of the term "information," Information Warfare means little more than any particular analyst wants it to mean. In what will become a seminal piece in discussing the relationship between information on the one hand and power on the other, John Arquilla identifies several distinct meanings associated with the word "information," at least two of which have meaning for students of the RMA generally, and Information Warfare in particular.

The oldest and most traditional meaning of information is simply as a message. "Reduced to its bare essentials, it regards information as an immaterial message or signal that contains meaningful (or at least recognizable content) and that can be transmitted from a sender to a receiver.[24] It is this kind of information-as-message that sensors provide to operators, for example, that staffs provide to their commanders, or that commanders provide to their subordinates in terms of orders or instructions. Upon the basis of messages received from these and a variety of other sources, commanders and operators formulate perceptions of the situation and act accordingly.

By interfering with these messages, friendly forces might be able to influence the perceptions, and hence actions, of their adversary. Deception operations, of course, are as old as warfare itself. But in an era when commanders depend so heavily on the flow of information to make decisions, to target their weapons, and to communicate with their forces, deception operations could become far more important than they have been historically. The nature of deception operations has also changed in the Information Age. In the past, forces attempting to deceive the enemy had to create a reality for the adversary to discover. This, for example, was the case in World War II when the Allies created a false Army complete with inflatable tanks and mock radio traffic. The advent of the Information Age, however, presents new opportunities. Rather than constructing a false reality on the ground, friendly forces might be able to construct it in the cyberspace alone. They might try to insert images into the enemy's databases, or into the flow of data between a satellite and its ground station.[25] There are any number of places where the talented information warrior might be able to add to or delete from the enemy's information system to change the adversary's view of reality.

In an information rich environment, commanders are not the only people making decisions. Individual soldiers make decisions every day, for example, on whether to stay and fight or to run to the rear. They do so based on their perceptions—perceptions on the worthiness of their cause, of their commanders' competence, of the attitudes of their fellow soldiers and hundreds of other factors. The purpose of psychological operations, of course, is to influence these perceptions by changing the information front-line soldiers receive. As the Gulf War illustrated, leaflets can still be a valuable psychological operations resource. But as front-line soldiers have access to more and more sources of information,[25] and as these sources are more and more vulnerable to modification by the enemy, psychological operations will come to play a larger role in military operations.

A second view of "information" relates not to the message itself, but rather to the system through which messages are sent. In what has become a classic work on information theory, Norbert Weiner argues that "...the amount of information in a system is a measure of its degree of organization.[25] Other analysts have pursued this approach, as Arquilla and Ronfeldt point out, equating "information with 'organization,' 'order,' and 'structure'"[28] In this view, the content of an individual message is less important than the medium through which the message passes. If there is an information structure for the message to get through, then an organization exists. Absent the structure, there is no organization, and in fact entropy reins.

To show how this view of information applies to Information Warfare, imagine the standard line-and-block diagram of any organization, whether a commercial enterprise, a civilian bureaucracy or a military force. The lines connecting the various boxes represent flows of information. Staffs use these line to talk to other staff sections and to their managers or commanders; leaders use them to talk to both subordinates and to superiors, etc. Now imagine for a moment that these lines—these channels of communication—are disrupted. The cohesion of the organization begins to erode and its ability to respond in a coordinated fashion declines. Indeed, if one could stop all information from flowing, the organization as an entity would cease to exist. If no one within a sub-organization can talk to peers, superiors or to subordinates, confusion will reign.

By deliberately interfering with information flows, the information warrior can degrade the cohesion of enemy organizations and deny enemy commanders the ability to coordinate their forces. Friendly forces can concentrate on one enemy element at a time, knowing that the adversary cannot send reinforcements. In many respects, this was the technique used by the Coalition forces during the Gulf War. Because the Allies had successfully denied, degraded, destroyed, and disrupted Iraqi information channels, enemy commanders could not receive reports or instructions from higher headquarters, they could not receive reports from their front line units, and they could not direct the actions of their forward-based forces. In short, because of the lack of information flowing between and among Iraqi units, Baghdad's front-line forces did not constitute an army. Rather, they were individual units vulnerable to destruction in detail.

Intelligence organizations can use both the notion of information-as-messages and information-as-medium to learn about the adversary. By intercepting messages, friendly intelligence can tell a great deal about the enemy's capabilities and intentions. By recognizing the importance of information-as-medium, intelligence organizations can identify the locations of enemy forces and construct the enemy's order of battle. Both these functions have long played a role in warfare. In an information-rich environment, they will become even more important. While the Intelligence Community generally objects to calling the gathering of this kind of intelligence "information warfare," exploiting the enemy's information flows must be an integral part of Information Warfare for very practical reasons.

It would be dysfunctional in an information campaign to attack a headquarters whose frequencies have been determined, whose codes have been broken, and whose telephone lines have been tapped. This has always been a potential problem in warfare, but with an entire campaign directed at influencing the enemy's information capabilities, the danger is far greater in an environment in which Information Warfare is taking place. Operators and intelligence officers need to plan the campaign together. Not only must the intelligence officer try to preserve his most fruitful sources, but the operator might be able to help the intelligence effort by knocking out certain means of communication, forcing the adversary into channels that friendly forces can more easily monitor. During the Gulf War, allied forces did everything they could to destroy the land lines linking Baghdad with the front. The object was to force the Iraqi High Command onto the airwaves where the U.S. could monitor the back-and-forth traffic.

In a sense, then, there are three types of Information Warfare. *Type I Information Warfare involves managing the enemy's perceptions* through deception operations, psychological operations, what the Joint Staff calls "Truth Projection," and a variety of other techniques. At the same time, one must protect against enemy perception management efforts. Even an adversary like Saddam Hussein managed to pull off some deception coups against Coalition forces during Desert Storm. *Type II Information Warfare involves denying, destroying, degrading or distorting the enemy's information flows in order to break down his organizations and his ability to coordinate operations.* This kind of information warfare can be fought with bombs and bullets to destroy headquarters and communications nodes, with electronic jammers and other electronic warfare devices to interrupt the flow of information, with "hackers" to break into information systems or insert malicious code into networks, or any of a number of other techniques designed to deny information or information functions to those who need it. *Type III Information Warfare gathers intelligence by exploiting the enemy's use of information systems.* A much larger challenge, however, may be in protecting friendly information systems from exploitation by other intelligence organizations.

Although almost all nations have some capability to conduct Information Warfare, combat against an emergent "information peer" might be the most demanding. In an environment where an adversary has sensor, processing and communications capability similar to that of the United States, the ability to conduct Type I Information Warfare—

to manipulate the enemy's perception of the battlespace—will be especially critical. Success in Type I Information Warfare would allow friendly forces to move on the battlespace without being seen, would allow the conduct of deception operations, and would sow confusion as to the general situation. Although technologies and new military systems will be important in this effort, new operational concepts that allow greater dispersion, that eliminate tell-tale unit signatures, and that encourage deception measures at the tactical as well as the operational and strategic levels may well be necessary. But just as these defensive techniques become more and more important, so will the ability to "see through" enemy deception efforts. The winner of this contest between "hiders" and "finders" will have an extraordinary advantage on the future battlespace.

Similarly, in the emerging information environment, competitors are likely to undertake psychological operations of far greater sophistication than they have in the past. Opponents of the United States, for example, will have, through CNN and other international news organizations, access to some of the highest communications technology in the world. They will be able to disseminate information and messages to the American home front, as well as to soldiers, sailors, airmen and marines on the "front lines" with the speed of light. Absent the ability to respond to these messages, or without some kind of a "counter-psychological operations capability," U.S. forces may be very vulnerable to this kind of attack. Even if the adversary cannot execute an operation capable of influencing American combatants, he might be able to achieve even greater impact by attacking perceptions in CONUS itself. Indeed, many opponents have already indicated that they believe public perceptions to be America's Achilles' Heel. The ability to execute Type I Information Warfare operations—in both offensive and defensive modes—will be a key to military operations in the future.

Although the discussion among advocates of Information Warfare frequently point to the potential effect of Type II U.S. offensive capabilities on an adversary, perhaps more important is the impact of enemy attacks on the Defense Information Infrastructure (DII). As U.S. military forces rely more and more on the flow of information, friendly forces will become increasingly vulnerable to an enemy's attempt to interfere with that information flow by denying, destroying, degrading, or distorting segments of it. With a substantial amount of information flowing over non-secured networks, with forward-based weapons increasingly reliant on data flows from CONUS, with forces depending on centrally-managed and processed intelligence collection systems, and with logistics depending on the smooth functioning of the civilian Public Switch Network, the Department of Defense needs to look closely at the vulnerability not only of the networks, but of the force it intends to send in harm's way. By cutting off these flows of information, an adversary might be able to put American forces at risk before they even fire a shot.

Analysts often think of the enemy's ability to prosecute Type II Information Warfare at the tactical and operational levels through the use of jamming, other electronic warfare techniques, and through the physical destruction of headquarters or other communications nodes. Very little thought has been given to the effects of an attempt to interrupt information flows at the military-strategic level. There is, however, no guarantee that an enemy would allow the U.S. to maintain an "information sanctuary" in the continental United States. Indeed, some analysts have suggested that, "One clear implication of warfare in 2015 is that almost any enemy will try to degrade the U.S. information system."[29] By attacking the National Information Infrastructure, not only could an enemy deny the U.S. military its use,[30] but a successful attack could also severely damage the U.S. economy and stun the American polity.

In time of war, Type III Information Warfare can be critical to success, as was demonstrated during the Gulf War. Various U.S. national technical means of intelligence collection, the RC-135 Rivet Joint, and various other ELINT systems were crucial to Allied success. But exploiting information flows is not limited to wartime. It takes place every day, as U.S. and foreign intelligence agencies try to learn about the others' military capabilities, their order of battle and their intentions. Nor does it always take place within the military domain. Foreign penetration of networks carrying research and development data from American corporations can be strategically useful to adversaries, as can databases containing information about the international marketing efforts and future pricing plans of defense contractors.

Although critical to military forces operating in time of conflict in an information-rich environment, Type I, Type II and Type III Information Warfare can take place across the spectrum of operations, ranging from everyday peacetime competition, to Operations Other Than War (OOTW), to full-fledged military conflict. In the military domain, it can include activity at all three levels of warfare—the tactical, the operational and the strategic. As the U.S. and other militaries rely more and more on information systems, they will become increasingly vulnerable. It may well be true that while today information warfare is a useful adjunct to the conduct of military operations, tomorrow it will be the *sine que non* of warfare: a nation without an Information Warfare capability will be a nation without a military capability.

In addition, of course, Information Warfare can also target national-level systems that are not directly connected to the military—like public opinion, the national information infrastructure, or commercial organizations with new high technology research in their databases. Figure 2, then, provides one way to think about the various dimensions of Information Warfare in the future:

A few things are notable about the matrix. First, it is clear that Information Warfare will not be limited to the military domain. Just as air power subjected the homeland of belligerents to destruction from the air, Information Warfare subjects countries to attack through the perceptual space and the cyberspace. Attacks on the national information space will have the dual effect of eroding military capability and of attacking the national will. A nation whose banking system has been credibly threatened, or whose financial system has been brought down may not be willing to pursue strategic goals abroad. *Whether or not the military is responsible for defense of the national information space is a matter for debate—a debate that needs to take place sooner rather than later. Right now, no one is responsible.*

Second, in thinking about Information Warfare, policy makers must address both the capabilities and vulnerabilities of the nation in each of the individual cells. While it may be easier and more in keeping with the military ethos to plan the conduct of offensive Information Warfare, it is far more important to be able to defend one's own information

	National			Military		
	Peace	Crisis	War	Peace	Crisis	War
Type I: Perception Mgt						
Type II: Denial, destruction, degradation, distortion of data						
Type III: Exploiting enemy information flows						

Figure 2: Information Warfare (Notional)

space. While it might be possible to mandate that the Services provide protection for all the new information-based systems they are in the process of developing, it clearly would not be possible, without the expenditure of tens of billions of dollars, to protect those legacy systems that will be with the nation for the next thirty or forty years. As a result, American military forces may have to change their way of doing business—their operational concepts—to reduce vulnerabilities.

Third, although the figure contains references only to national level Information Warfare, sub-national forces, including terrorist groups already employ crude Information Warfare techniques. If they were to develop a more sophisticated approach to the subject, their impact on the nation might be all out of proportion to their numbers.

Finally, a caveat. While Information Warfare will take place in each of these cells, far more important may be the interaction among them. A sophisticated Type I information attack against the U.S. national will, for example would have an effect on perceptions within the military. Thus, the Information Warfare matrix is not a panacea. It is designed primarily to demonstrate the breadth of information warfare as well as to eliminate areas of combat that do not belong.

Conclusions

In seems clear that the combination of new technologies and the military systems they have spawned have altered the battlespace profoundly. Recognizing these changes, analysts have proposed a number of alternative operational concepts at both the strategic and the operational level of warfare. Each of these operational concepts, however, and many others that have not been discussed, are *dependent on having an information advantage over the adversary*. To believe that all of America's future adversaries are going to allow the United States to operate unfettered in the information space—that they will not develop their own information capabilities, or that they are not going to employ offensive techniques to fight for control of the information space—is a path fraught with danger. There should be no doubt that future adversaries will develop military-information capabilities and systems of systems that rival those of the United States. There should be no doubt that components of the emerging system of systems will be targets of offensive Information Warfare. Future adversaries will fight for control of the information space in the theater of operations, as well as in the United States. This combat will take place in the physical space, in the cyberspace and in the perceptual space. The goal of both sides will be to obtain an information advantage that they can leverage into strategic gains.

As the U.S. military thinks through the implications of the coming RMA, it is crucial that they recognize the role that information will play in future warfare. The armed forces must develop operational concepts and organizational structures that are not only capable of fighting *for* superiority in this new environment, but are also proficient at fighting *in* it—of taking advantage of the enemy's mistakes in the information space and of capitalizing on friendly successes. To achieve this end, they must look closely at methods of fighting the information war, but also of exploiting advantages achieved by information warriors.

Endnotes

[1] In fact, one could make the argument—as I have elsewhere—that the most important military characteristic of the coming age is not that we are witnessing a revolution in military affairs, but that we are entering an "Era of Military Revolutions," with the First Information RMA followed by revolutions driven by bio-technologies, space technologies, directed energy weapons, and possibly many more. In such an environment, the key to victory is the ability to adjust procurement policies, operational concepts and organizational structures more rapidly than the adversary.

[2] John Arquilla and David Ronfeldt, "Cyber War is Coming!" *Comparative Strategy*, Vol. 1, No. 2, p. 143. See also Sproull and Kesler, *Connections: New Ways of Thinking in the Networked Organization*, Cambridge: MIT Press, 1991.

[3] Andrew F. Krepinevich, "Cavalry to Computer: The Pattern of Military Revolutions," *The National Interest*, No. 37 (Fall) 1994, p. 30.

[4] General Gordon R. Sullivan and Colonel James M. Dubik, "War in the Information Age," *Military Review*, April 1994, p. 47.

[5] U.S. Government, Department of Defense, *Conduct of the Gulf War Campaign*, Washington, DC: USGPO, April 1992, pp. 291-292.

[6] General Gordon R. Sullivan and Lieutenant Colonel James M. Dubik, *Land Warfare in the 21st Century*, Carlisle Barracks, PA: Strategic Studies Institute, 1993, pp. 12-14.

[7] Sullivan and Dubik, *Land Warfare in the 21st Century*, p. 22.

[8] Admiral William A. Owens, "System of Systems," *Armed Forces Journal International*, January 1996, p. 47.

[9] Cited in, Kenneth Allard, COL, USA, "Information Warfare and the Challenge to Corporate Culture," Presentation to the Annual Convention of the Electronic Industries Association, Phoenix AZ, October 11, 1995.

[10] See US Army Training and Doctrine Command Pamphlet 525-5, Force *XXI Operations: A Concept for the Evolution of Full-Dimensional Operations for the Strategic Army of the Early Twenty-First Century*, Ft. Monroe, VA: Headquarters, US Army Training and Doctrine Command, 1994), p. 3-5.

[11] They may even find that the very basis of military organizations needs to change away from traditional notions of battalions, brigades, etc.

[12] Joseph S. Toma, "Desert Storm Communications," in Alan D. Campen (ed.), *The First Information War*, Fairfax, VA: AFCEA International Press, 1992), p. 5.
[13] TRADOC Pamphlet 525-5, *Force XXI Operations*, p. 1-5.
[14] Col. John A. Warden III, "Air Power for the Twenty-First Century," in Barry R. Schneider and Lawrence E. Grinter (eds.), *Battlefield of the Future: 21st Century Warfare Issues*, Maxwell AFB, AL: Air University Press, 1995), p. 114.
[15] Some of the best discussions on different kinds of malicious programs can be found in Peter J. Denning (ed.), *Computers Under Attack: Intruders, Worms and Viruses*, New York: ACM Press, 1990.
[16] Jeffrey Cooper, "The Coherent Battlefield—Removing the Fog of War:' A Framework for Understanding An MTR of the "Information Age," unpublished paper, June 1993, p. 24.
[17] Quoted in John G. Roos, "InfoTech InfoPower," *Armed Forces Journal International*, June 1994, p. 31.
[18] Col. James W. McLendon, "Information Warfare: Impact and Concerns," in Barry R. Schneider and Lawrence E. Grintner (eds.), *Battlefield of the Future: 21st Century Warfare Issues*, Maxwell AFB, AL: Air University Press, 1995, p. 171.
[19] General Ronald R. Fogleman, "Information Operations: The Fifth Dimension of Warfare," in remarks to the Armed Forces Communication-Electronics Association, Washington DC, April 25, 1995. Cited in *Defense Issues*, Vol. 10, No. 47, p. 1. Fogleman argues that space is the fourth dimension of warfare.
[20] Martin C. Libicki, *What is Information Warfare*, Washington DC: National Defense University, 1995, pp. 3-4.
[21] See for example, George J. Stein, "Information War - Cyberwar - Netwar," in Schnieder and Grintner (eds.), *Battlefield of the Future: 21st Century Warfare Issues*, Maxwell AFB, AL: Air War College, 1995, pp. 153-170.
[22] John Rothrock addresses the issue in "Information Warfare: Time for Some Constructive Skepticism," SRI International, unpublished paper, July 1994.
[23] See Libicki, *What is Information Warfare*, pp. 94-96. For a different perspective on information dominance, see John Arquilla, "The Strategic Implications of Strategic Dominance," *Strategic Review*, Vol. 22, No. 3 (Summer) 1994, pp. 24-30.
[24] John Arquilla and David Ronfeldt, "Information Power and Grand Strategy," unpublished paper, July 1995 draft, p. 5. To be published in April 1996 by the Center for Strategic and International Studies.
[25] See especially the distinction between direct and indirect information warfare contained in the U.S. Air Force Paper, "Cornerstones of Information Warfare," unpublished draft, 11 August 1995, pp. 8-13.
[26] What will happen, for example, when U.S. soldiers can place and receive cellular telephone calls to and from anywhere via commercial satellites? What will happen when small units are plugged in to the global information infrastructure and soldiers receive different information there than they do from their own commanders?
[27] Norbert Wiener, *Cybernetics: or Control and Communication in the Animal and the Machine*, Cambridge: The MIT Press, 1949, p. 11. Cited in Arquilla and Ronfeldt, "Information, Power and Grand Strategy," p. 7.
[28] Arquilla and Ronfeldt, "Information, Power and Grand Strategy," p. 8.
[29] George F. Kraus, "Information Warfare in 2015," *Naval Institute Proceedings*, August, 1995, p. 42.
[30] Over 90% of all DoD communications takes place over the Public Switch Network. In addition, the military uses the Internet extensively, particularly for logistics and administrative functions. How well the military could operate without these various means of communications—whether for a few days or several weeks—is a matter of conjecture.

War, Information and History: Changing Paradigms

Elin Whitney-Smith

We are experiencing what some have called a crisis of will and others a loss of patriotism. War has become a spectator sport. For example, Scott O'Grady—American hero. The story of his ordeal and rescue have become an important part of American heroic history. Now, let us imagine for a moment what we would have felt if he had not been rescued. All the media attention would have been focused on how his friends and family felt at his loss. We do not just see heroes home and happy; we also see body bags. *It is difficult, if not impossible, for us to fight a war with such an individualized focus.*

The nature of what constitutes a threat has changed. We used to feel threatened by a foreign power's strength, by its weapons and armies. Now, we are threatened by a foreign power's weakness and poverty. We can be brought to the bargaining table by boatloads of sick and poor, instead of their young and strong—armed. It happened with Haiti and again with Cuba. This is a complete reversal of the ordinary power equation.

People's fears are increasing, as they are challenged by contact with a global world. The crimes of the inner city are in our living rooms. As the divergence between the "haves" and "have-nots" increases, both rich and poor are more likely to listen to demagogues who call for a return to societies defined by ethnic and religious values. The rich listen because they see the old values supporting stability, and the poor listen because they feel cheated and frightened.

All of these problems stem from the Information Revolution, because an information revolution creates a totally new world. If we want to function in this new world, we must understand the dynamics of information and war.

Information and War: two words. If we think about their meaning, they seem strange put together.

Information has a quicksilver quality. It can't really be defined. If I try to grab the meaning, it splits, rolls away and joins up with other bits. People try to define it in order to capture it in words, try to draw distinctions between data and information, or knowledge and wisdom, but it still eludes capture. Information doesn't obey the normal laws of physics. Information grows through sharing. It is not exclusive. I give you some information, and I still have it. Or you give me some information, and I don't get it. You give it to me again and again, and I still don't get it. Then suddenly, after you have given up, I get it! Information can't be quantified. I can count the words in a book or the bytes in a computer file, but I can't count how much information I get out of reading a paragraph or a book or attending a seminar. Information is unlimited. As I study any phenomenon, there is more to learn—more to know. Information is not absolute. It depends on context. It is in the eye of the beholder. Looking across a flat Alaskan landscape, I see nothing. I see emptiness. An Eskimo hunter sees a wealth of information about animals that have crossed it, the thickness of the ice, and as many as seven kinds of snow. By the same token, I can call a computer an information technology; but if I lack the skills to use it, it is just a big rock.

Some would say that War is about killing people and breaking things. Things and people are part of the world of matter and energy. They, unlike information, obey the laws of physics. Things and people can be counted. We may have many of a kind of thing, but each is one and one only. Things are exclusive. If you give me a thing, you no longer have it. Things are absolute. If one is lost or destroyed, that very thing cannot be replaced. Even it we make more things, the laws of thermodynamics tell us that in making something (work transforming matter to energy or vice versa) there is heat loss—entropy—that cannot be recaptured. The problems of material things are problems of scarcity.

We say that we are entering an Information Age, that we live in an information economy. But economy, like war, is involved with quantity and with scarcity. The problems of an information age are problems of plenty. And indeed, some of the problems of our time relate to plenty: Software piracy, intellectual property, how to quantify the "look and feel" of a piece of software or how to define information theft when the original owner still has the original information.

The problems of war are problems of scarcity. Information technology has shown us that Scott O'Grady or a child starving in Somalia or a couple on a boat from Haiti are all individuals. War has been about killing people, but those people were previously just numbers. We felt that it was all right for those numbers to be sacrificed to fix some scarcity—land, oil, wealth. The scarcity was more important than the numbers. But now we know these people for individuals, we feel their loss, we feel scarcity. Suddenly, the things we are being asked to sacrifice them for—land (especially other people's land)—seems less scarce and less desirable.

These problems arise because we are experiencing a shift from a world of scarcity to a world of plenty, while others, against whom we may have to fight, are still in the world of scarcity. We inhabit different perceptual worlds, and we don't know how to think about it or how to operate within it. It would be to our advantage for all to be in the same perceptual world. It would be a fitting Information War.

To begin to understand what we are going through, we need to understand that information revolutions have changed the perceptual world before, that these changes can be studied and understood and that we can use that knowledge to understand today's Information Revolution. We will start by looking at the last Ice Age and the death of the first information culture.

The First Information Culture

Ten thousand years ago, the first information culture perished along with the woolly mammoth, the giant bison, the mastodon, and the saber tooth tiger. It had been the dominant way of life for many millennia. It was, in comparison to all but the most recent standards, a global culture.

I call it an information-based culture because, if the people of the time were like recent hunter-gatherers, they got their living by knowing—not owning. They were secure, because they knew where the animals would be and when the plants would be ready to gather. The world they perceived was a world of plenty—there was enough to go around. An individual's status was based on stories, songs and knowledge rather than on what he or she owned.[1] Since anyone, regardless of gender or family, are likely to have good stories or songs, it was a relatively egalitarian society. There was no war amongst hunter-gatherers since: 1) it was not possible to take away a person's knowledge through force, 2) they owned very little, and 3) what they did own they shared.

From our perspective, the world of the Ice Age seems idyllic—new places to see and new people to meet, no war, the perception of plenty, sharing, and status based on telling stories, dancing dances, and singing songs. *The paradigm was that of plenty—Eden.*

Scarcity - The End of Eden

The extinction of the large herd herbivores suddenly made the perceived world of plenty into a perceived world of scarcity. There were massive famines.[2] It wasn't enough to know where something grew or where animals would pass; it became necessary to own, to control, and to restrict resources. Hunting and gathering became a marginalized life-style practiced by only a few. People started to create cultures based on owning material goods, not on sharing information. The strong who could take away things from others gained more status. Eden was no more.

The Invention of War - Jacob and Esau

In the new perceptual world—the world of scarcity—security was based on owning material goods. People used their knowledge of gathering to make crops grow where they wanted them—agriculture. Others used their knowledge of animals to gather together and domesticate herds of animals—pastoralism. Jacob and Esau. In both of these life-ways, people took their identity from their group and were secure because they were members of a group. *The paradigm was group membership.*

War is a response to scarcity. The forms reflect the kind of scarcity each group experienced.

Nomads (Esau) experienced periodic scarcity, and so became raiders. They used their knowledge of how to kill and how to herd and break up groups to kill and scatter their opponents. Since the scarcity they experienced was irregular, and since they did not plant, they did not have an attachment to owning geography. Thus, their form of war was brutal and brief.

Agriculturists (Jacob) settled and planted. As the populations grew, they experienced a scarcity of land and expanded outward to take over more and more land. They developed war based on standing and defending a piece of geography. First they built walled settlements, perhaps against the raiders, and then with the rise of a new information technology—writing—cities and empires. Their attachment was to geography, since wealth came from land. They developed defensive wars and then wars of imperialism.

Thus we have three paradigms: Eden, Jacob and Esau. The interactions between these paradigms each determined the kind of war that evolved.

Writing: The First Information Technology

Jacob's Line: From Writing to Rome

Scarcity created a need to know who was a legitimate member of a group and who was not, who worked and contributed, and who did not. Pre-literate groups were kin groups. The elders of a kin group knew who was related to whom and therefore who was a member in good standing. Many pre-literate groups are matralines; but even where they were not, women were valued, because they reproduced the kin unit [3] Group size had an administrative limit. It was limited by the ability to track membership and work. Security and identity was based on kin membership, not on individual effort or identity. Non-members were either adopted into the kin structure, which gave them an identity, or were considered enemies or slaves.

Scarcity leads to hierarchy. Those who are stronger can take things from those who are weaker. Tribute can be extracted from outsiders or from weaker members of the group. Those who can use information, might or charisma to gain a leadership position can restrict the means of survival to the members of his choosing.

The transition from small agricultural groups to civilizations begins the same way throughout the world. One of a number of similar, small agricultural groups is suddenly able to grow and dominate the surrounding groups. It is able to create irrigation projects and to make war. That group has some form of symbol system—Sumerian cuneiform, Egyptian hieroglyphics, Incan quipu, Chinese characters. Writing presents an organizing metaphor that creates the perception that things can be classified and organized. *The paradigm was class and organization—an information revolution.*

A symbol system made it possible to administer—to track membership and to tax. Group size could expand. Taxes may have taken the form of service in the military or of labor on state projects. Tracking people and membership and taxing wealth were necessary for war or irrigation projects to move beyond an amateur, part-time activity. Since membership could be tracked, kin units were less important for defining membership; and kin units were likely units of revolution, so women and their role as reproducers of the kin unit were devalued. Membership in the group as a whole was more important than either individual or kin identity.

Organizational ability and class structure came with writing. Writing presented an orderly, linear metaphor. People began to realize that they could organize things and people in a better, more orderly manner—things and people could be counted and classified. John Keegan[4] tells us that the military power of the early hydraulic societies was not based on any superiority in technology or in manpower, but in organization. Writing was a way to keep information private. Certain groups could dominate other groups based on their superior access to information. Writing limited access to information to those who could read—the elite—and thus consolidates their power. It created a different way of thinking for those who could read and those who could not. This validated and perpetuated the class structure. Class identity and group identity were important. A three-part elite developed:

• The king, pharaoh, inca or other political ruler was seen as a god or as a representative of god.
• Rulers were advised by priests or scribes who controlled information. They were often in charge of state projects and kept the tax records.
• The military defended the group against outsiders and kept the populace under control.

The purpose of war, for these groups, was to expand, to acquire more land, and to enslave and obtain tribute from those conquered. Through trial and error and clashes with other city-states and barbarians (the inheritors of the nomad raider tradition of war), this world view and way of life and war progressed through various city-states to empires culminating, in the West, with Rome.

Wars were fought either against the nomadic peoples or against other city-states or empires. The kind of enemy faced influenced how the military developed. If the threat was from nomadic raiders, then defensive war developed, as in China where there was emphasis on defensive structures (the Great Wall) and harassing the invader. The notion of decisive battles did not evolve. If the threat was from an equal, then tactics and strategies escalate and evolved. If there was no threat from an equal then little military development was necessary and, as with the Aztecs of the New World,[5] war could become largely ceremonial. War did not disappear, because the military elite had to continue to justify its place in the society and the three-part elite needed to control organized violence in case the common people rebelled.

Esau's Line: The Nomads and Horse People

Nomads kept more of the world view of the hunter-gatherers. They retained relatively egalitarian, kin-based social groups or alliance of kin groups led by a charismatic leader. They may have been the inventors of war, applying their knowledge of killing and cutting into a herd of animals to clashes with others. Over time, they too continued to evolve, inventing the chariot, cavalry and the stirrup. Their inventions were taken over by those whom they attacked. Nomads had no attachment to owning geography, because nomads did not plant. They swept in, took what was portable, and left. If nomads decided to settle and were successful, they took over much of the existing political structure and became part of the agricultural line, e.g., the Normans in France, the Jutes in the British Isles, the Manchus in China.

The Wars of Jacob and Esau

When the agriculturists (Jacob's line) made war on hunter-gatherers (Eden) or on nomadic peoples (Esau's line), the result was imperialism. When Esau's line made war on Eden, the result was enslavement of the people of Eden. When Esau's line attacked a similar society, the loser either became enslaved by or paid tribute to the winner. Only when the more advanced agriculturists (Jacob's line) made war against each other—either offensively or defensively—did "progress" occur in the nature of warfare. If Esau's line engaged in warfare with Jacob's through raiding, the defending agricultural society developed more sophisticated fortifications. When Jacob's line engaged in peer competition, regardless of outcome, there was a notable escalation of the development in technology, tactics, strategy, and military organization. At this point, we have a simple model of the evolution of war before the Fall of Rome.

Defense / Offense	Eden	Jacob	Esau
Jacob	**Imperialism** *Jacob attacks Eden*	Escalation of Technology, Tactics, Strategy, and Organization. Decisive battles, dominance by victor *Jacob attacks Jacob*	Imperialism, Expansion from city-states to empires *Jacob attacks Esau*
Esau	**Enslavement** *Esau attacks Eden*	Raiding, Defensive fortifications/walls Assimilation and Harassment. *Esau attacks Jacob*	Few highly violent encounters. Little escalation of tactics. Losers enslaved or tributary to winners. *Esau attacks Esau*

Figure 1: Jacob vs Esau vs Eden

Notes:
1) The type of response to scarcity determines what kind of war develops. Agriculturists develop defensive war over land. Pastoralists develop offensive raiding for booty to address periodic scarcity.
2) The type of competition determines how far the art of war evolves. Little competition against poorly organized or poorly equipped groups results in expansion with little or no evolution in the art of war. Competition against well armed, well equipped groups results in evolution of tactics, technology and strategy.

Information and Empire

The evolution of writing, the perception of organization and classification, and the development of the three-part elite, are administrative developments that allowed group size to expand beyond the kinship unit of the small agricultural group. Empires, too, have administrative limits.

The Limits of Empires: Rome and China

The Han of China swept out of their home area, conquering land for hydraulic agriculture, assimilating or enslaving some people, and pushing the hunting-gathering bands up into the hills or out of the area suitable for agriculture. They kept expanding until they reached the limit of cultivable land. As new technologies and new waterways were opened up, the empire and the limit of agriculture expanded. The Great Wall is roughly in the area where farming becomes unsuitable. Throughout China's history, there have been changes of dynasty. Periodically, nomads swept in from the north and either took over the government and took on the characteristics of the governed, or they simply took booty and went away. There were times of disorganization, when each area was ruled by its local warlord. But throughout, the Confucian civil service (information owners) played a role in balancing and shifting allegiances, sometimes having great power and sometimes less, but continuing to maintain a rough stability. *China reached the economic limit and thus did not exceed the administrative, organizational or information limits.*

Rome expanded too, conquering and moving on, demanding tribute from the conquered. The economy was dependent on the continuous expansion of the empire. Rome had evolved a civil service and the mechanisms of an empire. Roman citizenship was coveted. It provided a valued class identity. As the borders were pushed further and further outward, administration and maintenance of the military and the empire became more expensive and more unwieldy. Barbarians often found it profitable to join the empire, become citizens, and become part of the military. Despite the adoption of Roman citizenship, groups wanted to maintain their own customs and identities. They made different treaties with the empire. The administrative task grew with each new agreement. When the empire was attacked, individual groups of military might defend the empire, or they might make common cause with the attackers. *The Roman Empire outgrew the administrative or information limits before it reached an economic limit.*

After Rome: Esau in Jacob's World

In the West, there is a more developed notion of individual identity. Fewer people define themselves primarily in reference to their national or ethnic group. Their main source of meaning in life is based on individual fulfillment. The dynamic that started the evolution of the individual started with the fall of Rome. The evolution of the individual is based on the separation of the major information provider from the traditional power structure. *The fall of Rome initiated a paradigm of individuality and competition.*

With the fall of Rome, the Roman civil service disappeared, as did the political and military structure. The Roman Church was the only remaining information provider and the only institution that preserved its organization. The political and military functions had become so disorganized that each small town or manor had to provide for its own administration and defense. It was every small group and every individual against every one else; it was a highly competitive and individualized atmosphere.

The defense against nomadic raiders had been to build defensive walls. In the Middle Ages, we see individual raiders or small groups attacking increasingly elaborate castles, and the knights themselves becoming fortified in their armor.

The organizational paradigm was Esau's, but he was living in Jacob's world. Alliances were personal, following the form of the Germanic tribes. Wars in the early Middle Ages were individual feuds or rivalries between small groups. Any small-holder could set himself up as a military power.[6] There were no tactics or strategy as we would understand them today.

Unlike nomadic war, people of the Middle Ages fought for territory as well as booty. Although individual lords had priests to advise and to administer for them, the Church as an institution did little to create order out of the chaos of European politics. It supported one prince and then another, depending upon where its interest lay. This led to a kind of arms race between factions and factions of factions.

The Roman Church maintained its organization. It did not need the princes. It had a vested interest in keeping the princes relatively powerless and so could afford to promote the laity. It had the right of direct taxation—tithing. Tithing made it an advantage to the Church for the laity to be economically productive. Therefore it was to the Church's advantage to foster the development of technology and the spread of information. Monasteries of the Middle Ages often functioned as agricultural extension centers do today, to develop and spread information about techniques and technologies to increase productivity. The individual was encouraged to be productive and to give to the Church. Women as well as men were educated by the Church. In the early Middle Ages, many of the scribes were women. Literacy was more a function of class than of gender. The kind of Christianity that developed in the West supported good works and supported technology as a way of doing good works.[7]

In contrast, the Byzantine Empire continued the three-part elite structure that had obtained before the fall of Rome. The financial existence of the Eastern Church was dependent on the political power structure. Its interests lay in supporting the Empire. It developed a Christianity which supported mysticism, asceticism and submission to the will of God instead of good works. It did not encourage individual productivity or individual learning, nor did it spread knowledge to the laity. Thus, a notion of the individual did not develop. Identity was still based in group membership.

The fall of Rome broke the three-part elite structure. The Church could afford to use its power to support one faction and then another. It set up a highly competitive dynamic in Europe: princes against princes, the common people against the princes, and the church supporting one group or another and often supporting the development of individual wealth over that of political leaders.

Militarily, it led to an escalation of arms and the art of war—competition against similarly armed and equipped groups resulted in the evolution of tactics, technology and strategy.

It was an Information Revolution, because it increased information access for the non-elite. For the first time individuals were encouraged by their value system (the Roman Church) to use technology and learning to better their condition, regardless of their membership in a social group. Socially, it led to a more individualistic frame of reference.

We can begin to see a difference between contexts, where information was relatively free (available to people who were not members of the traditional elite) and where information was controlled by the traditional elite. *Free information leads to an increased sense of the individual.* As shown in Table 2, from the fall of Rome onward, the group with the freest information tends to win. They win because they are better able to invent, produce and economically survive any conflict.

Information Provider	Information Controlled	Not Controlled
Church	Byzantium	Europe
Printing Press	Spain, Italy, Portugal	Holland, England
Telephone & Telegraph	USSR	USA
Main Frame Computers	USSR	USA
PCs & Internet	???	???

Figure 2: Information Eras

The Print Revolution

The Printing Press: Phase I

Writing had introduced the notion of linear organization of thought. The fall of Rome introduced the notion of individuality; and the printing press, with its standard replaceable type, standard letters and standard editions of books, presented the people with a metaphor that they applied to all aspects of life. *The paradigm of standardization and replicability.*

The initial impact of the printing press was toward consolidation of the absolutist state. The nation-state replaced the city-state as the principal political unit. Increased access to books led to an increase in upper class lay literacy which helped the formation of the first nation-states. Kings founded universities to educate future government ministers. Ministers were needed to oversee the King's courts and the regulation and taxing of trade between towns and overseas. Demand increased for standard nation-wide law and regulation.

With the increased ability to tax and with the emerging consolidation, kings had access to treasuries and mercenaries. The military became more professionalized; it owed allegiance, albeit a purchased allegiance, to the king instead of being based on personal fealty to a feudal lord, as had been the case in the Middle Ages. Howard describes the army of the French invasion of 1494:

> With hindsight we can describe Charles VII's force as the first "modern" army, in that it consisted of the three arms deployed in various mutually supporting tactical combinations, and was very largely made up of men paid from a central treasury.[8]

War was still a matter of relations between princes, but increasingly those relations were based on economic and military power, not feudal obligations or rivalries. The political doctrines of the printer's son Machiavelli maintained that states alone could judge their own interests, and those interests were those of the prince.

The most powerful entities of the late Middle Ages in the West were the cities of Italy and the Iberian peninsula that were in closest contact with the major information provider—the Church. At first, they were in the forefront of the new information age. They explored, made new maps, learned and taught about navigation technologies and had an active, information-rich culture. The Church continued its support for learning and staffed the various state ministries and universities, founded for upper-class training.

The Printing Press: Phase II

With the coming of the Protestant Reformation, the Church lost its religious and information monopoly. It began to make decisions based on fear. Suddenly it felt it needed the support of the political and military powers. The western Catholic Church made alliances with the political powers in Spain, Portugal, and Italy, becoming like the Church of the Byzantine Empire. (Although France remained a Catholic nation, the alliance between the powers were not as strong as on the Iberian Peninsula.) During the Inquisition and the Counter-Reformation, the Church suppressed information and information technology. It stopped preaching a Christianity of individualism, withdrew support of technology to further good works, and began to stress obedience to authority and a more mystical Christianity.

The Protestant countries, Holland and England, did not suppress information technology. They became print-intensive cultures in the same way as we are a TV-intensive culture. A literate crafts-producing class developed—people who had grown up in crafts shops and then learned to read. They were able to use written records to keep track of raw material and finished goods. It set them free of the old style of family-based production. They invented the basic structure of capitalism based on the division of wage labor (standard labor producing a standard product) and the ownership of the means of production (replicability based on standard machines and standard measures). The power equation and every institution of life changed—an Information Revolution.

First Holland and then England became the most powerful nations in Europe. Many of the printers from Spain moved to the Netherlands. There they found people who wanted to know and wanted to buy every kind of printed material. How-to books, business manuals, pornography, music, maps, playing cards, and children's books all were printed and bought. The merchants used their new literacy to rationalize trading. Literacy allowed them to use book-keeping to follow good and bad investments and to track more merchandise than previously. The production of textiles could be put on a more productive footing as craftsmen tracked markets and styles.

England entered the Information Revolution later than the Dutch because of the persecution of Protestants and limits on the printing press imposed by the Catholic Queen Mary. With her death, printers again became active in England. Since the Dutch controlled trade, entrepreneurs in England had to find another niche. A new generation of businessmen arose, who were themselves sons of craftsmen, but who combined knowledge of the craft with literacy and numeracy. They were able to give out standard amounts of raw material and pay standardized prices for a defined, standard amount and quality of finished goods, because they could keep track of the transaction. These literate craftsmen invented the "putting-out" system. Some employed as many as 100 apprentices.[9] The new way of doing business made it possible for English goods to be made more cheaply than could be made by crafts production.

As more and more people who were formerly craftspeople became wealthy, they were able to purchase privilege. During the English Revolution, many of Cromwell's supporters and advisors were drawn from the new class of wealthy, literate sons of craftsmen. Increasingly, social place was seen as more related to wealth than to birth. With the restoration of the monarchy, wealthy merchants and manufacturers were able to gain access to political power. Social mobility increased.

Before the change in production, the family had been the major social and economically-productive unit. It included the biological family (often several generations), apprentices, journeymen and hired help, all of whom lived together. With the ability of the master craftsman to track work with writing and book-keeping, production moved out of the home. The family as a unit became part of the private sphere and second in importance to the economically-productive unit.

This change in the productive relations had repercussions for the family. Women and children of the master's family ceased to be active in production. They lost their economic importance. Literacy became the mark of adulthood, thus defining the non-literate as non-adults. Privacy became more important, as certain information could be kept from the non-literate. Children, who had been seen as small adults, emerged as a separate age-class that had to be protected from certain information.[10] As the home became separated from the place of production, distinctions arose between public and private, work and home, exterior and interior. Women, children and the old became part of the private, interior world; and, since they were all non-literate and not part of the activities related to production, they were increasingly seen as non-adult.

From the invention of writing to the rise of Rome, war evolved within the same paradigm. From the fall of Rome to the invention of the printing press, war evolved in the same way—groups forming alliances and coming together in larger and larger units, again within the same paradigm—*the paradigm of feudal fealty*.

From the invention of the printing press and the rise of the nation-state, war evolved to be increasingly standardized—professional, better organized and disciplined and including more people, culminating in the mass armies of the Napoleonic Era. The war paradigm was based on a standardized conception of armies—infantry, artillery and cavalry—led by officers who had some education in the art of war, facing each other using what tactics and technology they possessed to win on a particular piece of ground. The winner had better tactics, better technology, more men or had been able to choose the ground for an advantage. And like the two previous eras, competition against similarly armed and equipped groups resulted in an evolution of tactics, technology and strategy. But amongst these groups, there was no difference in how they believed the battle should be fought or what war was.

During the latter part of this period, armies did encounter different paradigms, and they were disconcerted. Napoleon's armies marched into Russia. The Cossacks, acting within Esau's war paradigm, attacked and harassed the troops, while yielding and even destroying territory, running away when Napoleon's army expected them to stand and fight. Their behavior did not conform to the standards expected of the military. Their activities disconcerted and disgusted the great European military thinker, Karl Von Clausewitz, who was sickened by their behavior and found it to be beyond the bounds of "civilized war."[11] Clausewitz was fully within the tradition of the European war paradigm.

The Electric Revolution: The Telegraph and Telephone

The Electric Revolution continued the evolution of the individual. Wars became even less a matter of courage and winning one encounter, and became more a matter of logistics, supply, production, communication, and technology. It shifted military power from state-sized units to the superpower-sized units—the United Kingdom, the United States and eventually the Soviet Union. Economic power shifted from Europe to the United States. It changed the identity of the family from a multi-generational, extended family to the nuclear family and defined the individual by his or her occupation, rather by family or class. By the time this revolution was completed, for the first time in the history of the world, it was expected that all adults could read.

The perception shifted from a merely standardized world to a world where flows of matter and energy were constrained into hierarchies. *The paradigm was continuity, progress and hierarchical organization.*

Phase I: The Telegraph

The most telling war of the early telegraph period was the American Civil War. The South was still a largely rural, even feudal, economy. What a person did and his or her position on the plantation, like the feudal manor, was based on class identity more than it was on occupation. They saw no need for interstate control, interstate ties or national identity.

The North had been tied together by the railroad and the telegraph. It had begun to think in terms of a national identity. It had lost the notion of crisp boundaries, because it had begun to come to grips with the necessity of incorporation laws, laws regulating railroads and national trade that would be applicable across state lines. The North had seen the development of a group of urbanized professionals that owed their positions to ability rather than birth, and the beginning of progress up the economic and social hierarchy. The North was part of the new Electric Era.

Victory in the Civil War gave the people of the North the blessing of fate. The opening of the West and the vista of a nation that stretched from sea to sea inspired them. Weibe writes of America at the end of the 19th century:

> By the early eighties publicists were savoring the word nation in the sense of a continent conquered and tamed. It was a term that above all connoted growth development and enterprise... An age never lent itself more readily to sweeping, uniform description: nationalization, industrialization, mechanization, urbanization.[12]

The basis of this information revolution was the telegraph. Railroads pre-dated the telegraph, but it was not until the invention of telegraphically-operated switches that they could operate safely. Organizationally, management costs were more than the income a railroad could make. It was impossible to operate a road of any consequence (longer than 50 miles) until rationalized management was invented. The structure of the telegraph switching network (communication moved both ways) suggested a new way to organize—*the constrained bureaucratic hierarchy.*

Daniel McCallum, an inspired user of the telegraph, introduced the familiar hierarchical organizational chart and modern business practice. He saw the organizational chart as a structure of communications and responsibility. He introduced the notion of a chain-of-command, in which an employee was responsible only to his manager, and stipulated that managers have the power to hire and fire.[13] This constrained the power of managers, reduced the information and decision-making bottleneck, and introduced accountability. The new organizational structure allowed business to grow. Others copied what the railroads pioneered.

The change in business structure increased social mobility. People could move up in the business hierarchy. People could "get ahead" without owning a business or farm. Factories needed cheap labor, a need largely filled by immigrants. The nation became more foreign and more urban. All of these changes eroded the large, rural, multi-generation, extended farm family and changed the definition of family to mother, father and children—the nuclear family.

These changes, along with improved communications, created the impression of a new society, much of which was seen to be strange and dangerous. There was widespread conservative reaction. The Know-Nothings, religious fundamentalists, isolationism, and the Granger movement—all products of this time—were ways of trying to return to a simpler age. Weibe writes:

> As men ranged farther and farther from their communities, they tried desperately to understand the larger world in terms of their small, familiar environment. They tried, in other words, to impose the known upon the unknown, to master an impersonal world through the customs of a personal society. They failed, usually without recognizing why.[14]

Hierarchies were not new, but they had been fixed and based on class. The military hierarchy shows the traces of pre-telegraph hierarchy: every non-commissioned person salutes every commissioned officer, and an officer is a gentleman—and communication moves one way. In business, before the introduction of the rationalized business hierarchy, managers or owners could tell an employee to mow his lawn or take out the trash. The employee was a servant to the owner. He was in a different class, and that class was fixed.

In a bureaucratic hierarchy, the job defines the person, not his or her class. The railroad conductor could tell the president of the company that he had to get on board or be left at the station, and a telegraph operator could break into meetings with important news or hold up a train. A middle manager had the power to hire and fire the people under him. A worker was only responsible to the manager directly over him, not the manager of some other department, and that manager was instructed to confine his orders to things within the employee's job competence. (Managers could not ask for personal service for their homes or families.) If a person did well, there was the possibility of moving up through the organization. These were all radical departures from the family- owned and operated business.

A sense of individual importance based on professional competence developed as a result of the new bureaucratic hierarchy. The individual at the bottom of the class ladder could give orders to those at the top at the class ladder by virtue of his profession. The conductor or telegraph operator was a person with importance, because he controlled information without which the whole system was imperiled. (The conductor was the time keeper. If the train did not run on time, the likelihood of a crash was increased, although telegraphic connections between stations helped.)

Businesses copied the railroad/telegraphic organizational structure, and they took the notion of continuity even further. First, distributors (Montgomery Ward, Sears and Roebuck, the Atlantic and Pacific Tea Company), and then manufacturers (Swift foods) began to think about how they could improve reliability and increase efficiency. They began to acquire their suppliers. Manufacturers began to visualize the production of goods in terms of continuous flow. Processes instead of units began to emerge in business conversation. The assembly line was created.

Phase II: The Telephone

Britain had used the telegraph and the railroad effectively to administer its empire, but it had not adopted the organizational changes developed in America. The introduction of the telephone extended the electric information revolution and shifted the balance of economic power from London to New York. It became possible to manage diverse holdings and check on many factories. It extended the paradigm of continuity organized into rationalized and constrained hierarchies.

The French and British did not adopt the new communications technology with the fervor with which the Americans did. The chief engineer of the British Postal Service, Sir William Preece, captured the British attitude:

> Few have worked at the telephone much more than I have. I have one in my office, but more for show. If I want to send a message, I use a sounder or employ a boy to take it.[15]

The French attitude was even more restrictive. Attali and Stourdze write of the problems in French economy:

> The growth of enterprises needing world markets made them more difficult to manage: the chain of production became unwieldy, requiring more time and space. To remain competitive, time lags in distribution had to be kept brief. The long technical processes of production and distribution had to be mastered, something that the local power structures (in France) unfamiliar with the workings of big industrial firms could not grasp. From then on, the telephone acquired vital importance. It helped bring the 1880 crisis to an end by winning new markets, and it played its part in the rampant competition in national and international markets until the 1929 depression.[16]

Politically the French government had a more controlling attitude toward information technology than the United States or Britain.

> Governments have always kept to themselves the exclusive use of things which, if fallen into bad hands, could threaten public and private safety: poisons, explosives are given out only under State authority, and certainly the telegraph, in bad hands, could become a most dangerous weapon.[17]

As a consequence, political, economic and military power (based on production efficiency) shifted from Europe to the United States. In Europe businesses remained family-owned and personally-run. During the late 19th and early 20th centuries, England's economic power was no longer based on her manufacturing might (between 1880 and 1890, U.S. steel production had overtaken that of Britain), but on her connection with her empire as suppliers of raw materials.[18]

With more and more goods manufactured and sold for cash, it was important to convince women to buy goods instead of making them at home. The new communications industry sold the *notion of modernity* even more effectively than it sold products. More and more of women's traditional work was done by factories and machines. The telephone further separated the home from the economic world. Suburbs arose, as it became possible for businessmen to remain in touch through the telephone. Women's lives became more restricted and isolated. As women felt the need to become re-integrated into the life of the nation, they turned to suffrage movements and social activism.

As the factories became more efficient, the demand for labor lessened. At the same time, people were getting more news and getting it faster. The city was seen as a den of evil, populated by foreigners. The fear these engendered created both conservative reactions and reforming reactions. Women agitated against child labor and championed education as a way to "civilize" and "Americanize" the children of immigrants. Child labor laws and public schools and professional education again changed and in the process extended the nature of childhood.

The revolution in production and the shift of economic power from Europe to the United States had political and military repercussions. The rate of social change and economic change made people feel insecure. The wars were partially economic and partially a conservative reaction of those still in the group/ethnic/class identity mode against the individualistic/pluralistic world emerging from the Electric Revolution. The wars of the Electric Revolution were won on the production line and in the research lab as much as they were on the battlefield. And out of those labs came the technology of the next Information Revolution.

The Digital Revolution

We are now in the midst of another Information Revolution, and there are similarities with its predecessors. The power equation has shifted to favor the most information-intensive culture. The Main-Frame Revolution, like the early Press Revolution and the early Electric Revolution, allowed the dominant powers—the United States and the USSR—to extend their administrative control. The USSR did not allow free information or freedom of information technology. The United States did. As a consequence, the electronic industry in the U.S. far outstripped that of the USSR.

The essence of the Digital Revolution is local control. The Soviet paradigm of central control prevented the notion of local information technology. As a consequence, the Soviet economy collapsed, because their production, ecological and social systems were far beyond the administrative limit of their information infrastructure.[19] That collapse, like the fall of Rome, has created a highly competitive situation between the inheritors of the traditions of the Byzantine Empire, who are still in the group identity paradigm, and those who are inheritors of a paradigm of individuality and competition.

As a consequence of economic devaluation of women's work at home, women have had to seek economic participation in the larger society. Women are regaining their place in production. The definition of gender is becoming more equal. The family has become less stable, as it has lost economic function. Thus, family size is again being reduced from children and the biological parents to the child and the care-taking parent.

As information technology moves us away from print, less information is kept private. Children experience sex and violence vicariously on TV and in their day-to-day lives. The age of sexual awareness is being lowered. At the same time, the need for increased and life-long education has pushed up the age of student learning. Both trends are blurring the distinction between adult and child. Childhood is disappearing. As in the time before the printing press, children are beginning to be seen as small adults. Evidence of this is the tendency to try children in adult courts and the lack of distinction between adult and children's fashions.

Television has brought the individual soldier, citizen and killer into our homes. This has two consequences. The individual has emerged from the faceless masses—as we see Baby Jessica or Scott O'Grady rescued, Rodney King beaten, or follow the Bobbitt case with horror or amusement, and we feel increasingly threatened. Crime statistics tell us our cities are safer than they have ever been, but we feel more threatened. As companies restructure for the Information Age, we lose jobs; and though we are the only "super-power," we feel more helpless than ever. This leads, as it has in the past, to conservative reactions.

We are seeing a resurgence of religious fundamentalism and of ethnic and national identity. There are twice as many private as public police. People live in walled communities. There is a call to a return to "family values." Isolationism and fear of foreigners are exemplified by the passage of California's Proposition 187, which seeks to deny the children of aliens education and health care. The class of people most likely to create new organizational structures and to innovate most widely are those who have the greatest need, coupled with access to new information technology. Congress passed and the President signed the Telecommunications Act of 1996 that makes Internet service providers responsible for indecency that passes through their systems. If the law makes it through the courts and is enforced, the model presented here would indicate that service providers, like Spanish printers in the Print Revolution, will move to countries where information and information technology is not restricted.

Leaving the Default Position

First, we must recognize that the change in paradigm is irreversible. We cannot go back to identity based on ethnicity, or on a simple definition of nationalism, any more than we can return to the small farm or the family business. We must instead wage a two-front information technology "war" to bring the rest of the world into the Information Age. We must accept that our current paradigm is based on Electric-Age, not Electronic-Age, thinking and redefine what national security means in the Information Age, based on our insights from previous information revolutions. And, we must wage a campaign to foster the emergence of the individual.

The first can be done by beginning conversations, by communicating through books such as this one, and by continuing the conversations internationally "on-line." The fostering of the individual can be done by making sure that information providers are not fettered, controlled by, or dependent on the existing political power structure. The peoples of Eastern Europe have never lived in information-free cultures. They went from the Byzantine Empire to various other forms of political control of information. The social system has been based on class, whether that class is based on birth, membership in the communist party, or membership in a certain ethnic or religious group. Because they have never lived in an information-free culture, they have never had the opportunity to develop individual identity or a social system based on competency and professionalism.

We can make "war" on these perceptual systems by giving and demanding, as a requirement for aid (military or economic), that we be allowed to blanket the area with modern information technology tied to the world-wide information super-structure. Connecting people to an independent source of information will foster economic and political development. It will develop individual identity. And, it will be cheaper, less invasive, and more effective than any of the dams, power plants, wells, and agricultural projects or weapons transfer programs of the past.

Endnotes

[1] See Colin Turnbull, *The Forest People: A Study of the Pygmies of the Congo*, New York: Clarion Press, 1967; and Richard B. Lee and Irven Devore, *Kalahari Hunter-Gathers: Studies of the !Kung San and their Neighbors*, Cambridge, MA: Harvard University Press, 1982.

[2] See Elin Whitney-Smith, *Pleistocene Extinctions: The Case of the Aboricidal Megaherbivores*, Electronic Publication http://www.well.com/user/elin; and *contra*, Paul Martin and Richard Klein, *Quaternary Extinctions: A Prehistoric Revolution*, Tuscon, AZ: University of Arizona Press, 1989.

[3] Christine Ward Gailey, *Kinship to Kingship: gender Hierarchy and State Formation in the Tongan Islands*, Austin, TX: University of Texas Press, 1987.

[4] John Keegan, *A History of Warfare*, New York: Vintage Press, 1994.

[5] Keegan, *ibid.*

[6] Keegan, *ibid.*

[7] Lynn Townsend White, Jr., *Medieval Religion and Technology: Collected Essays*, Berkeley, CA: University of California Press, 1979.

[8] Michael Howard, *War in European History*, Oxford: Oxford University Press, 1976, p. 20.

[9] Maurice Dobb, *Studies in the Development of Capitalism*, New York: International Publishers, 1932.

[10] Neil Postman, *The Disappearance of Childhood*, New York: Laurel Press, 1982.

[11] Keegan, *op.cit.*

[12] Robert H. Weibe, *The Search for Order: 1877-1920*, New York: Hill and Wang, 1967.

[13] Alfred D. Chandler, *The Visible Hand: The Managerial Revolution in American Business*, Cambridge, MA: Belknap Press, 1977.

[14] Weibe, *op. cit.*

[15] Ithiel de Sola Pool, et al, "Foresight and Hindsight: the Case of the Telephone," in Pool (ed.), *The Social Impact of the Telephone*, Cambridge, MA: MIT Press, 1977, pp. 127-158.

[16] Jacques Attali and Yves Stourdze, "The Birth of the Telephone and Economic Crisis: The Slow Death of Monologue in French Society," in Ithiel de Sola Pool (ed.), *Social Impact of the Telephone*, Cambridge, MA: MIT Press, 1977, pp. 109-110.

[17] Attali and Stourdze, *ibid.*

[18] Eric R. Wolfe, *Europe and the People Without History*, Berkeley, CA: University of California Press, 1982.

[19] Murray Feschback and Alfred Friendly, Jr., *Ecocide in the USSR*, New York: Basic Books, 1992.

Uncommon Means for the Common Defense

Alan D. Campen

"insure domestic Tranquility; provide for the common defence; and promote the general Welfare..."

"It's time for the government to sit down and re-evaluate what issues need to be addressed in terms of helping the government and private sector work together in controlling the flow of information and in the area of information security."

The Information Age is sweeping aside the physical and political barriers that once formed the bulwark of U.S. national security and is exposing a nation poorly prepared for intense global competition in cyberspace. Nascent recognition of our growing dependence on vulnerable information systems has set policy makers urgently pondering the source, form and ethical underpinnings of a new U.S. national security sanctuary: a new and totally different one to be forged not from traditional military resources, but drawn almost entirely from the private sector.

This new vision of the threat to national security presages an era of global competition dominated by a struggle for supremacy over *knowledge*: a contest that will penalize nations that depend upon telecommunications and computer systems, but are unable to defend those systems against attack.

Any highly industrialized society will be decidedly disadvantaged in this contest because its prime sources of strength and weakness are one and the same, and the assault is at hand. As Paul Strassmann sharply warned in recent congressional testimony, "I did not say *if* a devastating event will happen. I said *when*, because it is only a matter to time before crippling threats to the information integrity of the federal government will take place."

For over a hundred years our national security sanctuary had reposed firmly on patrolled ocean barriers, friendly borders, unmatched human and material resources, unlimited mobilization time, and, these failing, upon nuclear hegemony. But, knowledge warfare poses threats much different from hot or cold wars.

The *enemy* will be unseen and even unknown; acts of aggression may be launched from nation- or rogue-states, by religious fanatics, terrorists, criminals, or teen-agers insolently and ignorantly flouting their intellectual muscles in cyberspace. Our new sanctuary must shield us against conflict waged not by uniformed warriors locked in physical combat on sea, land and air, but, instead, fought in the *ether* through the manipulation, distortion and suppression of information. The weapons in will include directed energy beams, computer logic bombs and viruses, altered media images that distort perceptions of reality, and other psychological operations to influence the belief systems of peoples and, through that, the resolve of their leaders.

A white paper prepared in December 1995 by the U.S. Security Policy Board (SPB) notes that the Federal Government depends to an increasing degree on the National Information Infrastructure (NII) to carry out its national security, defense, law enforcement and public safety functions. It concludes "this is a national problem," and that business and industry will either provide protection commensurate with their perceptions of value of and risk to information, or "simply write off losses as a cost of doing business:" steps that do not adequately address national security concerns.

Initial efforts by the Clinton administration to craft a politically correct role for the federal government in securing the NII were soundly censured for their preoccupation with intellectual property and personal privacy issues, rather than confronting the overriding needs of the national defense establishment. These critics complain that the Federal government is abdicating its constitutional responsibility for the common defense if it persists in unprecedented reliance on the marketplace—seeking an uncommon means for the common defense.

The SPB paper finds "The Federal Government is poorly organized and resourced to ensure adequate NII security in terms of availability, integrity, and confidentiality...There are many different boards, commissions, working groups, forums, committees, advisory councils, etc., scattered throughout the Executive Branch, each of which has some aspect of information infrastructure assurance within its sphere...[but] no single entity with sufficient breadth of vision, responsibility and resources to effectively manage the Executive Branch's efforts towards the goal of information infrastructure assurance."

"The Day After"—a report on a national-level exercise conducted by the Rand Corporation for the Assistant Secretary of Defense C^3I—revealed that a deadly information attack on America was feasible, but, "because of the government/private and nationally distributed nature of the 'target,' we had no one in charge, or even capable of pulling the necessary defensive efforts together."

The SBP assessment finds "limited Federal Government resources to achieve Information Infrastructure Assurance appear to be inefficiently, ineffectively, and illogically scattered throughout the Executive Branch," and calls for establishment of a "Fair Court," one capable of making "security-related policy decisions which fairly balance—and are widely perceived to fairly balance the sometimes competing but legitimate interests of national security, law enforcement, commerce, and personal privacy in the national interest."

The Congress is pressuring the administration for a plan that addresses the "threats to, and vulnerabilities of, the NII." A report on the Intelligence Authorization Bill for FY96 (S.922) calls for the Director of Central Intelligence and the Secretary of Defense to prepare "a comprehensive report which identifies the key threats to U.S. computers and communications systems, and, [plans} to protect government or private U.S. information systems." Michael Nelson, of the White House Office of Science and Technology, announced on September 8, 1995 the formation of a working group to develop a road map to protect the NII, but the SPB paper concludes that "Given our current Executive Branch structures and resources, it appears unlikely that these Congressional concerns will be satisfactorily resolved anytime soon."

Ronald Gove and Ronald Knecht argued persuasively in their presentation to the 6-8 September InfoWarCon 95 conference that, "Given that is not possible to control the state of the globally interconnected information infrastructure, we must determine how to design information services that can operate safely in this inherently unsafe environment...[and this] will require fundamental changes in the approach to designing and operating an infrastructure."

The new security umbrella exists in name only, and is yet little more than a theology attended by a fuzzy vision of a "system of systems" to be designed, constructed, owned and operated by the private sector, with minimal Federal government direction and financing.

Unfortunately, the NII has embedded within it the Defense Information Infrastructure (DII), hosting the hard core of the military's non-tactical information systems and its sole means to direct transport and sustenance of its warfighting capabilities. It is not clear how the Defense Information Systems Agency can implement the necessary controls if its authority is constrained to the military only components of the NII.

The defense establishment must find a way to influence the design and construction of a robust, secure NII, despite vociferous opposition not only from a libertarian fringe—which sees conspiracy in every government security initiative—but also from an industry wary of government constraints and requirements that can only increase costs.

However, as *Business Week* reported in its September 11, 1995 commentary on the Aspen Colorado conference on Cyberspace and the American Dream, the libertarian-leaning panelists were admonished that "If the government does not play a substantial role to ensure the safety of cyberspace and mediate among competing interests...then the new frontier will remain a wilderness...Only a federal government could protect national security in the Industrial Age...When the devastating attack comes [on the Internet], then we'll want every resource of the government brought to bear."

That the commercial telecommunications industry should play a leading role in national security is neither new nor startling, but, that it should take that lead with minimal Federal policy and funding is unsettling to those who realize how dependent the military has become on vulnerable commercial information services for all of its functions. Estimates that over 90 percent of defense networks ride on commercial systems are probably conservative.

Dependence by the military on commercial information systems has been a fact of life since the Civil War, when both North and the South relied extensively on railroad telegraphy, and civilian cryptographers handed decoded dispatches directly to President Lincoln in the Telegraph Office.

Uniformed employees of the Bell Telephone system reconstructed French and German telephone systems for our combat forces during World War II, and the nuclear missiles planted across hundreds of square miles of our northern states were connected to their command centers by commercial microwave. AT&T's transcontinental coaxial cable was more deeply entrenched and routed around major cities to reduce collateral damage from nuclear attack. Those defenses were relatively straightforward, but the primary challenge now is no longer to prevent physical damage to communications. Instead, experience has shows that the task now is to detect the accidental or intentional translation of a single digit in a million lines of computer code, which, without instant remedy, can easily deny service to much of our national telecommunications system.

It is not the technical competence or patriotism of the commercial telecommunications industry that is in question, but the fact that it lacks both the incentive and the finances to build extra security and robustness into the NII. While Ma Bell surely kept one eye on the corporate bottom line during the Cold War, the other never lost site of Old Glory. But, these two objectives were never brought into serious conflict.

However, the NII will bring considerations of cost, competitiveness and security into direct confrontation. The additive costs to harden and protect the network in the 1960's were hidden in the rate base and paid by all subscribers. But now the defense establishment must deal not with one, but with an ever-changing host of information providers, who are themselves locked in a fierce struggle for survival: and that survival depends on low costs.

Martin van Creveld, wrote in *Technology and War*, that lower costs are produced by *efficient* systems that have no redundant or idle resources and which operate under highly centralized control, with a minimum of waste and friction. He wrote, "a certain amount of redundancy, slack, and waste must not only be tolerated but deliberately built in [to military systems]...and there are any number of occasions when military effectiveness is not only compatible with diminished efficiency but positively demands that it be sacrificed...the successful use of technology in war often means that there is a price to be paid in terms of deliberately diminishing efficiency." Such heretical notions are unlikely to long survive in the commercial marketplace unless buttressed by firm federal policy—and money.

It is one thing to design an information system against *statistical failure*; but quite another if it must withstand planned, malicious assault. As we have recently seen and as Frederick B. Cohen writes in *Protection and Security on the Information Superhighway*, "50 years of statistical downtime can disappear in a single incident," particularly when the cause is not random failure, but by a skilled opponent who is capable of learning. Cohen neatly summarizes the issue confronting the architect of the NII. "It is precisely the standards designers use to make technology efficient that make it easy to attack."

Cohen draws a sharp distinction between *efficiency* and *effectiveness* that quickly comes into view in the differences between the design of *systems*—where the engineer assumes things will work—and the design of *infrastructures*—where the architect must assume that they won't. He continues, "It is important to understand that efficiency under normal operating conditions almost never equates to efficiency or effectiveness under exceptional conditions. For this reason, any system designed purely for financial efficiency under normal operating conditions is highly susceptible to intentional disruption." Cohen contends "The infrastructure design issues of the NII are not now being addressed effectively and the implications on long-term information assurance may be significant."

According to Gove and Knecht, the NII must be engineered so that controllers can know the state of a system and when that state is being perturbed; have features that will enable ready restoration; and, the ability for decentralized control to limit cascading failure modes.

It must be recognized that a highly competitive industry facing unnerving, unpredictable changes in technology and uncertain markets for its enormous investments, cannot be expected to bear, unaided, that additional burden of ruggedizing the NII to meet national security requirements. The security differential must come from the federal treasury if we are to have an information service that can operate safely in an inherently unsafe environment.

An earlier and abridged version of this essay, entitled "Vulnerability of Info Systems Demands Immediate Action," appeared in the November 1995 issue of the *National Defense* magazine.

Creating a Smart Nation: Information Strategy, Virtual Intelligence, and Information Warfare

Robert D. Steele

INTRODUCTION: A Strategy Gap

The security of our Nation is at risk because our national leadership is attempting to manage 21st century threats with 19th century concepts, and has no strategy suited to our needs. The foundation of national security today is information—information as the critical element of military power and military vulnerability, and information as the critical element of national attractiveness for international economic investment.

When the Director of Central Intelligence (DCI), the most senior intelligence officer of the land, and a capable member of the Cabinet, states publicly that the Central Intelligence Agency (CIA) was created to conduct espionage (rather than its true, mandated mission: strategic analysis), and then tells Congress that "intelligence sources have only identified a handful of countries that have instituted formal information warfare programs," it is certain that our national intelligence community leadership is confused about both its mission and the threat—a "handful" is five; I count no less than 21 active information warfare (IW) threats.[2]

At the same time, within the Department of Defense, the very critical capabilities of the Defense Information Systems Agency (DISA) are being deprived of resources approved by the Secretary of Defense, but held hostage by the Services. Multiple counter-productive service programs in information warfare; an excessive effort to keep such programs in the black world as a means of obscuring their cost; and a general lack of leadership from the Assistant Secretary of Defense for C^3I, have seriously retarded our Nation's progress in addressing the information warfare threat *as a Nation*, and have made the Department of Defense contribution to electronic home defense and civil sector information security marginal at best.

Finally, on the civilian side of our government, within both the Administration and the Legislature, we have an approach to information issues which is both fragmented and—as is the American way—obsessed with technology and denial-of-service attacks, rather than content and data integrity.

It is in this context that we must examine the urgent need for a national information strategy which provides our Nation with both a virtual intelligence community, and a robust *national* defense against information warfare, *in all its forms*. A key premise is that in the age of information, information warfare depends more on maintaining a robust intelligence capability, and on electronic home defense, than on being able to deny electronic capabilities to enemies of varied sophistication. "Information peacekeeping"—my term—as well as a robust "information commons"[3] are the most important elements of both national security and national competitiveness.

Other great nations understand this, and there is evidence that non-state actors also are focusing on the dramatic advantages that can be derived from establishing information strategies that optimize the role of information in achieving political, military, economic, and cultural objectives.[4] We are in a state of neither war nor peace, and our existing bodies of governance are not able to meet our needs as they are now structured and defined—to enter safely into the 21st Century, we urgently need a *National Information Strategy*.

DIAGNOSIS: Four Warrior Classes

Our diagnosis of the conditions confronting us as we enter the 21st Century must focus on two areas which have very profound implications for national security and national competitiveness—the first area is that of threats, and the second area is that of the nature of war and peace in the 21st Century. Let us consider the first area, that of threats. Consider the illustration below:

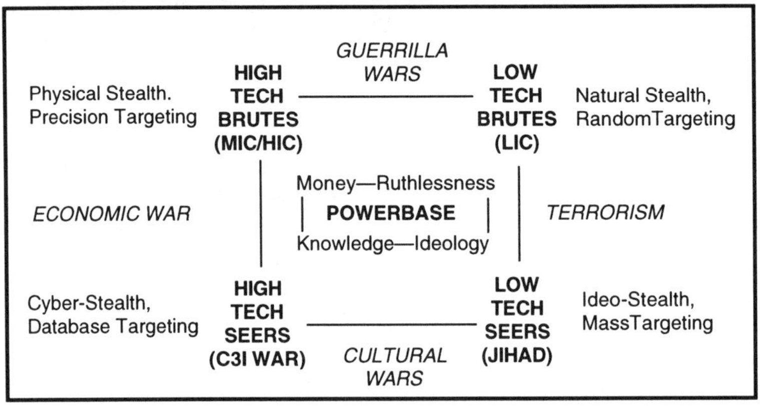

Figure 1. Four Warrior Classes

The High-Tech Brute is the "traditional" threat against which our national defense and our national intelligence communities have each organized. Virtually all of their funding is allocated to high-tech capabilities for unilateral warfare against strategic nuclear and conventional armed forces. We—the U.S.—are high-tech brutes, with very expensive and complex weapons systems which require huge and complex logistics trains, as well as precision targeting data, *which is not available*.[5] As we shall see this makes our capabilities largely irrelevant against the other three threat classes, and, at the same time it makes us extremely vulnerable to anonymous attacks from individuals, clans, gangs, and Third World "rogue" nations that once would not dare to act beyond their own borders.[6]

The Low-Tech Brute category is comprised of Criminals and Terrorists, and sometimes it is difficult to distinguish between them—and of course sometimes they form alliances, as when criminals procure weapons and other equipment for terrorists. What is most important about this target is that it is not threatened by our fancy weapons systems. It represents what we call a "low slow singleton" attack problem, for which signature and intelligence sensors are not available. It is also important to emphasize, as with the next two classes of warrior as well, that we are blind and deaf with respect to this threat, because we have not trained, equipped, and organized our intelligence community for these three types of threat.[7]

The Low-Tech Seer threat class is comprised of zealots, ideologues, mobs, and refugees, as well as the more sophisticated and coherent cultures of the Third World and the Eastern World, which Western intelligence communities have never been able to understand. It is worth noting that intelligence sources and methods associated with "indications & warning" (I&W) inevitably contain enormous cultural presumptions about both the motivations and the expectations of the opposing party. The same cultural presumptions at the policy level make it difficult to accurately anticipate, assess and respond to threats from this warrior class.[8]

The High-Tech Seer is represented by Hackers as individuals, and by Economic Warfare when conducted at the nation-state level. This warrior class is especially interesting because the battlefield is in the civil sector, the weapons are information and information technology, and the military in most countries has not yet realized that it must either be able to wage war "by other means," or find its role in the national defense significantly reduced in "The Age of Information." Perhaps of greater concern, civilian authorities appear to be ignorant of the urgent nature of this threat, and how to mobilize and organize civil capabilities to cope with potentially anonymous attacks on critical civil nodes.[9]

In concluding this section on diagnosis, it is necessary to provide one more illustration, one with three matrices—from war to peace, from here to there, and from long to short times.[10] Traditionally—and with little change today—U.S. national defense and national intelligence have focused on "war" beyond the nation's borders—"there." To the extent that internal threats to order existed "here" at home, this has been left to law enforcement. Now, however, we are discovering that war "by other means" is "here" inside the borders, in the civil sector, and occurring under conditions of nominal "peace."

I have added a third dimension to this matrix—the concept of time—because a major weakness of our existing defense and intelligence communities is that they have generally had the luxury of long periods of time to develop capabilities, to identify threats, and to conduct operations. Today, however, the enemy can be anonymous, can employ unconventional capabilities, such as electromagnetic or electronic attacks against key communications and computing nodes, *and can do this overnight, with no warning*. The single greatest challenge to both the defense and intelligence communities in the 21st Century is going to be this element of time: how does one train, equip, and organize a capability that is able to cope with "real-time threat"?

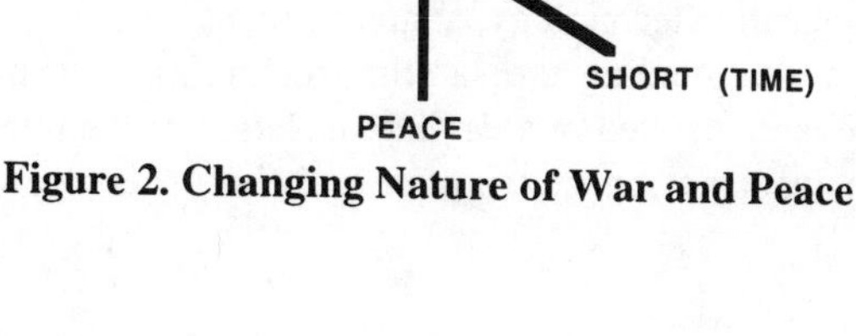

Figure 2. Changing Nature of War and Peace

Let me emphasize this, because it is so very important: in dealing with "chaos," threats emerge "spontaneously" and often unpredictably, and the ability to create "just in time" capabilities, and to react decisively "just in time," is going to be the single most critical aspect of successful defense and intelligence in the 21st Century.[11] Within the intelligence community, it will be impossible to maintain "central intelligence" organizations that collect everything—in the fashion of vacuum cleaners—"just in case." Instead, both intelligence and defense will have to be completely restructured in order to do "just in time" collection and take "just in time" action.[12] The remainder of this article will address our existing structural imbalances, the new forms of violence that will challenge intelligence, the need for new sources and methods of early warning, and, the national solution for prevention and action: national information strategies, virtual intelligence communities, and integrated civil-military information warfare and information peacekeeping programs.

STRUCTURAL IMBALANCE: Intelligence without Thought

In addressing issues of structural imbalance, I rely upon more than twenty years experience with the U.S. Intelligence Community. Although it has been my privilege to work with fourteen different intelligence communities world-wide in the past four years, and I see many parallels to my own experience, I will not draw generalizations here. My comments reflect the American experience.

Most distressing, and typically American, has been the substitution of technology for thinking, of bodies for brains. Two examples will suffice. A simple example: reliance on the polygraph machine ultimately has resulted in the destruction of the field of counterintelligence. Two of my classmates in the clandestine service were video-taped doing dead drops in Cuba because all of the Cuban agents had been doubled—and all of them had passed the CIA's polygraph tests.

A more complex example is satellite technology. While I continue to have great regard for signals intelligence technology, and good regard for imagery intelligence technology, there have been several negative outcomes to the American obsession with satellites as the primary source of "reliable" intelligence:

First, the development of satellites resulted in the creation of huge bureaucracies with vested interests in the extraordinarily vast funding for these programs, and these bureaucracies created narrow "pipelines" for Top Secret "CODEWORD" intelligence. In essence, the intelligence community in the United States became fragmented, and it became much more difficult for the policy-maker to receive an integrated intelligence product at a low enough level of classification to permit useful and timely dissemination and discussion.

Second, the secrecy surrounding the satellite technology—a secrecy that restricted sharing with even our most important allies such as France—severely hampered transnational cooperation and the sharing of intelligence against mutual enemies. This also led to an enormous waste of financial resources as the Americans sought to maintain a unilateral classified satellite capability, and eventually forced the Europeans and others to create their own duplicative technology, at great expense.

Third, the secrecy surrounding the satellite technology ultimately permeated all aspects of intelligence, and resulted in a *de facto* isolation of the intelligence community from the rest of the information continuum (all the other centers of unclassified intelligence available in the Nation and internationally, e.g., schools, universities, libraries, businesses, information brokers and private investigators, journalists, normal government offices, defense departments, *and other intelligence communities*). It is instructive that while the Americans have a number of classified burden-sharing agreements, they do not have any arrangements for sharing unclassified encyclopedic intelligence with counterparts in other governments, and they have very limited capabilities for providing their analysts with direct access to open sources of information.

Fourth, and most destructive, has been the impact of satellite cost on the funding of human expert analysts. Satellites have dominated the U.S. intelligence community budget, with the result that funds have not been available to hire true experts with ten to fifteen years of private sector experience. As the most recently retired Deputy Director of Intelligence for the CIA, Mr. Doug McEachin, has noted publicly, "It is difficult to do good analysis with a bunch of 19-year-olds on two year rotations." This is a devastating commentary on how the U.S. intelligence community has sacrificed thinking in order to afford technology.

The reality is that the *U.S. intelligence community is optimized for secrets, and believes that its mission is to produce secrets, rather than to inform policy*. This is why I am forced to point out that "the problem with spies is that they only know secrets!" France recently noted that several American spies were paying their nominal agents, actually under the control of French counterintelligence, for information that was available to the public. Although this is a common tactic when first developing an agent, the reality is that U.S. spies do not have the education, language capability, time, or incentive to follow what is available in the public domain, and they are therefore destined to continually waste valuable resources collecting information that is not and should not be classified.

Intelligence communities should not be in the business of collecting open sources; but if they are not able to establish themselves firmly upon a foundation of encyclopedic open source information available from the private sector, then it is my judgment that 75% of what they do in the classified arena is irrelevant at best, and, at worst, wasteful and counterproductive to policy. In essence, open sources provide the critical *context* for intelligence analysis—without such a context, classified intelligence is actually misleading and therefore dangerous to the policy-maker.

There are two other structural imbalances that I wish to address: the lack of attention to unclassified foreign-language hard-copy as a primary source of raw intelligence; and the lack of a coherent intelligence analysis model that distinguishes between the levels of analysis and the geographic, civil, and military spheres, and then ensures their integration. Implicit in this latter imbalance is the issue of whether intelligence is intended to broadcast generic information, or provide tailored "decision-support" to specific customers.

I continue to be astonished, when I am invited to review current plans for "modernizing" military communications, to find that everyone is very proud of their planning for "multi-media" digital systems. They stop smiling when I point out that 80% of the information that the commander needs has not been digitized—it is in hard-copy, generally has not been collected by the intelligence community, and is usually in a foreign language. Of course they have not planned for collection, translation, and digitization. Further, 80% of the civilian counterparts in their own country and military counterparts in other countries—with whom they must conduct coalition operations—cannot interface with the fancy technology. The reality is that "intelligence" must rely heavily on "ground truth" that has *not* been digitized, and "just in time" operations must rely on mixing civilian and military capabilities across political boundaries in such a way that *hard-copy* actually becomes the only acceptable common denominator for communications.[13] Intelligence communities must have global capabilities for rapidly identifying, collecting, translating, analyzing, digitizing and reproducing foreign-language hard copy.

The second imbalance is more subtle. When I first helped to establish the Marine Corps Intelligence Center in 1988, I undertook a personal examination of all available intelligence production from both the Central Intelligence Agency and the Defense Intelligence Agency. I came to two conclusions: first, I could not find a single product that supported any specific decision—everything was generic in nature; second, I found that none of the products were founded within any analytical model—they were more like classified journalism.

Regarding the first element, I offer three definitions which distinguish among data, information, and intelligence. In my view, *data* is the raw print, signal, or image that is collected; *information* is data which has been collated to be of generic interest; and *intelligence* is information which has been tailored to support a specific decision by a specific person at a specific time.[14] Newspapers are generic information—to my surprise, I discovered that all of the intelligence production which I reviewed was, in fact, nothing more than classified *information*. We have a long way to go in changing the day-to-day relationship between intelligence consumers and intelligence producers, and their capabilities, if we actually are to begin routinely producing intelligence which is useful to the policy-maker—that is, intelligence which can support *decisions* on a daily basis rather than by exception.

My second finding—the absence of a model of analysis—caused me to develop the model described below for our analysts—I did this for a very important reason: *the threat changes depending on the level of analysis*.

The most fundamental flaw in both intelligence and information today is the failure to establish, for each question (i.e., requirement), the desired level of analysis. There are four levels of analysis: strategic, operational, tactical, and technical.[15] These are, in turn, influenced by the three major contexts of inquiry: civil, military, and geographic. At the strategic level, civil allies, geographic location, and military sustainability are critical. At the operational level, civil instability, geographic resources, and military availability are important. At the tactical level, civil psychology, geographic terrain, and military reliability determine outcomes. At the technical level, civil infrastructure, geographic atmosphere, and military lethality are the foundation for planning and employment.

A simple example from the military sphere will illustrate the importance of this issue. Examining the capability of a specific Middle Eastern country in the mission area of tank warfare, it was found that, while the initial threat assessment (by someone unfamiliar with the levels of analysis approach) was very high because this country had a great many modern tanks, in fact, the threat varied significantly depending on the level of analysis. Only at the technical level (lethality) was the threat high. At the tactical level (reliability) the threat was very low, because the crews were not trained, had poor morale, and the tanks were storage and not maintained. At the operational level (availability) the threat increased to medium because there were large numbers of tanks widely scattered across the country. At the strategic level (sustainability) the threat dropped again to low, because it would be almost impossible for this country to carry out extended tank warfare operations, even on its own terrain.

The above only examines the threat from a military capabilities standpoint. When integrated with civil factors (such as bridge loading and tunnel clearance) and geographic factors (such as cross-country mobility and line-of-sight distance), the threat changes dramatically, depending on the specific area-of-operations and scenario. This *is why no intelligence product can be considered truly useful unless it reflects both an appreciation for the analysis model, and the specific scenario and decision being faced by a specific consumer*. This approach can and should be applied to every question for which intelligence—tailored information—is to be provided.

Our challenge is to thoroughly integrate classified intelligence, private sector open sources, and the information available to policy-makers, and to do so in a way which recognizes that we must provide *decision-support* at multiple levels of analysis. The availability of intelligence about threats, and the plans and intentions of enemies, is a far more important aspect of information warfare than is the now much in vogue: that is, ability to interfere with the electronic performance of selected weapons systems, most of which will not be used by our most likely adversaries.

NEW FORMS OF VIOLENCE: Challenges for Intelligence

There are four new main forms of violence—Socio-Cultural Outcasts; Information Terrorism; Information Crime; and Economic Competition—and today's Intelligence Community is not trained, equipped, or organized to detect and monitor these threats.

Of particular concern is the fact that we have created an enormously complex techno-sphere which is vulnerable to *anonymous* attack by individuals who are willing to resort to information terrorism or information crime. At the same time, this techno-sphere is vulnerable to penetration, distortion, and destruction by those who choose to resort to methods of economic competition, which many might consider illegal or immoral.

Professor Samuel Huntington's recent article on "The Clash of Civilizations"[16] is admirable, but I am of the opinion that, while civilizations may clash in epic terms, normal clashes today are between people as manifested through organizations. Today, as Trotsky would say, we have neither war nor peace, and we have, *within* civilizations as well as between civilizations, *clashes between forms of human organization*. The state, the corporation, and the gang are all vying for control of resources, and it is a cause for concern—and a legitimate mission for the intelligence community to understand—that today transnational gangs have more power, money, and computers than most corporations, and most corporations have more power, money, and computers than many states, *especially in their chosen areas of dominance*. This is increasing the chaos by fragmenting the battlefield, and aggravating external diseconomies that were once at least marginally addressed by the state.

Further, I have been impressed by an emerging literature on "national attractiveness," and have been persuaded that nations do not compete—but organizations do. It is the role of nations to provide for the best possible environment within which to develop and protect intellectual capital. Secretary of Labor Robert Reich, in introducing his concept of the American Workplace, defines "U.S. citizens" as any person or organization, *regardless of nationality*, which employs people within the borders of the United States of America, and/or which pay U.S. taxes. This is important. This means that nations "compete" by being attractive, *not* by undertaking campaigns of economic espionage, or by subsidizing their "national" industries. In essence, nations within a global economy should be striving to attract the most talented people and the most original ideas, with the result that "virtual nationalization" of *foreign* intellectual capital takes place. I find this an intriguing concept, and believe that one of the missions of the intelligence community will be to identify emerging talent and emerging opportunities, and to also identify the necessary incentives which would cause that talent and those opportunities to choose the United States—or any other nation—as a home base.[17]

EARLY WARNING: Virtual Intelligence Communities

I have emphasized the critical descriptive aspects of diagnosis and structural imbalance, because the hardest part of preparing for the 21st Century is admitting our deficiencies. There are too many apologists for the existing U.S. intelligence system who persist in believing that everything is fine, and that with just a few minor adjustments the existing capabilities can accommodate any threat. I suspect that most countries suffer from a similar obsession with the *status quo*.

There are four key points that I would make with respect to establishing early warning capabilities for the 21st Century.

First, if we accept that "central intelligence" is an oxymoron in the age of distributed information, then it follows that the ultimate Intelligence Community in the 21st Century, the most effective intelligence community, will be the one which mobilizes every citizen, every employee, to create a Virtual Intelligence Community. If threats emerge from chaos and must be dealt with in "real-time," then only a *total mobilization* of all citizens as *voluntary* civic sensors, will enable the national intelligence community to receive warning and develop estimates in time to respond appropriately and with accuracy. I emphasize *voluntary*.[18]

Second, if voluntary citizen sensors are to be effective as part of a virtual intelligence community, then it is essential that the state declassify the threat. In the United States, we have concealed from the public the terrible risks to our financial, power generation, and telecommunications infrastructures. This significantly increases our vulnerability and reduces the likelihood that innovative solutions will be communicated from those who are unaware of the need for improved security. In the more traditional areas, such as transnational crime, proliferation, terrorism, and drugs, there is a need for greater openness on the part of the state with respect to its concerns and its limitations.

Third, and a corollary to the first point: at the same time that we mobilize citizen-sensors, we must also harness the distributed intelligence of the nation. It is impossible for any government—or corporation for that matter—to maintain a cadre of experts on every topic, especially when the topics of interest change from day to day. Only by organizing an intelligence community which can draw quickly and with confidence on university experts, business experts, media experts, and others, can we create a Virtual Intelligence Community tht is truly comprehensive in its understanding and its ability to analyze threats as well as opportunities in real-time. Today, the U.S. Intelligence Community suffers from extremely unwieldy and inflexible security constraints, as well as procurement arrangements, that do not permit individual analysts to deal directly and frequently with experts in the "real world." This must change.

Fourth and finally, I wish to emphasize what I perceive to be a critical change in the nature of defense and law enforcement as the threat of general war with high-tech brutes recedes, and we are confronted with much more pervasive, relatively anonymous threats from ruthless, fanatical criminals, terrorists, ideologues, and criminal hackers. I believe that our national defense must be recast so that there is a seamless integration of defense options running from the streets of New York to the heart of darkness in Burundi. It is no longer possible to isolate "local" law enforcement from national counterintelligence, and general police capabilities from paramilitary, special operations, and conventional force capabilities. At the same time, the intelligence elements of the law enforcement, defense, and civil policy communities must be integrated, for there is too much overlap. Carrying this idea to its logical conclusion, and mindful of the fact that in the 21st Century most of the conflicts will be between states acting in coalition against non-state actors such as transnational criminal gangs or rogue Third World gangs, I suggest that we must create a Virtual Intelligence Community which is transnational in nature, and which utilizes open-source intelligence as the general foundation for integration.

NATIONAL INFORMATION STRATEGIES: Prevention and Action

Without a National Information Strategy, it is not possible to create a Virtual Intelligence Community, nor provide for the defense and prosperity of the Nation. It is imperative that we recognize that the center-of-gravity for information warfare is in the civil sector; and that "virtual intelligence" and "electronic home defense" are the critical and undervalued elements of survival in the age of information and information warfare.

The four essential elements of any National Information Strategy are: Connectivity, Content, Coordination, and Communications and Computing Security.

In my view, the existing national efforts to provide for *Connectivity* (of which the Global Information Infrastructure [GII] and National Information Infrastructure [NII] initiatives are examples) are good efforts, but they are severely limited, for they focus on tools rather than content. Connectivity without content is nothing but digital noise.

Organizations today have no incentive—and many disincentives—for sharing with others the unique *Content* that they have developed for their own programs. To take universities as an example: it costs money to allow the public to access university databases, and it increases the risk of damage to files from hackers or others who wish to play and may cause inadvertent—if not deliberate—damage.

Therefore, I believe that the government should provide incentives for all elements of the information continuum (K-12, universities, libraries, businesses, information brokers, media, government, defense, and intelligence) to put content online. A one billion dollar investment could yield enormous productivity and competitiveness gains across any nation's private sector. Within government, it is necessary to accelerate dramatically the structuring and digitizing of information in the possession of the government, but not available to the public. The incentives will be very cheap because they need only address the marginal cost of additional access, *not* the full cost of creating and maintaining a cadre of experts and their data. This cost is borne by the originating institution.

There are two ways in which billions can be saved each year through *Coordination*. The first is with respect to functional requirements for information technology, and the standardization of applications within organizations, industries, and the Nation. Billions of dollars are wasted by different organizations building variations of exactly the same workstation. Within governments, each department, and within departments, each bureau, spends millions for different or duplicative information technology capabilities. The lack of coordination becomes even more serious when one considers the absence of communications and computing security standards.

It is not safe today to work and play in cyberspace. One important U.S. government organization examined during one year all hardware and software reaching its loading dock and found 500 different computer viruses *in shrink-wrapped products coming directly from the factory*. This is unacceptable. The communication and computing industry today is not criminally negligent, only because there is no body of law which requires them to provide safe products and safe services. Significant cost savings and productivity improvements can be achieved through standards and testing and certification laboratories to assure the public and business consumers that communications and computing security standards are being met.

Finally, the fourth element: *Communications and Computing Security*. Our national telecommunications infrastructure is too vulnerable to interruption of services as well as destruction, degradation, and theft of data. Experts predict that we will see enormously costly electronic attacks on our major financial and industrial organizations, generally undertaken by individuals who stand to benefit financially from degraded or interrupted performance.

The current generation of systems engineers was not raised in an environment where security was a necessary design element. At every level, through every node, we are wide open—and in a networked environment, one open house contaminates the next. For this reason, one important initiative must be the legislation of "due diligence" standards which require that the communications and computing industry adhere to standards (most of which have not been established and need to be established quickly). At the same time, corporate managers must be held accountable for ensuring adequate security for the proprietary information stored on electronic systems; information upon which corporate profits depend. I anticipate a wave of lawsuits in the next five years, as stockholders realize that managers are not protecting their electronic information, and managers realize that they are not receiving "safe" products and services from the industry.

These four elements, like the four pillars of a building, must be developed and maintained together, or the National Information Strategy will not succeed. Such an integrated program could be established using existing resources. The cost savings from the elimination of redundant and counterproductive investments in information collection and information technology across government departments and into the private sector can also make a substantive difference against the federal budget deficit.[19]

How such a strategy is implemented, and what specific organizations or positions are created or modified, is less important that the *fact* of having a strategy which can serve as an umbrella for the coordination of existing resources and capabilities.

Today government information, including government "intelligence" (classified information) is *out of control*. Certainly a Chief Information Officer (CIO) would be useful, perhaps even authoritative, if dual-hatted as Deputy Director for Information in the Office of Management and Budget. Such a person should not, however, be expected to do more than coordinate resources and avoid counterproductive investments. The current position of Director of Central Intelligence should become the Director of National Intelligence (DNI), assisted by a Director of Classified Intelligence (DCI) and a Director of Public Information (DPI), and all committed to the fullest possible exploitation of open sources on behalf of both policy-makers and the public. The DPI should be dual-hatted as the Director of a National Information Foundation. This could fulfill the President's vision and—as the Vice President has often remarked—"harness the distributed intelligence of the Nation."

CONCLUSION: Smart Peoples + Dumb Nations = Bad Business

In the United States of America today, we are a smart people, but a dumb Nation, and this equates to bad business. Our national security and our national attractiveness as a site for international investment, which permits our citizens to prosper, are at risk. We have no alternative but to redefine the role of government and to emphasize its responsibility for the nurturing our "national information commons." We must redefine national intelligence and create a Virtual Intelligence Community in which every citizen is a collector, producer, and consumer. At the same time we must create the incentives to ensure that our "electronic home defense" is robust, and that our civil sector—the front line in all information wars—is trained, equipped, and organized for battle in the 21st Century.

To survive at the dawn of the 21st Century, we *must* have a National Information Strategy.

Endnotes

[1] This material builds on an original presentation in Paris to the conference on "Wars and Peace in the XXIst Century," co-sponsored by the *Foundation pour les Etudes de Defense* and the Institut des Hautes Etudes de la Defense Nationale. A complementary article with a more civilian focus is my "Creating A Smart Nation: Strategy, Policy, Intelligence, & Information," *Government Information Quarterly* (Summer 1996).

[2] The comment by the DCI about the CIA's "primary" mission was reported in a number of newspapers and posted on bulletin boards and reflects a disappointing lack of familiarity with the roots of both the Office of Strategic Services (OSS) and the CIA. The DCI's comment about information warfare, in his "Worldwide Threat Assessment Brief" to the Senate Select Committee on Intelligence, was reported in *IWR: Intelligence Watch Report*, Special Report Vol. 3, No. 3, 24 February 1996. While the DCI may have intended to exclude nominal allies, a simple review of countries based solely on open source reporting, would confirm that we should at this time be concerned about traditional opponents (Russia, China, North Korea, Cuba, Viet-Nam), traditional allies abusing their privileges (France, Germany, Israel, Japan, South Korea, Taiwan), and selected Third World countries with significant computer expertise (India, Pakistan, Iran, Iraq, Thailand, South Africa). When we add revolutionary organizations (Irish Republican Army), transnational criminal organizations (Russian, Vietnamese, Korean, and Colombian), and independent hacker organizations (e.g. from The Netherlands), we count at least 21 viable information warfare threats, even without considering countries such as Sweden, Singapore, and Australia, or the Arab coalition and the Palestinian Liberation Organization.

[3] Lee Felsenstein of the Interval Research Corporation, is the originator of the term "information commons".

[4] For over two years France has been developing its national economic and information strategy, and recently has transferred significant responsibilities into the *Secretariat General de'la Defense Nationale (SGDN).* In Sweden, a long history of close cooperation between government, business, and the academy has culminated in their first ever conference on national competitiveness, held 14 March 1996 in Stockholm. Other nations, such as Israel, have more limited and focused strategies.

[5] The precision-targeting problem consists of two elements: encyclopedic mapping, charting, & geodesy (MC&G) data at the 1:50,000 accuracy level for the area of operations; and an intelligence community able to both *acquire* the target, and provide a real-time "sensor-to-shooter" interface. Although SPOT Image Corporation can provide the necessary mapping data at the desired level of accuracy, the U.S. intelligence community has consistently failed to budget for SPOT imagery, or fully alert commanders to its utility, because of its obsession with maintaining dependency on a very expensive constellation of expensive classified satellites that are totally unsuited to wide-area surveillance or mapping support. Equally grave problems exist in the target acquisition arena when the target is anything other than a large conventional weapon that emits either heat or an electronic signature.

[6] A fuller examination of these four warrior classes is available in my article, "The Transformation of War and the Future of the Corps", published in *INTELLIGENCE: Selected Readings—Book One* (U.S. Marine Corps Command & Staff College, AY 92-93). My most detailed examination of U.S. intelligence community shortcomings in addressing the threat represented by these four warrior classes in the 21st Century is provided in "A Critical Evaluation of U.S. National Intelligence Capabilities", *International Journal of Intelligence and Counterintelligence* (Summer 1993).

[7] In the aftermath of the Oklahoma bombing the President was moved in improve law enforcement intelligence and domestic counter-terrorism intelligence. Unfortunately, the President did not—despite correspondence to him and to all Cabinet principals on this issue—come to grips with the fact that the "global village" requires the full integration of national, military, and law enforcement intelligence, and vastly improved methods of open source collection, warning methods against home grown as well as foreign "crazies", and sharing of information and intelligence across federal, state, and local organizational boundaries as well as national borders.

[8] One of the most fascinating opportunities which our refined understanding of the threat affords us, when combined with the "information explosion", is that of permitting the various departments of government to begin producing intelligence in their respective areas of expertise. The United States Information Agency (USIA), for instance, is ideally suited to fulfill most of our requirements for cultural intelligence, those that can be derived from overt contact and open sources. As I testified on 21 February 1996 to the Commission on Public Diplomacy, such diplomacy must be a two-way street, and great benefit can accrue from ensuring that both the Country Team elements and the various principals in Washington have the benefit of the rich cultural understanding characteristic of USIA officers—and not characteristic of CIA case officers or Department of State political officers. It is also important to note that "intelligence" is not synonymous with "classified" and more often than not is much more useful when unclassified. Data is the raw print, image, or signal. Information is data that has been collated and processed to be of generic interest. *Intelligence* is information tailored to support a specific decision by a specific person at a specific time and place.

[9] The seminal work in this area is Winn Schwartau, INFORMATION WARFARE: Chaos on the Electronic Superhighway (Thunder's Mouth Press, 1994. Thoughtful articles on the vulnerability of specific networks include: Maj. Gerald R. Hust, "Taking Down Telecommunications", School of Advanced Airpower Studies, 1993; Maj. Thomas E. Griffith, Jr., "Strategic Attack of National Electrical Systems", School of Advanced Airpower Studies, October 1994; and H. D. Arnold, J. Hyukill, J. Keeney, and A Cameron, "Targeting Financial Systems as Centers of Gravity: 'Low Intensity' to 'No Intensity" Conflict", *Defense Analysis* (Vol. 10, No. 2, 1994). It is with respect to this threat class that our government's incapacity to fulfill its constitutional responsibilities is most apparent.

[10] Mr. John Peterson, President of the Arlington Institute, developed the original matrix and definition; I have added the third dimension of time.

[11] I highly recommend the book by Brigadier Richard E. Simpkin, *RACE TO THE SWIFT: Thoughts on Twenty-First Century Warfare* (Brassey's, 1985).

[12] Paul Evan Peters, Executive Director of the Coalition for Networked Information in Washington, D.C., is the originator of the term "just in time collection", and has done some original thinking about how distributed information networks can provide "just in time" answers at a much lower cost *and with much greater currency*—distributed experts funded by distributed centers of excellence turn out to be more accurate, more current, and more responsive than bureaucratic analysts captive to a "central" intelligence organization. This is not to say that we must eliminate national intelligence—on the contrary, national intelligence organization must add the special value that comes from access to classified information and to the policy-maker—but must do so upon the foundation of distributed knowledge available throughout the Nation.

[13] To take one very important example, military maps, it merits comment that of the sixty-nine countries identified by the U.S. Marine Corps in 1990 as being "likely" candidates for contingency operations, there was no màpping data—hard-copy or digital—for twenty-two of the countries, old data for the ports and capital cities only for another thirty-seven, and very old data for the other ten. This was one of a number of critical intelligence shortfalls addressed in *Overview of Planning and Programming Factors for Expeditionary Operations in the Third World* (Marine Corps Combat Development Command, March 1990), for which I served as the Study Director.

[14] My most detailed work in redefining intelligence, funded by a European Ministry of Defense, is my white paper, *ACCESS: Theory and Practice of Intelligence in the Age of Information*", 26 October 1993.

[15] Edward N. Luttwak, *STRATEGY: The Logic of War and Peace* (Belknap Press, 1987). The author rendered an invaluable service to all intelligence and defense professionals when he created this extraordinary work. His discussion of how different combinations of weapons systems and tactics have varying levels of effectiveness when considered at different levels of analysis and in relation to one another is useful and thought-provoking. The remainder of the model is original to myself. A fully developed report, including definitions of high, medium, and low degrees of difficulty for the various military mission areas is available in my "Expeditionary Environment Research & Analysis Framework & Model 1990" (USMC Intelligence Center, 21 May 1990).

[16] See Samual P. Huntington, "The Clash of Civilizations?" *Foreign Affairs*, Vol. 72 (Summer) 1993, pp. 22-49. While I agree with the cultural focus of Professor Huntington, I think it is also useful to add the agricultural-industrial-information focus of Alvin and Heidi Toffler, with their books *PowerShift: Knowledge, Wealth, and Violence at the Edge of the 21st Century* (Bantam, 1990), and *WAR AND ANTI-WAR: Survival at the Dawn of the 21st Century* (Little Brown, 1993).

[17] See Robert B. Reich, *THE WORK OF NATIONS: Preparing Ourselves for 21st Century Capitalism*, (Alfred A. Knopf, 1991). A representative and leader of this school of thought is Professor Lars Oxelheim, "Foreign Direct Investment and the Liberalization of Capital Movements", in a book which he edited, *The Global Race for Foreign Direct Investment: Prospects for the Future* (Springer-Verlag, 1993).

[18] I once did a paper on torture, and was intrigued to find that you can torture someone to tell you what you know you want to know, but you cannot torture someone to tell you what you do not know that you need to know. In a complex world where threats cannot be anticipated, the civic sensor system *must* be voluntary, or it will not be effective.

[19] One authority, Mr. Paul Strassmann, estimates that $22 billion over seven years could be saved by the Federal government of the United States in information housekeeping costs alone. This is apart from policy savings derived from improved intelligence support. Mr. Strassmann has been Director of Defense Information and Chief Information Officer of the Xerox Corporation and other major companies. His books, including *The Politics of Information Management*, *The Business Value of Computers* and *Information PayOff* are all exceptional.

Protecting the United States In Cyberspace

Martin C. Libicki

Normally, the collapse of a mid-sized California mutual fund would have rated little news—until the reason for its failure was revealed: it had been looted by computer hackers, putatively from China. Because its founders were elites of countries disputing China for some islands, the attack was portrayed as a double blow—against these countries and against the United States, put on notice that its homeland was no longer a sanctuary. Within hours, several neighboring financial institutions, patrons of alternative local telephone service providers, found their phone (and thus data) services disrupted. Computer security experts, called in to help, reported that their universities' data networks had been invaded. An FAA node in Fresno mysteriously went off-line for several hours during peak morning traffic. A sudden reevaluation of systems integrity all over the West Coast followed. A computer chip firm discovered hidden bugs in a key product. The U.S. Pacific Command found anomalies in its Time-Phased Force Deployment data. Seven of the Command's flag officers, suspecting blackmail, decided to check their credit files; three had suspicious errors.

Panic reverberated. Many in Congress rose to demand a political response to what they deemed a "Digital Pearl Harbor" attack by the Chinese. The Administration was forced to ask China to prove its innocence in these attacks, a request indignantly rebuffed. Small investors fled the stock market, and the Dow fell hundreds of points. Mattress sales skyrocketed.

With every passing week, the United States appears to grow more vulnerable to attacks on its soft underbelly—its National Information Infrastructure (NII). As this vulnerability to attack is metamorphisized into military metaphors, the logic of national defense kicks in. Protecting the nation requires that someone be in charge. As comforting as such logic feels, such tasking would be a mistake. If seriously pursued, adherents would and should face opposition which would make them pine for halcyon discussions over the Clipper chip.

The problem is not that computer security is irrelevant. Quite the contrary. It is incumbent upon the Department of Defense to assume that its systems will be targeted by malicious hackers anytime it engages in controversial acts. Operators of commercial systems must be held responsible for the harm done to others, if their systems have been compromised. Those who introduce new commercial applications need to think through their potential for malicious misuse. Yet none of this supports the notion that the quotidian task of systems security against external foe can be assigned to a Commander-in-Chief and thereby placed firmly on the road to solution. To do so reveals a complete misunderstanding of both computers and national security. It suggests the problem is (in words used to describe the fin-de-siècle Austria-Hungarian Empire) "desperate but not serious."

Most of the NII is private, and the tools for computer security (even against determined attack) already exist. Thus, the nut of the case against an NII CINC is that self-defense offers by far the best security, and paradoxically, is vitiated if information security is considered a problem of national defense.

The NII and National Security

Why are people even worried about attacks on the nation's information infrastructure?

First the U.S. economy is growing more dependent on information systems. Analog systems are becoming digital; digital systems, themselves, are replacing humans (e.g., automated teller machines, voice mail systems). Staring at video screens—the portals to the infotainment face of the NII—may come to dominate America's non-business hours as well.

Second, information systems are interconnecting via phone and E-mail. Interconnection saves manhours, promotes workplace collaboration, and permits remote management (e.g., supervisory control and data acquisition [SCADA] systems) but also permits havoc to seep in from outside, or even abroad. When systems can infect each other, malevolence is harder to contain.

Third, more work is being taken away from mainframes and minicomputers. Both architectures, designed to carry a company's jewels, tend to make users second-class citizens, limit their access to software, and take security more seriously. PCs were designed to have everything accessible; UNIX workstations were designed for information sharing. The latter are far more vulnerable.

Fourth, many proposed system innovations carry new security risks. Some Web browsers and spreadsheet macros let the unwary download viruses into their system. Distributed objects over networks and software agents may introduce similar problems. If systems reconfigure themselves based on learning—a tried-and-true response to suspicions of corruption—starting afresh with original media will not work so well.

These four factors, especially when combined, suggest that the challenge of computer security will matter more to America's well being tomorrow than it does today.

Does this, however, make the protection of the NII a matter of national security? Yes, to some extent. First, the more this country depends on the integrity of its information infrastructure, the more it can be held at risk by attacks there. The threat of information warfare—massive disruption to some—may supersede the threat of nuclear warfare's massive destruction. Others see hacking as how an asymmetric competitor may keep the U.S. out of its backyard (and thus stymie our advantage at conventional warfare). Second, information warfare is terrorism writ less bloody, but potentially more effective. As porous as the U.S. is toward bad people, it is even more porous to bad bitstreams. A phone or E-mail connection suffices to access a wide variety of computers, hop-scotching from one node to another, until an important vulnerability is found. In cyberspace, the risk of detection is low; the risk of apprehension and punishment is even lower. Third, the DoD increasingly depends on the NII (95 percent of its communications go outside its own systems at some point) as its assets are repatriated and off-the-shelf becomes the rule. Thus, leaving this infrastructure unprotected may undermine conventional modes of national defense.

Information warfare has become the dark continent of threatdom. More is unknown than known. That alone should make the case for perspective rather than panic. As such, this essay makes several points:

- Most threats are ordinary (and thus self-contained).
- The tradeoff between risk and effect exists in information warfare as it does elsewhere.
- Defenses are, in theory, tractable if taken seriously.
- Vulnerability, although too high, is nevertheless easy to exaggerate.
- The benefits of attacking a nation's information infrastructure are unclear.
- System owners have to protect themselves; if they punt, the Government cannot substitute.

Do's and Don'ts for Government policy follow.

Ordinary and Extraordinary Threats

Systems abuse comes in many forms. Some are ordinary; they rely on normally present motivations (e.g., greed, boredom). Some are extraordinary and unpredictable. Systems owners can be normally expected to protect themselves against everyday threats whose future probability and patterns can be predicted from their past. More worrisome are the threats whose effect is exceptional because they arise from the concerted actions of a single malevolent source.

Deliberate systems abuses, many of which could be hacker attacks, come in roughly six forms:

- theft of service (e.g., cellular phone call fraud),
- acquisition of objective data (e.g., research results),
- acquisition or alteration of subjective data (e.g., a person's credit history),
- theft of assets (e.g., embezzlement),
- corruption of data in storage or motion (e.g., sabotage), and
- disruption of information service (e.g., telephony) or attached services (e.g., electric power distribution).

Disrupting an information service may be undertaken, not only for its own sake, but for secondary purposes; examples may include corrupting medical data to hurt individuals, seeking control for the purpose of blackmail.

Some attacks are no more than a high-tech version of carjacking and joyriding with little permanent consequence. Others are far more serious. For instance, because greed is eternal, the motive for breaking into and robbing a bank is ever present, whether or not the United States is under attack. Ditto for stealing services. Threats against individuals ("The Net"), although a potential tool of guerrilla war, are more likely to motivated by private gripes and grudges. A fourth case, stealing objective data, is the high-tech version of protecting classified information—something the DoD already takes seriously every day.

The last two, corruption and disruption, best characterize the unexpected and malevolent nature of information warfare. Because the perpetrator gains little for himself, its perpetration requires an external goal, and, for the most part, a concerted strategy and the time to carry it out.

Systems that face a known threat pattern (and which bear most or all of the cost of an attack) can determine an optimal level of protection. There is no reason to believe that they underprovide protection against information attacks than they do against other threats to their well-being (e.g., shoplifting, embezzlement, customer lawsuits). The real worry is a threat that does not exist in the ambient environment—and thus one for which there is less natural protection.

The Tradeoff Between Risk and Affect

Systems can generally be attacked in one of three ways: (1) through corrupted system hardware or software (2) by using an insider, or (3) by hacking—plus combinations thereof (e.g., having an insider reveal vulnerabilities that facilitate hacking). Physical attacks (e.g., jamming, microwaves, shot and shell) are also possible, but are generally useful only for service denial; they usually require on-site presence, and thus carry far greater risks. Thus, they are not the subject of this essay.

The first, corrupted hardware or software, may be epitomized by the myth of the rogue employee of a U.S. microprocessor firm queering some circuits in every PC chip which then goes bad simultaneously, just when most needed. How to ensure simultaneity without premature discovery is never explained. A slightly more plausible threat is a planted bug in a specific system (e.g., a jet computer that is disabled by a signal from the ground, an unauthorized patch onto systems software).

The second, the acquiescence or complicity of someone with the right privileges, is more likely. In this downsizing era, there is no shortage of disgruntled employees and ex-employees. Yet, not every bad egg will harm society. During the Gulf War, sensitive war plans had been left in a car and stolen; they were expeditiously returned with the comment that the perpetrator, while being a thief, was by no means a traitor.

Exploiting corruption, whether inside the system or among trusted users, has obvious advantages, particularly when used against otherwise well-secured systems. Yet, the risks of getting caught are far higher, because the chain of responsibility is more direct (and the number of suspects in either case is smaller than the several billion people with phone access). Recruiting such individuals from the outside involves risks akin to those for intelligence recruitment; they indicate a system is under watch for attack. The fact that no such conspiracy has come to light suggests the number of attempts to date has been small. The higher the risk, the lower the odds of being able to penetrate a large number of systems undetected; using insiders is a better avenue for opportunistic or intermittent rather than systematic attack.

This leaves the hacker route. Most systems tend to divide the world into at least three parts: outsiders, users, and superusers. One popular route of attack for Internet-connected computers is (1) to use a password attack so that the outsider is a user, and (2) use known weaknesses of UNIX programs so that users can access superuser privileges. Once a superuser, a hacker can read or alter files of other users or the system itself; control the system under attack; make it easier to reenter the system (even after tougher security measures are enforced); and insert rogue code (e.g., a virus, logic bomb, Trojan horse, etc.) for later exploitation.

The amount of damage a hacker can do *without* being a superuser depends on how systems allocate privileges. There is very little a simple phone user can do to the system.

Computer networks tend to be more vulnerable to abusers, especially when certain privileges are granted without being metered. Indeed, any system with enough users is bound to contain a few who can abuse resources, filch data, or otherwise gum up the works. While mechanisms to keep non-users off the system matter, from a security point of view, limiting what authorized users can do is of greater importance.

A variant attack method—applicable only to communications networks open to the public—is to flood the system with irrelevant communications or requests for service. Such an attack is particularly useful in a system where service is free or where accountability can be otherwise evaded. The weakness of such an attack is that it requires multiple separate sources (to minimize discovery) and that its effects last only as long as calls come in. Because communications channels in the United States tend to be much thicker than whose which go overseas, overseas sites are a poor venue from which to start a flooding attack.

Systems Can Be Protected

Even though many computer systems run with insufficient regard for security, they can nevertheless be made secure. The fundamental theory is that protection is a point to be sought on a two dimensional grid (see Table). One dimension is the degree of access: from totally closed to totally open. Needless to add, a system that keeps out every bad guy will make it difficult or impossible for good guys to do their work. Thus, the second dimension is resources (money, time, attention) versus sophistication. A sophisticated system keeps bad guys out without keeping so many good guys out, and vice versa.

Security Choices	Scrimp on Security	Spend on Security
Tighten Access	Users are kept out or must alter their work habits.	Users can get in with effort, but no hackers can.
Loosen Access	Systems are vulnerable to attack.	Users can get in easily but most hackers cannot.

To start with the obvious method, a computer system that receives no input whatsoever from the outside world ("air-gapped") cannot be broken into (and no, one cannot spray a virus into the air in the hopes that a computer acquires it). If the original software is trusted (and the National Security Agency [NSA] has developed multilayer tests of trustworthiness), the system is secure (efficiency aside). Such a closed system is, of course, of limited value. The challenge is allowing systems to accept input from outside without at the same time allowing core operating programs to be compromised. One way to prevent compromise is to handle all inputs as data to be parsed—a process in which the computer decides what to do by analyzing what the message says—rather than as code to be executed directly. Security then consists of ensuring that no combination of computer responses to messages can affect a core operating program, directly or indirectly (almost all randomly generated data tend to result in error messages when parsed).

Unfortunately, systems need to accept changes to core operating programs, all the time. Absent more sophisticated filters, a tight security curtain may be needed around the few superusers allowed to initiate changes (they might have to work from specific terminals hardwired to the network—an option in Digital's VAX operating system.)

The techniques of encryption and especially digital signatures provide other tools. Encryption is used to keep files from being accessed and permit passwords to be sent through insecure channels. Digital signatures permit very strong links to be established between message and messenger. A digital signature is used to create a message hash with a private key for which there is only one public key. If a user's public key can unlock the hash and the hash is compatible with the message, the message can be considered signed and uncorrupted. Thus computer systems can refuse unsigned messages (and rogue insiders can be more easily traced). The private key never has to see the network (where it could have been sniffed) or be stored on the system (where the untrustworthy could give it away). Digital signatures are being explored for Internet address generation, and for secure Web browsers. Not only users but also machines, and perhaps individual processes, may all come with digital signatures. (Unfortunately, a secure digital signature needs to be 512 to 1024 bits long—and is thus hard to memorize; human use may require hardware-encoded schemes coupled with PIN numbers so that stealing the hardware does not reveal the entire password).

Most problems of systems security can be parsed into user sloppiness, systems sloppiness, and poor software. User sloppiness includes poorly chosen passwords, or passwords left in public places. Systems sloppiness, likewise, includes a security regime that lets users choose their own passwords (or at least does not reject obvious ones), that does not remove default passwords or backdoors, that fails to install security patches, or that permits users enough access to total system resources to read or write files they should not have access to (particularly when these files control important processes). Poor software includes bugs that override security controls, or which permit errant users to crash the system, or in general, anything that makes security unnecessarily difficult or discretionary.

The head of the Computer Emergency Response Team (CERT) once estimated that well over 90 percent of all reported break-ins were made possible because hackers could exploit known but uncorrected weaknesses of the target system (for instance, the method hackers used to get into Rome Laboratory's computer in 1994 and Los Alamos's computers in 1996 was an unfixed bug in the Unix sendmail program that was used for the infamous Internet Worm incident in 1988). The rest came under the category of no-one-knew-that-could-be-done, but most of *these* were understood to be theoretically possible, even if the exact method used was not.

Because most PCs and workstation operating systems assume a benign world, rewriting them to make them secure against the best hackers is difficult; the more complex the software and security arrangements the greater the odds of a hole. In security, the primitive is often superior to the sophisticated; there are fewer configurations to test. Not all systems can be broken into in the face of a sufficiently large attack; the quality of the security system is what counts.

Nevertheless, against the terrorist, the virtual NASDAQ market can be secure with higher confidence than can the real NYSE stock floor—if for no other reason than technology permits a system's owners to control all of the access points and examine everything that comes through in minute detail. In the physical world, public streets cannot be so easily controlled, moving items cannot be so confidently checked, and proximity and force matters.

The Vulnerability of the NII

How vulnerable is the NII? Sadly, no one really knows. The publicized incidents of phone phreaks, Internet hackers, and bank robberies may or may not be the tip of the iceberg. The common wisdom is that victims do not like to talk about how they have been had, but Citibank's decision to prosecute (rather than overlook) perpetrators of a fairly large ($400,000 transferred with another $10,000,000 waiting to go) computer crime suggest a change in perception and prospects for better reporting.

What does computer crime cost? The FBI's precise estimate is between $500 million to $5 billion; in the same league with cellular telephone fraud (roughly $1 billion) and PBX toll call fraud. Many such estimates must be carefully understood. For instance, most embezzlement today is computer crime because that is where financial records are kept; but embezzlement clearly predates the computer. The cost of a stolen call is much less than its price, because the call otherwise probably would not have been made. Most phone systems have excess capacity; and the price of a phone call includes services such as billing that criminals do not need. The cost to a corporation of having its R&D looked at by competitors is generally far less than the cost of generating it in the first place: Most R&D is specific to a corporation's own products and processes and otherwise irrelevant; much of its value consists of implicit knowledge and what it teaches its researchers; and a good deal of the rest is published anyway.

CERT received over 2,000 reports in 1994 (a rise apace with the total Internet's growth—but CERT today is but one of over twenty incident centers, albeit the one everyone knows of). The Defense Information Systems Agency used publicly distributed tools to attack unclassified defense systems. It worked eight of nine times. Only one of twenty victims knew they were attacked; and only one of twenty of "them" reported it as they should have. If this 400:1 ratio is indicative—and Navy tests echo this—then 2,000 reports represent a million Internet break-ins, even if very few do real damage.

That said, the Internet is, with rare and unfortunately important exceptions (e.g., military logistics) not used for mission-critical tasks in the economy. Were some hacker, for instance, to invade and bring down the network here at the National Defense University, it would be difficult to distinguish the effects of doing so from the many times that the network goes down on its own. Similarly, someone breaking into NDU's computers for information (none of which is, of course, classified) would, at best, find draft copies of papers that their authors would have been more than pleased to circulate on request.

One reason computer security lags is that incidents of breaking in so far have not been compelling. Although many facilities have been entered through their Internet gateways, the Internet itself has only once been brought down (the 1988 Morris worm). The Internet, with its benign assumptions is, anyway, hardly indicative of systems in general; if it too becomes a mission-critical system whose compromise is a serious problem, it must evolve and will necessarily become more secure. Similarly, the phone system has never experienced a catastrophic failure, and no large phone outage has been traced to hacking (the most serious incident affecting phones in the Northeast in January 1991 was traced to a faulty software patch). No financial system has ever had its institutional integrity at risk through hacker attacks. A parallel may be drawn with the security of the nation's rail system: Unprotected rural train tracks are easy to sabotage, and with grimmer results than network failure, but, until recently, had not taken place for fifty years.

Nevertheless, computer security is too weak in too many places to withstand systematic attack. Systems were thought safe because really brilliant hackers were scarce; today, easy-to-use tools circulate on public hacker networks. Conversely, a system easy to abuse one way may not be easy to abuse in another. It is not the thousands of switches in the U.S. phone system that must be guarded, but the far fewer signal transfer point (STP) computers. Phone phreaks attack the system by getting into and altering the many data bases that indicate the status of calls and phone numbers. Presumably, with enough alterations, area telephone service can be terminated—but only so long as the data bases remain altered. It is far harder to plant a bug in the computer's operating system; access to such ports is very tightly controlled. Even though STP computers are interconnected through Internet protocols, serious study suggests the difficulty of one infecting another.

Can someone destabilize a nation's stock market by scrambling the trading records of the prior day (a la Tom Clancy's *Debt of Honor*)? Possibly, but it is easy to forget how many separately managed computers record every stock transfer (i.e., the trade company's, each of the two brokers' systems, plus perhaps each client's systems etc.). A simple expedient of archiving every transaction to an occasionally read archival medium (CD-ROM for the high-tech, paper printouts for the rest of us) will foil most after-the-fact corruption, detect consistent in-the-process faults, and sometimes see deliberately intermittent ones.

Can an individual's assets be stripped by erasing his bank account? A bank account is essentially an obligation by the bank to repay the depositor. This obligation does not disappear because the bank's record of it cannot be easily found.

Finally, a system's reliability involves not only its holes but its ability to detect its own corruption, the existence of backup data files and capabilities, the overall robustness of the system (including redundancy in routing), as well as the ability to restore its own integrity and raise its own security level on short notice.

A Digital Pearl Harbor

Although important computer systems can be secured against hacker attacks at modest cost, that does not mean that they will be secured. Increasingly common and sophisticated attempts may be the best guarantor that national computer systems will be made secure. The worst possibility is that the *absence* of important incidents will lull systems administrators into inattention, allowing some organized group to plot and initiate a broad, simultaneous, disruptive attack across a variety of critical systems. The barn door closes but the horses are gone. For this reason, a sequence of pinpricks, or even a steadily increasing crescendo of attacks is the wrong strategy; it creates its own inoculation. Strategic effectiveness requires that a nation's infrastructure be attacked in force, all at once. No such attack has ever happened, but as of 6 December 1941, no country had every been attacked across the Pacific Ocean either.

Irrational attacks need to be defended against, but what they can do is limited. Rational attacks are what matter because their purpose is not just to cause the United States pain, but gain a strategic political outcome, whose consequences are lasting. Such an attack may, as its purpose, seek to dissuade the U.S. from national security acts (e.g., intervening against the attacker), or hinder their execution (e.g., a mobilization, deployment, operation etc.).

In terms of leverage, hacker warfare may prove to be a pale shadow of economic warfare, itself of limited value. Suppose that hackers could shut down all phone service (and, with that, say, credit card purchases) nationwide for a week. The event would be disruptive certainly and costly (more so every year), but probably less disruptive than certain natural events, such as snow, flood, fire, or earthquake—indeed, far less so in terms of lost output than a modest-size recession. Would inconvenience prompt the public to demand disengagement from engaging the attacker? It is more plausible that the United States would desist before opponents whose neighborhoods are judged less worthwhile in the face of difficulty. It is less likely to withdraw before an opponent whose power to strike the U.S. economic system suggests why this opponent must be put down.

For instance, it probably would not have been in North Vietnam's interest to hire hackers to disrupt our systems. Doing so would have contravened the message that it was fighting only because the United States was in its (albeit incorrectly defined) territory. Such an attack would not only have compromised its drive to build support in the U.S. for the disengagement of its forces. It would have also portrayed North Vietnam as an opponent capable of hurting the United States at home, an act which would have eroded the cautions which mitigated U.S. air operations against North Vietnam itself.

How well such attacks can delay, deny, destroy, or disrupt military operations, is a more open question. An enemy at war should be expected to get at U.S. military systems as much as it can (subject to self-imposed limits noted above). But is there enough *military* potential from a concerted attack on the *civilian* infrastructure to merit concern?

Clearly there are vulnerabilities. Today's wars require a high volume of communication from the field to not only the Pentagon (say, to its Checkmate in the basement from the Black Hole in Riyadh) but also to various support bases, control points, logistics depots, contractors, and consultants. A prolonged power, telephone, and/or E-mail cut-off would hurt command and control. Given the multiplicity of communication media and links in the United States, such a disruption would have to be widespread, coordinated, and uniformly successful to have any effect whatsoever. Traditionally, a commander spent his time setting up a military operation and putting most of it on auto-pilot for a day at a time. In theory, real-time fingertip control from across the oceans is possible, but history does not suggest that establishing military operations with such long and vulnerable tethers is so wise. By this measure, a disruption that lasted hours, rather than days, would be unlikely to affect outcomes very greatly. Many services can be restored in that time unless some hard-to-replace physical item was damaged.

The effect of such an extended disruption on troop or supply mobilization is more difficult to gauge; these are processes that typically take weeks or months to reach fruition. Overnight deliveries aside, logistics should be able to take disruption with little ultimate impact—otherwise, it is already badly engineered to begin with (disruptions near the point of use, are, of course, an expected feature of warfare).

Granted, an enemy with a precise and accurate knowledge of how decisions are made and how information is passed within the U.S. military, may be able to get inside the cycle and do some non-trivial damage. But how easy is it for an adversary to know this? Not even insiders can count on such paths, and in an age where hierarchical information flow is giving way to networked information flow, the relevance of any one pathway is extremely suspect.

The difficulty of crafting a credible Digital Pearl Harbor is best illustrated by looking at the best and most widely reported scenario, RAND's "Day After in Cyberspace." In a basic Persian Gulf scenario, twenty-plus incidents befall U.S. and allied information infrastructures. In the end, despite major implausibilities (e.g., three separate incidents tied to identical logic bombs, the simultaneous blackout of the Washington area's heterogeneous phone systems, rogue subcontractors affecting what in real life are triple-redundant systems, market crashes following the manipulation of an unspecifiable computer), little results therefrom. The U.S. populace finds some grounds for mass panic should it so choose, but outcomes in the field are only modestly affected.

Can Security Be Socialized?

Is systems security a problem whose solution should be socialized rather than remain private? Consider some distinctions.

- If a foreign missile hits a refinery that blows up and damages its neighborhood, would the damage be the refiner's fault? No one wants to pay the cost of building refineries to withstand wartime attacks. It is far more cost-effective to socialize the problem of such incidents by providing a common national defense.
- What if a sniper hits a refinery tower to the same effect? This problem is partially socialized through public law enforcement, but a reasonable provision against faults somewhere in the system creating a cascade of events is well within reasonable expectations.
- Change the sniper to a random pistol wielder, and the responsibilities of the refiner are broader. Owners of dangerous equipment should be expected to take reasonable precautions (e.g., perimeter fencing, security guards).
- Finally, what if a hacker on the Internet were to gain access to the refiner's system and command a valve to stay open—again to the same effect. Should the refiner be faulted? Yes; it should know everything about its information systems whereas the government may know absolutely nothing. The refiner must both protect its internal systems from outsiders and ensure that software-generated events—including bugs—cannot do catastrophic damage.

Needless to add, none of this at all excuses the perpetrator, who, if caught, is and ought to be subject to the full force of the law. By the same token, if such responsibility can be ascribed to a group or even a country, the justification for similar sanctions thereby exists—insofar as judicial sanctions translate reliably into international sanctions.

The force of this example comes from the fact that most of the NII is in private hands; if their owners bear the total costs of system failure, they have all the incentives they need to protect themselves. Yet there are a few systems whose disruption carries public consequences: phone lines, energy distribution, funds transfer, and safety. If the threat is great enough, then they have to be secure—even at the cost of returning them to stand-alone status. True, this is a drastic step and less costly remedies (e.g., more secure operating systems) may suffice. Even the primitive solutions, though, are cheap compared to other steps the country takes to protect itself (e.g., nuclear deterrence). That said, the number of critical sectors is growing. Credit card validation is becoming as critical as funds transfer to hour-to-hour operations of the economy. Automated hospital systems are reaching the status of mission-critical safety systems.

Should there be a central federal policy maker for guarding the NII, and, if so, who? DOD has both the resources and national security mission. But its expertise is concentrated in the very agency fighting the spread of one of security's most potent tools, encryption. The military's approach of avoiding new systems that do not meet military specifications is costly when applied to technology with short life cycles, and difficult when applied outside hierarchies. NIST, the second choice, has the talent but not the funding, nor the experience at telling other federal agencies what to do. Beyond those two, the expertise and mission get thin.

The very concept of a single government commander for information defense is tenuous. Any attempt to "war-room" an information crisis will find the commander armed with buttons that attach to absolutely nothing. Why? Repair and prevention will largely be in the hands of system owners, who manage their own systems and rarely need to call on common resources (so that there is no scarce allocation problem). There is little evidence of any recovery or protection synergy that cuts across sectors under attack (say, power companies, and funds transfer systems). Second, in terms of policy, each sector is different, not only in terms of its vulnerabilities, and what an attack might do, but more importantly, in the range of policies that can be used to improve its security. Judicious coordination is, of course, always advisable. A high-level coordinator could ensure that the various agencies are doing what they are tasked to do; lower-level coordinators could work across-the-board issues (e.g., public key infrastructures).

Coda

Within weeks, another perspective on the hacker attacks emerged. Yes, the Fund had been looted by computer, but more evidence pointed to high-tech embezzlement from trusted insiders than to hackers. Subsequent incidents could have been the background noise of everyday events, amplified by panic. University computer systems are broken into routinely. With all the benefits of phone deregulation, it has pushed reliability to the edge of the cost-effectiveness margin. The FAA's old computers are failing and its new computers, like all new systems, will have break-in bugs. As computer chips get more complicated there are many more places for faulty logic to occur. No large data-base is error-free (particularly those that involve human data entry); one study found three in every seven credit reports had a least one fault. As it is, most systems errors are born as mysteries; some are solved, and some not. Yet, there is no more reason to believe that every unsolved bug proves malevolence than to suppose that every unexplained scientific mystery confirms the presence of alien creatures.

Things Worth Doing

Because the NII is, despite its largely private nature, a public resource, a role for the Government is not entirely unwarranted. But this role must be carefully circumscribed and focused. This section makes eight suggestions on things worth doing.

1. Figure out today's vulnerabilities. How vulnerable, for instance, *is* the NII? What can be damaged and how easily? What can be damaged through outside attack; what is vulnerable to suborned or even malevolent insiders? For what systems can attacks be picked up as they occur, and by what means? What needs to be done to increase the population of internal problems in a system? What kind of recovery mechanisms are in place to return operations after a disruption; after an act of corruption? How quickly can systems be patched to make them less vulnerable? Can a similar set of questions be asked on the military's dependence on commercial systems? How thorough would outages of the phone-cum-Internet have to be to system cripple military operations, and in what way: operations, cognitive support to operations, logistics (and if so, internal to the DOD or external as well), mobilization? What alternative avenues exist for military communications to go through? What suffers when the 95% of military communications that go through public networks travel on the DOD-owned grid? A third set of questions relates to the existing software suites on which the NII runs: Does, for instance, today's Unix need replacement, or are known fixes sufficient? How useful are test-and-patch kits for existing systems?

2. Fund research and development on enhanced security practices and tools, and promote their dissemination through the economy. The United States spends a hundred million dollars a year in this area (split among ARPA, NSA, and others). Areas of research include more robust operating systems, cryptographic tools, assurance methodologies, tests and, last, but by no means least, standards. We know how to secure systems; we don't know how to make such knowledge automatic, interoperable, and easy to use. Cyberspace may need an information security equivalent of the Underwriters' Laboratory, capable of developing standard tests for systems security.

3. Take the protection of military systems seriously. It should be assumed that any nation at war with the United States will attack military systems—especially unclassified logistics and mobilization systems—any way it can: and hacker attacks are among the least risky ways of doing so. Assume that foreign intelligence operatives are, or soon will, be probing U.S. systems for vulnerabilities. DOD may also have legitimate concerns over classified systems in contractor hands and defense manufacturing facilities. It may be useful to stipulate that contractors with the U.S. military (even phone companies) have a reasonable basis for believing they are secure. Perhaps DOD needs some method of examining a vendor's source code, while providing reasonable assurances that it will not be commercially compromised.

4. Concentrate on key sectors—or more precisely, the key functions of key sectors. Since the government cannot protect these systems, it may have to persuade (through its various devices such as contracts, regulation, technology assistance, the bully pulpit) their owners to take security and backup seriously, even if this means something as primitive as manual recovery. Several organizations are useful fora for discussing the threat (e.g., Bellcore or the National Security Telecommunications Advisory Council for

phones; the National Electric Reliability Council for power plants). Non-attribution incident recounting may be especially helpful.

5. Encourage the dissemination of threats data and the compilation of incidents data (and not just on the Internet where CERT does a good job). Raw data may have to be sanitized lest investigations be compromised or innocent systems maligned. Nevertheless, effective protection of the public information infrastructure must inevitably involve public policy, and no public policy that relies on "if you knew what I knew" can be viable.

6. Seek ways of legitimizing the "red-teaming" of critical systems, in part by removing certain liabilities from unintended consequences of authorized testing. Non-destructive testing of security systems may be insufficient until the state of the art improves; that is, only hackers can ensure that a system is hacker-proof. Unfortunately, hackers are not necessarily the most trustworthy examiners, and, tests do go wrong (the Morris worm propagated faster than intended because somewhere in its program "N" and "1-N" got confused with each other). Incidentally, such systems should be tested both with on-site access permitted, and without it, to better simulate national security threats.

7. Bolster the protection of the Internet's routing infrastructure—not because the Internet is so important, but because protecting it is relatively cheap. Critical national and international routers should be made secure and the Domain Name Service should be spoof-proof. Note this is not the same as protecting every system on the Internet—which is expensive and unnecessary.

8. Encourage the technology and use of digital signatures, in part by applying it to security systems and not just electronic commerce. Supporting policies may include research on private key infrastructures, enabling algorithms, and purchases that create a market for them.

9. Work toward an international consensus on what constitutes bad behavior on the part of a state—and what a set of appropriate responses may be. A consensus permits the rest of the world to handle states that propagate, abet, or hide information attacks, by limiting their access to the international phone and Internet system—in much the same way that a similar consensus permits similar trade restraints. That said, proof in these cases will be harder to come by, and otherwise respectable states that will be hurt by such an embargo can more easily convince themselves that the evidence has been fabricated or exaggerated.

10. Strengthen legal regimes that assign liability for the consequences of hacker attacks so that the primary onus rests with the system being attacked—subject, of course, to whatever can be collected from the actual perpetrator.

Things to Avoid

This section, which directly addresses the concept of an Information Warfare CINC, details what is more important: seven things to avoid.

1. Avoid harping on information warfare to the extent that warfare becomes the dominant metaphor used to characterize systems attacks (much less all systems failures). Porting the precepts of inter-state conflict to computer security tends to remove responsibility for self-defense from those whose systems have been attacked. It is not at all obvious that protection from attacks in cyberspace should be yet one more entitlement. Why?

• Promoting paranoia is usually bad policy. Most system problems stem from design flaws, human error, or both. Until systems reliability improves greatly, this will be true, even if malevolence is afoot.

• Once something is called war, a victim's responsibility for the consequences of its acts dissipates. A phone company, that may have to recompense customers for permitting hackers to harm service, should not be able to claim *force majeure* because it can argue that it was a war victim.

• Characterizing hacker attacks as acts of war creates pressure to retaliate against perpetrators, real or imagined. Reasonable computer security is not so expensive that the United States should be forced to go to war to protect its information systems. If, however, the United States needs an excuse to strike back—say, to forestall nuclear proliferation—the supposition that the target has sponsored information terrorism can be summoned as needed.

2. Don't, however, waste much more effort on traditional intelligence collection for hacker warfare. Crime requires means, motives, and opportunity. Means—cadres of hackers with some access to connectivity (e.g., not sitting in Pyongyang)—may be easily assumed. Sixty percent of all Ph.Ds awarded in computer security by U.S. universities went to citizens of Islamic or Hindu countries. Put some effort into motive, to understand plausible patterns of attack by other nations (so as to know what needs security work). Spend the rest of the time on opportunity, which is to say, documenting vulnerabilities so that they can be fixed.

3. Don't waste time looking for a Minimum Essential Information Infrastructure for the NII as a whole (as opposed to one for DOD). Such a list will be undefinable (minimum to do what—conduct a nuclear war, protect a two-MRC mobilization, staunch panic?), unknowable (how can outsiders determine the key processes in a system and ensure that they stay the same from one year to the next?), and obsolete well into its bureaucratic approval cycle (the NII is changing rapidly and has a long way to go before it gels). More to the point, the government has no tools to protect only the key nodes; what it might have are policies that encourage system owners to protect themselves (and they in turn will determine what needs to be protected first).

4. Don't sacrifice security to other equities. It is difficult, for instance, to see how the NII will be secure without the use of encryption; yet the Government is loathe to encourage its proliferation (thus Clipper chip and export controls). The controversy seems to be complicating the credibility of Government attempts to secure the NII.

5. Don't put so much emphasis on getting commercial systems to adopt existing security practices that they are unable to take advantage of tomorrow's innovations—particularly those that enable collaborative computing. Yes, some key systems (e.g., systems that control dangerous devices) must be secure regardless and, yes, many expected innovations have security problems that must be attended too. The entire systems field, though, is too dynamic for a straightjacket approach.

6. Don't eliminate heterogeneity unnecessarily; it makes coordinated disruption harder and preserves alternative paths. Common industry approaches to security matter less than standard protocols and application portability interfaces across industries.

7. Don't try to make policy without detailed understanding of how information systems are used. Strategic nuclear policy is where engineering details matter little (that

they explode is far more important than how they explode). With systems security, it is the very details that are the portals to, or barriers against, attack.

Conclusions

The trendy notion that 21st century warfare is likely to consist of alternating attacks on enemy information infrastructures is greatly exaggerated. Such an attack may happen—even if its perpetrators may come to understand how little is to be gained and how much is to be lost by doing so. The more important point is that they need not happen if a modicum of attention—and that probably suffices—is paid to the possibility.

So, who *should* guard the NII? If it's yours, then you should. The alternative is to have the Government protect systems, which, in turn requires knowing the details of everyone's operating systems and administrative practices—an alternative which, even if it did not violate commonly understood boundaries between private and public affairs—is in any way impossible. Forcible entry in cyberspace does not exist—unless misguided policy mandates it.

The Role of the Media

James Adams

On Saturday, February 3, Sergeant First Class Donald Dugan became the first American soldier to die during the NATO peacekeeping operation in Bosnia. It was no concerted enemy attack or precision sniper fire that killed Dugan. That might have jeopardised the fragile peace agreement and be a serious cause for concern. Instead, he had picked up a discarded piece of ammunition which then exploded in his hands. In other words, it was an accident and the kind of accident that happens frequently in every army.

Yet, that night, the death of Dugan was the lead on every network news broadcast, and it was the front page lead in every major newspaper the following morning.[1] According to the Lexis-Nexus database, in the course of the first 24 hours after his death newspapers and magazines devoted more than 50,000 words to this single fatality and accorded Dugan the kind of national stature that might have been given a general fallen in battle in another age.

The difference in the coverage now compared with coverage then is the immediacy of the news and the ease with which it is transmitted around the world. Within minutes of Dugan's death, the information had been relayed from the U.S. Army headquarters in Bosnia to the NATO force headquarters and from there via a press conference to the world's media. With CNN leading its half-hourly news shows with the death, the agenda for the rest of the nation's media had been set, and they all dutifully followed the lead that had been established for them.

This kind of group feeding is a hallmark of news operations that began with the development of the wire services and has been honed by the revolution in international communications brought about by the growth of the Internet. But it is also a graphic illustration of the collective ignorance of the media and the politicians about how warfare actually works. Conflict today is judged not so much by victory or defeat, but by the numbers of casualties on the allied side, where deaths above single figures are routinely seen as a political, and thus a military defeat.

There was a graphic illustration of this during the deployment of U.N. peacekeepers to Somalia. Six Cobra helicopter gunships lifted off an American Navy vessel off the coast of Somalia just before midnight on December 9, 1992. Their mission was to provide cover for the U.S. Marines and U.S. Navy SEALs who were landing in the country as part of Operation Restore Hope, the mission to get aid through to millions of starving Somalis. In the briefing just minutes earlier, the pilots had been told that intelligence about the threat facing them was limited. What little was known suggested that some of the armed gangs might have rocket propelled grenades and small arms.[2]

As the lead Cobra came within sight of land, the pilot saw through his night vision goggles dozens of flashes from the beach. Assuming this was enemy fire aimed at him, he armed his weapons system and prepared to fire a salvo of rockets. Then, over his headphones came an urgent message: the lights on the beach were not enemy fire but the flashes from photographers taking pictures of a landing that was supposed to be a well-kept military secret.

To the normally camera-shy SEALs, the landing was an embarrassing farce. Instead of successfully launching a covert operation in hostile territory, they were shocked by hordes of journalists and photographers eager for a snapshot of the Pentagon's finest in action. To the Bush Administration and some senior military officials, Operation *Restore Hope* was too good a photo opportunity to miss. News of the landing had been leaked to the media to ensure maximum coverage for a military operation that was a certain winner back home. After all, the operation's goal of getting aid to the starving was laudable enough. The opposition to American might was just a few poorly armed local gangsters, and the open terrain favored American technology and firepower.

But as the operation unfolded, an apparently compliant media turned hostile, and those poorly trained and equipped gangsters managed to defeat the United States of America, the last remaining superpower and the strongest military force in the world. The facts of the reversal of American foreign policy are not in dispute. For America's allies, the reversal of U.S. fortune in Somalia caused concern about the strength of American political will in prosecuting foreign policy. These concerns are justified. But underlying such questions is a new reality that exists in the media and in government that helps explain why peacekeeping, peacemaking, and war fighting in the future may be impossible if we apply the criteria that once worked so effectively.

Peacekeeping and warfare today are taking place in a world the likes of which we have never seen. All the old certainties have disappeared; there is no Cold War, no superpower rivalry to provide both tension and stability. Instead there has emerged a series of relatively small, unexpected crises. These have provided some fresh challenges for the policy makers, the politicians, and the media that report on them.

But it is not just the end of the Cold War that has transformed the debate. The end of that era has heralded a new generation in the political leadership in many democratic countries, and it has consolidated changes that have been under way for some time in the media. Consider this: The President of the United States is 48; the Prime Minister of Britain is 50. The average age of staff working in the White House is around the mid-thirties. The heads of British intelligence are now appointed in their late 40s. Even the average age of staff on my own newspaper has fallen in the past 10 years from around 45 to 30, as we struggle to reach the younger readers we need to win the fierce battle for circulation.

This means that many of the political leaders and most of the advisers have no concept of the political and personal consequences of warfare. There have been no world wars to devastate families, none like those that so scarred our parents and grandparents. Thus, there is no true conception of the real horrors of war. In the media, there are now very few reporters and editors who have covered conventional conflicts. In 15 years of reporting on wars, revolutions, and terrorism around the world, I have only covered two conflicts that might be considered conventional: the Iran-Iraq War and the Gulf War against Saddam Hussein. The balance was made up by a large number of smaller wars, low-intensity conflicts, and acts of terror.

It is hardly surprising, then, that the current generation that is leading the media and politics has a very limited vision of war and the capability of the armed forces. It is a view formed by each individual's experience, which is confined almost entirely to television, movie images and, to some extent, what they have read in the newspapers. This is a small world, where action is concentrated on the human drama, the big picture writ small so that it is understandable to the average person. It is a world where attention spans are short.

For example, the way news is reported has undergone a striking transformation in the past 25 years. The average length of a Presidential statement on a network evening news broadcast fell from 42 seconds in 1968 to less than ten seconds in 1988. The three major networks gave to George Bush and Michael Dukakis one fourth of the air time they gave to Richard Nixon and Hubert Humphrey. In the last election and since the inauguration of President Clinton, there has been even less time allotted to the attempts by the President and his staff to communicate directly to the people.[3] Gone are the days when the networks were suitably deferential when the White House called. Instead, a cult of personality has evolved, built around the anchorman and woman who help present, refine, and make the news. The reason for this is that Presidents are, by and large, rather boring and do little for the ratings, while a network's own staff can present material in a way that suits them and enhances the ratings. Or, as Dan Rather put it in a speech:

> They've got us putting more fuzz and wuzz on the air, cop show stuff, so as to compete not with other news programs but with entertainment programs—including those posing as news programs—for dead bodies, mayhem, and lurid tales.
>
> We have allowed this great instrument, this resource, this weapon for good to be squandered and cheapened. The best among us hang our head in embarrassment, even shame. We should all be ashamed of what we have and have not done, measured against what we could do—ashamed of many of the things we have allowed our craft, our profession, our life's work to become.[4]

This *mea culpa* by one of the very people who has replaced Presidents with punditry is well founded. As the television media have trivialized the news, newspapers also have to seek ways of presenting their information in a lively and exciting way to retain their audience. That has meant not just a narrowing of the focus but a concentration on the trivial, the marginal, and the irrelevant in the search for excitement. In warfighting terms, this means that sound bites have replaced sense. There is no longer a search for an understanding of the bigger picture—the "strategic vision," if you like. Instead, what matters is the here and now, and modern communication means that what happens over there is presented here and now to the millions of Americans who form the body politic.

This narrow focus means that there is an obsession with detail, with every nuance of a story. That means that politics matters more than it has ever before. A united national front is a thing of the past. Never again will America stand united as a nation against an aggressor. Instead, the President may try and stand tall, but there will always be others sniping on the sidelines who will get equal time.

The reporting of conflict has changed as the media have evolved, so that the camera and the laptop bring home the single image of casualties, civilian or military. The news media and political elite demand that these casualties be counted in single figures to be acceptable. For example, it was striking in both the Falklands and the Gulf War that casualties were extraordinarily light. Even so, every single one was analyzed and agonized over and investigated in an attempt to find unrealistic certainties in the chaos of war. It is that drive to minimize loss of life that is going to be a primary factor of decision making in the foreseeable future.

There are two examples of this from the Somalia operation. First, the consensus that drove Congress and the Administration to support the deployment of American forces into that country at the beginning of this year evaporated when the body of a single American soldier was dragged through the streets of Mogadishu. That image, broadcast and rebroadcast by all the media, produced a wave of reevaluation across America. By all accounts, the President of the United States was shocked—even surprised—by the sight, as if warfare is not about suffering and horror but is somehow kinder, warmer and more generous than reality. Congress, too, immediately lost its nerve, sensing with the extraordinary antennae with which politicians seem to be born that public sentiment would no longer support the troop deployment. Of course, as Congress backed away and the White House wondered aloud about the rationale behind the commitment, the media caught the smell of panic and jumped in with both feet to complete the circle of self-absorbed indecision.

The result of that single incident was that the President ordered U.S. troops to be effectively confined to barracks, ceding control of Mogadishu to the armed gangs the Administration and the United Nations had committed to control only a few weeks earlier. At the same time, to buy off Congress, the President set a deadline for withdrawal from Somalia. Imposing a deadline and announcing it to the enemy is a cardinal tactical error which demoralizes your own force ("Why should I risk my life when we are going to leave anyway?") and hands tactical control to the enemy ("If we just wait until the deadline, we can get everything we want"). That the world's most important military and political power should have its foreign policy dictated by a television image of a single dead American is extraordinary. That the policy then should show such ignorance of military tactics and history is a cause for concern for allies and Americans alike.

The second image from Somalia is that of Michael Durant, the captured helicopter pilot. His bruised face was featured on the cover of newspapers and magazines across the nation, and he became a symbol of the apparent impotence of America in the face of an intransigent Somali warlord. Then he was released, and reporters and cameras followed him from Mogadishu to Germany and then home where, of course, he made the required appearance on the Larry King show.[5] This was one man, one prisoner in a country that is strategically irrelevant to the future fortunes of the United States or even the world—yet he assumed a symbolic importance far beyond his value as a man, an airman or an American citizen. Of course, reducing casualties is a laudable goal. But death and injury are unfortunate consequences of committing military forces to a conflict. Soldiers are trained to kill people, and yet there seems to be a broad view that crisis management today can somehow be handled without loss of life.

The media have played a large part in developing this view. The media always demand excellence in others; in terms of crisis management this translates as a successful resolution with minimum cost to "our" side. In the past 10 years, the way the media form opinion has changed dramatically. CNN is everywhere, and where CNN goes, all the other media outlets swiftly follow. Censorship today is virtually impossible, what with backpack satellite broadcast systems and telephones that allow reporters to file their copy from anywhere in the world.

While competition among different media remains superficially fierce, much of it is artificial, with an increasing number of stories covered by correspondents who are paid for their name or their face rather than for the content of what they can deliver. The growth of major cities with single newspapers has actually reduced competition, producing a kind of corporate arrogance that places much less value on the old-fashioned scoop and more on establishing a reputation as a "newspaper of record." This in turn has made for a different kind of reporting, where CNN and the wire services begin to set the agenda, and where they are followed by the newspapers and magazines whose editors and writers take their ideas and their leads from the those who fed at the news trough first.

News has an immediacy that drives the political process in ways that can be very unhealthy, particularly when so many of the decision makers have no experience of the world about which they are taking decisions of life and death. However, as much as both the military and politicians would wish it otherwise, that is the new reality of the media covering crises today, and it will remain so.

This is not just a one dimensional view of the media as news gatherers. Others who are part of the violence also have a much better understanding of how the media operate. I remember covering the takeover of the American Embassy in Tehran in 1979 by militant students. Many of those holding the Americans hostage had been educated at American universities and had a good understanding of the vulnerabilities of that society. The daily press conferences were carefully timed for the American networks so that interviews could be obtained, fed to the satellite, and reach the New York anchors in time for the evening news. It was skillful propaganda that proved very effective.

But the world has moved a long way from those early days. In the same way that the Pentagon routinely establishes a sophisticated public affairs operation for every military deployment, so protagonists understand the value of media attention. A good example of this came in a *New York Times* report of February 6, 1995 which described the activities of the Chechen rebels fighting the Russians:

The Chechen military commander, General Aslan Maskhadov, sitting serenely in his headquarters here (Novogroznensky, Chechnya), a recent model Motorola walkie-talkie in one breast pocket...They gave interviews and then they gave out their satellite phone numbers to reporters and left...When Russia's most wanted men were done talking to the journalists, politicians and relatives of the hostages, General Maskhadov made a couple of brief telephone calls on his portable phone....

That use of modern communications has been matched by the proliferation of different systems that give people all over the world access to the same kind of information at almost exactly the same time. A bomb goes off in London, and the fact of its detonation is flashed around the world by many different wire services and television stations, and information about that explosion is exchanged among journalists on the spot and by others in different cities. For example, when the IRA cease-fire broke down in February 1995 with the detonation of a bomb in London, I reported the story from Washington using contacts I have in the intelligence community and governments in America and Britain. Because I have some knowledge of the subject, I in turn was contacted by several wire services in a number of different countries, the major news magazines in America and television stations around the world. A single source thus becomes a resource for a vast number of news outlets.

That trend is exaggerated by the developments on the Internet. According to the Associated Press, the numbers of North American newspapers offering information through on-line computer services tripled in 1995 to 175 and is expected to double again in 1996.[6] Some newspapers have established sites on the World Wide Web; others offer stories and photographs through commercial on-line services; and a few others have launched their own stand alone on-line services. And this is just the beginning. Every major newspaper group has plans to provide a complete download of its newspaper or magazine to portable laptop computers which will interface with video and databases that will be accessible at a very low fee to any customer interested in getting more information on a given subject that is reported that day.

For the public, politicians and the military planners who have to confront the problem of an ever more intrusive media, the new world also poses some difficult challenges. Christopher Dunkley, the television critic of London's *Financial Times*, put it like this:

> Members of the television generation have no cushion against reality. We know how usual are pain and suffering, because the are brought to us, day in, day out in graphic pictures and detailed speech. To live with the sadness and pain of the whole world is something else. Half a century into the age of television, you begin to wonder whether this is not perhaps insupportable. What we are trying to do in living with global television is unlike anything that any previous generation has attempted.[7]

Prime Minister John Major of Great Britain gave this a political perspective in an interview with the *Los Angeles Times* on June 20, 1993. He was asked: "Leaders today are disadvantaged by that which might be called the CNN Syndrome. Everything has to happen so quickly. Does it get on your nerves?" He replied: "It doesn't get on my nerves. It is a fact of life. I think it is bad for government. I think the idea that you automatically have to have a policy for everything before it happens and respond to things before you have had a chance to evaluate them properly isn't sensible."

However "sensible" or not it may be, the media now have a power to effect the course of events and the decision-making of politicians that is greater in scope than at any time in our history. Consider how the role of the journalist has changed this century. In 1916, the British Foreign Office set up its first public relations department, and for the first time journalists were officially admitted into the hallowed halls of Whitehall—much to the chagrin of the doorman, who had managed to keep them at a distance until then.

"Well, sir, this is a change from what it used to be," he said. "Before the war, those Press gentlemen used to line up in the courtyard outside the office at about 4 o'clock, and one of us would come and say, "Nothing doing today, gentlemen, and they went away."

From that subservient beginning, the press have developed a voracious appetite for news and information. This seems to have occurred in a cycle that began in the first half of the century when the media began to understand the range of their power and influence. When Ian Fleming was the Foreign Manager of *The Sunday Times* in the 1950s, my newspaper maintained 150 correspondents around the world, with reporters in nearly every country. When I took over that position 15 years ago, *The Sunday Times* had eight cities manned by staff correspondents, a figure we maintain today. This pattern of expansion and contraction has been matched by every media organization in the world which was first seduced by the possibilities of global coverage and then faced with the financial realities of maintaining such a network.

What that means today is that media coverage is highly selective and driven not necessarily by the importance of a story, but by the cost of covering it, or even by something as simple as who happens to be in the area at the time. The column inches and television time devoted to Somalia versus Liberia, Angola or Burundi bear no relation at all to the scale of the tragedy unfolding in any of those countries. Strategically and economically, Angola is a more important country than Somalia; and the human tragedy in Burundi is arguably worse than Somalia. Nevertheless, the media herd goes to Somalia because it captured the imagination of editors, it made good and colorful copy, it was accessible and—perhaps most important of all—everyone else was there and the lemming instinct that drives so much of the media prevailed.

This selective media focus, which tends to be extraordinarily intense and of limited duration, has the effect of driving policy. That in turn has led the media to believe that they have not only a duty to report the news but also the power to influence events. As the British Prime Minister Stanley Baldwin said of the press barons of his time: "What they aim at is power and power without responsibility—the prerogative of the harlot throughout the ages."[8]

This power without responsibility has been refined to an art form in Washington, where news reporters frequently become news makers, and the line between reporting, commentating, and policy making has become so blurred as to be almost indistinguishable.

The politicians and the public have pandered to the media in a way that has encouraged this evolution. When I first came to live in Washington two years ago, I had a choice of what title I would assume, and eventually settled on Washington Bureau Chief. I assumed—rightly as it turned out—that others would see in the title an undeserved stature and see behind me a large staff eager to do my bidding.

In fact, I am chief of myself and my hard-pressed researcher. But this small conceit has given me access to the corridors of power in a way that would not be possible in London. It has also given me access to a social life among the political and media elite, where Bureau Chiefs are sought-after dinner companions. By contrast, in England, where journalists are just as distrusted as they are here, but politicians see little need to pander to them as they do in America, dinner party hosts would never boast of a reporter coming to dinner for fear the other guests might cancel.

Yet it is in Britain and not America where historically bargains have been struck with the media that have been proved to work. During the war against the Irish Republican Army in the 1980s, several undercover operations were established by the British security forces that were designed to trap IRA terrorists. This involved establishing observation posts in close proximity to potential targets such as politicians, businessmen and journalists. In some cases, these observation posts were inside the subjects' houses. Inevitably, news of this huge operation leaked, and every single significant media organization was briefed on the details of the operation and asked to keep it secret. That secret lasted for nine months when the operation was shut down.

There is an assumption that a similar bargain can work in America, and information officers in the Pentagon will cite examples where this has worked. For example, a number of reporters were briefed in advance about Operation Uphold Democracy, the military plan for taking control of Haiti, and there were no leaks.

That success with a small and controllable group should not be used as an illustration of how a larger, international group would work, particularly over an extended period of time. In Britain, there is a special word used to describe the activities of a number of tabloid journalists chasing a single subject. The activity is known as "monstering," and the hapless subject is "monstered," which aptly conjures up the right image of a pack of baying hacks hard at work. War—real war—will be just like that, with hundreds and probably thousands of reporters from different countries, different cultures and with different deadlines all chasing the same story and searching for a scoop. The military will become the enemy, because they will not provide a scoop that might not exist, rumors will become fact in place of real facts, and stories will bounce around the world with bewildering speed from laptop to editor's desk to the Internet and back to the laptop of a reporter sitting perhaps a few feet away from the original transmission.

Bosnia is perhaps the best example of the power of the media to influence the debate. In the 1992 Renaissance Weekend, when the American political establishment gathered to celebrate the New Year, much of the discussion, which included President Clinton and several others who are now senior members of this Administration, was focused on the unfolding tragedy in the former Yugoslavia. I was struck by the passion with which people argued that "something must be done" and the lack of specifics that people brought to the debate. This was the media, heart on its sleeve, arguing that the politicians and the military could do something—anything—to stop the killing. Such criticism is all too easy. Douglas Hurd, the former British foreign secretary and one of the Europeans so roundly criticized in America for his Bosnia policy, addressed the issue this way:

> Suppose we had launched air strikes...as a measure of our indignation and determination to resist aggression. Suppose that the result was not to help the effort for peace but to destroy it. Suppose that the result was not the saving of little girls...but the maiming of many other little girls. Suppose that the result was the halting of the humanitarian airlift to Sarajevo and of course the ending of all evacuation of casualties. Suppose that the result was retaliation against British and other U.N. troops within range of artillery, so that after many had been killed all had to be withdrawn. Who would be the first to denounce the lack of judgment, the failure to foresee, the recklessness of the disastrous misadventure? No prizes for the answer. And I would add that no real blame would attach to the critics who then switched position. That is their profession. Ministers and those who advise them have a different profession...Those who argue from outside government that "something must be done" are in a different position from those who actually have to make the decision and then impose the consequences of those decisions on others.

Hurd argues for a better understanding of the relationship between the media and government:

> Those who do need those who report and comment because in a democracy it is through the medium of the reporter and commentator that the people learn and judge. The reporter and commentator have a different angle of vision and different preconception from those who have to decide and act. It is no use the Minister or the serving officer assuming that reporters will see his problem his way. They will see it their way and report accordingly. It is no use resisting this or resenting it, but equally it would be wrong to be seduced by the apparent lure of favorable press comment. The relationship will be fruitful provided each side recognizes the difference between the professions. The general should not fancy himself as a commentator or the commentator as a general or a Cabinet Minister. If we each keep reasonable self-confidence in our own profession, then we shall do very well together.[9]

This clarion call for the maintenance of a division between the media and the policy makers is rooted in history and not in the current reality. Today, the evolution of the media as policy maker, the commentator as not just opinion former but also policy driver, is almost complete. This is an era when governments are not run by principle and conviction or even a clear strategic vision. Instead, politicians are increasingly driven by newspaper headlines and the results of opinion polls which are formed by those very same headlines.

A century ago, a single incident that was deemed to impinge on national sovereignty would provoke an immediate and violent act of retribution. When General Gordon was killed in Khartoum, the British dispatched a punitive expedition that years later punished the perpetrators of the act. Today, when the body of a single American is dragged through the streets of Mogadishu, the American government reverses its foreign policy and begins a withdrawal from the country. This momentous change in the way foreign policy is handled bodes ill for the future.

With an attention span so short and a world view so limited, it is difficult to conceive how a consistent policy for crisis management can be developed by the world's leading democracies. Is it conceivable that the world's only remaining superpower would deploy forces to an area like Northern Ireland to keep the peace in the way the British did 30 years ago? Is it conceivable that the American administration would send any troops to a similar environment? Under the present circumstances, the answer is no.

War, peacekeeping, and crisis management haves never been about consensus and about opinion polls. Those factors may have had influence, but they have never been paramount. The successful prosecution of any military operation is about leadership and a strength of resolve that allows principle and conviction to ride over the often ill-formed media criticism and the snapshot reporting.

These developments will all have a critical impact on the future of war fighting in the Information Age. The proliferation of information sources has been matched by a reduction in the number of sources supplying raw information. The proliferation of methods of controlling information flow has been more than matched by the development of systems that allow information gatherers to communicate at will. It is quite clear that the days of effective censorship designed to impact public opinion in support of a government's policy are over. No longer can governments control the flow of information, however much they might wish to do so. It would be foolhardy indeed for any government to plan for the control of information in the event of tension or conflict. On the contrary, planning must be devoted not to controlling by the suppression of news, but controlling by the manipulation of information.

Yet, it is one of the paradoxes of the Information Age that military planners and political leaders have more need now than ever before to try to maintain public support for political and military action. It is no longer the case that public support for national endeavors will be granted automatically. On the contrary, gaining public support for any kind of military action will be very hard. As Bosnia demonstrated, winning over Congress is tough, and winning over the public at large is tougher still. Yet, taking action is only the first step on what will almost always be a very tough road. Casualties in any deployment of forces are inevitable and, as we have seen, there is simply no public, political or media awareness of what warfare is about, and therefore little tolerance of any cost, let alone the costs that are inevitable in a full-scale conflict. The challenge then is to try to create an environment that at the same time bolsters public support at home while undermining public support in the enemy camp.

In an ideal world, the military and political leaders would enlist the assistance of the media to propagate a view that would help the national interest. In reality, such a bargain is almost impossible to sustain, especially when the media are so diverse and modern technology makes a mockery of "national" borders. To those familiar with the concept of Cyberspace and who are comfortable operating there, the very idea of "nationalism" is alien and has little place in their world which exists without any of the conventional boundaries that have given the traditional world its coherence.

The most comprehensive review of the relationship between the media and the military was conducted by the Freedom Forum First Amendment Center in 1995. Among the findings, which were based on a poll of about 1,000 military officers and 350 members of the media were:

—Fifty-five percent of military officers polled believe that the media should be allowed to report whatever they want from the battlefield, without censorship, as long as guidelines developed jointly between the military and the news media are honored.

—More than 80 percent of the officers say the news media as "just as necessary to maintaining U.S. freedom" as the military.

—Only 2 percent of the officers and 18 percent of the media think reporters should be free to report "anything they want, with no restrictions."

—Seventy percent of officers and 74 percent of the media agree that: "few members of the media are knowledgeable about national defense."

While all that suggests a healthy mutual respect between the military and the media, there are still enough grounds for disagreement and conflict:

—Sixty percent of the military officers, but only 8 percent of the media, agreed "military leaders should be allowed to use the news media to deceive the enemy, thereby deceiving the American public."

—Sixty-four percent of the officers, compared to 17 percent of the media, believe the news media harmed the war effort in Vietnam.

—Ninety-one per cent of the officers, compared to 30 percent of the media, think the media is more interested in increasing readership or viewership than in telling the public what it needs to know.[10]

Valuable as this study is, it reflects an old order that no longer exists and a debate that is largely irrelevant to the future of warfare. It is a fact, accepted by every public affairs officer in the military, that most reporters are extraordinarily ignorant about the subjects they cover. It is an accepted fact among the journalists that whatever they might say in reply to a survey, the military will fight to suppress the news once casualties mount and focused criticism begins in wartime. But even given those prejudices, in the Information Age it matters little what the American media or military think about each other. Equally, for the Pentagon and the media to earnestly debate about which reporters have access to which pools and when and exactly how much information is to be released is irrelevant. In the real world in a real conflict, there will be thousands of reporters on the ground from every country that possesses a media. Censor one reporter from Washington, then his competitor from Tokyo will get the information; file it back and it will be published within hours and be back in Washington. That is how the Information Age works.

During the Gulf War, there was an extensive pooling system for all war correspondents that was designed to control the information flow. Yet my newspaper provided some of the best coverage of the war operating almost entirely outside the pool system and by deliberately avoiding all the press conferences and formal briefings. For every reporter controlled by the pool system, there were four or five roaming around the Middle East and western capitals trawling for information that was readily accessible. And, of course, information supplied to one reporter is almost immediately available to every reporter.

The reality is that information flow in the Information Age cannot be controlled. What can and should be done is to design a new architecture that uses cyberspace and the information revolution to help prosecute warfare. This need not involve lying—a short term solution to a tactical problem that has few long term strategic benefits. What it can involve is the manipulation of information so that the focus and flow of data are controlled.

During the Gulf War both the CIA and Britain's MI6 had an active campaign of disinformation that specifically targeted the Arab press, so that articles appeared that were damaging to Saddam Hussein and the Iraqi cause. But in England and America, the intelligence agencies were more careful not to attempt to manipulate or deceive on their home turf.

There are techniques and tactics now available that allow allied forces to take some control of an enemy's broadcast media and to play a significant part in controlling the print media. That is a valuable asset that improves what used to be propaganda into an important part of the strategic and tactical equation. In the future, every force commander should have available to him an array of such tools so that he can plan, knowing that, at a minimum, the enemy's morale is going to be very fragile.

Winning the hearts-and-minds campaign at home or in the homes of allied nations is a much tougher prospect. In part, this can be achieved by open briefing, but that will be unrealistic once the shooting really starts and the fragile coalition between the media, the politicians and the military that allowed the deployment in the first place begins to fragment. As the British discovered in the Falklands, the press in their drive for information and news and the military in their need for secrecy and the maintenance of morale are natural and often deadly competitors.

Too little attention has been paid to using the opportunities presented by Cyberspace. Instead, the focus has been on how to control the information flow, something that every professional reporter knows is impossible. The arrival of electronic media means that there can be huge force multiplication by inserting the right information in the right part of the network. For example, a video feed made accessible to every news story appearing on every newspaper on the Internet that accurately portrayed a government's position might be of more value than a conventional press briefing. But, instead of embracing the new technology and the opportunities it brings, conventional thinking about war fighting and the manipulation of public opinion continues to predominate. This is very dangerous traditionalism that makes no allowance either for the changing perception of wars among the media and political elite, or the proliferation of information sources that are impossible to control.

However, as we look around the world today, it is difficult to find the leadership qualities that successful crisis management demands. With this lack of resolve, it is difficult to see just what future peacekeeping faces. The Pentagon and all the other defense ministries around the world have been war gaming the almost infinite number of scenarios that the current unstable world can produce. There is no doubt that the military can change its tactics and train its people. But what is it that will persuade this new generation of leaders in the media and politics to understand that peace has a price? I fear there are not enough politicians with the courage to pay the price, or enough members of the media who respect the bold decisions that may cost lives. Instead, there is a drive for quick, easy solutions to complex problems, and if those easy solutions do not work, then there appears to be no will to find the real answers.

Endnotes

[1] *Los Angeles Times*, February 5, 1996.
[2] *Time,* December 21, 1992.
[3] *The New Republic*, June 21, 1993, p. 30.
[4] *The Boston Globe*, October 7, 1993.
[5] *The Associated Press*, November 5, 1993.
[6] *The Associated Press*, February 6, 1996.
[7] *Financial Times*, July 7, 1993.
[8] *Financial Times*, July 6, 1995.
[9] *The Guardian*, September 17, 1993.
[10] *The Tennessean*, September 22, 1995.

Grounding Cyberspace in the Physical World

Dorothy E. Denning and Peter F. MacDoran

We live in a physical world and depend on that world for our sustenance. Over time, humans have partitioned this world into a hierarchy of nations, states, counties, cities, districts, public and private property (land, buildings, rooms), and other geographical areas, each with its own governance and subject to the governance of encompassing jurisdictions. Various federal, state, and local governments supply basic infrastructure and services (e.g., military forces, monetary structures, roads, fire and police, schools, water) for those residing within their borders. Many of these benefits are essential to promote economic development and the well being of residents.

All human activity takes place in this physical world. This includes action in "cyberspace," that vast array of public and private networks connecting computers and users all over the globe. Indeed, it is often characterized as a "virtual world" that transcends space. People log into computers and on-line services without regard to their own geographic location or the location of the system they enter. Computers are addressed through domain names such as "abc.xyz.com," which give no indication of physical location (though many non-U.S. addresses identify the country in the top level domain, e.g., "abc.xyz.fr" for a system in France). Similarly, individuals correspond using domain-based addresses such as "smith@abc.xyz.com." Although some addresses such as "denning@cs.georgetown.edu" suggest a geographic location, there is no guarantee of its accuracy and many addresses do not even give a clue (e.g., 12345.678@compuserve com"). Moreover, because a user may be able to log into a computer from any place in the world (e.g., using telnet or a dial-up line), there is no way of identifying the geographic location of a user even when the location of the computer where the account is held is known. With mobile phones and computing, the location of a user becomes even more difficult to determine. Anonymous remailers make it possible to conceal even logical locations in cyberspace.

The consequence of this lack of grounding in physical space is that actions can take place in cyberspace without anyone knowing exactly where they originated and the jurisdictions effected. Although this has not adversely affected many activities, for example on-line discussion groups or the dissemination of public information, it has caused numerous problems. It has been difficult to prevent unauthorized access to computer systems and to restrict access to privileged accounts (e.g., "root") and sensitive information. Finding the perpetrator of a computer intrusion or any crime in cyberspace has been extremely difficult and often impossible, especially when the perpetrator has "looped" through numerous machines throughout the world to get to a target. It is not unusual to read a news story such as the following, which appeared on July 4, 1995:

SEATTLE (AP) —An Internet provider with about 3,000 subscribers shut down after a computer hacker defeated security measures on the system. The electronic intruder entered the system through an Internet link in North Dakota, but his actual location is unknown....

In some instances, hackers have been able to hijack network connections and spoof the network addresses of machines within a security perimeter. Software has been downloaded and distributed in violation of export controls. Controlling transborder data flows has been nearly impossible.

As electronic commerce takes off, the problems could get much worse. We are quickly approaching a time when a substantial portion of the economy will be completely on-line, involving only the sale and purchase of information goods and services. If this segment of the economy is divorced from the physical world and beyond any control by local and federal governments, the effect could be widespread fraud, tax evasion, money laundering, and other economic crimes along with an erosion of the tax base needed to provide basic services and ensure law and order. If that happens, the physical world in which we reside could degrade significantly, potentially causing economic instability and social disorder.

This article presents a new paradigm for cyberspace that is grounded in the physical world. We will first give a short description of grounded cyberspace, its benefits and applications, and some privacy considerations. We will then discuss how the paradigm can be realized with new technology that makes use of the microwave signals transmitted by the twenty-four satellite constellation of the Global Positioning System (GPS). We will describe some current limitations of GPS technology and how these could be accommodated. We will conclude with a few observations about the future of GPS and the prospects of grounded cyberspace.

Grounded Cyberspace

In grounded cyberspace, the physical location of a particular user or network node at any instant in time is uniquely characterized by a *location signature.* This signature, which is created by a *location signature sensor* (LSS) from the microwave signals transmitted by the GPS satellites, can be used by an independent device to determine the geodetic location (latitude, longitude, and height in a precisely defined geocentric coordinate reference system) of the LSS to an accuracy of a few meters or better. For reasons described later, the signature and its derived location are virtually impossible to forge. An entity in cyberspace will be unable to pretend to be anywhere other than where its LSS is actually situated.

Benefits and Applications

Grounded cyberspace offers precise and continuous identification and authentication of the geodetic location of physical entities in cyberspace. Such information can be used to address the limitations of cyberspace noted earlier. The following describes specific applications:

Controlling login access. In order to determine whether persons attempting to log in are as claimed, most systems require users to provide information confirming their identities. This process of confirmation is called user authentication. To date, user authentication methodologies have fallen into one of three categories: information the user knows (e.g., password, PIN, or private encryption key), possession of a device (e.g., access token or crypto card), or biometrics (e.g., thumb print or retinal scan). None of these methods are foolproof. Passwords and PINs are often vulnerable to guessing, interception (e.g., by "sniffer" programs on networks), and brute force search. Users frequently write them down in places that are not physically protected. Hardware devices can be stolen. Cryptographic systems can fail even when the algorithms are strong. Typically, their security reduces to that of PINs or passwords which are used to control access to keys stored in files and activation of hardware tokens. Biometrics devices can generate false positives (letting in unauthorized users) and false negatives (denying legitimate access). Most are vulnerable to interception and replay of the transmitted data by masqueraders (e.g., a thumb print never changes).

Geodetic location, as calculated from a location signature, adds a fourth and new dimension to user login authentication. It can be used to determine whether a person is attempting to log in from an approved location, e.g., a user's office building or home. If a user is mobile, then the set of authorized locations could be a broad geographic region (e.g., city, state, country). In that case, the login location serves to identify the place of login as well as to authenticate it. If unauthorized activity is detected, it will facilitate finding the individual responsible for that activity.

Unlike other authentication devices, a user's location signature sensor cannot be stolen and used elsewhere to gain unauthorized entry. The LSS will simply create a signature for the thief's location. In addition, intercepting the location signature transmitted during login does not allow an intruder to replay that data from some other place in order to the spoof the location and gain unauthorized entry.

Authentication by geodetic location can be performed continuously so that a connection cannot be hijacked, for example, if a user forgets to logout or leaves the premises without logging out. It can be transparent to the user. A user's location also can serve as a common authenticator for all systems that the user accesses. The user need not remember multiple authenticators or passwords or own multiple authentication devices. Geodetic location is fundamentally different from other methods of authentication. It could be used alone or in combination with other methods. Its value added is a high level of assurance against intrusions from any unapproved location regardless of whether passwords have been compromised or devices stolen. In critical environments, for example, military command and control, telephone switching, air traffic control, and banking, this extra assurance could be extremely important in order to avoid a potential catastrophe with reverberations far beyond the individual system cracked. In work environments where the principle threat is outsiders, the use of geodetic location combined with simple, fixed passwords might be sufficient. In those cases where an entire group has full access to a system, location authentication could be all that is necessary and provide a less expensive but more secure approach to access control than other methods.

Controlling access to privileged operations and sensitive information. Geodetic location can be used to ensure that users can perform sensitive operations (e.g., switch to root, modify system files, or initiate electronic funds transfers) or access valuable information only from approved physical locations. It can be used to prevent corporate secrets from being downloaded into employee homes or motel rooms and to reduce the chances of a hacker breaking into a system and gaining root privileges.

Geodetic location could be extremely valuable for authenticating financial transactions, as illustrated by a $10 million computer fraud perpetrated in 1994 against Citibank. A Russian and his accomplices obtained the identification numbers and passwords for the Citibank accounts of three banks in Argentina and Indonesia. The Russian then dialed into Citibank's computer from his office in St. Petersburg, and transferred funds from the victims' accounts into accounts opened by the accomplices. If access to the accounts had been limited to the banks' locations, he never would have been able to perform these operations from Russia.

Locating the perpetrators of cybercrimes. One of the biggest obstacles to investigating computer intrusions is tracing an intruder back to a physical location so that an arrest can be made. If the intruder has looped through several hosts, it is necessary to get the cooperation of the system administrators operating each host in addition to the cooperation of the telecommunications carriers. With knowledge of the precise geodetic location of anyone logged in, the problem is readily solved. In many cases, an intruder could be located and apprehended during a first attack, making it unnecessary to allow an intruder back into the system several times in order to conduct a trace. Knowledge of geodetic location can be used in other types of cases as well, for example, to find the originator of a fraudulent transaction, a libelous or harassing message, or a death threat. Moreover, the requirement to reveal physical location would itself be a deterrent to the commission of cybercrime because of the loss of anonymity. In addition, each of the sites through which a user passes could add its own location signature so that the complete physical path is readily discernible.

Location information can provide evidence not only for the purpose of conviction, but also to absolve innocent persons. If illegal activity is conducted from a particular account by someone who has gained unauthorized access to that account, then the legitimate owner of the account may be able to prove that they could not have been present in the location where the activity originated.

Anti-spoofing of host computers. A major threat to network security is spoofing of host computers. Location signatures can be used to prevent such spoofing and limit execution of certain protocols to machines that are inside a security perimeter. Location information effectively transforms any logical security perimeter defined by a set of host identifiers into a physical one defined by a set of geodetic locations. Even if a host name can be spoofed, its location cannot.

Enforcing site licenses. The location of a client requesting to download or execute licensed software from a server can be used to restrict access to clients affiliated with an organization having a site license. With this approach, the server need only know the geodetic location(s) of the site.

Electronic notary. An electronic notary could attach a location signature (stamp) to a document as proof that the document existed at a particular location and instant in time. In order to prevent someone from altering a document that has been stamped or using the location stamp with another document, the notary could digitally sign the stamped document. Alternatively, the LSS might be programmed to make the signature a function of the document as well as the GPS data. The notary could be implemented as a stand-alone device or network service.

On-line orders and emergency "911" services. When ordering products or signing up for services, it would be unnecessary to type in one's physical address because this information could be derived from the geodetic coordinates. Similarly, with knowledge of geodetic location, computer networks could offer access to 911 services through the click of a button. It would not be necessary to break the phone connection and dial 911 for help.

Export controls and transborder dataflow. Enforcing export controls on software that is posted on a server is essentially impossible today because a foreigner can access the software by logging into any computer in the United States, download the software to that system, and then download it to the foreigner's personal computer. With knowledge of the geodetic location of a user attempting to access export-controlled software or other information, it would be possible to restrict access to persons within national borders.

Taxation. The geodetic location of a person buying or selling information goods or services could be used to levy federal, state, or local taxes and export/import taxes on commercial transactions.

GPS applications. There are numerous defense and civil applications of GPS, including navigation, fleet monitoring, and surveying. Many of these applications depend upon computer networks, where they become vulnerable to spoofing and network intrusions. They will require a grounded cyberspace for security and safety and can be designed so that their use of GPS supports that goal. As described later, GPS receivers used for navigational purposes are not suitable for grounding cyberspace, as they are readily spoofed.

Privacy Considerations

It is not intended that grounded cyberspace be used to track the physical locations of individuals in ways that would be invasive of privacy. Thus, it would be important to administer safeguards to prevent this from occurring. One safeguard would be to strictly limit access to and the dissemination of geodetic information that has been collected for some purpose. In fact, existing laws already control government access to such information. Government agencies must obtain subpoenas to get subscriber information and court orders to get on-line transactional records (e.g., the addresses on electronic mail messages). Access in the private sector can be controlled through contracts and other commercial agreements or, if needed, through additional regulations.

Another safeguard would be to use and retain only that information which is needed for a particular application. Even though a geodetic location can be known at the meter level, for many applications, the location could be "rounded," for example to a country level for the purpose of controlling transborder data flows or to a country, state, or city level for the purpose of taxation.

A third safeguard would be to give users some control over the release of their geodetic locations, analogous to capabilities for "opt-out" and caller-ID blocking. Such blocking could protect against misuse by persons who have no need for such information. Providing one's geodetic location could be voluntary, although some actions might be prohibited if location is not supplied (e.g., access to particular host computers or export-controlled software).

Technological Basis

The technological means for grounding cyberspace lies in special GPS receivers that create location signatures. GPS consists of a constellation of twenty-four satellites operating in six orbital planes. Each satellite transmits two bands of microwave signals designated as Ll (1575.42 MHz) and L2 (1227.60 MHz). These signals can be picked up by GPS receivers connected to small antenna and used to determine latitude, longitude, height, and time. Because there are four unknowns, the signals from at least four satellites are needed to solve for these parameters.

The L1 band carries two channels: a narrowband channel occupied by a Coarse/Acquisition (C/A) code and a wideband channel occupied by either an unencrypted P code or an encrypted Y code. The L2 band contains only the P or Y codes. The Y code, which is intended for military use, provides a Precise Positioning Service with accuracy's better than 20 meters. The C/A code, which is open for civilian use, is intentionally degraded for security reasons through a process known as selective availability (SA) to provide a Standard Positioning Service. Conventional code correlating receivers which process these signals have accuracy's limited to 100 meters. Accuracy's better than that are possible, however, through Differential GPS (DGPS).

DGPS technologies achieve greater precision by using at least one additional receiver, deployed at a regional reference station whose location has been geodetically surveyed and is known with high accuracy. The reference station receives the GPS signals and uses knowledge of it own location to determine the errors in the signals. It then disseminates differential corrections, which can be picked up by receivers anywhere in the region and used to correct the GPS signals. In some cases, DGPS methods achieve accuracy's of 1 to 10 meters.

Because they compute geodetic location directly from the GPS signals, conventional (code correlating and differential) GPS receivers are not suitable for grounding cyberspace. Anyone could report an arbitrary set of coordinates, and there would be no way of knowing if the coordinates were actually derived by a GPS receiver at that location. A hacker could intercept the coordinates transmitted by a legitimate user, and then replay those coordinates in order to gain unauthorized entry. To ground cyberspace, one needs receivers which create location signatures.

CyberLocator

International Series Research, Inc. has developed a GPS-based technology, called CyberLocator©, which could be used to ground cyberspace. Rather than using a conventional GPS receiver, CyberLocator uses a location signature sensor (LSS) to form a location signature from bandwidth compressed raw observations of all the GPS satellites in view (perhaps as many as twelve satellites). Because the GPS signals are everywhere unique and constantly changing with the orbital motion of the satellites, the signature is unique to a particular place and time. As currently implemented, the location signature is 20,000 bytes and changes every five milliseconds. However, there are options to create a new signature every few seconds.

To ground cyberspace, client (user) and server (host) computers are each connected to a LSS utilizing a small (7 cm x 7 cm) antenna. For the moment, we will assume that each LSS can receive signals from at least four satellites at any given time. To authenticate the location of a client, a host challenges the client to supply its current location signature. The signature is then configured into packets and transferred to the host. The host, acting as the reference station, then uses its own simultaneously acquired GPS signals to compute the differential corrections and calculate or verify the client's location to within an acceptable threshold (a few meters to centimeters, if required). For two-way authentication, the reverse process would be performed. Authentication can be transparent to the user.

A host could challenge a client for its location signature at the time of login or when access to an application or file is requested. In some environments, location signature data might be transmitted continuously at a low bit rate (e.g., 20 bytes per second) for the purpose of continuous authentication and access control. Re-authorization can be performed every few seconds or longer.

A location signature is virtually impossible to forge at the required accuracy. This is because the GPS observations at any given time are essentially unpredictable to high precision due to subtle satellite orbit perturbations, which are unknowable in real-time, and the intentional signal instabilities (dithering) imposed by SA. Further, because a signature is invalid after five milliseconds, the attacker cannot spoof the location by replaying an intercepted signature, particularly when it is bound to the message (e.g., through a checksum or digital signature). Continuous authentication provides further protection against such attacks.

Unlike conventional code correlating receivers which use only the civilian C/A signals, the CyberLocator technology also uses the military Y signals. The signals are processed using a patented codeless method that does not require decryption of the Y code or knowledge of the classified telemetry.

Limitations of GPS Technology

GPS technology has two fundamental limitations that affect its application to cyberspace. Neither of these is serious enough to undermine the basic objectives, but they both require some accommodation.

Obstruction of signals. Because the GPS signals do not in general travel through walls and other physical objects, a GPS receiver will not function if its antenna is inside a closed room without windows. Even if the antenna is placed on a window, trees and other buildings can obstruct enough of the sky to preclude receiving signals from four or more satellites. The preferred location is a rooftop.

One solution is to place the antenna on the roof and run a cable from the roof to the receiver device. In that case, the location signature will identify the building, but not the exact location of a particular user or computer within the building. Thus, it is like a street address. With a single family home, this would probably be sufficient. With an office building, the GPS receiver could be attached to a network gateway computer (e.g., firewall) within the building and used to provide a common location signature for all employees attached to the (physically protected) network. Whenever a user ventured outside the protected network, the gateway would supply the location data. It would also authenticate all attempts to enter the protected network.

It is possible to uniquely distinguish the users within a building using a single antenna placed on the roof. Here, the antenna might be connected to a phone line. Users would have their own LSS devices, which would dial into this line to receive the wire-connected GPS signals Each LSS would be programmed with a unique value that would parameterize its processing of the signals and serve to distinguish its positioning data from that of other receivers sharing the same antenna. This value would not be determinable except through the GPS signals.

Although it is desirable for an antenna to be positioned with full view of the sky, this is not always necessary. If the location and environment are known in advance, then the antenna can be placed on a window with only a limited view of the sky (and thus capable of receiving data from fewer than four satellites). The environment would be taken into account when the signals were processed at the host to authenticate the location. For example, knowing that a window faces north, the host might be able to verify the building location and floor. This technique would not work, however, if the geodetic location is unknown and the objective is to determine it.

Distance. A second limitation of GPS technology is that DGPS methods require that the two receivers (at the host and remote sites) be within 2,000 to 3,000 kilometers so as to receive signals from at least some of the same satellites at the same time. This would be problematic if the sites are on opposite sides of the globe (e.g., a user in Amsterdam could be attempting to gain access to a host in Colorado). The limitation could be overcome by deploying regional LSS, which would make their location data available on request. With an LSS in London, a host in New York, for example, could authenticate a client in Milan by verifying the location of Milan relative to the London LSS and the London LSS relative to its own location in New York. However, in environments where the users are all on one region though not necessarily in fixed locations, this "shortcoming" would be a benefit as it would prevent foreign intrusions (e.g., the person in Amsterdam would fail authentication).

Conclusions

GPS technology offers a promising approach to grounding cyberspace in the physical world. Its initial application is likely to be in the area of network and information security because the potential benefits are enormous and an organization can use the technology to enhance its own security independent of what other organizations do. As the technology is integrated into more and more systems, its application to other areas could be realized. When that happens, GPS will transform cyberspace from a world that potentially undermines nations, states, and other geographical communities to one that better supports these communities within a global, networked world.

Adapted from a paper written for the National Academy of Public Administration and National Research Council, May, 1995.

New Approaches to DOD Information-Systems Acquisition

Michael Loescher

As we move deeper and deeper into the Information Age, the infrastructure of moving information is becoming more and more homogeneous. The command and control plans of the 1970s were 200-page compendia of disparate communications wiring diagrams. Today command and control is increasingly embedded in four common functionalities: data repositories; software applications; carriers, from satellites to fiber; and end-terminals, from radios to laptop computers.

Increasingly all four are being built in the commercial marketplace, not in government laboratories and systems commands. Moreover, ten years from now, almost certainly we will move past buying the infrastructure of command and control to buying information itself. When we do, command and control will have been transformed from a system to a commodity that will have value in the marketplace only with respect to time and place.

Over the next decade, therefore, it will become critical that we sort out what *genuinely unique* systems government must build, and develop the means to produce them more efficiently—and most importantly—faster to leverage the commercial products that are becoming the mainstay of command and control systems.

Amateurs study strategy; professionals study logistics—the old saw is still true. But on the modern battlefield an increasingly relevant question is, what is logistics? For the last 50 years, logistics has meant focusing on the importance of *materiel depth*, in terms of fuel, parts, ammunition and, ultimately, industrial base. As we move further into the Information Age, however, it is becoming increasing apparent that in post-Cold War campaigning much—perhaps even the definition of effective battle space itself—will depend on information, the critical commodity of modem warfare.

Information, in turn, depends on building, operating, and sustaining an infrastructure that can deliver it. Yet, in electronics production, design, sales and distribution, times have changed. DoD no longer is driving research and development, and industry is seeking markets outside the military. In a world in which state-of-the-art is off-the-shelf-industry, and potentially our foes, can obtain better information systems (IS) technology cheaper and faster than DoD because our current acquisition system buys computers in the same way we buy bullets.

It is urgent, therefore, that we rethink our approaches to IS acquisition. Technology and tactics have always been inextricably tied; from maneuver warfare to strategic bombing to carrier warfare, one has fueled the other. In modern warfare, it is information technology, in one form or another, that fuels modern tactics. When targeting, C^4I—and a hundred other considerations—depend on information and IS technology, logistics equals "come-as-you-are" acquisition. In the Information Age, acquisition has become a *tactical* issue.

There are really three defense issues arising from the global information revolution, all inextricably related. The first centers on the *emergence of Information Warfare*, the emerging doctrine of warfare resulting from the proliferation of, and dependence on, new IS technologies. The second revolves around *what kind of information infrastructure* DoD needs to conduct modem warfare. The third issue, addressed in this paper, concerns *how we will obtain the infrastructure*. This paper presents such a future framework: three new principles that together create a model for how DoD might more efficiently acquire IS. Without it, we cannot build the first two.

Information-systems acquisition is a little like national health-care: we need new ideas, and we need a Government-private sector partnership. In the presence of both, Government will be able to take advantage of the global revolution in information. In the absence of either, the taxpayer and DoD both will suffer. Despite our growing understanding of the importance of Information Warfare on the battlefield, technological opportunities are often harder for Government to exploit in the marketplace. This is due to two factors:

- Our current acquisition system is maximized for large programs that yield products typically both stable in design and bought for more than a decade of use. Neither is characteristic of electronics in general, nor of IS specifically;
- There is a widening gap between the delay of the acquisition process and the much greater rate of technological change today in computing and electronics.

The stakes are high. Since 1980, DoD software expenditures have risen dramatically, until for the past 5 years the annual expenditure had reached $30 billion, much of which is now obsolete. Moreover, a computer hardware generation is now 18 months long, with the cost of computing dropping at 6 percent annually. Increasingly, we are actually paying R&D for commercial, off-the-shelf (COTS) hardware integrated by contractors, while our role in real R&D has precipitously dropped. In 1962, the U.S. Navy alone was responsible for over 50 percent of the nation's R&D expenditures on electronics. Thirty years later, DoD as a whole provides less than 10 percent. Industrial development of IS has exploded beyond ability of Government to plan—we have to learn instead to go along for the ride.

Yet, this should be good news, not bad news, for we in Government are presented with three important opportunities today.

- First, in the 1990s, the taxpayer should no longer have to pay for the high cost of technology. As we have seen, today, much, if not most, of the R&D in computing and electronics needed for the military is being accomplished in industry—by industry. Moreover, COTS use will increase as the level of technical expertise and awareness is raised among operators. The idea that Operational Requirements (ORs) can be divorced from the detailed understanding of their implementing technology is surely an engineer's, not an operator's. "Tell us what you want, and we'll build it" has a tinny ring. The assumption on which it is based is neither born out in practice nor in history. In practice, the best ORs come from operators who understand technology in detail and who can, in their mind's eye, envision the new tactics it makes possible. Increasingly, we are entering a time in which more ORs will reflect the application of COTS technology than Government RDT&E invested in genuinely new technology.

• Second, we can now solve many operational problems that have been extremely difficult in the past. Examples abound: in communications, data processing, data display, sensor fusion, electronic combat devices, guidance systems—we are reaching levels of such technological sophistication that operational problems seemingly so difficult to solve 10 years ago are now much easier. So much easier in so short a time that, in some cases, we refuse to recognize the opportunities.

In the operating forces, tens of thousands of people work everyday with communications and ADP equipment that was conceived in the early 1970s, bought in the 1980s, and fielded in the 1990s. The genuinely serious impact of this is not just in manpower inefficiency or cost savings, but in operations itself. When we are accustomed to using this kind of antiquated equipment, envisioning the power of information requires an active imagination.

Thus, at the very moment of the global information systems revolution, we who pride ourselves on the use of high technology are blinded to its opportunities, both in efficiencies and operations, by an outdated and inappropriate acquisition system. But if we in Government can devise an *operational and acquisition framework* within which we can foster innovation, we will succeed in capturing the dynamics and direction of the information revolution.

• And, therefore, the third opportunity presents itself following from the first two: if we devise a means to capitalize on these first two developments, DoD can have better technology, faster and cheaper.

This last conclusion sounds wistful in Government circles. Yet we see it daily in our homes. From televisions to computers, from CD players to watches, technology is better, more available, and more economical each year. Yet we are only now beginning to see the obvious: computers and software are not like torpedoes and airplanes. What, then, might be a new operational and acquisition framework for information systems? Three key concepts are proposed.

Pyramidal Programming

The first, which we might call *Pyramidal Programming*, deals with the DoD Program Objective Memorandum (POM) planning. The purpose of an acquisition system is to relate *technological means to operational ends*: warfare is inextricably tied to technology. Technology and doctrine are components of the same cycle. In an acquisition system, linkage between technological means and operational ends is achieved through a programmatic structure.

But both are changing with IS. As we move away from single-arm warfare to combined arms (i.e., joint) warfare, our *operational ends*—our doctrine and the systems to implement it jointly—will change. As for *means*, the change in technology is all around us—we are moving from many hand-crafted software and hardware artifacts to fewer, more universal technology building blocks.

Pyramidal Programming is a relational model that relates operational goals in the form of *architecture* to *resources* and *technology*. The idea is to bring the operator, the programmer, and the engineer to a common model to quantify the consequences of change for all decision makers. By relating programs to architecture, it eliminates standalone stovepipe programs, which in turn reduces the sheer number of building blocks to be produced and, wherever possible, reduces the blocks to standards.

Most importantly, the building blocks become linked to operational ends, making joint technology a norm rather than an anomaly. Standard building blocks, both hardware and software, go to build what we might call *Electronic Platforms*, the analog to airplanes, tanks, and ships. Electronic Platforms can have clearly identifiable operational goals, production quotas, interfaces and technological composition. Thus, we can identify precisely what it is we want to build, why it must be built, how it fits with other joint efforts operationally, programmatically, and technologically, and the building blocks from which it will be built.

In addition, the ability to articulate Electronic Platforms clears the way for modular installations on a grand scale—meaning all we need in aircraft, vehicle, and ship construction is space, power, and fiber. We can then insert into that parent platform the corresponding Electronic Platform and subsequent upgrades with proper form, fit, and function. This is a way of keeping high-cost defense forces at the electronic cutting edge over the 30-year life of major platforms. Pyramidal Programming implies a cultural shift from *building systems* to *buying systems. It changes our notion of what acquisition is.*

Perhaps most importantly, as we transition from stovepipe programs to building-block programs (and from building to buying), Pyramidal Programming can provide an orderly set of managerial tools to *DoD decision makers and Congress alike* so that the Services can make the transition into the Information Age in lockstep and with wholesale cost savings.

Cyclical Acquisition

Pyramidal Programming identifies technological building blocks that make up Electronic Platforms, but it doesn't get them built. To do that, we need a second new idea, perhaps best called *Cyclical Acquisition*, by which we mean a process that captures *all funding appropriations* in the design, procurement, fielding and support of a building block. The idea is a dollar saved—whether RDT&E, OP, or O&M—is still a dollar earned. The strategy behind Cyclical Acquisition is that of an engine that can be accelerated or decelerated, and which has four statistical and fiscal entry points, and conserves all appropriations at those critical points.

Think of acquisition as an engine. The input is money. The output is technological building blocks. The engine's purpose is to produce output from input as efficiently as possible. There are four sets of effectiveness measures: effectiveness, suitability, affordability, and sustainability.

Effectiveness has to do with operational value: does the building block work well, can it be improved, is it interoperable? *Suitability* is a technological issue and is a measure of maturity, functionality, and modularity. *Affordability* addresses such concerns as percent of funding applied to the block, procurement strategy, economies of scale. *Sustainability* involves maintenance, provisioning, installation, and training.

The more we work with these four sets of measures of effectiveness (MOE), the more we find in IS that the boundaries between them start to pale. Suitable technology, for example, depends on affordability. Sustainability depends on the specific technology, not a monolithic ILS philosophy: surely repairing a howitzer is different than repairing a computer. Similarly, new technology improves sustainability and lowers costs: the development of plug-in telephones saved telephone companies millions in installations and manpower costs.

From this, we can draw three important conclusions:

• The ideal acquisition engine must be cyclical to capture the interrelationships of all four measures of effectiveness.

• The engine, therefore, can and should be fueled by all four MOEs—and all appropriations.

New RDT&E expenditure can be linked to reduction in logistics-related O&M savings. A system like the existing acquisition system, which inputs only ORs, misses *both* technological and fiscal opportunities; and,

• Such an engine, if made to measure and conserve costs throughout the cycle, can put cheaper technology in the operating forces faster (because we shopped for it) that costs less to support (because its mean time between failure is longer than its mean time before obsolescence.)

Unlike our cyclical engine, the current acquisition system can be divided in practice (if not precisely by instruction) into four separate processes: the development of ORs; the development of the POM; the acquisition and procurement of systems; and the support of systems, which includes installation, training, maintenance, and provisioning.

These four processes, while intended to be iterative, in practice have become linear, and are managed in isolation from each other. As they become more linear and less iterative, *the entire cost of a program rises higher, and yet becomes less visible*: The total amount of RDT&E, OP [procurement], O&M, MP, and other funds used to build, buy, install, operate, and maintain a system or a group of systems often is simply never calculated.

When a system becomes difficult to maintain or operate—or expensive to install or train personnel—it is rare that the problem surfaces; rarer still that a timely requirement is generated to replace the system; and, rarest that a system is restructured to capture technological opportunities. There are identifiable reasons for this.

In practice, linear acquisition responds directly to an OR: budgets for it, acquires it, fields it, and typically leaves it stranded. Life cycle support is too often simply life support. This has been especially true of electronics and computing systems in the last 30 years, during which systems engineers built end-to-end stovepipe systems from a large menu of what were, in hindsight, unstable building blocks. These systems required diverse hardware, often used proprietary or other unique software, lacked standards, and required high training and maintenance costs. Interoperability seemed a labyrinth.

Moreover, there is often a disincentive operating. When an organization decides to spend a percentage of limited RDT&E and OP to buy a new system, it does so in response to an OR, the starting point of the linear system. If that organization is not also responsible for the installation, logistics, and support of the system, it has no incentive to seek statistics on those costs. If statistics were obtained, the funds saved by fielding a new stovepipe system would not be recouped by the same organization that paid for the new system. Therefore, from an organizational view, there is no incentive to modernize. In the 1970s, when old stovepipes required new stovepipes for replacements, this mentality was understandable if not laudable.

In 1990s, open systems standards and architecture make functional replacements cost-effective. By merging the four processes of today's linear acquisition into Cyclic Acquisition for rapidly developing technologies like IS, we can build better, more universal, and cheaper building blocks faster.

Assembly Line Fielding

The final consideration becomes fitting the building blocks into an assembly line approach so that industrial techniques can be brought into government. For that, we need the third and final new idea in IST acquisition, which we shall simply call *Assembly Line Fielding*. The Assembly Line is focused on three problems:

• Migrating IS engineering into *definable functionalities* (i.e., building blocks into Electronic Platforms) so that modular approaches to ship, tank, and aircraft building can be achieved;

• Changing the pace of technology injection into the operating forces to respond to *operational tempos and generational changes in technology rather than individual program funding*; and

• Conservation of funding through 'Just In Time" (JIT) assembly.

Fielding IS is a classic example of where Total Quality Management techniques best apply. Our current fielding system is like an automobile factory in which doors, transmissions, engines, and bodies are bought independently, based on the budget of individual organizations, and then stacked on the line without respect to their requirement on the line or sometimes even understanding the overall car design.

Buying 500 components in a year when only 200 can be installed usurps funds for other raw materials urgently needed in the line that year. This is a somewhat simplistic view—there are, of course, economies of scale to be considered. However, economies of scale versus costs of storage, obsolescence in electronics, and other considerations are calculable—and, more to the point, should be calculated.

When we create an assembly line paced by operational tempo and the availability of raw materials, we conserve dollars because we bring to the line only the raw materials needed when they are needed. When we provide those raw materials to the line through Cyclical Acquisition, we ensure their cost is the lowest possible and foster their continued improvement through the four requirements points in the cycle.

In manufacturing terms, *the assembly line can be accelerated or decelerated in response to the customer*. As the operational tempo is increased, equipment can be inserted into deploying forces—whether division, air wing, battle group or MAGTF—as they depart. This, in fact, was done during Desert Storm, but only at great cost and significant disruption, because programs had been paced to reflect their individual funding levels without overall context.

By pacing the assembly line to the deployment schedules and by fueling the Cyclic Acquisition engine to produce incremental improvements, we can inject cutting-edge technology systematically and cheaper with each deploying force. This is so because the variable in the equation is the *generational change of technology, not the technology itself.* Whether weapons or microchips—or microchips in weapons-we can field equipment into operating forces as they need it, as the technology is available—just in time.

Business Strategies in the Information Age

R. T. Goodden ©

Immediately following the breakup of AT&T, American business use of telecommunications to link the computers of the emerging digital age really took off. The integration of telecommunications and the computer was well under way in 1986 when a West Coast astronomer by the name of Clifford Stoll chanced upon an intruder who had broken into his mainframe from, he eventually learned, far-away Germany.[1] This was more than the hacker mischief that had begun to plague telephone carriers and switches; it was the beginning of what today is a sustained attack upon digital research, commerce and governance. The simple relationship between growth in bandwidth and subsequent economic growth, if it ever really existed, was over as fast as it began.

Today we see a reach for maximum bandwidth to support a global telecommunications grid, moving terabits of voice, data, images and video between continents. But in many cases, the grid has a foundation of sand. It continues to be vulnerable to service disruption, malicious destruction or theft of content by individuals, criminal cabals, and state-sponsored agents. The threat is as real as the growing body of documentation on bank losses, service disruptions, and theft of intellectual property. For companies whose viability depends on the production and flow of information, strategies are needed to protect equities as well as to create opportunities. The purpose of this paper is the organization and discussion of basic information-age business strategies.

The status of 21st century business on the wide-open information highway is akin to that of the individual whose needs were documented almost fifty years ago by Abraham Maslow. In a ground-breaking sociological text, Maslow found that people operated on needs at three general levels: personal survival, family/societal reinforcement, and self-actualization.[2] He formulated the now famous pyramid model of human needs wherein, upon settling a basic need for food and shelter, man could move up to taking a place in a community of peers, possibly rising to a status where accomplishment of unique and rewarding achievement was possible at the apex of a pyramid of growth solidly underpinned from below.

The analogy between the position of Maslow's individual and the businesses of today may be an appropriate one from which to investigate modern business needs. Clearly, there is a down-side risk to pursuing a growth plan aimed at the top of a pyramid for which no foundation has been put in place. If, in Maslow's terms, modern business requires first that its survival needs be met, what are those needs?

Information production and use is the modern, measurable inventory of assets, the medium of exchange, and the target for growth in the post-industrial age. If this assertion is true, there are three levels of business needs. The first, most basic need is secure storage of core digital assets. The second need is access to cooperative development via reliable and secure channels of communication. The third is a supportive environment for intellectual risk-taking to achieve the highest level of creativity in new products, solutions and processes from which wealth may be compounded. Maslow would require that these needs be examined in more depth.

Core Security—The Basic Universal Need

The analogy is to the bank which must secure its core asset, depositor funds. Arguably, today the basic needs for security of assets of contemporary banks, for example, are not being met, in view of the growing numbers of computer attacks. This has been going on for some time, and the losses have mounted into the hundreds of millions of dollars. Little has been acknowledged publicly for understandable reasons. Banks appear more willing to write off painful amounts than foreclose future depositor confidence by acknowledging repeated losses. These un- and under-reported losses constitute a serious denial of the problem which serves only to compound the numbers and sizes of loss.

Surveys suggest the pattern behind the banking example repeats throughout commercial industry, in research centers and in government. The Computer Security Institute has found that commercial systems administrators report rising instances of illegal entries or attempts. The Computer Emergency Response Team (CERT) service of Carnegie-Mellon University regularly issues alerts regarding increases in the number and sophistication of attempts to illegally enter commercial computer networks. Behind the closed doors of meetings of the President's National Security Telecommunications Advisory Committee (NSTAC) and other industry/government-exchange fora, the fact of vulnerability and loss is partially acknowledged and discussed in the most general terms, but not with the specificity needed to identify the threat and begin counter-measures. What accounts for the reluctance to seek help?

Three reasons are postulated here. First, the competitive nature of business understandably limits the timeliness and extent of acknowledged loss. For example, if a telecommunications carrier admits to loss of service or compromise of transiting information, customers can switch their traffic to an alternative carrier. Often it only takes a phone call. Banks have the same problem. The real differences in the quality, price and reliability of service between providers may be largely in the perception of the customer, as readily demonstrated by the fiercely competitive marketing campaigns these competitors launch to merely maintain market share. Who has not seen the carriers vie on television for our individual long-distance accounts? But competition in a mature market is only the first reason for reluctance to discuss commercial losses.

The second reason for the reluctance to seek help is that CEOs are loath to admit they are not in full control of their operations. The modern, right-sized, lean corporation was an early adapter of digital computing and telecommunications technology. The system is in place. Additions and changes are costs that must be justified to external boards and stockholders. Up to this point in time, it has been easier to quietly write off attacks than to take the heat for a marginally adequate network.

This reticence is also found at the Information Systems Manager's (ISM) desk and constitutes the third reason for corporate reluctance to acknowledge loss and seek help. As chief architect of the system in place, the ISM is already invested heavily in the status quo. With industry trends toward out-sourcing the ISM function, only the most courageous manager would approach the CEO and the board with a request for an engineering change order to improve a flaw in his carefully crafted design.

In a nutshell, based on an analysis of current trends and attitudes, culled from numerous interviews and meetings, the three major blocks to government and industry admitting the seriousness of the attacks are competitive position, executive intransigence, and staff equities in the status quo. There are other, lesser motives. A recent survey shows that a major source of computer attack and loss is internal, the work of the disgruntled or criminal employee.[3] Security against the internal threat may be only marginally effective without draconian compartmentalization in basic business communications. Combating internal attacks requires a variety of measures that militate to formalize and close off the internal coordination necessary to the modern, re-engineered business.

Elsewhere, corporations may see a tie between the increase in attacks and the increase in use of the Internet. Stay off the Internet, they reason, and the threat goes away. Never mind the body of evidence that shows the Internet is the global network of communication and commerce. This is where the reluctance to confront the core security issue breeds a wider problem. Knowledgeable analysts understand that the point of entry for attack is any remote port, not just an Internet port. This is where certain businesses, like operators of utilities and pipelines using System Control and Data Acquisition (SCADA) networks to tie together many remote sites, are so vulnerable. The threat today has moved from the teenage hacker-nemesis of credit-card telephones to sophisticated criminals and terrorists who appear to be looking to steal what is available and to destroy what is not.

In terms of Maslow's model, the basic requirements for security of company assets as a basis for expanded commerce are not being met wherever there is a remote, unsecured access points into the core network. The losses have apparently been tolerable thus far, but this situation cannot last. As costs arise from losses, they will marginalize costs of repair. But, in most cases, without analysis, the crossover point between continued toleration of loss and marginal cost to repair will be passed without option to act. What is the strategic business answer?

The answer may lie in the growing accumulation of anecdotal evidence which acts as surrogate for the underlying, unacknowledged quantitative data of growing loss. Recently, several users of commercial Private Branch Automatic (telecommunications) Exchanges (PABX) have gone to court for relief from tens of thousands of dollars of toll fraud caused by hackers entering unshielded remote access points for further dialing around the world. PABX manufacturers, some of whom were also carriers, have defended themselves by pointing out that system manuals specified requirements for shielding and, further, that hacker use of these remote ports was common public knowledge. Hence, owner beware. In turn, courts have held that he who chooses to operate a PABX is responsible for all calls that transit it. Is he who chooses to operate a LAN responsible for all attacks against it? It would seem so. This precedent is being built on regularly and within view of stockholders and customers. It offers a compelling analogous rationale for CEOs and ISMs to alter their avoidance of the issue of information attack.

The accumulation of anecdotal evidence of the fact of, the seriousness of, and the remedies available for, the menace of computer attack grows, and with it grows a requirement of corporations to exercise an appropriate standard of *due diligence* in the protection and conservation of stock-holder assets. This may be the key to resolving the problem of unreported and underreported attacks. The process is slow. Precedence is built a case at a time. But there is a coming inevitability of assignment of liability to corporations and their officers for losses incurred because of failure to act. Here the power of courts to pull internal memos and reports detailing losses will become a strong tool for forcing an industry-wide minimum standard, as well as a tool for analyzing the total costs of information attacks across national economic sectors.

Business strategy for the basic security of corporate information assets becomes a matter of anticipating the evolving, de facto standard for due diligence, or risking malfeasance by waiting for its formal imposition. Consider, for example, recent DoD requirements for use of the Clipper Chip as a condition of doing business. Clearly, CEOs and ISMs alike have a narrowing window of voluntary compliance. The smarter corporations have embarked on a deliberate plan to assess the current risk, adopt methods in contemporary corporate use to combat internal and external attack, and document a living policy and procedure (P&P) for periodic review and improvement to insure demonstrable improvements in compliance with evolving standards.

A contemporary basic strategy, proceeding as it must from a comprehensive risk assessment, should include the following basic components. First, a physical security plan must be emplaced to control entry into corporate property. Within the corporate facility, core computers such as network servers must be secured from casual access. An individual must be assigned the responsibility for corporate security policy and procedures. Second, a P&P manual must be available to each employee so that each understands they have an individual role and responsibility. Third, where computers are open to remote access, a firewall to control electronic access must be emplaced. In practical terms, these three elements—physical security, a document that explains each person's role and responsibility, and a firewall barrier where ever computers are remotely accessed, constitute a minimum set of protections to meet core survival needs and *due diligence*.

Intermediate Needs—Business in Community

Maslow defined his next higher level of human need, beyond that of basic survival, as forging relationships in family and community for mutual support and growth. Again there are useful analogies for business strategies. At a higher level than basic business survival, an information age company can hardly stand alone and unsupported against the escalating sophistication and numbers of computer attacks. Few companies can remain competitive in the market place and simultaneously fund, from "overhead accounts," an in-house capability for improving defense of its computers against the onslaught. Mutual support is the most efficient answer.

CERT, NCSA, and CSI are all examples of voluntary groups set up to provide some degree of mutual support in information network and computer security for businesses. Arguably, the capstone of these organizations is the NSTAC because it functions at the strategic interface between the Defense Information Infrastructure (DII) and the National Information Infrastructure (NII) on which much of the DII rides. An explanation is in order.

NII refers to the total interconnected national telecommunications network of the U.S. which is made up of the private lines of major carriers, more numerous minor carriers and interconnection companies, and thousands of local exchanges which connect private telephones to the national network, and the world. The NII originated as a telegraph network, highly subsidized by federal money. Therefore, it has always carried U.S. government message traffic, including defense traffic. Overseas, the military evolved a doctrine for separate telecommunications networks to carry their message traffic for greater communications security. The total defense network is referred to as the Defense Information Infrastructure (DII). Within the U.S. the DII historically has ridden on the NII, except for the small set of highly survivable minimum essential telecommunications necessary to respond to nuclear attack.

Because of the dependency of the DII on the larger NII, CERT and NSTAC have enjoyed a government subsidy in return for assuming an important role in guaranteeing the reliability of the NII for government needs. In today's austere times, the subsidy for the CERT, and eventually the NSTAC, is at risk. Consequently, recent reports suggest that Carnegie Mellon may be rethinking its commitment to CERT.[4] Part of the reason appears to be the drying up of a DoD subsidy.[5] Feeding the issue is frequent public criticism of the CERT for its alleged reticence to openly discuss the frequency and seriousness of information network attacks. The effect of loss of the CERT on business strategies for the information age would be significant.

Having already made the point that few corporations can afford the overhead investment necessary to craft effective internal defenses against information attack, it may be useful to examine alternatives in a world without a CERT response team. A successful strategy which hedges against unforeseen risk might have three components; partnerships (consortia) for mutual defense and support, supporting membership in industry associations and a stable of consultants for surge or special requirements. Each addresses many similar risks, but each also contributes unique protections.

Partnerships, or consortia in the contemporary vernacular, require formal exchange of contractual documentation committing the partners to timely exchange of data, expertise, and resources. At the macro-level they resemble the chip industry initiatives of the 1980's established to pool U.S. expertise against an onslaught of superior foreign products. Historically, the problem with these industry consortia was that they often brought together competitors within the same sector of industry, such as two or more long-distance telecommunications carriers, who had much to gain by exploiting a competitor's weaknesses. This predatory aspect of competition forced a fatal chill on most of these projects for pooling assets.

More appropriate for modern times are the new global telecommunications consortia such as Concert, the British Telecom-MCI partnership, which features one representative corporation from each of several complementary, non-competing sectors (or nations). Each formally contributes expertise, data and such other resources as may be necessary to open new markets or, perhaps, combat a threat against the interconnected partners. Some of the larger consortia are massive enough to be capable of market manipulation.

They bear a resemblance to the old European mercantile alliances such as the Hanseatic League in that membership in one consortium evolves an exclusive, multinational, economic tie that permeates deeply into the tiers of vendors and suppliers that contribute to the larger systems integrator. This exclusivity both contributes to the defense and the insularity of the partners.

Within each consortium, timely notice of information attack provokes defensive response, and set in motion countermeasures development. A global competitive edge accrues to the consortium with the best response. Irrespective of size, the best of consortia have (or will have) facilities and media protection, encryption schemes, and key-escrows superior to that of any rival, or many governments, which may be unable or unwilling to invest the sums necessary to achieve parity.

Here emerges the crux of the issue of the middle ground of business strategy; loyalties to global consortia versus loyalties to national government. If history is prologue, the winner is the consortium which so carefully manages perceptions as to create the image of superior national loyalty in each of multiple members in multiple nations. Impossible? No. But historically, such perceptions are easier to manage in the short run than over time. A sinusoidal pattern of consortium strength, plateauing, decline in the face of political miscalculation, and painful political rehabilitation is the common result.

Overseeing the competing consortia may well be the International Telecommunications Union (ITU), the 130-year-old United Nations organization charged with maintaining interoperability, equity and reliability in the Global Information Infrastructure (GII). The ITU is made up of the governmental delegations from each of 194 nations which operate a telecommunications system that interconnects with the GII, together with the carriers and manufacturers that make up the several global consortia, and the "independents." These numerous non-consortium "independents" marginally compete with, or occupy niches that do not threaten, the giants. Having outlined the role of partnering for defense in the form of a formal consortium in a contemporary business strategy, attention turns to the second, less formal type of mutually supporting alliance, membership in an industry trade association.

Industry trade associations offer the prospect of data sharing and occasional, less formal alliances, which can assist in the formation of an effective business strategy for the information age. Through journals, symposia and trade shows, associations offer a window on industry-wide trends, developments and threats, though on a more generalized basis. The chief role of an association historically has been as spokesperson in the government/industry policy and programs interface. The use of such a forum for lobbying and information-sharing makes sense for a business strategy that must economically leverage beyond internal capabilities.

Associations must be carefully chosen to assure common goals. The key is the concept that these are mutual support organizations. The association contributes a collective storehouse of support and expertise. The business contributes time and individual, often narrowly specialized, expertise. One of the most important offerings an association can make is as a ladder to larger organizations with more clout and greater depth in mutual support.

For U.S. businesses, there are two organizations of broad information industry charter which exist at the interface between the NII and the GII. The first is the formal

FCC, chartered by government to devise and enforce standards in the information carriage industry. The second is the informal and more narrowly focused NSTAC. The FCC oversees participation by U.S. industry in the various working parties and committees of the ITU, wherein standards are set for incorporation of new technology into the GII. Industry representatives act as proxies for U.S. policy makers in technical areas where the FCC cannot hope to sustain an in-house cutting edge technologist. Politically, the FCC mission with regard to ITU standards can be simplified to: *insure that US. industry is not hobbled by development of ITU standards that U.S. venders cannot meet in a timely, competitive fashion.* Major U.S. consortia members and lesser independents from various trade associations vie for assignments to ITU groups for the purpose of ensuring that their developing R&D or extant design will preferably be, or at least meet, developing standards for GII use.

Membership in the group of FCC proxies is a meritocracy, often based on work on more specialized industry standards groups like ANSI, the Electronic Industries Association, and others. This is where the FCC interface of NII with GII differs from that of the more narrowly defined NSTAC. The NSTAC, as is now constituted, dates from the Bell divestiture of 1984 and comprises a fixed number of members, each of whom is an officer of a member corporation.

The function of the NSTAC is evolving to a slightly broader one than from earlier days when it was a cooperative body designed to aid reconstitution of the DII and restore government [control] following a major natural catastrophe, or an attack on the U.S. Committed to rapid reaction, NSTAC members must be able to commit significant corporate assets to the common national need on very short notice, actually a telephone call. As losses to external information attack mount, they resemble in value the losses due to the major calamities for which the NSTAC was created and supported. As cycle times diminish between warning (if any), digital attack, and initiation of defensive countermeasures, the defensive strategy of both consortium and independent more nearly resembles that of the NSTAC.

For the NSTAC to evolve to a clearer role as emergency respondent to external digital attack, two things must happen. First, the arbitrary membership ceiling must be lifted. Second, the organization must be moved closer to the executive reins of government than its current position as a ward of the Director of the National Communications System (NCS)— a DoD function. If, for example, it were a dependency of the National Security Council (NSC) or the Office of the Vice-President (in those administrations where he acts as domestic policy executive) a broader, permanently staffed NSTAC could provide all of the functionality necessary to support the timely defense of the NII and its component DII from external information attacks. It needs a permanent staff, paid for by member contributions, and responsive to the organization as a whole, not the individual competitive organizations of which the larger body is composed.

The NSTAC is the ideal organization to achieve the necessary synergy, sense of mission and timeliness of response because it has the capacity to draw upon the cream of industry talent, and the acme of corporate power and decision making, while being managed by industry for the mutual defense of the NII and the DII. The government role in such an organization is as a partner, prepared to use the power of the State to enforce confidentiality and neutrality, while minimizing predatory competition among members in the reporting, analysis and disposition of threats.

Compared to the CERT, an expanded NSTAC, by its proximity to the Office of the President, has a superior ability to set membership rates, draw members and staff talent, and manage the timely exchange of information. Moreover, coupled with government partnership at the NSC level, the power of government in the form of an Executive Order could be used to ensure the protection of those reporting attacks from the predatory competition of the marketplace. Here specifically, the power of the Espionage Act of 1917 could be used to ensure that any report of attack, any system vulnerability, and any response to attack is made a matter of national defense security. That Act, which lives today as Title 18 U.S. Code (specifically 18 USC 793a) is still the primary means by which we protect from sabotage the telephone and telegraph lines carrying military communications.

Whether a business chooses formal partners or relies on the hierarchy of membership industry trade associations, the contribution to mid-level information security strategy of the third defensive measure, access to a stable of consultants must be considered. As each escalation of more sophisticated attack is answered by more elaborate software defense products, there arises both a need and a niche for consultants to recommend improvements, train staff and provide surge or recovery support. By their nature, consultants are able to escape the administrative distractions that sap the ability of the corporate ISM to focus on the escalating sophistication of the attack-countermeasure cycle.

The high and increasing number of quality information security products coming to market, and the overhead investment required to compare solutions, to procure new software, and to train staff, generally limits the ability of a corporation to keep up with market improvements. The margin of vulnerability to new attack therefore waxes due to new attack methods and then decreases due to adoption of new countermeasures. Consultants serve a valuable role as industry scouts, searching out and adapting new technology early enough to make profit in the sharing of their temporary information edge.

Highest Needs—Self Fulfillment

At the highest point of Maslow's pyramid of needs stands the notion that, even after basic and mutual support needs are met, most people have a need to excel in some manner which allows one to stand out from the mass of contemporary society. So it is with some businesses. These may be characterized as searching for a niche or an identity that sets them above the median in one or more attributes.

In the information age, at the apex of business are those which pioneer the recognition, identification, and countermeasures necessary for information security, or information attack. Some concentrate on narrow sectors of information security research and development, such as design of encryption systems, firewalls, network monitoring and alarms, and/or countermeasures development. Others, assuming there is a customer for such developments, may be working on code and channels for delivery of code to disrupt, co-opt or otherwise insert some modicum of non-cooperative management of someone else's data stream and decision cycle.

Business strategies for "information attack" must be founded on security policies that mimic government Cold-War compartmentalization of "black" programs. More than just draconian security, these businesses must settle for themselves the issues of legal responsibility for their actions, especially since they may not be cloaked by "national security needs." An analogy may be drawn with a case study in laser warfare.

About twenty years ago, a large corporation found that illumination by certain lasers could change the crystalline structure of glass or quartz structure. It was realized that this had great implications for battlefield tanks which use periscopes to allow operators to view the external world and serious implications for the eyes of anyone peering through glass when the laser beam impinged. Corporate managers soon found that the stockholders did not see such developments as within the range of products they envisioned for the corporation. More than mere liability, there were moral issues. In the end, the corporation quietly withdrew from these endeavors.

Had the corporation stayed, possibly they would find themselves in a position today, not unlike the tobacco giants who are slowly being brought to atonement for past business practices and resultant public injuries. The tobacco analogy is not perfect. Most smokers derive pleasure from the process. In the case of information warfare offensive developments, it is hard to imagine what justifiable good comes from the creation of a destructive virus, worm, Trojan horse, sub-carrier vector for infection, or clandestine chipset for destruction upon remote activation. Perhaps a more apt analogy is to the corporation which sets out to build lock picks. The corporation which sets out to build an offensive device—perhaps for use by a clandestine agency—probably violates the law of the nation in which the device will be used, and probably is liable for damages in a world court should a nexus even be established.

The patterns which emerge in charting the history of corporate product developments and personnel changes make it impossible to shield the corporation from eventual liability for actions that could be reasonably construed as intentionally injurious. People change jobs more often and may carry with them a wide range of feelings about the old corporation, key executives, and key developments. Secrecy agreements cannot be made to protect corporate wrongdoing. How then does a corporation, bent on cutting-edge devices for information mischief, inoculate itself against the inevitable leak and subsequent lawsuit?

If precedence is prologue, the strategy for defense has not been found. Hence, the corporation seeking to perfect mischief for profit charts new ground at essentially unbounded risk. Strategies for protection of capital and profit, while creating the means to deny or destroy another's intellectual property or chattel, must evolve around the convoluted tactics of "shells" and "fronts" by which organized crime has long sought to insulate itself from liability. Recent Congressional investigatory history, laced as it has been with base politics, should not induce any entrepreneur to believe that government could long shelter and protect such activity, even in the name of national defense.

Legal and stockholder's moral considerations aside, businesses which seek to lead the development of state-of-the-art methods for perception management, non-cooperative influencing or manipulation of external decision cycles, C^3I/telecommunications service disruption and denial, and/or deception, must found their strategies carefully. Business strategies for these kinds of offensive information warfare products and services must be based on cutting-edge technology, well-defined victim profile information on which to operate, and innovation on demand. These businesses may need the epitome of flexible, adaptive, just-in-time production, as they operate in a dynamic vortex of measure/counter-measure escalation. Chances are good they will not long remain hidden from victims, nor immune from Hammurabian retribution.

However, the application of methods of information attack require more than technology. Business strategy for the development of offensive devices must include carrying hard technology from concept to application—in the context of the political/military, economic or societal domain in which a particular attack will be launched. For example: what most often trips up the hackers most elegant software manipulation is detection by a victim, because of failure to understand basic business methods or corporate culture. While the corporate developer of information attack methods may not necessarily be the final perpetrator, the product is fatally flawed if it cannot perform, with repeated high reliability, in a known envelope of victim ambient conditions. The developer is thus driven to an early, long-term relationship with the eventual attacker, and by extension, the victim.

The global telecommunications infrastructure is evolving closer to ubiquitous use of fiber for distance transmission and RF (radio frequency) for local bridging to mobile users. SATCOM will always occupy an RF niche for private networks and temporary expansion to austere areas pending installation of cable. Hence optical transmission, cellular/PCS systems, VSATs, their underlying switching matrix and supporting software network will, for the foreseeable future, be the focus of engineering for information attack.

Apart from offensive-minded business, strategies for businesses seeking to perfect the means of protecting data for profit by developments such as encryption, firewalls, intrusion detectors and the like, have considerably lesser liabilities. In this arena, success is dictated by possessing the cutting edge in both software engineering and "hacking." Here is the legitimate blending of information attack with defense. The defensive system design team works against a strictly internal offense, or attack team, for the purpose of perfecting a defensive product. Information attack, where used, is supplied by an internal "B team," in a controlled environment. Contemporary manufacturers have begun using such product development strategies with mixed results. At issue is the internal "hacker" especially when procured from the outside. Can his/her energies be controlled and channeled? Can the corporation's core networks be shielded from retribution in the event he/she is dismissed?

A few corporations have recently posted developmental software to Internet bulletin boards to draw impromptu external "hacker invitational" attacks. Prizes have been offered for a successful breach. Marketing plans have been built around successful defenses. Evidence of some potential customer backlash has been noted as net "wags" have been observed to opine that the hacker who could do the most harm will not be tempted by modest one-time prizes when the real gold is to be had when the new system is widely fielded. This vignette drives home the point that product development must be controlled internally. Reliance cannot be placed on external, voluntary cooperation. The gut issue then becomes bounding the risk that the internal corporate hacker is the cutting edge or ensuring against liability if he/she isn't.

Bounding such risk for cutting edge corporations must involve assembly of an in-house emergency team to swiftly stem any customer-reported breach. The contemporary model is the "CERT cycle." A breach is reported, triggering emergency response, countermeasure development and broad, rapid dissemination of warning and response. Whether CERT remains or not, product developers have essentially been drawn into a new, more permanent relationship with customers who invest in promises of information security. No developer can promise omnipotent protection. No customer may claim injury if he/she has not routinely incorporated all CERT/corporate public notices of latent defect.

In this complex environment, the role of government will remain customer, regulator, and arbiter of disputes via the courts. Despite efforts in some quarters to grow intelligence and warning organizations to detect, quantify and assist in countering threats, the government can neither afford nor perfect such a role, even for the DII. The expense of cultivating and maintaining cutting-edge emergency response teams can neither be carried alone by industry nor by government. It must be a cooperative investment. Because the NII is privately owned and managed, the lead must go to industry. Niche strategies may be devised for contractual support of a larger combined effort by small companies possessed of sole expertise. Few if any large scale integrators will have all of the expertise to lead the combined effort. At the heart of the defensive effort will always be the rapid escalation of the next product and the newest threat or flaw.

General Considerations

The core of business strategy for the information age must be the bounding of risk between the assurance of the security of corporate assets, against the need for communication and currency in the evolving state of the competitive market. More elegant strategies to accommodate positioning of the corporation in the diverse and growing information marketplace must incorporate continuing investment in upgraded protection, threat recognition, measured response, and due diligence, according to evolving, informal public standards. Strategies should not rest upon single points of failure, but should allow for graceful degradation of networks and partial survival by compartmentalization. Product development and marketing strategies must be cognizant of the state of published threat capabilities, because product liability will evolve as fast as products themselves. Here, "published" must be broadened to include informal, near real-time notice on Internet boards.

This last point must be understood. The cycle of attack, detection and countermeasure is highly compressed in the information age. At the point of product launch, the detection and countermeasures team must be poised for action. Typically, the attacker may be an early adapter, possibly even a beta-test observer. The first attacks may be more nuisance than substance, but are sure to escalate. The point is that the attacker is honing his methods and possibly sharing them with a few associates. If countermeasures are not in place by the knee of the product deployment cycle, the resulting loss to the developer may be more than a loss of public confidence and an early plateau in sales. The most significant loss to the developer may be in a rash of lawsuits from legitimate, early adapters who have sustained significant losses due to faulty product security or unforeseen vulnerabilities.

Clearly, a main line of defense against corporate product liability is good people. The traditional corporate model which is built around early acquisition of good people on whose lifework the corporation can grow is changing. The state of the art in information systems and practice is evolving much faster than the ability of any person to maintain cutting-edge currency while still producing new products. Few corporations can afford the investment in retraining the last product development team to tackle the newest requirement. Out-sourcing for training and the supplement skills must be a part of even core business development strategies. New systems for assessing the knowledge, aptitude and reliability of people resources must be treated as base-line investments.

Methods for recycling or compensating past contributors must be deliberately thought out. Potentially one of the highest order threats against the corporation is the disgruntled contributor, whether currently separated or simply shoved aside. Statistics show that the capital required to set up a sole proprietorship may be in the $50,000 range of initial capitalization. Is this too much to invest in a formerly valued employee being moved out due to obsolescence? Wouldn't it be best to train the employee on the latest company product and launch him/her on an independent career as a training partner? Such "post-service" investment can be an effective part of a basic business strategy.

Conclusions

In the information age, business is confronted with a host of new threats centered around the same digital access, storage and flow which characterize the new age. Maslow offers a convenient model for applying strategy to the complex information-age business. The model calls for basic methods to secure core business information, while the business positions itself for the market place. Methods and implementation of strategy increase in complexity as the market position of the corporation, and its potential threat profile, increases.

Decision times compress both internally within the business, and externally within the market place. What were five year, or greater, cycles in the development, marketing, fielding and harvesting of new industrial-age products and services have compressed to less than 12-18 months. Micro-cycles in development and production become critical to business strategy and require new levels of prescience in strategic planning for the information market place. Of numerous new micro-cycles, none are more critical to a product or service launch than the timely detection and cure of flaws which are vulnerable to information attack.

The heart of business strategies to meet the new age is the security of core information networks and data bases. Building comprehensive security is an analysis of risk from full, open market access, versus overhead resources available for investment in protection of core functions. Properly bounded risk may exceed available resources, thereby requiring external cooperative measures such as membership in trade associations and/or mutual defense consortia. Paradoxically, external assistance adds to the security risk which was initially brought on by increasing external information access and flow.

Market leaders face the greatest threats from information attack. Corporations investing heavily in cutting-edge R&D for early market share must be capable of rapidly countering both product development flaws and unanticipated weaknesses which may accrue from technological leaps in methods of attack. Corporations investing in the development of tools for information attack face significant additional burdens and liabilities resulting from public exposure of such activities and/or victim lawsuits.

Regardless of business mission, state of the technological art, or market position, *people* are the greatest resource of and potentially the greatest threat to the information-age business. Compression of product development cycles hasten both burnout and skills obsolescence. Rapid retraining and post-service investment to keep personnel productive go far in reducing damage done by disaffected or cast-off workers.

In the last analysis, business strategy for the information age is an iterative process as dynamic as the market place itself. Few road maps exist. Few guarantees may be had, except the guarantee that information attacks will be made and will increase both in sophistication and severity. Liability for loss due to information attack will increase as public knowledge of losses is found and acknowledged. More than ever the decision deferred becomes the liability incurred.

Endnotes

[1] Clifford Stoll. *The Cuckoo's Egg: Tracking a Spy Throughout the Maze of Computer Espionage,* New York: Doubleday, 1989.
[2] Abraham Maslow. *Motivation and Personality*, New York: Harper Row, 1954.
[3] See, for example, a review of a Michigan State University survey reported in *Datamation Magazine*, December 15, 1995, p. 20.
[4] Elizabeth Sikorovsky, "CERT Shifts from Incident Response to Research Role," *Federal Computer Week*, December 4, 1995, p.8.
[5] According to an article in the May 1996 issue of *SIGNAL*, the ASD C^3I is considering some means to continue funding the CERT effort.

From InfoWar to Knowledge Warfare: Preparing for the Paradigm Shift

Philippe Baumard

Successful firms, such as Intel, maintain an innovative environment, seek continuous performance improvement, favor customer orientation through partnerships with customers and suppliers, enhance results orientation, and place speed of creation, defense and development of value-chains at the core of their strategic focus.

To maintain its leadership, Intel developed "war rooms," and encouraged informal relationships that crisscrossed organizational boundaries. Nevertheless, when Intel had to face InfoWar practices, it had to acknowledge that the company failed to prevent and to anticipate large-scale Info-destabilization.

New businesses live on the brink of disasters. Yet, "organizations have many stabilizers, but quite often lack proper destabilizers."[1] We will argue in this paper that InfoWar (informational arena-based warfare) has been thought within the boundaries of old schemata that will no longer be accurate in the XXIst century. These schemata includes misconceptions of management, organizations, economics, welfare and of purpose of development. We will investigate, in the footsteps of Hedberg, Jonsson, Starbuck, Steele, Wilensky, and many others, design principles that worked, and no longer worked. Founding our comments on observations of real-world experiences, we end with recommendations to prepare nations, organizations and people for the forthcoming paradigm shift from InfoWar to Knowledge Warfare (K-Warfare).

Why Policy Makers Got Trapped in the Information Paradigm

World leaders, who mostly belong to a generation that is not born with a computer at home, have been strongly influenced by cybernetics. In a cybernetic world, economic and social life is seen as a system; values are categorized; economic systems are modeled; social structures are typologized, and ideologies are invented to put all these systems together. In such a world, policy makers are not wrong to assume that information is power, and systematized information, the structure of power itself. History has been, so far, consistent with such implicit assumptions. Power was centralized, and, therefore, needed centralized intelligence. The world was organized into blocks, and therefore, needed compartmented information. Economic and social systems were hierarchical, and therefore, hierarchical information made sense.

From the starting point, this cybernetic view of the world was quite erroneous. As Varela and Maturana pointed out,[2] neurons that participate in the building of "vision" account only for 20% from the eyes' retinas, whereas 80% of them come from other parts of the brain. In other words, 80% of our "vision" is internally constructed. Vision is mostly knowledge, not information. Furthermore, this knowledge is mostly tacit; it escapes our individual or collective awareness.[3]

Eventually, people—including policy-makers—learn without being aware of what is being learned;[4] code without being aware of coding;[5] and most dramatically, learn without having intended or planned to learn.[6] Most learning is incidental.

Emerging "Information Warfare" doctrines fail to acknowledge this fragility of learning. Mapping without knowing is nonsense. Mapping, as an act of "vision," is mostly derived from these 80% of neurons, in our brains and not in our retinas, that participate in the construction of images, and help us to transform noticed and unnoticed stimuli into sense-making. Such weapons as "private-sector communication satellite constellations that instantly link individuals, on-demand high-resolution imaging spacecraft, and rapidly evolving gigabit/sec-class networks"[7] are no less than phantasmagorias, if we neglect to take care of these disturbing—yet remaining—autonomous neurons of our brains.

A small firm of less than 12 employees, named Indigo, is an exemplar. Indigo produces and publishes five confidential newsletters, including the Intelligence Newsletter,[8] a well reputed source of intelligence among policy makers in Europe. Myths and rumors circulate, seeing in Indigo's high accuracy a ploy of obscure foreign intelligence. French readers suspect foreign intrusions. Foreign readers suspect French manipulation. In fact, Indigo is nothing else than an efficient "knowledge-refinery,"[9] that is to say a firm purposefully designed for the efficiency of its knowledge generation. On site observation shows that "far from being pliable, knowledge generates its own path of transformation, while simultaneously transforming and being transformed by its organizational settings. An implication is that those who would manage knowledge should respect this propensity for autonomous development."[10] Cautious towards systematized information gathering, Indigo's staff is operating within a "community of practice"[11]—i.e. an intensive and highly-contextualized socialization process—and favors HUMINT. The whole organization is focused on sense-making instead of information-collection. Intensity and depth of internal and external socializations are considered as the core organizational competitive advantage. The rate of defaults is close to zero. The overall performance, in terms of growth and return on investment, is twice higher that similar organizations such as the Economist Intelligence Unit.

To understand such a performance, let us recall that information is not knowledge, and then let us investigate how to deal with knowledge, instead of information. As General Franks pointed out, "Vietnam was the first battlefield use of computers. The Univac 1005, which the 25th Infantry Division installed in 1966 at Cu Chi, filled an entire van. "Images" of the enemy and terrain were captured with conventional cameras and television, with light intensification devices, radar, and infrared devices. Sensors and high altitude reconnaissance scanned 100,000 square miles per hour, providing commanders with a heretofore unknown view of the battlefield." [12] Meanwhile, the Vietnamese population were digging tunnels. Similarly, the French Foreign Legion was settling its command outposts on hills, so as to dominate battlefields. Meanwhile, Vietnamese soldiers were digging the crops and burying themselves in the face and "vision" of the enemy—proving, if necessary, that neurons from the retinas only account for 20% of vision. What was dramatically missing was not information, but knowledge in general, and an adequate form of "knowing" in particular. "We are on the threshold of an era where order can be achieved largely through knowledge—not necessarily through physical order."[13]

Knowledge vs. Information, Knowing vs. Knowledge

Understanding the differences between 'knowledge' and 'knowing' is essential to a successful entry in this new paradigm. "One contemporary cliché is that more and more turbulent settings are requiring organizations to use more and more knowledge, and that this in turn forces organizations to process more and more information."[14] A knowledge-base is all the learning of people and institutions, more or less explicitly encapsulated in minds, brains, models, signals, culture, rules and guidelines.

Greek philosophers used to categorize this human knowledge in three ensembles: the *techne*—the embodied technical know-how; the *episteme*—the abstract generalization derived from knowing-how, and the *phronesis*—the wisdom of social practice, (i.e. the ability to derive aggregates from social learning.) In modern management literature, the investigation of knowledge within and in-between organizations is merely derived from the same twenty-four centuries old conceptualization. The conventional view is that the relevant knowledge comes from explicit situational analysis; that is, it is objective knowledge. As Detienne and Vernant pointed out,[15] education in the Judeo-Christian world has been strongly influenced by the pursuit of Truth as the sole goal of knowledge generation. Starting in 400 BC, knowledge is systematically understood as "objective knowledge," leaving 'meaner' forms of knowledge and knowing—such as conjectural knowledge—disregarded and low-grade. The governmental intelligence cycle itself is a pursuit of objective knowledge. Intelligence generation is driven by an objectivation force that discards unreliable information and sources according to truth-setting rules.

As Wilensky put it, the intelligence bodies are overcrowded with "facts-and-figures men," who "introduce a 'rational-responsible' bias." "Facts-and-figures men are preoccupied with rational argument and criteria; their technical competence compels opposing parties to be more careful or honest in their use of information, to match each other expert for expert, fact for fact."[16] Thus, current doctrines of InfoWar are all implicitly based on a biased assumption that large-scale truth seeking is superior to depth and differentiation of knowing modes. Such doctrines are based on the belief that the process of organizations and nation's 'getting into difficulties' is essentially one of the degradation and increasing disutility of their knowledge-base.[17] Yet, when doctrine generators are asked to define such a "knowledge-base," they have to face their incapacity to describe and to qualify it.

Knowledge-base, as a matter of fact, is a static concept. It assumes that knowledge can be systematically put in the form of a representation, and neglects all various forms of tacit knowledge in general, and collective tacit knowledge, in particular. Thus, the same Judeo-Christian bias applies to the representation of knowledge. Knowledge is assumed to be merely a long-term representation; is seen as a commodity; is talked of in terms of volume and stocks; is described with a vocabulary borrowed from hardware management. In such a biased conception of knowledge, one usually distinguish short-term, or procedural, representations that can be immediately acted on one side, and long-term, or structural, representations, whose access and development need several apprenticeships.[18]

As a consequence, focus should be put on the advancement of "knowing," instead of the accumulation of "knowledge." Development of national intelligence capabilities should therefore target the improvement of interpretation and sense-making skills, instead of pursuing the utopia of the ubiquity of a knowledge seen as a commodity. Such a self-deception has its roots in the reproducibility of information. Redundancy of information is a serious waste of resources in most industrial democracies. For instance, in France, no less than 80 administrative bodies distribute the same information ,again and again, to small and large businesses This redundant information eventually leads to redundant intelligence administrations, leading to the hypertrophy of bureaucratic, and inefficient, intelligence bodies.

The 1996 reorganization of the U.S. Intelligence Community is an example of this lack of focus on "knowing" capabilities, and of the exaggerated attention given to the accumulation of "knowledge." In 1992, Ernest R. May "urges the Committee to think of individuals in the Intelligence Community as well as of their organizational boxes."[19] Frank Carlucci, a former Assistant to the President for National Security Affairs, underlines that "Congress could render a valuable service if it would lead the Intelligence Community through the process of cultural change that many of our businesses have gone through."[20] As Orton and Callahan noted, "unwarranted duplication remains a problem; and intelligence remains too isolated from the governmental process it was created to serve." [21]

The focus on "knowledge as a commodity" vs. the "improvement of knowing" can also be observed in the conceptual frameworks that are judged to be a good basis for knowledge-based warfare. Colonel Steven J. Sloboda, formerly in charge of long-range planning for U.S. Space Command asserts: "Space is literally the fabric upon which we will weave our approach to knowledge-based warfare. Space is the enabling ingredient. Fortunately, the convergence of our experience in space operations, communications networking, and information processing seems to make the move to knowledge-based warfare achievable." [22] Unfortunately, human souls and minds are not fully readable from outer space. The "folk theory" that trust moves, not words, might well be misleading in a knowledge-based paradigm. The Vietnam, Gulf and former Yugoslavia experiences—three modern war theaters with intensive use of satellite information—are exemplar cases of the limits of satellite cartography in penetrating human intents. Moreover, such experiences underline the limits of InfoWar. As Dragnich noted, the "so-called information war" that has been proposed "to wage against the Serbs is ridiculous. The Serbs do not need the outside world to tell them that communism and Slobodan Milosevic are bad." [23]

Misconceptions of management

Thus, management should be designed and understood as primarily a knowledge-generation process. Many companies tend to follow management practices that take the physical world for granted. When the Berlin Wall fell, Finland believed that the announced geostrategic shift would require the acquisition of combat fighters. The market was estimated at around 3 billion U.S. dollars. Four French companies, Snecma, Matra, Dassault and Thomson, and the Defense Administration, decide to enter the race for this competitive bid. When the newly settled French Economic Intelligence and Corporate Strategies Commission, at the French Office of Planning, decided to develop a few exemplar case studies, the case of the Mirage 2000-5 was selected.[24] The audit revealed that lack of coordination and knowledge sharing was at the root of the commercial failure. Managers who negotiated the contract were chosen according to corporate criteria. Internal competition prevented any attempt of crisscrossed knowledge transfers. Another French firm, the Aerospatiale, which has an in-depth knowledge of the Finland aeronautics market, was not consulted by the competing pool. In the absence of a long-term knowledge strategy, the State was unable to display any capitalization of knowledge on Finland. The lack of longitudinal capitalization of geostrategic knowledge led to the incapability of designing required distinctive attributes in the competitive bid. In the middle of the negotiation process, the political turmoil in Finland was perceived as an obstacle, whereas the American companies reinforced their coordination and lobbying to use these elections as a leverage for their offer. Indeed, the French consortium was competing with a hypothetical F-16 offer, while the American were proposing the F-18. As Wilensky warned, "in all complex social systems, hierarchy, specialization, and centralization are major sources of distortion and blockage of intelligence." [25]

However, it seems that this analysis can be put a step forward. In this intelligence failure, the main cause was the inappropriateness of management practices to a non-market environment. The French consortium failed to recognize and acknowledge forces that acted outside the narrow borders of the targeted market. In a transversal environment (i.e. that implies geopolitical, geoeconomical, local politics, technology and society), with a transversal offer (i.e. typically a consortium of different firms, proposing dual technologies), traditional "market management" fails to grab critical issues. As R. D. Laing noted, "the range of what we think and do is limited by what we fail to notice." If nonmarket knowledge is not integrated in management duties and skills, it is bound to be neglected. Thus, "nonmarket strategies result from a management process that incorporates knowledge of the market and nonmarket environments, information about specific issues, and conceptual frameworks that guide strategy formulation and implementation." [26]

Misconceptions of organizations

Most organizations are unfit for the management and capitalization of intangible assets in general, and counter-productive in terms of knowledge generation. However true, one "must analyze the flow of information along the value chain as well as the movement of goods." [27] It might be quite insufficient to cope with the new conditions of competitiveness.

The whole concept of value-chain, and the education given to managers for that matter, should be revised. Managers and scholars are used to thinking of organizations as stable contractual bodies, with physical locations (headquarters, plants, departments, etc.), while the new economics call for a focus on industries as systems, rather than buildings and walls. Bo Hedberg introduces the concept of "imaginary organizations" to picture these new economic conditions.[28]

An "imaginary organization" is a knowledge-infrastructure concerning markets, potential opportunities for production and creation of value-chains. Hedberg uses the example of Gant, an American garment brand that was bought by Swedish investors, and developed worldwide. Gant had no proprietary plants. The whole organization consisted of a team of managers that coordinated market needs and channels with a constellation of independent suppliers. The core competitive advantage of Gant lies in the corporation's ability to coordinate market needs with independent systems' inputs. Gant used its knowledge infrastructure to define and find matches between independent production and design capabilities and market needs.

This whole perspective of "knowledge infrastructures" is likely to be the dominant paradigm in the coming century. Hewlett Packard in France got rid of local middle management supervisory staff and replaced it with a centralized information platform at its headquarters. The "information infrastructure" collects customers' needs and requests, and dispatches the information directly to managers and maintenance engineers' notebook screens through Electronic Data Interchange. Locally, Hewlett Packard suppressed many subsidiaries and branches. Managers and maintenance engineers work at home, being constantly on the move to meet customers' needs and specifications on sites. The whole organization is transformed in a knowledge-generation node, with many peripheries where action is taking place.

Could such a model be implemented on a national scale, and what would be the social and welfare consequences? It is quite probable that such a "knowledge infrastructure" could be designed and implemented on a national scale. It would require administrations, large and small corporations and individuals to share a communal information infrastructure, where demands and supplies of tangibles and intangibles would find their matches. In such a perspective, competitive advantage of nations would eventually lie in national ability and speed to generate (and discontinue without social and economic costs) virtual value chains to operate them. Attempts such as the Department of Commerce's Advocacy Center in the United States, and the Committee for Economic Security and Competitiveness (CCSE), attached to the Secretariat General de la Defense National (SGDN) in France, are evidently pursuing such a model. Both the Advocacy Center and the CCSE pursue an objective of coordination and alertness between administrative bodies and private organizations. However, while the Advocacy Center is located at an operational level, with a direct link with the intelligence community, the French CCSE is placed under the authority of the Prime Minister, and its main focus is a supra-coordination of administrative bodies (Ministries of Finances, Defense, Foreign Affairs, French Office of Planning) that already fulfill, more or less properly, a coordination role. Political ambitions, in France and in the United States, and intelligence communities' internal conflicts, are however impeding the performance of both the French and American experiences.

Misconceptions of economics & welfare

Economics theories mainly failed, for they either never succeeded in addressing the benevolence issue in economic development, or rapidly lost focus when attempting to grab it. Myths that surround the development of InfoWar or InfoEconomics, are mainly myths of malevolence: 'cyberwarriors,' 'viruses,' 'logic bombs,' etc. Whereas we leave the paradigm of economics of forces, physical order, heaviness and superiority of gender on genius, we tend to bring with us the bad habits of past and history. InfoWar experts and analysts react to the emergence of the 'knowledge paradigm' with a defense attitude towards the unexpected. Whereas a global knowledge infrastructure could have been an opportunity to substitute a threat-equilibrium with 'integrative power,'[29] policy-makers tend to project ideologies and doctrines that proved to be wrong, instead of inventing the conceptual framework that will fit the new economics.

Two biases lie behind the design and mission of these governmental-level information coordination bodies. The first bias could be pictured as an "intelligentsialization" of the information infrastructure. Both governments have chosen a top-down implementation of their information infrastructure, thus applying obsolete governmental schemata to the management of knowledge. While experts are calling for the development of the largest "knowledge sharing culture,"[30] national knowledge-infrastructure projects are being drawn with an elitist bias. It might occur, around 2010, that such decisions were historical self-deceptions. Doing so, governments tend to confuse information logistics (a structural perspective) with knowledge sharing (an interactionist perspective). In other words, artificial efficiency is reached today because decision makers and policy makers, who share information, already hold the requisite knowledge to make this information actionable. Thus, it gives the illusion that the development of an information structure is a necessary and sufficient condition to attain a national knowledge infrastructure. On the contrary, such a policy will prove to be counter-productive. It will eventually create an isolated body of upper-level knowledge, disconnected from the reality of social development and learning, and therefore, increasing the gap between people who act, learn and talk, and people being acted, learned and talked. Economic performance might be reached through an routinized logistics of generic knowledge amongst business leaders, industrialists and politicians, but social performance is already doubtful. Research findings suggest that permanent improvement and continuous learning cannot be achieved in situations of disarticulated socialization.[31]

Information infrastructures, as designed in American and French projects, favor information exchange, including possible use of information highways, and neglect to design proper socialization devices that would enhance permanent and collective sense-making. Furthermore, such knowledge infrastructures are already perceived by the population as jobs-destructive, in opposition to almost all fourteen points of Deming's principles of continuous transformation.[32] One of these principles says that fear should be driven out, so that everyone may work effectively. Surrounded by myths of malevolence, economic intelligence sharing-infrastructures, on the contrary, announces a quest for economics of coordination costs, worldwide economics of scale, and the birth of a knowledgeable elite, with privileged and discretionary access to uprising knowledge infrastructures. Hewlett Packard was an example of that point. Local managers disappeared, leaving their place to management technicians "being acted" by electronic data interchange. Many firms, more or less consciously, took this curve. Asea Brown Bovery (ABB) reduced its corporate staff, after its fusion, from more than 4000 to less than 300 "global managers." Given the fact that middle managers already live and work in suburban areas, the effect is an increasing gap between geographically-concentrated conceptual knowledge, and geographically-dispersed procedural know-how. Instead of encouraging a cooperative culture, knowledge infrastructures may implement a perennial rupture between an exclusive and very small knowledgeable suprastructure, and a very large, fragmented and desocialized, cognitively-taylorized substructure.

In Deming's theory, effectiveness is derived from continuous efforts "toward the simultaneous creation of cooperative and learning organization to facilitate the implementation of process-management practices, which, when implemented, support customer satisfaction and organizational survival through sustained employee fulfillment and continuous improvement of processes, products, and services."[33] Similar thinking can be found in intelligence history in general, and in the XVIth century Elizabethan doctrine of governmental intelligence in particular: "Elizabeth was intellectually the most enlightened monarch of her time." Francis Bacon writes that she was "undued with learning," and "to the end of her life she sets hours for reading (more than) scarcely any student of her time." One way to please her was to talk "In Praise of Knowledge," as Essex did with his essay, most probably written by Bacon."[34] Queen Elizabeth I's intelligence shadow adviser, Sir Francis Bacon, was the author of the Advancement of Learning in 1605, and also authored an essay entitled "Followers and Friends" in 1597. The other intelligence doctrine advisor, Sir William Cecil, authored on his part, a forward-looking memorandum entitled Matters Necessary to be Done, Troubles that all May Presently Ensue, Things Necessary to be Considered, With Speed, With Foreboding, With Foresight, Plots and Designs.[35] Speed, consistency and sharing of knowledge-generation processes on a large-scale base were already put at the center of national development strategies.

The difference between 16th century Great Britain and current industrial democracies, however, is a fundamental shift from obedience to commitment of the governed. To continue to design information infrastructures in the Elizabethan style, is overlooking that knowledge is nowadays widely distributed. "Cooperation, in this context, is synonymous with collaboration among different individuals, groups, or organizations, where all entities are engaging in noncompetitive, mutually beneficial, win-win activities."[36]

Why Shifting from I-War to K-War: A case-study

As Wilensky once put it, "information has always been a source of power, but it is now increasingly a source of confusion. In every sphere of modern life, the chronic condition is surfeit of information, poorly integrated or lost somewhere in the system."[37] Roots of such failures can been found (a) in the persistent confusion between knowledge and information, (b) on the large scale focus that has been given in education to cumulating of knowledge-bases vs. permanent improvement of the diversity and flexibility of modes of knowing, and (c) in the failure of scientists in integrating in new organizational forms and purposes, the advancements of social cognition and collective learning. Yet, "managers are becoming increasingly aware that informed adaptability is at a premium and to attain it they may need different modes of organization to find and solve different types of problems."[38]

Nevertheless, and consistent with a perception of knowledge as a commodity, "organization" on one side, and "knowledge' on the other side, are systematically organizational forms, but leave managers with the duty of generating adequate knowledge to operate them. Knowledge sociologists put much emphasis on the many forms of socializations that participate in the building of cognitive skills, but are reluctant to study how organizational design and knowledge generation interact. German definition of the world "Intelligenz" could shed some light on such an intricated issue. The Wirtschafts-Lexikon, a principal German dictionary, in defining intelligence, puts "an emphasis on mental processes geared to adaptation, integration, and recognizing significant relationships. These processes are interesting: were we to consider them as characteristics of some organizational form, we would come very near to the 'intelligence system' definition." German thought also recognizes the importance of the perception of causal connection and of capacity for combination."[39] To achieve the integration of "knowing" and "organizing," German authorities have historically put a strong focus on the continuity of education to intelligence in the society. After World War II, the Economic Police was reintegrated in national industrial infrastructures. Today, German students receive education from German generals and senior military officers in most business schools as to maintain a longitudinal awareness of the role played by intelligence and military art in the understanding and design of business organizations.

The Perrier case illustrates the importance of "the perception of causal connection and of capacity for combination," so much favored by German intelligence.[40] On July 3, 1989, Perrier and PepsiCo. were negotiating the creation of a joint-venture, in which Perrier would hold 65% of the shares. The negotiations were disrupted on July 16. In August 1989, Perrier sold its subsidiary, the Societe Parisienne de Boissons Gazeuses, which distributed PepsiCo in France to its main competitor, Coca-Cola. This competitive move was perceived as retaliation. In November 1989, PepsiCo denounced the poor performance of Perrier in the management of its license and announced the disruption of all contractual arrangements for December 1990. PepsiCo took Perrier to court on November 8, 1990; and announced, a day after, that it would be eventually interested in taking over the soft-drinks activities of Perrier, if stock price would be more attractive. Meanwhile, the Coca Cola stock reached the historical price of $72 on November 18, 1989.

On January 19, 1990, a laboratory in North Carolina discovers traces of Benzene in samples of Perrier mineral water. Experts suspect the information to have been transmitted through a mole in a Perrier production plant in Vergeze. "Causal connection" can be made between the test results, and the nearby location of a Coca Cola plant. The laboratory Manager does not remember having replaced its test equipment, but "combined" information shows strong evidence of all test equipment being graciously replaced by a Coca Cola sponsoring of the laboratory. On February 2, 1990, the Food and Drug Administration warned Perrier that mineral water being distributed in the United States contained Benzene.

At that time, Perrier was a potential target for a take-over. Nestle would eventually be interested, and had made aggressive competitive moves on the European market. In particular, Nestle had managed to sign an exclusivity with Walt Disney Europe; walking on Coca Cola traditional proprietary territory. On February 5, 1990, the Food and Drug Administration confirmed the presence of Benzene in Perrier mineral water. On February 10, Perrier was forced to acknowledge, but reacted very quickly by announcing that all bottles would be withdrawn from the market. On February 12, Perrier's stock lost 14%.

bottles would be withdrawn from the market. On February 12, Perrier's stock lost 14%. Suntory, the Japanese distributor of the brand announced the withdrawal of 10,000 bottle cases from the Japanese market. On February 14, German authorities forbid Perrier mineral water on their markets. The French Commission of Stock Operations (COB) announced an investigation on suspicious stock movements that occurred on February 9. Sales were stopped in the United States, Canada, Japan, Germany, Switzerland, Denmark and Hong Kong.

The InfoWar could have found its end in this last event, but Perrier held 25% of the American sparkling waters' market, with an annual sales of $500 millions. Perrier reacted with great dexterity, facing such an Info-destabilization. Financial market observers were promptly reassured of the integrity of the natural water source. The human error was fully explained with a worldwide dissemination of accurate counter-information. Sanitary authorities announces the results of scientific investigations: "The daily consumption of half-liter of Perrier during 30 years do not increase the risk of cancer." The Perrier stock gained 6.3% on Paris stock exchange.

The second phase of this large-scale InfoWar arose on February 20, 1990. A 36 years old Athenian woman asked Perrier for 7.5 millions Francs for the damage caused by the explosion of a bottle that supposedly led to the loss of her eye. Evidence shows that the incident occurred on August 25, 1986—four years before. Several similar court cases appeared in different places of the globe: a lawyer in Bridgeport defended Mrs Vahlsing and eight similar cases of Class Action appeared in Connecticut and Pennsylvania. Perrier discovered that Kroll, the investigative consultancy that took care of its information in the United States, had withdrawn key-information from its reports.[41] In 1991, Nestle finally took over Perrier.

Very similar cases of InfoWar, such as the Shell-Greenpeace Brentspar's case, or the case of "benzene threat" for Octel Co. Ltd. in the United Kingdom,[42] lead to the same conclusions: (a) an isolated organization cannot cope alone with large-scale Info-Destabilization without considerable loss; (b) successful large-scale InfoWars involve interorganizational agreements, and collective manipulations of worldwide information infrastructure (mass media, scientific institutions, customer groups, etc.), and most importantly, (c) ability to rapidly make sense (i.e. generating knowledge) is superior in counter-fighting InfoWars to systematic collection and compilation of open information, already coming from a corrupted or contaminated information infrastructure.

Preparing for the K-Paradigm

Sweden might be an examplar of a country that already engaged in the preparation for the paradigm shift towards Knowledge Warfare. In 1977, Dr. Stevan Dedijer started a business intelligence course at Lund University, educating and training many graduate students who would later become the men and women in charge of economic intelligence in such groups as Skandia, Volvo, or Ericsson. The latter company has organized a strategic group with the university of Karlstadt, that investigates strategic issues of long-distance education and information highways. Participants of this group also participated in the 1992 Swedish Ministry of Defense seminars on the application of the C^4I^2 to strategic development. In a well-defined and well-applied strategy, another strategic group that put together economic, social, political and military leaders, such as Lars Hallen, the head of scientific attaches; Bjorn Wolrath, AB Skandia CEO; Goran Pagels-Fick, from Ericsson; Peter Nygards, State Secretary for Industry; and, Jan Foghelin, head of the Defense Research Center (Fosvarets Forskningstantalt)[43] started to build an "economic intelligence community" among business leaders in 1991. Originally named "BISNES" (after Business Intelligence and Security Network of Sweden), on a proposed idea from Dr. Dedijer, the network adopted a more discreet strategy by inviting, for large debriefing sessions, economic intelligence thinkers and leaders of the open world. General Pichot-Duclos, the head of Intelco, the French InfoWar and Economic Intelligence think-tank, was among the early guests of these sessions with businessmen, the academia, and the military.

Sweden also holds the first rank in systematized intelligence activities in large companies in Europe.[44] Observations of Astra-Draco, Electrolux, Ericsson Radio, Gambro, Celsius Tech, Skandia, SCA Graphic, SAS, Telia and Volvo, as compiled by Hedin, show a good balance between strategic and operational objectives, a systematic supply-and-on demand intelligence for corporate management, a focus on information-sharing culture (e.g. systematic community meeting around the BISNES network), and a particular focus on knowledge acquisition processes.[45] What can be learned from the Swedish experiment?

First of all, the Sweden knowledge infrastructure does not seek publicity. Proceedings of the first open conference on Swedish nation-scale economic intelligence were not translated, and not available on any Web servers, although Sweden displays one of the highest rates of electronic information and telecommunications in the world. While Sweden is claiming to be behind with the knowledge warfare agenda, young Swedes can do their military service in economic intelligence activities. Second, the Swedish experiment is culture-driven. Information-sharing is a long-standing cultural practice among expatriate Swedes. Emphasis is put on a culture of knowledge sharing, rather than on the constitution of specialized administrative bodies. Third, the core of the Swedish knowledge infrastructure is not hardware-based, but it is a "community of practice and sense-making." The BISNES informal network meets regularly, and sense-making is a communal and face-to-face process. Sweden, however, has favorable conditions that could be hardly met by other countries. It is highly culturally-homogenous, and its population is less than 10 millions. The level of reading is, with all Scandinavia countries, one of the highest in the world.

Conclusion

"Making the simple complicated is commonplace; making the complicated simple, awesomely simple, that's creativity."[46] Preparing for the knowledge warfare paradigm requires a strong focus on reengineering of the whole education process of industrialized democracies. It is that simple; but policy makers will face strong resistance, especially from academics. Integration of strategic issues assessment into education should take place as early as possible. The current process is cumulative. The required process is interactionist. Instead of thinking of education in terms of sequentiality, policy makers should design education in terms of interconnectivity and interoperability. Many organizations would like today to increase the awareness of strategic issues among their engineer population, and vice-versa, to increase the awareness of technological issues among their commercial task-forces. To do so, they design new systems, centralized economic intelligence units that dispatches technical market information to both communities. Some firms, like Intel, encourage hybrid teams of engineers and managers as to fertilize crisscrossed issues. This is a result of a Taylorized learning and knowing. Emphasis should put on judgment, cognitive skills, cognitive flexibility, incongruity and ambiguity tolerance at the youngest age. In the knowledge warfare paradigm, strategic advantage does not lie in the concentration of facts-and-figures, but in the complementarity and singularity of the brains who interpret them. National widespread sense-making capability matters more than electronic information highways.

Endnotes

[1] Bo Hedberg, Sten Jonsson, 1978, "Designing semi-confusing information systems for organizations in changing environments," *Accounting, Organizations and Society*, Vol. 3, No. 1, pp. 47-64.

[2] F. J. Varela, H. R. Maturana, 1994, *L'arbre de la connaissance*, Paris: Addison-Wesley.

[3] H. Helmholtz, 1867, *Treatise on Physiological Optics, Vol. III*, translated from German by J.P.C. Southall (Ed.), 1962, New York: Dover.

[4] E. L. Thorndike, R. T. Rock, 1934, "Learning without awareness of what is being learned or intent to learn it", *Journal of Experimental Psychology,* Vol. 19, pp. 1-19.

[5] L. Hasher, R. T. Zacks, 1984, "Automatic processing of fundamental information", *American Psychologist*, 48, pp. 1372-1388.

[6] J. G. Jenkins, 1993, "Instruction as a factor of incidental learning," *American Journal of Psychology*, Vol. 45, pp. 471-477.

[7] W. B. Scott, "Information Warfare demands a new approach", *Aviation Week & Space Technology*, March 13, 1995, p. 85.

[8] http://indigo-net.com/lmr.html. Archives since 1993 are available in English on the Net.

[9] J. S. Brown , P. Duguid, 1991, "Organizational Learning and Communities of Practice Toward a Unified View of Working, Learning and Innovation", *Organization Science*, Vol. 2, No. 1, pp. 40-57.

[10] W. H. Starbuck, in the preface of P. Baumard, 1996, Organisations deconcertees. La gestion strategique de la connaissance, Paris, Masson. Forthcoming: London, Sage, 1997.

[11] J. E. Lave, E. Wenger, 1991, *Situated learning. Legitimate peripheral participation*, Cambridge: Cambridge University Press.

[12] General F. M. Franks, Jr., "Winning the Information War: Evolution and Revolution," speech delivered at the Association of the U.S. Army Symposium, Orlando, Fl., February 8, 1994, in *Vital Speeches of the Day*, Vol. 60, Issue 15, p. 455.

[13] General F. M. Franks, op. cit., p. 456. It is noticeable that Harry Howe Ransom's "Strategic Intelligence" article (1973, General Learning Press), when using the Viet Cong guerilla as an exemplar, and using an intelligence estimate NIE 143/53-61, "Prospects for North and South Vietnam," dated 15 August 1961, does not mention the existence of the Vietnamese underground logistics, and suspects the "Bloc to build up the eastern part of south Laos, improving the roads, mountain trails, and airfields, as a major supply channel." (p. 7) This is an exemplar of applying a cultural mode of knowing that projects ethnocentric schemata on a singular reality.

[14] W. H. Starbuck, op. cit,

[15] Detienne M., Vernant J.P. (1978), *Cunning Intelligence in Greek Culture and Society*, translated by J. Lloyd, Atlantic Highlands, NJ: Humanities Press.

[16] H. Wilensky, 1967, "Organizational Intelligence," in *The International Encyclopedia of the Social Sciences*, David L. Sills (Ed.), Vol. 11, New York: Macmillan & the Free Press, p. 321.
[17] J. C. Spender, Ph. Baumard, 1995, "An empirical investigation of change in the knowledge leading to competitive advantage," Research Paper, presented at the Academy of Management Annual Meeting, in Vancouver, August 5, under the title "Turning troubled firms around: Case-evidence for a Penrosian view of strategic recovery." 18. J.F. Richard, 1990, Les activites mentales, Paris: Armand Collin.
[19] Ernest R. May, statement before the Senate Select Committe on Intelligence, 4 March 1992.
[20] Frank Carlucci, testimony before the Senate Select Committe on Intelligence, 4 March 1992.
[21] J. Douglas Orton, and Jamie L. Callahan, 1996, "Important 'Folk Theories' on Intelligence Reorganization," *The International Journal of Intelligence and Counterintelligence*, Volume 8, No. 4.
[22] W. B. Scott, 1995, "Information Warfare Demands New Approach," Aviation Week & Space Technology, March 13, p. 86.
[23] Alex N. Dragnich, "Containing Serbia," letters to the Editor, *Foreign Affairs*, November/December 1994, Vol. 73, No. 6, p. 198.
[24] The final report under the presidency of Henri Martre, and co-authored by Ph. Baumard, Ph. Clerc and C. Harbulot, was published by *La Documentation Franaise* in Februrary 1994, under the title Intelligence economique et strategie des entreprises. The Mirage 2000-5 case study was withdrawed from final publication.
[25] H. Wilensky, op. cit., p. 323.
[26] David P. Baron, Fall 1995, "The Nonmarket Strategy System", *Sloan Management Review*, p. 75.
[27] T. A. Stewart, 1995, June 12, "The Information Wars: What you don't know will hurt you," *Fortune*, p. 119.
[28] Bo Hedberg, *Imaginary Organizations, forthcoming*, New York: Oxford University Press, 1996.
[29] For developments on integrative power, see Kenneth E. Boulding, Three Faces of Power, London: Sage Publications, 1990.
[30] See Ph. Baumard, " Guerre éonomiqué et Communaute d'Intelligence," *La Revue Politique et Parlementaire* (Political and Parliementary Review), Paris, January 1992; Ph. Baumard, *Strategie et surveillance des environnements concurrentiels*, Paris: Masson, 1991 and Ch. Harbulot, *La machine de guerre economique*, Paris: Economica, 1993.
[31] J. C. Spender, Ph. Baumard, op. cit.; I. Nonaka, H. Takeuchi, 1995, The Knowledge Creating Company. *How Japanese Companies Create the Dynamics of Innovation,* New York: Oxford University Press.
[32] W. E. Deming, 18986, *Out of Crisis*, Cambridge: Massachussets Institute of Technology, Center for Advance Engineering Study, pp. 23-24.
[33] J. C. Anderson, M. Rungtusanatham, R.G. Schroeder, "A theory of quality management underlying the Deming management method," *Academy of Management Review*, 1994, vol. 19, No. 3, pp. 480.
[34] S. Dedijer, 1989, "British Intelligence: The Rainbow Enigma," *The International Journal of Intelligence and Counterintelligence*, Vol. 1, No. 2, p. 82.
[35] quoted by S. Dedijer, op. cit, p. 83.
[36] J. C. Anderson, M. Rungtusanatham, R. G. Schroeder, op. cit., p. 483.
[37] H. Wilensky, op. cit., p. 331.
[38] Dale E. Zand, 1981, *Information, Organization and Power. Effective Management in the Knowledge Society*, New York: McGraw-Hill, p. 58.
[39] F. T. Pearce, and S. Dedijer, February 1976, "The Semantics of Intelligence," Research Paper, Lund University, p. 11.
[40] Ch. Harbulot, P-J. Gustave, November 1995, "La contre-information ou comment repondre une attaque," *Cahiers de la Fonction Publique et de l'Administration*, No 140, pp. 11-13.
[41] Source: M. Najman, 1995, "Intelligence economique," a special television broadcast, Strasbourg: Arte (Franco-German Television).

[42] D. Knott, "Views conflict on benzene threat," *Oil and Gas Journal*, May 23, 1994, p. 41.
[43] Source: *The Intelligence Newsletter*, march 7, 1996, "First large public conference on economic intelligence in Sweden," No. 283.
[44] H. Hedin, 1993, "Business Intelligence Systems: systematised intelligence acitivities in ten multinational companies," *The Journal of the Association of Global Strategic Information*, pp. 126-136.
[45] Lars Bengtsson, Jessica Ohlin, 1993, "Strategy Formation and Knowledge Acquisition Process," in Larsson et al., Research in Strategic Change, Lund Studies in Economics and Management, 21, Lund University Press.
[46] Charlie Mingus, 1977, "Creativity," *Mainliner*, 21(7), p. 25, quoted by W. H. Starbuck and P. C. Nystrom, 1981, "Designing and understanding organizations," in the *Handbook of Organizational Design*, Vol.1, Oxford University Press, p. 9.

Thoughts About Information Warfare

Ronald J. Knecht

The concept of information dependency provides the proper context for the consideration of offensive and defensive information warfare.

Unrecognized information dependency, not the known or potential flaws in the technology used in the communications and computing infrastructures, is the fundamental challenge to business or military operations in today's interconnected world. Information-based activities are replete with such unrecognized dependencies.

Information-based Warfare

The warfighting doctrine of the United States says that "The Joint Campaign should fully exploit the information differential, that is, the superior access and ability to effectively employ information on the strategic, operational, and tactical situations which advanced U.S. technologies provide our forces."[1] This doctrine reflects the shift from industrial warfare to information-based warfare.

The application of this doctrine is seen as yielding a Revolution in Military Affairs (RMA) enabled by the marriage of precision munitions, high speed computers, high capacity communications, and remote sensors providing a "God's eye view" of the battle space. In the vision of the advocates of RMA, the U.S. side will use information more efficiently than the enemy and thus will enable the military to operate "inside the information cycle" of the adversary, disrupt the command and intelligence processes of the adversary, and deliver decisive blows with high-probability-of-kill weapons.

The concept of an RMA flows from an earlier visionary concept from the defense research and development community called Global Grid. Global Grid envisioned the aggressive worldwide distribution and processing of data to allow any consumer—civil, intelligence, and military—to connect to any data. This would provide the U.S. a strategic advantage and enable flexible, scalable, interoperable, and timely information operations.

The benefits promised by Global Grid were not limited to the military. The path from Global Grid led also to a vision of a government-inspired, industry-developed National Information Infrastructure, or NII. As spelled out in the September 1993 *Agenda for Action,* the focus of the NII initiative was on economic rather than on military benefits. To their credit, however, the proponents of the Global Grid concept did lay out a technology path to information-dominated warfare and to the bright promises of the RMA.

Information Dependency

However, some of us then in the office of the assistant secretary of defense for (command, control, communications, and intelligence), (OASD(C^3I) believed the proponents of Global Grid were not giving sufficient attention to the increased dependency on technology that would result from the initiative. This was not an anti-technology bias, but a belief that the increased risks must be understood and managed. This concern was a key factor in the decision by the Department of Defense leadership to issue DoD Directive TS3600.1, Information Warfare (U), dated December 21, 1992. [2]

This directive states that the central role of information in modern warfare requires that U.S. forces to be prepared to operate in an information-hostile environment; cautions not to plan to fight in a manner that requires more information bandwidth than can be protected; instructs commanders to understand what will happen to the forces under their command if they are denied the information they expect to have available; and, to gain an appreciation of their information dependency, requires the military to exercise in information-hostile environments.

The Structure of Work

The implications of information dependency can best be shown by examining the design of work. Work is defined as an effort directed toward the production or accomplishment of something. All work, whether digging a ditch, building an automobile, selling a product, or mounting a complex military operation, can be considered within a common organizational or architectural framework.

At the highest level of the architectural framework (Figure 1) is a business model. The business model encapsulates the answer to the executive-level question "What business are we in?" This model can be made explicit but more often is implicit.

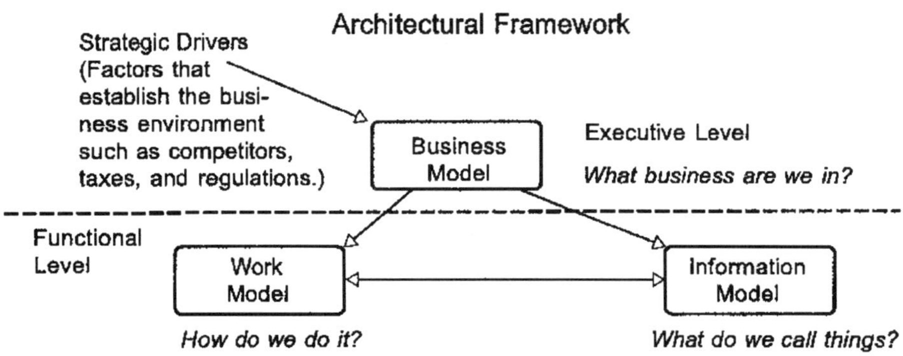

Figure 1

The business, in addition to being defined by the business "owner," is shaped by factors present in the environment within which the business operates. These external factors include the actions of competitors, the tax structure, laws and regulations, and the technical aspects of the work environment. When the business model does not accommodate the reality of the exterior environment, whether in original design or by failure to adapt to changes in the exterior environment, the business suffers and may fail.

At the next level of the architectural framework is the functional level of work. This level consists of both an organization model and an information model. The work organization model reflects the structure and flow of the functional activities of a business (people, process, and procedure) and answers the question "How do we do it?" The associated information model answers the question "What do we call things?" Needless to say in a complex enterprise these models can be very, very complex.

The structure of work as a business model, a work model, and an information model has always existed. The introduction of the computer into the work environment caused a profound change.

In the computer-assisted enterprise, a new "application model" is inserted into the functional level (Figure 2). Some of the process and work rules of the business are now embedded in application software tailored for that business. This enabled the work model to be modified to take advantage of the power of the computer and, if desired, the benefits of linking to other computers in a distributed environment. (The modification to the work structure should not be thought of as simply the addition of a computer. Usually, many of the processes and procedures of the work, including the role and behavior of the people in the enterprise, change significantly with computerization.)

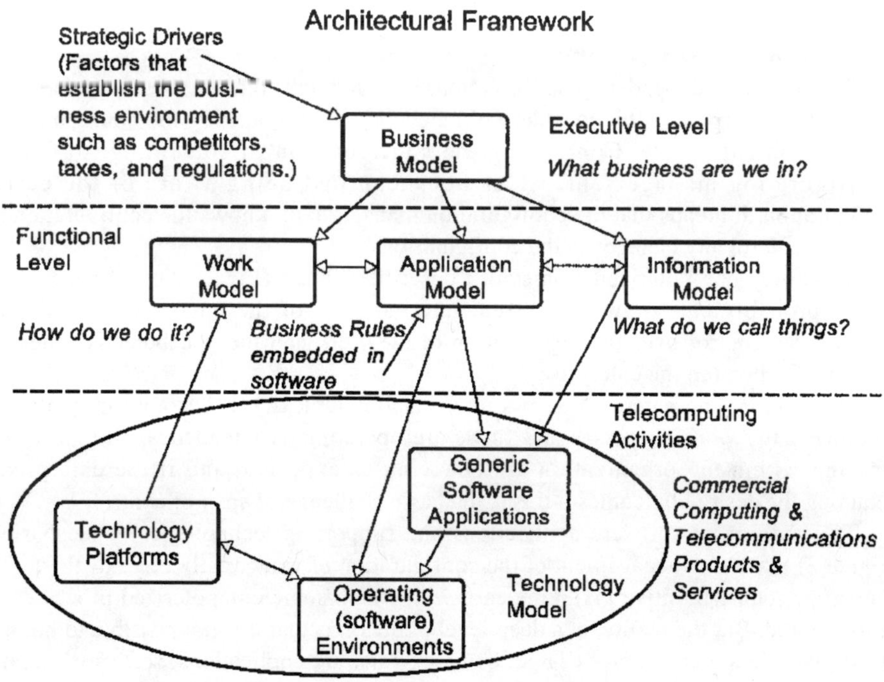

Figure 2

The introduction of the application model at the functional level requires the addition of a new lower level to the architectural framework: the technology model. The technology model is made up of the computer and communications hardware, the operating systems and related software, and any common-use software applications that are needed to support the higher level software application model. In almost all cases the components of the technology consist of commercial computing and telecommunications products and services.

The addition of the application model and the supporting technology model enabled profound improvements in the efficiency of work, but also introduced new vulnerabilities and risks. Because the technology in the telecomputing components is "generic," the knowledge of any defects in these components is widely shared. (This is to the advantage of the Hacker and Cyberwarrior. They only have to know what kind of computer and software an enterprise is using in order to exploit all that is commonly known about the flaws in the technical model of the particular enterprise.)

Further, once software applications and supporting computers were added to an enterprise the executive surrendered significant control over much of the enterprise. The behavior of many of the supporting information technologies are under the control of others. And the more distributed the telecomputing structure used, the greater the dependency on the decisions and actions of others.

Configuration Managment

This increased dependency on the actions of individuals outside the enterprise can be brought into sharp focus by considering the challenge of managing the configuration of work in the enterprise. Controlling the configuration of something, to conduct "configuration management," does not mean just being aware of the current configuration. It means that the configuration manager both knows the configuration and is able to control any changes to the configuration.

In the non-computerized framework described above (Figure 1), the executive in charge probably can know the current internal state of the business and will have considerable control over the organization of the work and the vocabulary of the work accomplished within the enterprise.

Of course, as an enterprise grows in size and complexity, it becomes more difficult to know if the work processes and flows are operating as intended, if the individuals laboring within the organization are behaving as expected, and if the enterprise is obtaining the desired outcomes—this is the basic challenge of span of control. [3]

The addition of software applications and supporting technologies to the business (Figure 2) make the management of the configuration of work vastly more difficult. This may seem counterintuitive given the ease with which some computerized processes can be monitored. But the reality, at a deep level of detail, is that it is not possible to know all of the possible logical states of large, complex software applications, software operating systems, or even the internal components of the computer hardware. (Software developers test for suitable operation in a desired state but have no means by which to know all the possible undesirable logical states that may exist and which an adversary—criminal or warrior—may know and exploit. [4])

When internetted, packet-routed telecommunications are included in the mix, the challenge of configuration management becomes even greater. In this situation neither the business executive nor military commander (or their staffs) has any way of knowing the moment-by-moment configuration of the external telecommunications infrastructure upon which the enterprise depends. [5]

The lack of configuration knowledge and configuration control in a distributed computing environment is amply demonstrated by the ease in which hackers and criminals routinely penetrate many commercial (and unclassified military) enterprises. Although the application of the computer and interconnected telecommunications to the conduct of work has fostered significant economic growth, it has also led to a global telecomputing environment without law and order, a state of technical complexity where few of the many electronic break-ins are detected and where data transiting the world-wide communication networks are often compromised, and to a dangerous circumstance where very sophisticated, user-friendly software tools for breaking into computers are freely available on the Internet.

A primary factor contributing to the ongoing criminal exploitation of information activities is the rate of change in computing and communications technology. Technology has far outstripped the development of security safeguards and the security awareness of the majority of users of the new technologies—and the gap continues to widen. (This widening gap applies as well to information warfare defense.)

Alternative Definitions of Information Warfare

The concepts of the design of work, and the dependency on information and information systems described above, lead directly to the following definition of Information Warfare: "The preparation for and use of physical or logic-based weapons to disrupt or destroy information or information systems in order to degrade or disrupt a function(s) that depend upon the information or information systems." This can be restated as an attack on work that is mounted through the information or information systems required for the performance of that work.

This definition focuses attention on the functions that depend upon information and information systems, not the supporting infrastructure. On the defensive side this enables one to identify the individual(s) that is responsible for the conduct of a function and thus to hold that individual(s) accountable for undertaking those actions necessary to ensure suitable performance of the function in an information-hostile environment. On the offensive side it tells the information warrior to turn his or her attention to the military or political value of disrupting or defeating a function that can be reached through its supporting information or information system.

Compare this with the current definition of information warfare being used in DoD: "Actions taken to achieve information superiority by affecting adversary information, information-based processes and information systems, while defending one's own information, information-based processes, and information systems. This definition focuses on achieving an unspecified level of "information superiority" over an adversary.

In order to define information superiority, the identity of the adversary must be known. Only if an adversary's use of information and the adversary's means to attack the information operations of foes are understood will it be possible to determine what mix of offensive and defensive actions have to be applied in order to achieve information superiority over that particular adversary. If an unknown attacker mounts an information warfare attack, these conditions cannot be known

The DoD definition has been heavily influenced by the concepts of command and control (C^2) warfare, a subset of information warfare. C^2 warfare is an American adaptation of a Russian-developed concept of warfare. The Russian theory postulated a C^2 war between commanders, supported by force. The American military has postulated the decisive application of force enabled by dominant battlefield knowledge.[6] Both pose conflict between opposing forces.

The fact that one party in a conflict depends upon efficient information activities invites an information warfare attack upon those activities by the opposition. The opposition, however, may not depend upon information-based processes and may not have any information systems that can be reached with an information warfare attack. (Achieving more efficient and effective information operations than a potential adversary is a sound goal; it just should not be labeled information warfare.)

The value of offensive information warfare attacks is determined by the value of information operations to the adversary. The value of defensive information warfare actions is determined by the degree of dependency that the defenders have on their own information operations, irrespective of how efficient those operations may be.

Offensive Information Warfare

By the first definition given above, an offensive information warfare attack would normally be targeted on disrupting a specific function(s) [a targeted attack]. Many assume that, because it is easy to break into a computer by exploiting known flaws in the technical model, then it follows that it is easy to conduct meaningful information warfare. This is not so. Knowing exactly what to attack and when to attack can be a very complex and a very intelligence-intensive process. Information warfare targeting requires an understanding of the adversary's function(s) to be held at risk:

- What is being done (business model)?
- How and when is it done (work and information models)?
- What computing and communications infrastructure, and supporting facilities, does the function(s) depend upon (technical model)?

The preparation for a significant information warfare attack requires the information warfare planner, in effect, to determine the "As-Is" model of the target function(s), in the jargon of business process reengineering. Through a combination of intelligence collection and process analysis the planner gains a degree of understanding of the steps in the work flow of the targeted function. This enables the planner to deduce what will happen to the work flow, and thus the function(s) of interest, when particular elements of the underlying information or information systems are subjected to various digital or physical forms of attack.

Developing a sound "As-Is" model in a cooperative business process reengineering environment is hard work. Attempting to develop an "As-Is" model of a foe's functions from afar by using the tools of the various intelligence crafts can be very difficult, particularly for those steps in the process that do not depend upon technological support, but only reside in the heads of the workers. Seldom are human-related processes and procedures neatly spelled out in the documentation of a supporting software application that can be easily downloaded from a target computer.

An easier approach is to obtain, by purchase, subversion or through deception, is the cooperation of an individual(s) who is working or has worked within the process of interest. This can have a very high payoff as an insider can explain the internal processes and procedures and even assist in the attack. [7]

Notwithstanding the thrust of the first definition given above, an offensive information warfare attack does not always have to target a specific function. An attack could be mounted to simply degrade the operation of various elements of the shared information infrastructure of the adversary without knowing how or if the attack will degrade a specific function(s) [an entropy attack]. [8]

However, carrying out broad entropy attacks is a bit like trying to catch a trophy bass by randomly dynamiting lakes. Lots of fish may be killed without any assurance of catching the specific, tagged fish needed to win the fishing contest. Often computer technologists propose digital attack techniques for use in the conduct of information warfare (for example, many forms of computer viruses) that are like trophy fishing with dynamite—the benefits cannot be predicted with any degree of certainty. Unlike mob violence, warfare applies or threatens to apply violence—physical or digital—in a focused manner to support the attainment of a defined military goal or political objective.

The Command and Control of Information Warfare

The need to achieve a useful military or political outcome leads to the consideration of the command and control aspects of offensive information warfare. Normally, before an individual in authority is willing to approve a military action, he or she wants to understand to some degree of precision the anticipated results of the proposed attack(s). The decision authority may want to know many things:

- Is the proposed action consistent with the laws of war and treaty obligations that the particular actor is interested in observing?
- Can the scope of the attack be controlled?
- If the enemy sues for peace, can the actions set in motion be stopped?
- Can the attack be countered?
- In some circumstances, can the attack be detected?
- Can the attack be attributed to the attacking party?
- If the attack depends upon surprise, what is the risk of compromise?
- What information dependencies does the attack itself have? (What has to be known? When does it have to be known? What confidence do you have that you will get the needed information?)
- How will damage assessment be done?

In short, can the purpose for attacking and the process of executing the attack be explained to the decision maker as a rational military action?

Means of Attack

Do not assume from the earlier discussion of the design of work and the increased risks associated with distributed computing that attacks on information operations (work model and technical model) are limited to "over-the-wire" digital techniques. Information warfare can be carried out by a variety of means to include:

• Physical attacks on the components of the information infrastructure, e.g., computers, communications devices, software, cables, control devices, etc.

• Physical attacks on the components containing or supporting the information infrastructure such as buildings, power systems, environmental services.

• Physical attacks on or the subversion of the people (witting or unwitting) who operate elements of the information infrastructure.

• Physical destruction of information (erasure or over-write) without harming the infrastructure components.

• Logic (malicious code) attacks on the components of the information infrastructure, e.g., computers, communications devices, software, control devices, etc.

• Logic attacks on computer-controlled components supporting the information infrastructure. These may include air conditioners, air handlers, power distribution, and cooling water.

• Attacks on information provided via the information infrastructure that is used by a specific function(s) (e.g., deception and false information introduced into the infrastructure).

• Corruption of information using logic or digital attacks without harming the components of information infrastructure. (The greatest harm may result from an attack which corrupts or injects false information in a manner that cannot be detected by the users of that information who subsequently take actions based on the corrupted or false information.)

• Combined attacks where both physical and logical attacks on the information infrastructure or supporting elements are undertaken in combination either to mask one or the other types of attack or to obtain the benefits of a combined attack.

Information Warfare Defense

The concepts sketched above apply also to the defensive side of information warfare. At a macro level, in order to defend against information warfare threats to a function(s), the work flow, processes and procedures, information, and information infrastructure used by the function(s) must be understood.

Unlike on the offensive side, the defender, by applying the process capture tools of business process reengineering, can directly gain an understanding of the functions and the dependency relationships. (With some foresight this analysis can be a very economical "two for the price of one" process. Ways to obtain greater functional efficiency can be discovered at the same time that information dependencies in the existing "As-Is" model are identified.)

The BPR-like analysis should enable the defender to: 1) know the information assurance dependencies of the functions for which he or she is responsible; 2) understand what happens to the work processes if the action of an adversary, act of nature, or error by a worker with authorized access to the enterprise's information and information systems disrupts some portion of the telecomputing environment; 3) design a means to monitor the enterprise's information and information systems for the detection of intrusions, containment of attacks, and restoration of service; and 4) know what to train for and practice in realistic exercises such that the workers in the enterprise can recognize a failure within the work process and are prepared to take appropriate remedial action.

These steps are easy to state. They may be very difficult to accomplish.

Defensive Actions

The questions of importance then are how to adjust the business and business model, how to design the processes and procedures used in the work flow model, how to apply technology, and how to train the work force in order to obtain the advantages, economic or military, of using a globally interconnected telecomputing infrastructure without succumbing to the risks endemic to the conduct of operations within this interconnected environment. A partial list of possible answers to these questions follows.

Enclaves

One approach to control the functional activities that have to be monitored, controlled, and defended is to create information enclaves within the global infrastructure and a means to safely communicate information between the enclaves of protected information users, when needed. Firewalls, when properly configured, can be used to create enclaves and provide some degree of isolation from potential adversaries.

Operating more secure—never absolutely secure—enclaves in the larger global infrastructure will be possible only if access to the enclaves can be controlled, including the behavior of the workers with authorized access to the enclave. If a desire for openness in government, a desire to obtain the lowest possible price in computational or communications services, or indifference to the activities of the workers in the enterprise result in unfettered access to the enclave by anyone in the global population, then a meaningful defense cannot be obtained at any price.

Of course, the easiest means to eliminate the risk associated with operating within the globally interconnected telecomputing infrastructure is to simply disconnect from it. If the business or military function does not depend upon the interconnection to the shared information infrastructure, then it probably should not be connected, as this just adds risk with no offsetting benefit.

Risk Analysis

If the execution of a function must depend upon using the shared information infrastructure, then the executive responsible for the function should plan to operate with some degree of risk. In this circumstance, informed risk-benefit analysis should underpin all proposed defensive actions. A factor to consider when making the risk-benefit calculation is that, while the benefits—economic or military—normally scale in a predictable manner, the risks can lead to very nonlinear outcomes. (When a proponent for the benefits to be gained from assuming or increasing functional dependency on shared telecomputing activities or distributed computing activities makes his or her case, always ask what is the worst thing that can happen to the work flow and business model as a result of the proposed action.)

Additional Considerations for the Defense

Now, the risk management situation is not totally bleak. Lots of smart things can be done for low cost to reduce risk at the computing and telecommunications levels.

By far the most cost-effective steps are to provide a sufficient number of well-trained staff and adequate monitoring equipment to administer the telecomputing environment within the operating enclave(s). As long as system administration is treated as a part-time job that can be assigned to untrained individuals, the ability to achieve any meaningful level of protection or capability to react to an attack is problematic.

Once the processes and procedures of the function are understood, a capability to monitor their configuration can be put in place. The monitoring activity should be external to the processes being monitored and be supported by a robust computing and communications capability. The defenders should be able to undertake triage activities to limit the spread of an attack and manage the restoration of operations without being dependent upon the very infrastructure they are defending (a key lesson from the Morris Internet incident).

A word of caution. Dependency on overly centralized defense activities is dangerous. The cost may be very low for an attacker to send a centralized defensive staff on an expensive wild goose chase. A layered approach to gaining configuration knowledge and control, with some process for aggregation of knowledge to detect patterns of activity not observable at lower levels, is the preferred approach to designing a defensive information warfare (or information security) management capability.

Those responsible for monitoring the state of the business and mounting the defense should be made aware of any perturbations to the physical plant housing the computing and communications elements they are charged to defend. Service outages from fire, cable cut or other physical damage that may be viewed locally as "accidents" may be recognized as an information warfare attack when viewed in aggregate.

Smart system design will position critical software and data on servers that are physically and logically separate from those used to house software and data that are useful but not essential to the survival of a business. Such separation will ease the process of repair and speed the restoration of essential processes. Maintenance of protected "clean" versions of software also can speed recovery.

Careful attention to the backup of data may be essential to recovery from an attack. Safe backup and archiving can be more difficult than many suspect. A long duration preparation phase for an information warfare attack may have reached the stored data or even have subverted the process used to perform data backup and archiving.

Information replication can assist the defender. (Replication means that it is possible to copy information without changing the original information. Replication is the feature of information that separates it from the world of physical artifacts. Replication is also the feature that allows the undetectable theft of information because, unlike physical assets, the information custodian may retain his copy of information, but so does the thief, and the custodian may not even know it.) By placing multiple copies of information on distributed servers, it may not be possible for an adversary to know which server is being used at any particular moment in time to support a function and thus, eliminate the adversary's ability to destroy the information with an attack on a single location.

The encryption of the information used by a function, in transit or in storage, is another technique that can be used to enhance the defense of the function. However, some means of encryption provide an easy path to an attacker who does not intend to read the enciphered information but simply wants to mount a denial of service attack. By attacking certain elements of a signal or an encryption system, the attacker may be able to prevent the intended user of the information from being able to decrypt and read the information [9].

Software and systems designers should be asked to design software and information systems that provide dynamic configuration awareness, enable configuration management, and ensure ease of repair. (Currently such features get little attention, and the design methods to achieve these objectives are not well understood.)

The manufacturers of telecomputing hardware and software could (and probably will) vastly improve the defensive circumstance if each device or software program was equipped to provide a secure digital signature to identify itself when queried by to the system administrator's management tools (I'm workstation serial number xxxx).

Likewise, biometric devices that uniquely, continuously, and passively identify each individual engaged in telecomputing activities within the enclave would go a long way toward eliminating the presence of intruders masquerading as legitimate participants in the functional activity.

Taken together these and other similar steps would greatly improve configuration knowledge, enhance the control of the telecomputing environment, eliminate many trivial (hacker class) attacks and enable a more robust defense. However, the use of distributed technology means these steps can never deliver a totally safe environment for information operations.

Likewise, as long as people are part of the functional process, then the state of human nature places an upper bound on the perfectibility of configuration knowledge and control. Thus, notwithstanding the benefits of technology sketched above, the recommended approach to achieving a robust information warfare defense is to focus on the design of resilient work.

Design for an Environment of Uncertainty

Rather than continuing to search for a technological silver bullet, or vainly attempt to achieve error-free human behavior, the very design of the function or business model should be modified to enable the business to function in an environment of risk. The first step is for the business-owner (or military commander) to accept the fact that any business that operates in an environment that includes the fast-paced introduction of technology cannot be completely protected. Sooner or later bad things will happen by accident or intent.

The business model should be adjusted to accommodate the inherent, unknowable vulnerabilities that accompany the beneficial use of telecomputing technologies. To that end, the work flow should be understood in sufficient detail such that it is possible to describe and measure acceptable bounds on the output of each intermediate process or procedure in the work flow, including the behavior of the workers in the enterprise. [10] (This design approach would enable the manager or commander to better address the insider threat. If a well designed and operated configuration management process had been in place, someone would have been obligated to ask: "Mr. Ames why are you getting data from that location as you don't need it for your job?")

When monitoring detects that the acceptable limits on intermediate work outputs are approached, automated work processes and the workers in the enterprise should "know" what alternative mode of work to switch into until corrective actions have made it possible to return to the preferred state. This ability to shift between processes to preclude failure is the essence of resilient work. If unable to quickly respond, the enterprise can succumb to a fatal, nonlinear failure. [11]

Again, the process of designing work itself so that its configuration can be monitored, the tools needed to aid in the management and control of work process, and the means to dynamically switch between work processes are not well understood.

Deterrence

The successful executive and military commander of the 21st century operating in an information warfare environment will understand what he or she can know about the enterprise for which he or she is responsible. He or she will also understand what cannot be known because of the technology used. With this knowledge the executive will be prepared to manage any unwanted change in the process of work—whether caused by systems failure, error, or attack. That executive will ensure a robust means to detect a change in the work environment before it becomes sufficiently large that it cannot be controlled and the enterprises fails. Obtaining this degree of understanding of the operational characteristics and the information dependencies of the enterprise is the greatest possible deterrence to a successful information warfare attack on the enterprise.

Endnotes

1 Joint Pub. 1, p. 57.

2 DoDD TS3600.1 is not limited to computer-based information activities. It defined "Information" as data or knowledge relevant to a particular circumstance or task and defined an "Information System" as the organized collection, processing, transmission, and dissemination of information, in accordance with defined procedures, *whether automated or manual. [Emphasis added]*

3 From a configuration management viewpoint the issue of span of control raises several interesting design questions. How does one design work so that its state can be known? How does one design control mechanisms such that, when unwanted changes in work processes and flows are detected, the work can be redirected to the desired state? If computers are used, how does one design a software application such that its operation ensures the desired outcome? To date, there is no general theory of design, at the level of work flow, to guide the creation of distributed functional activities such that total configuration management is possible. This is because, at some level of detail or degree of granularity, complex activities that involve the dynamic interaction of people, process and information are in a continual state of change. It is not possible nor would it be affordable to attempt to know every detail of every transaction. Thus, the granularity at which the state of work is to be monitored and the precision of the control measurements become important considerations in the design of configuration management mechanisms—and to the conduct of information warfare.

4 See Judith Hurwitz, "Testing the Untestable," *Computerworld Client/Server Journal*, February 1996

[5] Some enterprises mandate the use of specified fiber optic paths for communications so that they can maintain improved configuration knowledge and better control over sensitive communications. Such concerns are well founded as by 1993 packet theft had become endemic on the Internet. A primary target was the tuplet consisting of user address, user identity, and user password. Intruders used the identity and password that had been copied from the network to masquerade as legitimate computer users. Once the intruder gained entry into a computer he, or less commonly she, could apply other readily available software tools to read, steal, or destroy data, insert or change software, install a backdoor to facilitate subsequent reentry, eradicate any traces of the previous activities, or actually destroy the system. This is not a reason to abandon passwords: They still have use for controlling direct access to computer terminals. This form of password theft can be easily countered by using passwords only one time. However, the generation of one-time passwords requires the addition of a physical device or special software to the computers at some marginal cost. Until the use of one-time passwords, or some other solution that prevents the theft of user identities and the access privileges associated with those identities, is widely adopted, the globally shared communications networks will remain a path for hackers, criminals, saboteurs, terrorists, and cyber warriors to gain easy entry into interconnected computers. In addition to the theft of static passwords, other well known defects in the design of computer operating systems, routers, switches, and transmission protocols are exploited by cyber-intruders to gain unauthorized entry into computers. The reader interested in exploring some of these defects in the non-technical literature may want to look at *Computer Related Risks*, Peter G. Newmann, ACM Press, 1995; *Protection and Security on the Information Superhighway*, Frederick B. Cohen, Wiley, 1995; and, *Computers Under Attack*, edited by Peter J. Denning, ACM Press, 1990.
A current example of the widening gap between technology and security is industry's competitive rush to promulgate advanced network browsers that enable individuals to roam the World Wide Web and download information. The latest browsers enable end-users to download into their desktop computers information and small computer applications called "applets" that are tailored to manipulate the information. These applets are touted as the low cost solution to all kinds of distributed information operations including viewing graphics, conducting commercial transactions, and searching remote data bases. This new technology is being eagerly embraced by computer users who want the benefits promised but who do not have a clear understanding of the significant risks associated with downloading information and active software applications of unknown parentage into their local computing environment.

[6] Much has been made of the information warfare implications of Alvin Toffler's concept of Third Wave Warfare. Many have not grasped that the third economic wave co-exists with the first and second waves of economic civilization and associated means of warfare. It is quite permissible for a country that has a third wave economy to undergo an information warfare attack from a first or second wave civilization that may have rented some third wave information weapons. The third wave victim may chose to respond to this information warfare attack with the dagger of the first wave warrior or with the high-explosive weapons of second wave industrial warfare.

[7] Such "social engineering" is a preferred approach for both hackers and criminals who wish to subvert a business process. Although less straightforward, another approach used by criminals is to exploit the known flaws in the generic telecomputing technologies to gain entry to a firm's computer(s). They then find and download the firms' application software (and even the working notes of the software designers) so that they can spend time off-line studying and gaining an understanding (reverse engineer) of the work processes they intend to subvert.

[8] The 1988 Morris Worm incident on the Internet is an example of an indiscriminate attack. It caused a lot of temporary inconvenience, but Mr. Morris (who apparently just lost control of or did not adequately comprehend the potential reach of his "experiment") could not have ensured that a particular function was disrupted at a particular time to satisfy a specific warfare objective.

[9] A concern with commercial encryption, circa 1996, is the risk of unforeseen design flaws. Although the designers of some of the most widely used Internet browser programs are very creative, subsequent security failures showed that the encryption engines contained in some of these browsers were flawed. These recent real world demonstrations that skilled software designers

are not necessarily skilled crypto-mathematicians is fair warning of the risks of using unproved software products to protect critical functions. Further, some of the encryption applications used for protection of information in transit leave an unprotected plain-text copy of the information on the source or destination computer storage device where it can be obtained by intruding into the computer. Another risk is encountered when individuals download "free" encryption software from the Internet without any assurance that it has not been "doctored" for the benefit of someone interested in reading their supposedly secure communications. In another variant of encryption-facilitated attacks, the attacker replaces the encryption software on the target's computer system with doctored software which appears to operate normally but which produces "encrypted" messages that the attacker can read. Basically, *caveat emptor* applies to free goods from the Internet and to the software encryption of high value information.

[10] A simple example of the application of process knowledge to bound an outcome is people who learned to solve computational problems using slide rules. As a part of the process of learning to solve such problems, they had to learn to be able to estimate the outcome of their calculations with sufficient accuracy to be able to correctly place the decimal point. In other words, they understood the expected limits of the outcome of a computational process within an order of magnitude. Many of the people who learned to solve identical computational problems with digital calculators were not required to learn this estimating process. They enter numbers via a keypad and an answer with a correctly positioned decimal place was automatically displayed. Repeated experiments have shown that these people can be fooled if given a defective calculator because their model for solving computation problems does not include a process for estimating the limits of an acceptable solution.

[11] The theft of funds from Citibank required the subversion of the bank's software applications and money transfer processes. However, the bank contained the problem so that it did not go non-linear [Citibank Fraud Case Raises Computer Security Questions, *NYTimes*, Aug. 19, 1995]. In contrast, the subversion of internal audit processes by Nicholas Leeson led to a non-liner escalation of loss and the total failure of the 233-year-old Barings investment bank [New Areas in Finance, New Kinds of Crimes, *NYTimes News Service*, January 2, 1996].

Information Warfare

George J. Stein

We need to state up front that much of what is discussed in this essay on information warfare is unofficial speculation. There is no official, open-source U.S. government definition of information warfare. The Department of Defense calls its current thinking and approach to information warfare "command and control warfare" (C^2W).[1] There is little agreement among the services about either information warfare or C^2W; and among civilian defense analysts looking at the issues of information warfare, there is even less agreement. Why, then, should we be thinking about this new and strange idea? The chief reason, of course, is that while we don't know just what we've got here, all the services agree that information warfare is something important.[2] Was Desert Storm the first war of third-wave information warfare or the last war of mechanized second-wave industrial warfare?[3] We're not sure, but a lot of people, including potential rivals, are trying to figure it out.[4] This article attempts to make some sense of this new idea called information warfare. We'll look at four sets of ideas: (1) A definition of information warfare; (2) How we should start thinking about developing a strategy of information warfare; (3) Why current Air Force doctrine may be the best framework for developing a doctrine of information warfare; and (4) A very brief comment on the danger of failing to develop information warfare.

Defining Information Warfare

Information warfare, in its largest sense, is simply the use of information to achieve our national objectives. Like diplomacy, economic competition, or the use of military force, information in itself is a key aspect of national power and, more importantly, is becoming an increasingly vital national resource that supports diplomacy, economic competition, and the effective employment of military forces. Information warfare in this sense can be seen as societal-level or nation-to-nation conflict waged, in part, through the worldwide internetted and interconnected means of information and communication.[5] What this means is that information warfare, in its most fundamental sense, is the emerging "theater" in which future nation-against-nation conflict at the *strategic* level is most likely to occur. Information warfare is also changing the way theater or operational-level combat and everyday military activities are conducted. Finally, information warfare may be the theater in which "operations other than war" are conducted, especially as it may permit the United States to accomplish some important national security goals without the need for forward-deployed military forces in every corner of the planet. Information warfare, then, may define future warfare or, to put it another way, be the central focus for thinking about conflict in the future.

Information warfare, in its essence, is about *ideas and epistemology*—big words meaning that information warfare is about the way humans think and, more important, the way humans make decisions. And although information warfare would be waged largely, but not entirely, through the communication nets of a society or its military, it is fundamentally not about satellites, wires, and computers. It is about influencing human beings and the decisions they make. The greatest single threat faced by the Air Force—and by the services in general, as we begin to think about information warfare—is that we will yield to our usual temptation to adopt the new technologies, especially information technologies, as merely force multipliers for the current way we do business.[6] It would be a strategic mistake of historical proportions to focus narrowly on the technologies; force the technologies of information warfare to fit familiar, internally defined models like speed, precision, and lethality; and miss the vision and opportunity for a genuine military revolution. Information warfare is real warfare; it is about using information to create such a mismatch between us and an opponent that, as Sun Tzu would argue, the opponent's *strategy* is defeated before his first forces can be deployed or his first shots fired.

The target of information warfare, then, is the human mind, especially those minds that make the key decisions of war or peace and, from the military perspective, those minds that make the key decisions on if, when, and how to employ the assets and capabilities embedded in their strategic structures. One could argue that certain aspects of the cold war such as Radio Free Europe, Radio Martí, or the US Information Agency were a dress rehearsal for information warfare. One could argue that certain current capabilities in psychological operations (PSYOP), public affairs and civil affairs, together with the intelligence agencies, satellite drivers, communications specialists, computer wizards, and the men and women in agencies like the Air Intelligence Agency or the new Joint Information Warfare Center, represent some of the key learning environments in which we'll develop some of the new capabilities for information warfare.[7] And while the concept of information warfare in its computer, electronic warfare, and communications net version is most familiar in military operations involving traditional state-to-state conflict, there are new and dangerous players in "cyberspace"—the battlefield for information warfare. There has been a proliferation of such players- nonstate political actors such as Greenpeace, Amnesty International, rogue computer hackers like the Legion of Doom, some third world "rebel" who stages a "human rights abuse" for the Cable News Network (CNN), or ideological/religious inspired terrorists with easy access to worldwide computer and communications networks to influence, to exchange information, or to coordinate political action on a global basis. All of this suggests that the military or governments of a traditional nation-state may not be the only serious threat to our security or the driver of our national security politics.[8] Cyberspace may be the new "battlespace," but the battle remains the battle for the mind. There must be no confusion of the battlespace with the battle.

Let's take a look at this in a context we think we're familiar with: propaganda as an effort to influence national morale and support for the nation's armed forces. The Vietnam War taught us the consequences of winning every battle in the field and losing the information war on the home front. Before the advent of information warfare, propaganda was traditionally targeted through various mass media to influence a mass audience. One key change made possible by the new technologies is the potential for customized propaganda. Those who have received individually targeted political advertising from a company specializing in "niche" marketing research must have had a momentary shudder when they realized that there are private companies who seem to know everything about their buying habits and tastes, whether they support the National Rifle Association or attend Tailhook conventions, and what television shows they watch. Every credit card purchase adds data to someone's resources, and not everybody is selling just soap or politicians. Contemporary public and commercial databases and the constantly expanding number of sources, media, and channels for the transmission of information, essentially available to anyone with a bit of money or skill, have created the opportunity and "target sets" for custom-tailored information warfare attacks on, to take just one example, the families of deployed military personnel. Think about the morale implications of that for a minute. Computer bulletin boards, cellular telephones, video cameras, and fax machines-all of these provide entry points and dissemination nets for customized propaganda assaults by our opponents on military, governmental, economic, key civilian strategic structures, or even the home checking accounts of deployed troops.[9] Operations security (OPSEC) is increasingly a most vital military security issue. However, information warfare should not be confused with or limited to just propaganda, deception, or traditional electronic warfare.

A major new factor in information war is the worldwide infosphere of television and broadcast news. Information warfare at the strategic level is the "battle off the battlefield" to shape the political context of the conflict. It will define the new "battlespace." We face an "integrated battlefield," not in the usual sense of having a global positioning system (GPS) receiver in every tank or cockpit but in the Clausewitzian sense that war is being integrated into the political almost simultaneously with the battle. Many people suspect that the national command authorities (NCA) are in danger of becoming increasingly "reactive" to a "fictive" universe created by CNN, its various international competitors, or even a terrorist with a video camera.[10] This media-created universe we live in is fictive rather than "fictional" because although what we see on CNN is "true," it is just not the whole, relevant, or contextual truth. Nevertheless, this fictive universe becomes the politically relevant universe in which the government or the armed forces are supposed to "do something." Members of Congress, the national command authorities, and our mothers all watch the "instant news" followed by "instant" second-guessing commentary. This is increasingly the commander's nightmare. First, 15 congressmen are calling the chairman of the Joint Chiefs to ask whether retired admiral so-and-so's critical analysis on "Nightline" of the CINC's ongoing theater air campaign is valid. More importantly, 300 congressmen are also getting 10,000 calls, E-mails, faxes, and even letters from angry families who've just seen the television report (carefully "leaked" to French television by an unhappy defense contractor and innocently repeated by CNN) that the U.S. military-issue antimalaria pills don't work in Bongo-Bongo. All this without the real "bad guys" trying their hand at information war. Use your imagination. Somalia gets in the news, and we get into Somalia despite the reality of equally disastrous starvation, disorder, and rapine right next door in Sudan. The truth is that there were no reporters with "skylink" in Sudan because the government of Sudan issued no visas to CNN reporters. We all know the impact of the pictures of the failed raid to capture Mohamed Farah Aidid in Somalia. The potential, then, for governments, militaries, parties in a civil war such as Bosnia, or even religious fanatics to manipulate the multimedia, multisource fictive universe of "the battle off the battlefield" for strategic information dominance should be obvious.[11] The armed services are just beginning to think about how these new technologies of instant communication will change the battlespace, and, quite frankly, there are not many good answers yet.

Fictive or fictional operational environments, then, whether mass-targeted or niche-targeted, can be generated, transmitted, distributed, or broadcast by governments or all sorts of players through increasingly diversified networks. The information war potential available to states or other players with access to the universe of internetted communications to use the networks over which banking information is transmitted to suggest that a "hostile" state is about to devalue its currency could easily provoke financial chaos.[12] Direct satellite radio or television broadcasts to selected audiences, analogous to central control of pay-per-view programs, again offers the potential for people in one province or region of a targeted state to discover that the maximum leader has decided to purge soldiers from their clan or tribe from the army. Your own imagination can provide many examples of how the increasingly multisource communications systems offer both the armed forces and the national command authorities countless new possibilities for societal-level information warfare to shape the information battlespace to our advantage.

Let us take just one example of how current technologies could be used for strategic-level information warfare. If, say, the capabilities of already well-known Hollywood technologies to simulate reality were added to our arsenal, a genuinely revolutionary new form of warfare would become possible. Today, the techniques of combining live actors with computer-generated video graphics can easily create a "virtual" news conference, summit meeting, or perhaps even a battle that would exist in "effect" though not in physical fact. Stored video images can be recombined or "morphed" endlessly to produce any effect chosen. This moves well beyond traditional military deception, and now, perhaps, "pictures" will be worth a thousand tanks. Imagine the effect of a nationwide broadcast in banditland of the meeting between the "digitized" maximum leader and a "digitized" Jimmy Carter in which all loyal soldiers are told to cease fighting and return to their homes. The targets of information warfare, remember, are the decisions in the opponent's mind, and the battlespace of the human mind is also the zone of illusion.

Let's play with this a bit. Through hitching a ride on an unsuspecting commercial satellite, a fictive simulation is broadcast. This may not be science fiction, and readers of Tom Clancy's latest novel *Debt of Honor* will suspect it's not. Simultaneously, various "info-niches" in the target state are accessed via the net. Some of the targets receive reinforcement for the fictive simulation; others receive slightly misleading variations of the target state's anticipated responses, and the whole of the opponent's military is subject to a massive electronic deception operation. What is happening here?

At the strategic level, this is the paralysis of the adversary's observation, orientation, decision, action (OODA) loop.[13] The opponent's ability to "observe" is either flooded or very slightly and subtly assaulted by contradictory information and data. More importantly, his ability to "orient" is degraded by the assault on the very possibility of objective reasoning as we replace his "known" universe with our alternative reality. His "decisions" respond increasingly to our fictive or virtual universe, and, most importantly, military "actions" within his strategic structures become increasingly paralyzed as there is no rational relationship of means to ends. What he does is not based on reality because we've changed his reality. This is real war fighting. It would seem, then, that if we can develop a strategic vision and real capability for information warfare, we can bring American strategic power within sight of that elusive "acme of skill" wherein the opponent is subdued without killing as we destroy his ability to form or execute a coherent strategy. How, then, do we think about developing information warfare strategy?

Developing Information Warfare Strategy

Developing a strategy of information warfare starts with serious, creative, and "color-outside-the-lines" thinking about current information technologies and ways in which these might be turned to strategic purpose to serve the national command authorities and military use. This will involve thinking about information in new ways: What information is needed? What organizational changes would occur in the way we gather, process, distribute, and use information? What information-based operational changes could then happen?[14] The services are starting this new thinking under the label "command and control warfare."[15] This, however, is only the first step, as the "digitized battlefield" fails to revolutionize strategic thinking. Let's illustrate this with a bit of history. As Speaker of the House Newt Gingrich observed, some time before the American Civil War, the Prussian general Helmuth von Moltke was thinking about railroads and telegraphs:

> *If we used the telegraph to relay mobilization orders quickly and then used railroads to concentrate troops from bases scattered throughout Prussia, we could concentrate the main effort at the key battle location of a campaign. We wouldn't have to mobilize the army, then concentrate it, then march it to where we hoped the key battle would occur.*[16]

Good insight. And this, unfortunately, is about where we are when we think of information warfare as only command and control warfare.[17] That is, how does this technology permit tanks, ships, and aircraft to do what they do now a bit better. It was Moltke's next insight, argues Speaker Gingrich, that the Joint Staff and the services need to imitate:

> *But the Prussian army is not organized, nor does it operate in a way that would permit it to respond to telegraphed orders to get on trains and show up somewhere else. That's not how we organize, train, and equip. What I need to do is reform the way to get the information needed to do this, the way we're organized so we can use this information, and figure-out new ways to operate; what I need is a new General Staff system.*[18]

Count von Moltke realized that before he could make revolutionary use of the new technology, he had to solve the higher-order question of what changes in information, organization, and operations would be needed. This is the challenge we face now. The armed forces have a good idea that information technologies just might be the driver in future warfare, but we haven't yet articulated the strategic vision or identified the higher-order changes we need to make to really make this all come together.

Now, let's add another idea—this time from the Air Force heritage. In some ways, "info-warriors" are like Gen William ("Billy") Mitchell and the pioneer league of airmen. They see the potential. Mitchell's vision of the potential for airpower drove, at great cost to himself but great benefit to the nation, the development of a new form of warfare. Now here's the key point. Once the vision of strategic airpower was presented clearly, once people were able to say,"Yes, I see how this could change warfare," then the technologies followed:"Oh, air bombing—you'll need a bombsight." "Oh, enemy aircraft—we'll need some kind of detection system; let's call it radar." This is the point—the technology is not just a force multiplier. It is the interaction of strategic vision with new technology that will produce the revolution in military affairs and a new warfare form.

This, then, is the challenge of information warfare. Is there something about information and the information technologies that would permit us to create such a mismatch between what, when, and how we and our opponents observe, orient, decide, and act or such a level of "information dominance" that the opponent is helpless—and not just on the battlefield? Is there a way we could use information, like current theories of airpower, to create an"information campaign" that engages an opponent simultaneously in time, space, and depth across the full range of his strategic structures so that the result is strategic paralysis (he is deaf, dumb, and blind to anything except that which we permit him to hear, say, or see)?[19] Not that we just blind him, but that he sees what we wish him to see without realizing that it's "our" reality, not his. Can we envision that kind of strategic information warfare? And, as was the case with airpower, technology will follow strategic vision. It's OK if we can't insert computer viruses by direct satellite broadcast—today; fry every air defense radar with an electromagnetic burst from a remote unmanned aerial vehicle (UAV)—today; transfer all the dictator's Swiss bank accounts to the internal revenue service (IRS)—today; project holographic images, complete with proper electronic signatures, of 15 squadrons coming in from the north when we're coming in the back door-today; or beam the Forrest Gump interview with "El Supremo" into every radio and television in banditland—today. Develop the strategic theory of information warfare, and the technology will come.

Information Warfare Doctrine

There is, of course, no official information warfare doctrine and the efforts of the various services to describe command and control warfare as the military application of information warfare remain incomplete. For the Air Force to focus almost exclusively on C^2W that is defined as the "integration, coordination, deconfliction, and synchronization" of OPSEC, deception, PSYOP, electronic warfare, and physical destruction efforts targeted against the opponent's fielded military forces, represents a failure to appreciate either air and space power or to appreciate how airpower doctrine could guide the development of an information warfare campaign. How, then, might we use current Air Force doctrine as presented in Air Force Manual (AFM) 1-1, *Basic Aerospace Doctrine of the United States Air Force*, as a template to start thinking about information warfare?

First, assume that information warfare is warfare in the information realm as is air warfare in the air and space realms. As the objective of air warfare is to control the air realm in order to exploit it while protecting friendly forces from enemy actions in the air realm, so the objective of information warfare is to control the "infosphere" in order to exploit it while protecting friendly forces from hostile actions taken via the information realm. Thus, as air control is usually described as counterair, with offensive and defensive counterair, so any strategy and doctrine of information control must address counterinformation in terms of offensive and defensive counterinformation. Offensive counterinformation, like offensive counterair, could be seen as involving information exploitation through psychological operations, deception, electronic warfare, or physical attack and information protection as, again, physical attack, electronic warfare (EW), and, often overlooked, public and civil affairs. Defensive counterinformation, like defensive counterair, would include active protection such as physical defense, OPSEC, communications security, computer security, counterintelligence, and, again, public affairs. Passive protection would include standard ideas like hardening sites and physical security.

If control, or dominance, of the information realm is the goal, like air control, it is not an end in itself but the condition to permit the exploitation of information dominance for, as in air doctrine, strategic attack, interdiction, or close "battlefield" support through C²W attack. Information dominance of both the strategic "battle off the battlefield" and the operational "information battlespace" is, like air and space control for traditional surface warfare, the key to strategic effect. The relevance of airpower doctrinal thinking for information warfare now becomes obvious. A review of the history of the airpower debates would show, in part, that those who insisted that airplanes were merely a force multiplier to provide close air support for the "real" effort would never recognize the strategic potential of airpower or support the acquisition of technologies for strategic air missions. As long as information warfare thinking is dominated by a doctrine that argues that the only information warfare mission relevant to the armed forces is command and control warfare and that C²W is merely a force multiplier against the communications and information assets of the fielded enemy forces, the potential for the exploitation of information dominance for strategic information warfare and, again, the identification and acquisition of key technologies will be missed. C²W, like close air support, is a vital military mission. It is, in fact, a central component of information warfare, but, like close air support and other "traditional" battle-oriented missions, not the whole story. The challenge is to use Air Force doctrine as the foundation to envision the "Information Campaign," which, like the "Air Campaign" in the Gulf War, is of strategic significance. What, for example, would "speed, precision, and lethality" be in an "info-strike?"

Epilogue: Danger of Not Developing Information Warfare Strategy

If the world really is moving into a third-wave, information-based era, failure to develop a strategy for both defensive and offensive information warfare could put the United States and the US military into the situation of being on the receiving end of an "Electronic Pearl Harbor."[20] Information is fluid; the advantages we now have, and which were demonstrated in the Gulf War, could be lost because we have very little control over the diffusion of information technology.[21] Second, it's a smaller world, and our potential opponents can observe our technologies and operational innovations and copy ours without them having to invent new ones for themselves.[22] Remember, the biggest center for developing new computer software is not Silicon Valley but Madras, India. What will they sell to whom? Finally, and to return to an earlier point, if the U.S. military approaches information warfare merely as a force multiplier and adapts bits and pieces of technology to just do our current way of warfare a bit better-if we "digitize the battlefield" for an endless rerun of mechanized desert warfare-the real danger will be that someone else will refuse to play the game our way. What if they, like Count von Moltke or General Mitchell, think real hard, purchase the dual-use technologies on the free world market, alter their whole strategic concept, and make the leap to a strategy of information warfare?

We do not yet have a strategy of information warfare, and we have not answered the higher-order questions of how we would reorganize, retrain, and reequip for third-wave warfare. But if any of this has made even some sense, you now know the urgent requirement for developing the vision that produces the strategy. The strategy will identify the technologies, organizational changes, and new concepts of operations. We must really become like von Moltke and Billy Mitchell—"If we could use this to do that, then we could...."

Endnotes

[1] Joint Chiefs of Staff, Memorandum of Policy 30, subject: Command and Control Warfare, 8 March 1993.

[2] Gen. Gordan R. Sullivan and Col. James M. Dubik, "War in the Information Age," *Military Review* 74 (April 1994): 46-62.

[3] Alan D. Campen, ed., *The First Information War: The Story of Communications, Computers and Intelligence Systems* (Fairfax, Va.: AFCEA International Press, 1992).

[4] Mary C. Fitzgerald, "Russian Views on Information Warfare," *Army* 44, no. 5 (May 1994): 57-59.

[5] John Arquilla and David Ronfeldt, "Cyberwar is Coming!" *Comparative Strategy* 12 (April-June, 1993): 141-65.

[6] Carl H. Builder, *The Icarus Syndrome: The Role of Air Power Theory in the Evolution and State of the U.S. Air Force* , (New Brunswick, N.J.: Transaction Publishers, 1994).

[7] "Information Dominance Edges toward New Conflict Frontier," *Signal* 48 (August, 1994): 37-39.

[8] Winn Schwartau, *Information Warfare: Chaos on the Electronic Superhighway* (New York: Thunder's Mouth Press, 1994).

[9] Peter Black, "Soft Kill: Fighting Infrastructure Wars in the 21st Century," *Wired*, July-August 1993; 49-50.

[10] Douglas V. Johnson, *The Impact of the Media on National Security Decision Making* (Carlisle Barracks, Pa.: Strategic Studies Institute, US Army War College, 1994).

[11] John Arquilla, "The Strategic Implications of Information Dominance," *Strategic Review* 22, no. 3 (Summer 1994): 24-30.
[12] H. D. Arnold et al., "Targeting Financial Systems as Centers of Gravity: `Low Intensity' to `No Intensity' Conflict," *Defense Analysis* 10 (August 1994): 181-208.
[13] John R. Boyd, "A Discourse on Winning and Losing," 1987. Unpublished set of briefing slides available at Air University Library, Maxwell AFB, Alabama.
[14] Maj. George E. Orr, *Combat Operations C3I: Fundamentals and Interactions* (Maxwell AFB, Ala.: Air University Press, 1983); and Frank M. Snyder, *Command and Control: The Literature and Commentaries* (Washington, D.C.: National Defense University Press, 1993).
[15] Lt. Col. Norman B. Hutcherson, *Command and Control Warfare: Putting Another Tool in the War-fighter's Data Base* (Maxwell AFB, Ala.: Air University Press, September 1994).
[16] Newt Gingrich, "Information Warfare: Definition, Doctrine and Direction," address to the National Defense University, Washington, D.C., 3 May 1994.
[17] Joint Publication 3-13, "Joint Command and Control Warfare (C^2W) Operations," second draft (Joint Chiefs of Staff, Washington, D.C., 15 January 1994).
[18] Gingrich address.
[19] John A. Warden III, *The Air Campaign: Planning for Combat* (Washington, D.C.: National Defense University Press, 1988).
[20] Alvin and Heidi Toffler, *War and Anti-War: Survival at the Dawn of the 21st Century* (Boston, Mass.: Little, Brown and Co., 1993).
[21] V.K. Nair, *War in the Gulf: Lessons for the Third World* (New Delhi, India: Lancer International, 1991), see especially chap. 4, "Role of Electronics in the Gulf War," and chap. 5, "Desert Storm: Air Power and Modern War."
[22] Jean Pichot-Duclos, "Toward a French `Economic Intelligence' Model," Defense Nationale, January 1994, 73-85 in *Federal Broadcast Information Service*: West Europe, 25 January 1994, 26-31.

This article originally appeared in the Spring 1995 issue of *Airpower Journal.*

Strategic Information Warfare and Comprehensive Situational Awareness

Daniel T. Kuehl

Two terms that have coming into increasingly widespread use within the Defense community in recent months are "dominant battlefield awareness" and "system of systems." Both owe their origins primarily to the work of Admiral William A. Owens, the former Vice Chairman of the Joint Chiefs of Staff and one of the leading proponents of the need for fundamental structural change in the Department of Defense.[1] Both concepts are being driven in part by the emerging and evolving "Revolution in Military Affairs" (RMA), of which Operation Desert Storm was the harbinger.[2] This, in turn, is being driven by the ongoing revolution in information technologies that has brought about the current interest and debate over Information Warfare as another environment in which future military, economic, social and political systems will contend.[3]

Admiral Owens has stated that Dominant Battlespace Awareness (DBA) "involves everything from automated target recognition to knowledge of an opponent's operational scheme and the networks relied on to pursue that scheme."[4] The question immediately raised is whether this perspective is too narrow. The term *battlespace* is a significant improvement over the original term *battlefield,* which was far too narrowly focused on a tactical, terrestrial, geographic space such as 200 by 200 nautical miles, roughly equivalent to the Kuwait Theater of Operations during the Persian Gulf War. Initial discussions of DBA (or the closely related concept Dominant Battlespace Knowledge [DBK],[5] in fact, focused on "the locations of emitters, armor concentrations [and] field headquarters." While these are certainly important to the theater commander, they hardly satisfy the needs of the political leadership. Even *battlespace* is tied too closely to events and problems at the tactical level.

This paper emphasizes, instead, the need for comprehensive situational awareness,[6] defined as *having sufficient information about an adversary's national-level political, economic, military and social systems to successfully operate against those systems and accomplish strategic political and military objectives; the means used may include diplomatic and economic actions, as well as destructive or non-lethal military operations.* This definition *certainly* includes information on where such typical military assets as "emitters, armor concentrations, field headquarters" and the like are located. But it will also include possessing knowledge and comprehension (i.e."situational awareness") of strategic centers-of-gravity such as the critical nodes in the enemy's national infrastructure; how their political and other vital systems function; whether these systems possess exploitable vulnerabilities; how their informational and financial networks function, etc.

Although comprehensive situational awareness is not the same as information dominance, it is critical to attaining such an advantage. I use "information dominance" in the same sense that one would use the traditional terms "air supremacy" or "command of the seas", i.e., having such a marked degree of superiority in the medium of conflict that we can use it virtually at will for our own purposes, while denying its use to the enemy. This paper is based on the premise that attaining "information dominance" over a future enemy will provide us with a degree of military (and political, economic and even social) advantage analogous to that provided by aerial and maritime supremacy.

At the strategic level, informational needs and military capabilities extend far deeper than a paradigm focused on traditional battlefield-level assets and functions. Considerations such as the locations of emitters, armor concentrations and field headquarters constitute a paradigm that is constructed too narrowly. Such an approach would drive us to a tactical-level perspective focused on that location where military forces physically meet and struggle for battlefield "victory" in the traditional sense. This means that the "victor" retains possession of the field of contest and the "loser's" forces must flee the field of battle and suffer the preponderance of casualties, etc.

Such a paradigm would constrict Information Warfare (IW) into a smaller and even less-than-optimum version of its smaller construct, Command-and-Control Warfare (C^2W). C^2W, originally defined in 1993 in JCS Memorandum of Policy (MOP) 30, has five essential elements, sometimes called the "five pillars:" deception, operational security (OPSEC), electronic warfare (EW), psychological operations (PSYOP), and physical destruction. C^2W is the strategy that implements the military elements of IW.

Information Warfare will, almost by its nature, be conducted at the strategic level. It will take advantage of American technological capabilities that become increasingly pronounced and provide commensurately greater leverage at that level of warfare, while simultaneously requiring that we deny our adversary the opportunity to act against one of our strategic vulnerabilities; namely our growing dependence on the transmission of critical information (economic, military, etc.) digitally over electronic networks. If we stay with the paradigm suggested by "battlespace," we will merely make marginal improvements in our tactical capability to conduct "second wave warfare," as the Tofflers would term it.[7] These improvements will have progressively less influence as we move up the scale of warfare from tactical, through the theater/operational level, to true strategic operations. If we possess the degree of comprehensive situational awareness postulated as the basis of this paper, we should strive to operate at the strategic level of warfare, for it is at this level that our operations can have the greatest opportunity to directly influence the enemy leadership.

By focusing at the strategic level of war, however, we are immediately forced to answer several basic questions: what national security objectives (political, economic, social and military) are we trying to accomplish? What military objectives will support attaining these overriding national security objectives? What elements of our adversary's "system of systems" offer the greatest vulnerability, and how can we exploit that vulnerability?

The military does not dictate the security objectives in a conflict, but in most cases the military does informally influence the shaping of those objectives. Current and evolving information technologies provide vastly improved command-and-control capabilities, which of course have both advantages and disadvantages. A key advantage is the ability of senior political and military leaders to track the development of a situation and assess the impact and effectiveness of our operations on a real-time basis. This will enable us to make decisions based on current and accurate information and to disseminate those decisions to all necessary levels of command quickly and confidently. The main disadvantage is that the interagency nature of information warfare will involve an increasing number of actors, with the accompanying potential for slowing down or otherwise affecting the decision-making process. For those so inclined to view senior level involvement in the operational process as a nightmare, the image of what LBJ could have done with a laptop personal computer linked into all the databases is sobering.

If the Gulf War is a paradigm, the military will be given significant latitude in determining the military objectives that are the fundamental factors in selecting the targets and target sets we wish to influence or negate. Is there a paradigm we can use for establishing what these target sets should be?

John A. Warden has suggested that a useful way to think about this problem is to envision the enemy state as a series of rings or shells that contain or consist of different elements of the state and society: his well-known "Five Strategic Rings."[8] The enemy leadership will almost always be at the *center* of this paradigm, for in the Clausewitzian concept of state-vs-state warfare, the leadership controls the state's actions; and it is thus the leadership that we must influence.[9] This holds true even if the adversary is not a state in the international sense of the term, for any significant actor (whether military, political, economic, or even criminal) will have some form of leadership function. At the *outermost* ring or shell are the nation's fielded military forces. "Second-wave warfare" would make this an intermediate objective of the highest priority,[10] for in the age of mass production/destruction warfare one could not "get at" the opposing leadership without first breaking down the nation's military line of defense. This century's two world wars were perhaps the ultimate paradigm of this mode of warfare. The implied promise of "third-wave warfare" is that it will enable us to bypass, penetrate, or otherwise overcome all or most of these forces to strike or directly influence the leadership and the other intervening rings: the state's infrastructure, populace, and industrial base.[11] All of these can be the focus of strategic information warfare. Some of these fall within the construct of the Joint Staff's paradigm of C^2W as contained in Memorandum of Policy (MOP) 30, but others lay outside of its relatively narrow parameters that concentrate on the *military* application of information warfare against traditional targets, the opposing military forces.

Viewing the enemy state as a "system of systems" provides insights into the relationships and synergy between the state's different elements or components. Instead of a reductionist approach that breaks the system apart and views it through increasingly narrow and isolated lenses, the holistic approach aggregates the disparate parts of the system to see how they build upon and influence each other. This approach, Warden argues, is useful whether the system is a state, a living organism, an organization, or an infrastructure network.

The attached list of hypothetical targets for strategic information warfare is drawn from a variety of sources, most of them surprisingly traditional. Indeed, a review of targeting during the Gulf War air campaign clearly indicates the types of assets and

John Warden's Concepts: Rings and Systems
(Source: "The Enemy as a System", Airpower Journal, Spring 1995

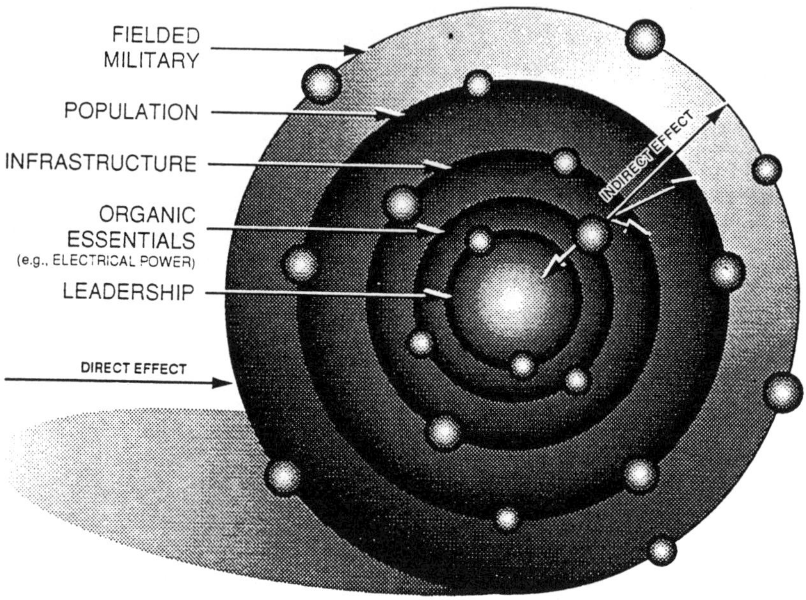

	Body	State	Drug.Cartel	Electric Grid
Leadership	Brain • eyes • nerves	Government • communication • security	Leader • communication • security	Central control
Organic Essentials	Food and oxygen (conversion via vital orgrans)	Energy (electricity, oil, food) and money	Coca source plus conversion	Input (heat, hydro) and output (electricity)
Infra-structure	Vessels, bones, muscles	Roads, airfields, factories	Roads, airways, sea lanes	Transmission lines
Population	Cells	People	Growers, distributors, processors	Workers
Fighting Mechanism	Leukocytes	Military, police, firemen	Street soldiers	Repairmen

Figure 1. Warden's Rings and Systems Concept

capabilities that might be included in any sort of strategic warfare. Almost any discussion of strategic air operations, for example, will include many of these target sets as traditional, indeed commonsensical, strategic bombing and aerial attack.[12]
A great deal of conceptual thinking about the application of strategic airpower against vital national centers-of-gravity has been done at the Air University since the Gulf War, much of which is directly applicable to the postulated employment of strategic information warfare against the very same elements.[13] The initial draft of the Air Force's effort to develop doctrine for IW addresses the issue of strategic attack in the information "realm" within the context of Warden's five strategic rings, and makes fractionalizing the coherence of national centers of power as the basic objective of such attacks. Facilities such as microwave towers or telecommunications facilities (both of which were key target categories attacked during the Gulf War air campaign) are cited as examples of critical national information systems.[14]

The need to conduct information warfare at the strategic level is as obvious to other countries as well. The Chinese, for example, note that the "main purpose of information warfare is to weaken the enemy's command ability...which includes command of the state."[15] Russian publications also speak of the need to disrupt "all important and vital national systems [such as] civilian and military control, communications, energy, transport, etc."[16] Studies by the DoD's Infrastructure Policy Directorate highlight the obvious fact that modern nations are extraordinarily complex systems of networks that depend on the synergistic interplay of their various components to function effectively.[17] The increasing dependence of these networks on "supervisory control and data acquisition" (SCADA) systems interlinked by digitized and computerized information transmission systems in telematic networks[18] introduces a potential vulnerability into the nation and creates a new strategic center-of-gravity.[19]

Although a variety of means will be available to act against these targets sets, two key factors seem most important. For those targets or capabilities which we determine must be physically destroyed, precision destruction will be required in almost all cases. The Gulf War clearly highlighted the need for precision intelligence in an era of precision weaponry.[20] If we have "comprehensive situational awareness" we thus have precision intelligence and will need weaponry or devices that can exploit it. Other targets or capabilities may be more vulnerable to a soft-kill mechanism, such as a computer virus that disables the enemy's computerized national telephone switching system, an intrusive IW attack that wipes out the enemy's computerized logistics inventory database, or even an electromagnetic pulse to disrupt electronic systems on a widespread basis.[21]

Comprehensive situational awareness will be required not only to locate the target and establish targeting parameters, but also to gauge the effectiveness of an attack and determine its impact on the enemy. The synergistic effect of this blend of advanced capabilities will enable us to operate well inside of the enemy's "OODA Loop" (observe-orient-decide-act) at all levels of conflict, tactical through strategic, and render them incapable of responding effectively and intelligently to our operations. It also requires, however, a depth of understanding of the enemy that extends well beyond the level of most of our current intelligence systems and personnel. Waging information warfare to the fullest extent will require the development of improved methods of performing "battle damage assessment" using innovative measures of effectiveness for significantly different types of operations that might employ radically new types of technologies.

It will be equally vital to protect ourselves from enemy attempts to interfere with our own "rings." Comprehensive situational awareness will be necessary to detect such efforts and either deter or defeat them. This is critical to "our way of war", which has become increasingly dependent on electronic linkages for information transmission and effective command-and-control. Electronic links and networks not only provide efficiency; they also can provide vulnerabilities to enemy penetration and exploitation. What could be termed "information interdiction" is a viable concept that could provide decisive leverage at all levels of future conflicts. Although the concept of the "information superhighway" has conceptual flaws and is an imperfect metaphor for the expanding worldwide information network of networks, it does have one very useful connotation: There are no "one-way streets." Every electronic path that we use to transmit information, coordinate the actions of our forces, or store data, is also open to electronic intrusion and possible destruction.

It cannot be safely said that every agency or organization that relies on information for its daily functioning recognizes either the threat or the criticality of protecting our information networks.[22] The crucial paradox of the information age is that while computerized information processing and transmission networks must be as open and accessible as possible in order to fully utilize their speed and volume for efficiency and effectiveness, this very openness is a vulnerability against which we need to be protected.

The current effort by the Joint Requirements Oversight Council (JROC)[23] includes IW as one of the several areas in which it will evaluate U.S. war fighting capabilities and requirements. There are, however, critical aspects of the IW issue that fall outside of the JROC's focus and mandate yet still influence our ability to wage offensive or defensive strategic Information Warfare. For example, one aspect is the legal status of IW and how IW-related actions or operations will be considered under existing international law. If another nation disables a U.S. military or civilian satellite with a ground-based directed energy weapon or by use of a satellite uplink to "take over" the satellite, is this an "act of war" analogous to an attack on a sovereign warship at sea? There are historical precedents for such actions, of course. At the outset of World War I, for example, the Royal Navy retrieved from the ocean floor and cut all the submarine telegraph cables that linked Germany to the rest of the world, thus preventing independent [wired] communications between Germany and the neutral nations. This would seem analogous to disrupting a nation's communications satellites today—a complex legal issue that needs much greater exploration.

What if a nation employs a computer attack to disable the Federal Reserve or Wall Street for a day? If such an operation hurts or kills no one and "merely" costs hundreds of millions of dollars in stock losses and trading confusion, what are the legal ramifications? Is this an act of war? What retaliatory measures would be appropriate? Is protection from such a strategic attack even a mission for the military, or does it belong in the area of civil law enforcement? These are critical issues that need to be thought through, but that fall outside of the mission of the JROC process.

The interrelationship of what we call "the laws of war" and the impact of new technologies developed decades after the laws were codified, is complex and loaded with legal, operational, and emotional time bombs. The submarine and the bomber are two early 20th Century examples of the difficulties faced when the technology of war evolves faster than the law of war. What would have happened, for example, if during the Gulf War an Iraqi fighter carrying two radar-guided Exocet air-to-surface missiles had managed to penetrate to within firing range and launched its missiles at the U.S. fleet. Sixty seconds later, after the aircraft had turned away, well beyond visual range, its two missiles locked onto the largest radar return they found and sunk a hospital ship: its large red crosses and aids to visual identification being useless and irrelevant. This is just one hypothetical example of how technology is racing beyond the bounds of the accepted legal conventions regarding the laws of armed conflict. The technologies involved in IW will exacerbate this problem significantly.

Related to the legal issues involved in information warfare is its interagency nature. The "purple" of joint operations is being provided to the DOD elements that perform IW through the publication of JCS MOP 30, which provides guidance for some aspects of IW, namely the C^2W portion, and the recent approval of Chairman JCS Instruction (CJCSI) 3210.1, titled "Joint Information Warfare Policy," which provides broader guidance to the Services and Joint elements. Additionally, joint doctrine is being developed for all of the specific C^2W activities,[24] but these address only a portion of what IW encompasses. The Services are working on doctrinal and operational concepts for IW or, as the Army calls it, Information Operations,[25] but these are clearly tied to their military roots and thus are unable to reach into the interagency nature of IW. To use the previous example, what if a hostile nation attempted to interfere with the telecommunications systems in the Northeast U.S., to degrade our military systems and serve up a "warning shot" to the populace and bring pressure on our government. This would most certainly be a threat to our national security, but any sort of effective response would involve both military and other federal agencies, plus significant elements of the private sector, in what could be termed "strategic defensive IW." How will this be coordinated and who will plan, control and execute the responses, both defensive and offensive, especially if the response involves actions on the part of the military? This is the sort of problem that we are unprepared to solve and which the JROC process is probably not designed to discuss.

Focusing the concept of comprehensive situational awareness and information warfare solely on "bringing fire to the battlefield" is too limiting and may preclude us from providing the theater commander (and thus the National Command Authorities) with war-winning tools and strategies that both increase his effectiveness and enable him to win faster and at less cost in lives and resources. Strategic information warfare may provide us with the capability to dominate future adversaries and quickly meet our military and political objectives by using technologies and strategies that minimize bloodshed and destruction and thus emphasize American strengths, while exploiting enemy weaknesses.

Notional Critical Target Sets

Political

- National governmental apparatus and centers
  - — Headquarters, administrative offices, and ministries
  - — Supporting C^3 nodes (hard or soft)
  - — Command posts (mobile/fixed; air/land/at sea)
- Internal state police and control forces
  - — Headquarters, Intelligence technical collections systems
  - — Supporting databases
- Propaganda systems: domestic and international
  - — Public affairs, public diplomacy, and Psyop organizations and production facilities
  - — Cultural centers/networks
  - — Links into area/international telecommunications nets

Infrastructure

- Information infrastructure
  - — Public and secure telecommunications switches
  - — Radio relay facilities and telephone exchanges
  - — Fiber optic networks, nodes, and repeater stations
  - — Microwave transmission networks and nodes
  - — Computer and data processing centers
  - — National C^3I centers and Satcom links
- Energy and power sources
  - — Production centers, transformer stations, distribution and control centers
  - — Pumping stations and backup systems
- Transportation
  - — Ground traffic control at choke points
  - — Air traffic control centers
  - — Supporting computer and electronic systems
- Financial centers and networks
  - — Banks and trading centers and institutions
  - — Currency controls and depositories and supporting databases
- Population stability
  - — Food and water distribution systems and control points

Military Forces

- Strategic national defenses
  - — Warning systems sensors
  - — Defense command & control centers
  - — Satcom links to space-based systems
  - — Deployed forces
- Strategic offensive force projection systems
  - — Conventional delivery systems
  - — Unconventional weapons systems
  - — Control centers, command posts and R&D centers

Endnotes

[1] See, for example, Admiral Owens' "Introduction" to Stuart E. Johnson and Martin C. Libicki (eds.), *Dominant Battlespace Knowledge* (Washington, DC: National Defense University Press, 1995).

[2] For Admiral Owens' views see his "JROC: Harnessing the Revolution in Military Affairs" in *Joint Force Quarterly* (#5, Summer 1994), pp. 55-57. For another view see Eliot A. Cohen, "A Revolution in Warfare," in *Foreign Affairs*, Vol 75, No. 2 (March-April) 1996, pp. 37-54.

[3] Although some agencies and organizations use differing terminology for this situation (the Air Force calls it a "realm," while the Joint Staff refers to it as a "domain;" I call it an "environment"), the terms are synonymous and they all boil down to the same thing.

[4] William A. Owens, *Dominant Battlespace Knowledge*, p. 7.

[5] There is an ongoing debate over the definitions and delimitation's of DBA and DBK, which has somewhat the flavor of "how many angels can dance on the head of a pin?" Attempting to define DB is terms of "90% certainty of knowing X..." and DBK in terms of "95% certainty of knowing X + Y..." is a fruitless and sterile argument that can never have a satisfactory resolution because it is an argument over an unknowable and unquantifiable concept, i.e., information.

[6] Although the original discussions that led to this paper used the terms "total" situational awareness and "dominant battlefield awareness" I have focused on "comprehensive" situational awareness for two reasons. First, the word "total" is too absolute and immediately deflects the discussion into a minefield that concentrates on how such awareness could be obtained and the difficulties that might make such a goal unobtainable. On the other hand, "comprehensive" clearly indicates that, while such awareness will be sufficient for our needs, it will not—and need not—be absolute. Secondly, the original focus on the battlefield is too narrow, for reasons explained in the body of this paper.

[7] See Alvin and Heidi Toffler,*War and Anti-War: Survival at the Dawn of the 21st Century* (NY: Little, Brown, 1993), pp. 38-43. The Tofflers would define "second-wave war" as that form of conflict that features mass destruction between industrial powers whose strength and power is based on mass production of industrial goods. This is in contrast to what they term "third-wave warfare", of which the Gulf War was a presage, emphasizing precision targeting rather than mass destruction, operational effectiveness based on the transfer of massive quantities of information, and the use of information dominance to generate an operational tempo inside of the enemy's "OODA loop," his ability to "observe-orient-decide-act." This concept is based on the writings of John Boyd.

[8] Colonel Warden was the architect of "Instant Thunder," the conceptual strategic air campaign against Iraq that became the basis for the final Desert Storm air campaign plan. See John A. Warden III, "The Enemy as a System," *Airpower Journal*, Vol. 9, No. 1 (Spring) 1995, pp. 40-55, from which these graphs were extracted.

[9] In some cases we may be willing to continue dealing with the existing leadership after the war, as we did in Vietnam or (if not by desire) Iraq. In other cases, we have insisted on a change in the enemy leadership as a wartime objective, such as the end of the Hitler regime in Nazi Germany. In still other cases we may be willing to work with a modification of the existing leadership, as with the Japanese Emperor after World War II. In all cases, however, the leadership is at the core of the situation, and this is especially true for scenarios involving non-state actors such as terrorist, religious, or criminal groups. These groups or organizations may not have industries, infrastructures, or populations, but they all have leadership elements against which we can direct information operations.

[10] This construct intentionally mirrors the task assigned the 8th Air Force by Operation POINTBLANK, the Combined Bomber Offensive of 1944. This called for achieving air superiority over Europe as an intermediate objective of the highest priority, necessary before either the invasion of Europe or the full weight of the strategic bombing campaign could take effect.

[11] See John A. Warden III, "Employing Air Power in the 21st Century", in Richard H. Schultz, Jr., and

Robert L. Pfaltzgraff, Jr. (eds.), *The Future of Air Power in the Aftermath of the Gulf War*, Maxwell AFB, AL: Air University Press, 1992, pp. 57-87. For a discussion of how the "5 rings" concept influenced the development of the Gulf War air campaign plan see Sandy Cochran, et al., *Gulf War Air Power Survey (GWAPS), Vol I, pt 1, Planning*, Washington, DC: Government Printing Office, 1993, pp. 94; also see Daniel T. Kuehl, "Thunder and Storm: Strategic Air Operations in the Gulf War," in William Head and Earl H. Tilford, Jr. (eds.), *The Eagle in the Desert: Looking Back on US Involvement in the Persian Gulf War*, Westport, CT: Praeger, 1996, pp. 112-115.

[12] See for example, *GWAPS Statistical Compendium*, Table 177 "Strikes by AIF Categories," Which includes four pages of target categories. For narrative discussions of air campaign targeting and additional graphic depictions of targeting objectives, target sets, and component categories, see Cochran, *GWAPS Vol. I, pt. 1*, p. 193, Table 22 "CENTAF Target Sets by OPLAN 1002-90 Objectives," and Barry D. Watts and Thomas A. Keany, *GWAPS, Vol. II, pt. 2, Effects and Effectiveness*, p. 271, Table 22, "Examples of Core Target Categories."

[13] To cite several examples: Jason B. Barlow, *Strategic Paralysis: An Airpower Theory for the Present*, Maxwell AFB, AL: Air University Press, 1994, especially Chapter 5, "The National Elements of Value Model," pp. 55-78; Gerald R. Gurst, *Taking Down Telecommunications*, Maxwell AFB, AL: Air University Press, 1994, especially Chapter 2, "Telecommunications," pp. 5-28; and Steven M. Rinaldi, *Beyond the Industrial Web: Economic Synergies and Targeting Methodologies*, Maxwell AFB, AL: Air University Press, 1995, especially Chapter 3, "Synergies and Infrastructure Elements," pp. 25-34. These three studies were all student theses at the School of Advanced Airpower Studies. Another relevant effort is H. D. Arnold, J. Hukill, J. Kennedy, and A. Cameron, "Targeting Financial Systems as Centers of Gravity: 'Low Intensity' to 'No Intensity' Conflict," in *Defense Analysis*, Vol. 10, No. 2, 1994, pp. 181-208.

[14] "Air Force Doctrine Document 5: Information Warfare" (first draft, 18 November 1995), Chapter 4 (IW Application) and subparagraph 4.2 (IW Targets).

[15] Foreign Broadcast Information Service (FBIS) translation of "Exploring and Analyzing Characteristics of Information Warfare" by Wang Huying, summarized by Publication Translation Section of U.S. Consulate General in Hong Kong in message 130402ZFEB96.

[16] Grigory Smolyan, Vitaliy Tsigichko, and Dimitryiy Chereshkin, "A Weapon, Perhaps More Dangerous than a Nuclear One: The Reality of Information Warfare," in *Military Supplement* (18 November 1995), translated by Rob Hughes, Institute for Conflict, Ideology and Policy, Boston University. Also see Mary C. Fitzgerald, "Russian Views on Electronic Signals and Information Warfare," *American Intelligence Journal*, (Spring/Summer) 1994, pp. 81-87, for Russian perspectives on IW, EW and the Gulf War.

[17] Briefing by USD(P)/Infrastructure Policy Directorate.

[18] "Telematics" is a relatively new term that refers to the conjoining of computerized information storage and manipulation systems with long-distance telecommunications networks such as phone systems.

[19] The degree to which this dependence is expanding is not widely recognized. For example, during the aftermath of a fatal train crash in Washington, D.C., in February 1996, news reports mentioned that all of the switching signals (red and green "stop-go" signals) that control train traffic in the entire Eastern portion of the United States are controlled from one central location in Jacksonville, Florida. During discussions about possible signal "failure" as a cause of the accident, however, none of the news commentators mentioned the possibility that the SCADA nets that actually controlled the signals might have been intentionally tampered with. This is not meant to suggest that they were, but rather to highlight that no one even thought to ask the question.

[20] The precision weaponry is the easy part of the equation: the precision intelligence by comparison will be the tough part. For a discussion of the operational impact of this development see Thomas Keaney and Barry Watts, *The Gulf War Air Power Survey (GWAPS), Vol II, Pt 2,*

Effectiveness, Washington, DC: Government Printing Office, 1993, pp. 348-355. Evolving discussions of "precision warfare," however, go beyond merely physical destruction, even when that destruction is caused by non-explosive means, to include precise knowledge of causative factors within enemy systems and precise predictions of intended effects.

[21] Gerald R. Hust, "Taking Down Telecommunications" (Student Thesis, School of Advanced Airpower Studies, Air University, Maxwell AFB, AL, 1993); also Lawrence G. Downs Jr., "Digital Data Warfare: Using Malicious Computer Code as a Weapon" (Student Thesis, Air War College, Air University, Maxwell AFB, AL, 1995). If these examples sound far-fetched, one need only consider a recent incident, described in the Pentagon's "Early Bird," in which a sixteen year-old English computer hacker penetrated numerous computer databases worldwide and moved extremely sensitive information halfway around the world from one nation into another. The hypothetical examples postulated here have all been cited as potential American vulnerabilities to a determined IW attack.

[22] See, for example, the situation described by Cliff Stoll, in which a KGB-sponsored computer hacker managed to penetrate U.S. defense computer systems to gather intelligence: Cliff Stoll, *The Cuckoo's Egg: Tracking a Spy Through the Maze of Computer Espionage*, New York: Simon and Schuster, 1989. For a fuller description of this threat, see Winn Schwartau, *Information Warfare: Chaos on the Electronic Superhighway*, New York: Thunder's Mouth Press, 1994. Also see the Joint Security Commission's "Redefining Security: A Report to the Secretary of Defense and Director of Central Intelligence," 28 February 1994, which noted that "Networks are already recognized as a battlefield of the future."

[23] See William A. Owens, "JROC: Harnessing the Revolution in Military Affairs," p.56.

[24] These include Joint Pub 3-13 (currently being drafted), which will be Joint Doctrine for IW, and Joint Pub 3-13.1, the recently approved doctrine for C^2W. For the individual elements or pillars of C^2W see 3-51 for Electronic Warfare, 3-53 for Psychological Operations (PSYOP), 3-54 for Operational Security (OPSEC), and 3-58 for Operational Deception. Obviously, there is none for the fifth pillar of C^2W, physical destruction of key C^2 nodes.

[25] The Army has a draft Field Manual 100-6, "Information Operations" out for comment, and the Air Force is working on its own IO concept that may be included in the next iteration of its basic doctrine manual, Air Force Doctrine Document 1 (the old AFM 1-1). Lt General Ralston, former USAF DCS for Plans and Operations, briefed these concepts to a public audience at the Air Force Association's "Airpower and the Revolution in Military Affairs" symposium held 17 January 1995. The Air Force has recently published, under the joint signatures of the Secretary of the Air Force, Dr. Sheila Widnall, and the Chief of Staff, General Ron Fogleman, "Cornerstones of Information Warfare," a sixteen-page white paper that is the most farsighted view of IW of any of the Services.

The Information Warfare Campaign

Michael Loescher

We are in the midst of the Information Age; our children's children will learn in school that computers simply were the harbingers. Information has become a commodity that permeates and strengthens the foundation of our everyday activities—from music to commerce to science.

War and the conduct of it will be affected profoundly. The opening gambit and possibly the war termination strategy will be an Information Warfare (IW) campaign focused on the decision maker. Surveillance will dominate commanders' decisions, and C^4I will be the underpinning of all action. Information has become a principal commodity of modern war.

Just as the airplane proved more than just "better scouting" for the gun line or the battleship in the 1920s, IW is not just better electronic warfare for better C^4I or better surveillance. It is a fundamental alteration of the tactical continuum that permanently has changed the face of warfare. Information Warfare marks a collision between technology and doctrine, creating a new direction with revised tactics from what was previously evident.

In the last several years, much has been written about the coming importance of IW. Yet little has been written about *how to conduct it.* This paper provides a doctrinal framework for planning the IW campaign—how a commander, regardless of his geographical location, force size, or technological sophistication, should come to think about IW and how he should go to war in the Information Age.

Targets

IW is about the attack and defense of information, There are two key concepts in that simple definition. First, IW is a *tactical mind set* that incorporates parallel functions, each equally important: the protection of own-force information and the exploitation of the foe's. History does not teach that better technology necessarily leads to victory. Rather, victory goes to the commander who uses technology better or who can deny the enemy his technology. Thus, IW has the potential not only to be a *force multiplier*, but also to be a force *equalizer*. A large, technologically dependent force is a perfect target set for a small, technically sophisticated foe.

Second, while the hostile information infrastructure (e.g., command and control systems, communications links) may be chosen as target sets, they are not in themselves the target. *The target is the information itself.* The significance of this differentiation lies in the nature of modem information systems technology. In the past, cryptology, deception, manipulation, and destruction all have been disciplines aimed at the unique military communications of a foe. In the future, as the worldwide explosion in commercial information systems increases, friend and foe alike may be using the same satellite carriers.

In such a world, C4I and counter-C4I take on different meanings than they have in the past. The complexity of a future global commercial communications infrastructure will present both obstacles and opportunities in war. For example, the best place to conduct IW may be 6,000 miles from the location of tactical forces, a concept we will explore below. Thus, in planning the IW campaign, it is vital to focus first on what information we wish to exploit before choosing the means to destroy or otherwise utilize it. This maxim has a direct parallel to the principles of war—economy of force, mass, and surprise apply to IW as well.

Nor should the targeted information be solely in the format of traditional communications. As sophisticated weapons proliferate, sensors also must proliferate, whether indigenous, provided through commercial means like LANDSAT or French SPOT, or made available—"leased"—by other nations. Since the range and capability of sensors vary significantly, from fire control to wide area surveillance, the information they provide the commander similarly ranges from intelligence and warning to precision targeting. Like the communications infrastructure, the surveillance infrastructure of the future, both for friend and foe, will be exceedingly complex.

The essence of the IW campaign, therefore, can be distilled to six planning concerns, that address both the attack and defense of information central to the concept of IW.

- Precisely *what information* is vital to friend/foe at each functional (e.g., surveillance, C41) and organizational (e.g., division, airwing, naval force) echelon?
- What is the *purpose* of the vital information (e.g., command and control, weapons targeting, diplomatic exchange)?
- Through *what infrastructures* does it flow?
- *Where in those infrastructures* is it most vulnerable?
- Through what means can it best be *protected/exploited* (e.g., soft kill, hard kill)?
- If exploited, *to what end* (e.g., strategic or tactical; manipulate or destroy)?

Campaign planners face two significant obstacles, however. Planning the campaign, especially for exploitation purposes, itself necessitates large amounts of information about the enemy. Planners will need to know a great detail about the various hostile infrastructures to answer thosee questions. At first glance, it is a formidable task. But such information, in fact, has exact parallels with traditional intelligence—what is required is an order of battle and an estimation of capabilities, expressed in no more technical terms than we use today for hostile weapons profiles. As a result, requirements for technical intelligence for the campaign can reasonably be expected to grow in the future. (It should also be said that the task is not much less formidable when planning the information-protect campaign. In a multinational, combined arms task force, recognizing one's own order of battle can be difficult.)

Battle Space

The second obstacle lies in the ability to *perceive* friendly and hostile information infrastructures. Hostile communications can range in spectrum from VLF to commercial satellite, encompass a mix of old and new technologies, and include voice, data, and video (including commercial television) in format. As we have seen, sensors may be commercial or on loan, making the rules of engagement for destruction problematic at best. Weapons mixes similarly vary. For communications and sensors especially, the physical components will probably reside thousands of miles from the commanders who use them.

The battle space in which IW is conducted, therefore, is a complex abstraction—it can exist as a planning and operating reality only in its reconstruction as a model. Moreover, like traditional battle space, it is a terrain in which both friend and foe expect to operate. As they operate—manipulating or destroying—they change the battle space. As a result, IW has to be conducted dynamically both with respect to time and space.

To choose a simplistic example, when a blue commander jams an orange satellite transponder, he effectively produces a large hole for a time in the IW battle space—and one that is obvious to both parties. An orange counter by moving to HF, for example, changes the tactical spectrum again, but can only be countered again by blue *if perceptible* (i.e., able to be sensed) and *modeled in at least near real time* (i.e., exploitable time). Just as concrete, but far more subtle, blue's injection of a software virus into orange's database creates a potentially well-timed hole in the IW battle space, which blue desires to see and desires orange not to see.

As with other elements of the IW campaign, these moves have direct parallels with traditional warfare and with the principles of war. The objects are:

• To gain control of the IW battle space and deny or control the enemy's use of it (*Initiative, Surprise*);

• Having done so, to project power by conducting offensive warfare in that dimension (*Mass, Economy of Force, Simplicity, Maneuver*); and

• To simultaneously protect own systems (*Security*).

For campaign planners, however, one obstacle is, how can we perceive the target set? How can we conceive of a hundred geographically and electronically diverse targets as a cohesive IW "battle space" to exploit and protect?

The Grid Concept

A prerequisite for joint warfare is that a combined arms commander possess the means to sense the entire battle space as a whole, with the transition across the air, land, sea space and spectral interfaces transparent. Only through such comprehensive surveillance can he move his forces in set and sequence through a multidimensional campaign area. As a practical matter, however, his surveillance assets are likely to be operated by diverse organizations, many of which are geographically and organizationally distant from him. Some will be part of a national or commercial inventory of sensors, others will be operated at the theater level. Some will be operated by allies and others physically attached to his various tactical platforms.

Thus, the commander's force surveillance *system* will consist of borrowed parts that must be *focused* on the tactical problem—it is impractical and inappropriate programmatically for a component service to seek to construct such a force-wide sensor system—even if it were technically possible. The question, then, becomes: how can diverse sensors, many of which are neither owned nor operated by the commander, nor even in-area, be employed to appear to act as an effective *force surveillance system*?

For IW planners, the answer begins with a shift in perspective—away from the sensor itself to the battle space it senses. In making such a shift, we may conceive of the sensors as a *grid of capabilities* overlaying the battle space instead of a series of independent single sensors. Such a "grid" would have variances over the battle space—the number of sensors, detectables in the environment, location of sensors, their individual precision and resolution, and revisit times—to name a few. By conceiving of sensors as a virtual grid, we can arrive at some useful operational constructs.

First, at any given time, place or frequency, the variances can be viewed (and modeled instantaneously) as assets or lack of assets. These variances can be further equated to predictive targeting probabilities when the grid is brought to bear against a track (whether blue or orange.) Second, thinking of sensors as a grid of capabilities allows planners to use them efficiently, pitting operational requirements against an appropriate set of sensors. Economy of force applies here: sensor targeting need only be as precise or as timely as required by the weapon selected.

Third, when we understand that sensors have operating envelopes as unique to them as those of a particular aircraft, we also can understand a grid can be manipulated effectively, and perhaps dynamically, to compensate for (or create) "holes" or unacceptably low probabilities.

Finally, by conceiving of sensors as a grid, the center of gravity—the right place for the right weapon, whether software in a New York switching center or command center in enemy—becomes more obvious. This is because the enemy also has a Surveillance Grid. Similarly, his grid can be studied, with strengths and weaknesses becoming apparent to his opponent. By such a conception, planners can consider and exploit in detail the technology of the hostile IW infrastructure dynamically and reduce its complexity to doctrine—and ultimately to campaign plan (in this case, surveillance and counter-surveillance.)

In the same way we can conceive of a Surveillance Grid, we can also conceive of blue and orange Communications Grids. In the past decade, the worldwide telecommunications revolution has exploded, and it is now evident that a robust communications infrastructure will be available globally by the turn of the century. A military communications technician who retired in 1988 and one on active duty in 1998 will have worked on entirely different communications infrastructures.

Not only is the number of communications transponders increasing, but breakthroughs in multiplexing, the move to digital formats, and most importantly, the advent of virtual networking will provide military commanders with a communications capability that not only will be jam-resistant (by virtue of network switching) but also several orders of magnitude larger.

By the close of the decade, both the U.S. and a hostile commander can expect robust communications with restoration options and, with the advent of computer workstations, more flexible command and control. But these capabilities—because of the footprints of communications (both satellites and the shore infrastructure; e.g., the local telephone and data services) and the geography of the campaign—will vary from place to place on the globe. Thus, as with sensors, we may conceive of communications as virtual grids overlaying the tactical area.

Execution, Technology, and Battle Management

Finally, in planning the IW campaign, it is useful to think of all weapons available to both forces as a, sorted by third abstract "grid," a tactical grid that consists of shooters—weapons available to the commanders, sorted by suitability and availability against a hostile order of battle. In doing so, IW planners can conceive of the various grids' instantaneous interaction as a sort of momentary "core sample." That is to say, the correct connection in time of the *Surveillance Grid* with the *Communications Grid* and the *Tactical Grid* is what is required to affect a kill. Disruption of the interaction—the three-grid core sample—at the appropriate place and time—even if out of the tactical area—will prevent the kill.

Thus, with IW, disruption of the firing solution can now be moved back from the actual force interaction in both time and space—we can do it in New York on a schedule instead of the last minute in country as platform defense. The essence of IW campaigning becomes planning when, where, how, and why.

In effect, the IW battle space is the instantaneous product of blue on orange interaction of geographically and electronically diverse assets that make surveillance, C^4I and targeting possible. Conceiving of these as grids that interact allows planners to accomplish two critical functions: to identify in time and space the right target (i.e., where and when to disrupt) and to monitor and model the interaction in real time, creating sequenced set of operational events—the IW campaign.

Such a campaign, because of the protect/exploit duality, must be planned down two parallel paths:

• *Protect:* a sequenced set of operational security, surveillance, C^4I, and information security plans;

• *Exploit:* a sequenced set of operational deception, counter-surveillance, counter-C^4I, and counter-targeting plans.

Because of its complexity and speed, IW will require the *technological and organizational focus* to manage it —to perceive it, to conduct it, and to avoid its conduct against us. In terms of technology, there are three requirements:

• A doctrinal, organizational, and technological battle management system that is applicable across all echelons to all components of the force, regardless of their position in it. The systems must be readily scalable across the levels of conflict as the force structure expands from on-scene commander to joint task force to full campaign-level command.

• The system must incorporate a force-wide surveillance system, the interfaces of which are synergistic and seamless across the battle space and operationally transparent to the user regardless of echelon or component.

• The system must integrate hard kill (e.g., weapons on target), soft kill (e.g., saturation, deception), and very soft kill (e.g., intrusion).

Organizationally, IW must be effective and be coordinated *across the air, land, sea, space, and spectral battle space* and *vertically up and down echelons*. The grid construct also serves us well here, for if we can conceive of own-force IW assets as three grids over the operating area, then the commander's IW protect functions reduce to managing all three grids in a manner that provides operational continuity vertically through them.

If we have weapons and communications, but no surveillance, we cannot fire the shot. This situation occurs today (though we may not recognize it as a grid problem) when the revisit time of a sensor will not allow us to target. If we have surveillance and weapons, but we can not connect the two, the solution is still zero. This is what we experience in today's non-virtual, circuit-specific communications when a targeting network fails. Similarly, surveillance and communications are no good without the weapons. This is the situation when a weapon failure occurs or when a targeting solution cannot be passed to the optimum shooter.

Thus, a critical part of the IW campaign plan is ability to manage own force grid continuity and that of analogous hostile grids in tactical time. Given the protect/exploit duality, four IW battle management functions can be envisioned:

Sensor Management—which is to say, Surveillance Grid integrity. The functional responsibilities include sensor management, collection management, and surveillance coordination for the echelon in which the commander is positioned (i.e., Navy CVBG, Army EAC, JTF, theater commander). Personnel assigned these functions must have an operational and technological understanding of all sensors that can impact the battle space—national, theater, platform; allied, component or joint; friendly or hostile.

Information Management. The functional responsibilities include managing the Communications Grid and the force C^4I system. Personnel assigned these functions must understand communications—national, theater, platform; allied, component or joint; commercial and military; and friendly and hostile jamming and interference potentials.

Battle Space Management. The functional responsibilities include track and targeting coordination throughout the battle space, whether air, land, sea, or space. Personnel assigned these functions must understand weaponry and surveillance—national, theater, platform; allied, component or joint; friendly or hostile.

The conduct of Electronic Warfare and its related disciplines. The functional responsibilities include maintenance of the electronic offensive and defensive capabilities, including counter-surveillance and counter-C^4I capable at the force level. Personnel assigned these functions must have an operational and technological understanding of all Electronic Warfare systems that can impact the battle space—national, theater, platform; allied, component or joint; friendly or hostile.

SOFTWAR

Chuck de Caro

In the first half decade of the 1990s, the United States emerged as the only remaining superpower. Yet, instead of reigning over a *Pax Americana*, the U.S. has been unable to stem the constant erosion of its real and perceived ability to protect its national interests. Consider the following:

- Five years after the U.S.-led military victory over Iraq, Desert Storm has become Desert Drizzle and has faded to an asterisk in the history books. Saddam Hussein, the alleged vanquished, is growing again in stature, requiring a continued U.S. military presence in the region.
- A pair of fifth-rate Balkan despots for years thumbed their noses at the U.S. and NATO, while making a mockery of U.N. efforts to preclude continuing acts of genocide. A huge multilateral effort backed by billions of dollars is currently attempting to create equilibrium.
- A tenth-rate sub-national tribal leader inflates a bloody tactical defeat and makes it appear to be a U.S. disaster, resulting in the ignominious U.S. withdrawal from Somalia.
- A military junta in Haiti uses the Somali example, staging a riot and managing to make a U.S. warship, carrying U.S. and Canadian troops on a U.N. mission, turn tail and head home.

These startling, illogical outcomes point out that *the very nature of war is changing*. The Clausewitzian view of war as an extension of politics using violence to "constrain the enemy to accomplish our will," reflected the technology of his time. In the early 19th Century there was a sharp line between diplomacy and belligerent conflict, because constraint of another society's will was possible only through massive application of gunpowder and cold steel.

But a product of late 20th Century technology, *global real-time television,* has opened the line between diplomacy and war and left a sizable gray zone where the wills of nations can be bent and major changes in international politics can be effected without resorting to lethal means. This type of conflict is here defined as SOFTWAR: *The hostile use of global television to shape another nation's will by changing its vision of reality.*

SOFTWAR can achieve the same objective—the constraining of the enemy's will—as 19th Century warfare had sought to do. It brings forth the possibility of the most efficient kind of warfare as defined centuries ago by the Chinese military philosopher Sun Tzu: "To win 100 victories in 100 battles is not the acme of skill; to subdue the enemy without fighting is the acme of skill" [1]

The Nature of the Medium of Television

Television, by its nature, is an extremely effective, insidious and dangerous medium for delivery of propaganda. As Marshal McLuhan first noted in the 1960s, television is a "cool" medium that defines events by the viewer's *perception of images and sound,* rather than of reality. Perception can be further distorted by various aspects of telegenics: lighting, sun angle, "star" quality, voice quality, production values, wardrobe, video quality, transmission quality, hue, tint, background setting and other factors that have little to do with reality.

The Nixon-Kennedy debate during the 1960 Presidential election is one example. The transcripts show a fairly even contest; those listening on radio felt strongly that Nixon had won. To the millions watching television, however, Kennedy's natural camera appeal was enhanced by makeup and a dark suit and contrasted with a perspiring Nixon with a five-o'clock shadow, leaving the perception that Kennedy had won decisively.

Desert Storm proved that the image can become reality. Nowhere was that idea better demonstrated than on CNN, the only *global* network. The war on CNN was often simply *televised* in real-time; it was not edited or thoughtfully put into context and *reported.* Thus the narrow focus and random selection of unfiltered, real-time images distorted the true scope and nature of events. What was really known about the enemy's relative strengths and weaknesses was often erroneously shaped by television.

Idiosyncrasies of the Medium of Television

B-Roll Magnets. "B-Roll," TV slang for images of the actuality being discussed, automatically skews the reportage around itself, like a magnet in a saucer of paperclips. Unlike the print medium, where the photographs support the written words, television has a built-in difference, where words are used to support the pictures. Thus, the best action-oriented videos get the best supporting wordage and hence the most play. For example, spectacular B-Roll of a Scud being intercepted by Patriots over Israel at night is better than a long, hazy shot of the shelling of Khafji. Though the counter-attack at Khafji was militarily far more important than the destruction of an inaccurate missile, reality was skewed, because there was more action, drama and suspense in the Scud tape.

Short-hand Feedback. TV coins phases to reduce the time it takes to project a thought, for example: "OJ," "Whitewater," "Watergate," "Iran-Contra," or "Reaganomics," for example. Once used, the phrase spreads everywhere to identify the "everything" around the idea. In Desert Storm, the words "Elite Republican Guards" were used by the press, especially the TV press, to identify every piece of B-Roll which contained an image of just about every Iraqi in uniform. Who reported that the Republican Guards were "elite" in the first place? Saddam or the Western press? Who checked it out? The reality is that in eight years of combat with Iran, the "*eliterepublicanguards*" couldn't take and hold one, repeat one, Iranian swamp. Yet Republican Guards, whom most reporters couldn't identify in any case, were often reported as being elite.

Media Amplification. Media amplification denotes the phenomenon by which any side-by-side comparison on television implies rough parity, if not outright equality.[2] A murderous dictator of a fifth-rate country is accorded the same stature as the democratically elected President of the most powerful nation on Earth. The television images of fleets of Iraqi tanks manned by the aforementioned legions of "eliterepublicanguards" implied great military might, but belied the reality that, during Desert Storm, they became so many waiting targets for the *really elite* USAF B-52 crews. The perception of invincibility was so strong, however, that many well-informed Americans really believed that the "*eliterepublicanguards*" would make the U.S. forces swim in a river of blood in the "Mother of All Battles." In reality, it was the Iraqis who did the blood-swimming in the "Mother of All Defeats."

Political Throw-Weight. What matters is maximizing the amount of air time that an issue can garner: the more air time, the more likely the audience will be convinced. Like a MIRVed missile which can hit several targets simultaneously, a single strong piece of B-Roll can cause a number of major downstream events—the Rodney King video is an excellent example.

In the run-up to the Gulf War, Saddam Hussein got the maximum throw-weight from the global media. He dressed in well-tailored statesmanlike suits when being interviewed by Peter Arnett, for consumption by the Western audience; in battle dress when being photographed with his troops; and in Arab garb to maximize his effect on the regional Arab audience. He used this same technique specifically for the television cameras, by having his "eliterepublicanguards" fake a return to Baghdad soon after they invaded Kuwait. The perception was that the Iraqis were leaving Kuwait; the reality was that they were reinforcing their grip on that conquered country. The result was global confusion about his intentions.

Using this television idiosyncrasy is not limited to adversaries. ABC's *20/20* reporter John Martin demonstrated[3] that a Kuwaiti government-backed organization hired the American public relations firm Hill & Knowlton to hype the story of Iraqi soldiers yanking Kuwaiti babies out of incubators. It turns out that the eyewitness—who's name was not disclosed at the time of the Senate hearings—was the 15-year-old daughter of the Kuwaiti Ambassador to the U.S. Martin's investigation found little proof that what Nayirah al-Sabah said was anything more than propaganda. At the time, however, the perception was strong enough to get President Bush to mention the "incubator atrocities" eight times in 44 days and strong enough for seven Senators to mention the incident during debate over the war. (Note that the war resolution passed by only five votes.)

Quality Roulette. The quality and veracity of information vary greatly; but because presenters "anchors" tend to have a universally high telegenic factor (called "Q"), the news audience is often unintentionally misled. Think of news reports as sausage: they all look the same, but the quality of the ingredients varies tremendously. Under wartime pressure, human factors enter the equation more noticeably, with even greater effects upon the end-product. Some examples:

- On Day Two of the war, as Israel came under Scud attack, CNN went live to its Jerusalem Bureau showing the bedlam of newsmen who believed they were being gassed, trying to don protective masks, ear pieces and microphones simultaneously, while the camera bucked and panned wildly. Bureau Chief Larry Register, seemingly in shock, kept trying to pry open a window until somebody else yelled at him to desist. They were completely wrong about the gas attack, but the perception scared the watching global TV audience.

• In Saudi Arabia, CNN's Charles Jaco, overworked to the point of delirum, imagined a gas attack, reported it without corroboration, tried to put on his mask and passed out live in front of the whole world, causing more very anxious moments.

• In Baghdad, CNN's Peter Arnett's reports were not only skewed because of heavy Iraqi censorship, but also because he could not cross-check information freely due to restrictions imposed on the numbers and length of his satellite phone conversations.

• In Jerusalem, CNN's Richard Blystone, on Day Three of the war, tired and unable to find out that the fiery trail in the sky was actually a Soviet booster burning up on re-entry after orbiting a reconnaissance satellite, was quoted by the *Washingtonian* as babbling, "I don't know what it is, but it sure looks strange."

Idiosyncrasies of the Global Television News Media

Distinct from the perception-versus-reality distortions of the *medium* of television itself, are the daily operating vagaries of global *television news media*, of which CNN is the prototype. These systemic phenomena, known as "glitches in the web," further distort reality. Far worse, these glitches can be used by a foreign power to its advantage.

Operating Realities. What is seen on television is often driven by *budget*. It costs a lot of money to move crews around and transmit reports. Therefore, bureaus are established; and, as a natural consequence, the closer to the bureau that a story occurs, the more likely that it will make it on the air. If the story is a long way off, hard-to-get-to, and dangerous, there will be fewer stories. Hence, the weight of the news is skewed. Worse, in very dangerous areas, foreign crews of unknown quality and motivation are increasingly used.

Naive Editorial Stance. Media amplification can be re-amplified by the editorial policy of a news organization. When CNN aired Iraqi government-provided and -edited video, live as-received, of Saddam visiting some of his hostages, CNN was vehemently condemned for becoming a propaganda vehicle for a madman. Writing in *Washington Journalism Review*, Jeff Kamen noted that CNN Executive Vice President Ed (no kin to Ted) Turner said to the Canadian Broadcasting Company, that airing Saddam and the hostages is the "same as airing a live speech by the President [of the U.S.] or a football game."[4]

CNN President Tom Johnson, queried by Barbara Mutasow of the *Washingtonian* about the same incident, said, "We take President Bush without knowing what he is going to say; we take Secretary Baker without knowing what he is going to say; we take Margaret Thatcher live. So why not Saddam Hussein?" Johnson added, "This is a global network. Why should I censor Saddam Hussein? Isn't the audience sophisticated enough to see we should present all sides?"[5]

This "neutral" (in reality, naive) editorial stance implies that there is no difference between dictatorship and democracy. Hitler reading aloud from Mein Kampf is the same as FDR talking about his dog Fala. The downstream effects on national will are obvious.

Random Access Coverage. During Desert Storm, CNN became, in effect, a global party line where leaders of the PLO, the Israelis, the Saudis, the Jordanians, the

Kuwaitis, and just about everybody else in the world struggled to get across their propaganda message. Even Muammar Quadaffi himself called the "International" Desk (Turner-speak for the Foreign Desk) and got on the air, live.

The "International" editor acted more like a Barnum & Bailey ringmaster than an editor. When the PLO complained that CNN was becoming a propaganda machine for the Israelis, the *Washingtonian* reported that Eason Jordan, the then 30-year-old CNN vice president for "International" news and his colleagues decided their coverage was unbalanced and put the word out: "Let's get some Arabs on the air."[6]

Hence, global information flow decisions were made on a reactive, shoot-from-the-hip, time-critical basis. Who gets covered (and who doesn't) depends on who's on what shift in Atlanta.

Capricious Override. Teddy Roosevelt called the Presidency a "bully pulpit" which could exert a great deal of moral suasion over the course of events. During Desert Storm, CNN chief Tom Johnson was asked by President Bush to pull his reporters out of Baghdad. Johnson agreed, but was overruled by Ted Turner, who, according to Howard Kurtz of the *Washington Post* and Peter Boyle of *Vanity Fair*, said, "We have people there that want to do it and, by God, *I'd* better not be overturned." [Emphasis added.][7] So much for the "bully pulpit!" By happenstance of ego, then, the flow of global television information is randomly changed.

Warped Mirroring. The use of CNN as an *ad hoc*, real-time situation update system in all major U.S. military war-rooms during Desert Storm, left U.S. planners with a warped mirror. Among U.S. officers interviewed by the author after Desert Storm, of those who watched CNN as part of their daily update procedures, not one knew that the CNN received in the U.S. is different from the CNN received in the rest of the world. Cable News International (CNI) has a mix of CNN and CNN Headline News and foreign news features; and, therefore, the political throw-weight of CNI is very different from CNN.

Thus, U.S. planners reacting to their perception of events by political throw-weight are working against the rest of the world's planners whose views are similarly skewed. (Note that the DIA/JWICS teleconference system has similar flaws.) Further, Ted Turner has stated flatly: "I'd eventually like to see all of our overseas bureaus staffed by people of that country or at least people of that race or nationality..."[8] Not only does this policy affect the issue of quality assurance and credibility, but it swings open the door to a future Dr. Goebbels who can covertly co-opt CNN in any number of nefarious ways.

Mandatory Balanced Coverage. In order to provide balanced coverage, CNN and other networks always add an opposing view as standard procedure. Thus, any U.S. view could be parried or negated by a skillful sound-bite or B-Roll clip from the opposition. Ted Turner mandated the word "international" instead of "foreign" news as part of his "one-world" philosophy. Bernard Shaw, CNN anchor, has been quoted to the effect that his work is viewed in 105 countries and must be free of bias: "There is no 'enemy,' there is no 'friendly.' I can't take sides."[9]

SOFTWAR Scenarios: On the Receiving End

Television: The Poor Man's I&W

An early indication of the effect of Information Age or Third-Wave institution of global television is that it gives developing nations the equivalent of a multi-billion dollar indications and warning intelligence system for under $100 a month. CNN Headline News, for instance, delivers half-hourly reports on the status of the U.S. government, from which U.S. action is easily predicted. For example, if the President is calling for immediate military action, and the Speaker of the House and the Senate Majority Leader both vociferously disagree, the probability of action is less likely than if all three are in agreement on the policy.

Recall that during the Desert Shield phase of the Gulf War, the news media covered, broadly but anecdotally, U.S. military preparations and mobilization. This coverage aired American popular and Congressional reactions to the crisis, mobilization procedures, and the prospects of armed conflict, including disaffected reservists and families of military personnel. The fact that this coverage might have provided the Iraqi leadership with an inaccurate portrait of ultimate American resolve does not lessen the validity of the point.

The Poor Man's C^2W

Global television also provides an instrument for Command and Control Warfare (C^2W). While DoD uses direct methods such as jamming, spoofing, or attacking enemy military command-and-control organizations to render them ineffectual, some Third-Wave-oriented foreign powers use an indirect method against the political side of the nation.

An adversary has only to generate very strong video that is designed to negatively stimulate the U.S. body politic. By instantly creating domestic political pressure, an opponent often can preclude our political leadership from acting, thus freezing the U.S. military and by default rendering U.S. policy and military capabilities ineffectual. This can be done in a number of interesting ways.

Balkan Jacks. The Milosevic regime used advanced information warfare techniques in the Balkans: The regime fanned the fires of pan-Serbism by taking over the national television system and using it to magnify semi-dormant hatreds. In the words of Stojan Cerovic, commentator for the liberal Belgrade weekly *Vreme*,

> "It is not true that the Serbs and Croats lived in constant hatred under Tito and were just waiting for the moment when they could start killing each other. Hatred had to be created artificially, and the key instrument was television. Before we had the real war, we had a *television war*."[10]

Milos Vasic, one of the founding editors of *Vreme* Magazine, pictured the effect of TV thusly:

> "It's an artificial war, really, produced by television. All it took was a few years of fierce, reckless, chauvinist, intolerant, expansionist, war-mongering propaganda to create enough hate to start the fighting among people who had lived together peacefully for forty-five years. But nobody was killed.

> You must imagine a United States with every little TV station everywhere taking exactly the same editorial line—a line dictated by David Duke. You, too, would have a war in five years."[11]

Moreover, the Serbians and Bosnian Serbs have brilliantly adapted CNN and other real-time TV services to provide a feedback mechanism for judging military-political moves. Given that CNN provides a real-time view into the inner workings of the American executive and legislative branches, any move in the Balkans can be accurately judged. In effect, for four years the Serbs played the child's game of Jacks with towns and cities in Bosnia. The upward toss of the ball represented a timing mechanism in the duration of which the Serbians made judgments of how much territory they could sweep with a single stroke. They varied the air time of the ball by injecting peace talks, U.N. negotiations and other feints into the political stream; or they took U.N. peace-keepers hostage on global television, and used the concern in the troops' home countries to prolong the evolution. If the U.S. threatened, they withdrew. When the U.S. was focused on budget hearings, a crisis elsewhere in the world, or some other significant or emotional issue, the Serbs moved forward. By continuing to play Jacks, the Serbs swept up by *fait accompli*.

The Haitian Variation. A tenth-rate tin-pot Haitian dictator, using global TV as the "Poor Man's I&W" in a game of "Balkan Jacks," judged the likely U.S. reaction in the wake of revulsion at the video-tape of Rangers being killed and mutilated in Somalia. He optimized his political-military moves to forestall U.S. intervention by having a handful of rabble assemble on a pier, mug angrily-on-cue for global TV while waving English-language placards. He thus turned away a U.S. warship—on a U.N. mission—with nothing more than the video of an alleged mob that generated the perception of imminent bloodshed projected and amplified by TV. The perception was worsened by video coverage of the warship sailing away.

Saddam Time Live. During the Gulf War, Saddam's propagandists were able to cause anti-U.S. and anti-Alliance riots in Jordan because they could directly access the audience via the friendly Jordanian government's TV system. The global political effects, even when allegedly filtered through CNN and other networks, ranged from riots in Morocco to demonstrations in Europe and the United States. These effects pale in comparison to those that can be generated in a DBS-based scenario.

The L.A. Hop. This phenomenon could be described as a *skipping ignition pulse*. In 1965, the Watts area of Los Angeles was a tinder-box, with an "ignition temperature" set by local conditions of poverty, crime, racism and escalating tensions between the populace and the police. All that was needed was a localized ignition pulse; a spark that ironically came when the police arrested an intoxicated black motorist. Once ignited, the riot spread in the classic manner, outward from the center by word-of-mouth to the edges of Watts. By contrast, the 1992 Los Angeles upheaval, broadcast as-it-happened on global real-time TV sent an ignition pulse that set off simultaneous fires wherever the same ignition conditions existed, without a localized spark. The result was a "hopping phenomenon," generating riots in San Francisco, Seattle, Atlanta and then even to Toronto, Canada.

Virtual Nations

The nation-state is no longer the ultimate expression of a people's geopolitical identity. Information Age means and methodologies now enable groups to be formed without overriding regard to physical borders. These amoebae-like organizations, using cellular phones and the Internet, can easily span oceans and continents, control vast amounts of money or information, and change form over time.

Communications-Type Virtual Nation. In the future, the concentration of information assets such as gateways, comsats, microsats, video and data bases, and fiber distribution systems will put enormous amounts of power in the hands of a single corporation or person. The power of such a person would be that of a *de facto* nation without borders or very many people that could affect *de jure* nations simply by constricting or releasing the information flow. If the concentration were held or back-stopped by a niche-competitor, it could be leveraged into the role of king-maker against the U.S. engaged in a peer-competitor struggle.

Criminal-Type Virtual Nation. The amount of economic power controlled by a drug cartel amounts to the GNP of a niche-competitor nation, again without boundaries and without very many people. The Cali cartel is already, in effect, a virtual nation organization with tendrils throughout the Americas and through much of the world, including some strategic chokepoints. In the role of an anti-U.S., part-time alliance with a peer-competitor, niche-competitor or ideological enemy, they could provide an instant on-the-ground logistics and C^3I system that covers most of the U.S. on a block-by-block basis. Think of the Cali cartel cocaine, money and arms flow to the Bloods or Crips nation-wide gangs, using the Internet and cellular telephones.

Slow-Motion War.

The U.S. has always reacted to clear and present danger. But what if an enemy has learned the chink in the American armor is that it is slow to react to threats that are not immediate. A subtle informational campaign, combined with economic and political efforts, perhaps even aided by a demoralizing war-by-proxy, could achieve what direct confrontation cannot. Americans react to long-term TV advertising campaigns which often contain subtle inner messages. If a concerted effort were made by an adversary via various corporate entities that over time convinced the population that a method other that the American way was a better idea, the end result of a war, changing a population's will over an issue, would have been achieved. If the adversary is willing to take a generation or two to achieve a goal that it considers important enough, what in the American culture can prevent him from doing so?

Implications of Near-Term Technological Developments

Direct Broadcast Satellite (DBS)

The nascent SOFTWAR battlefield of today's global television is dwarfed by an emerging technology called DBS, best described as a television relay station in geosynchronous orbit 25,000 miles out, with a signal so powerful that it can broadcast clear television signals to a small, flat or parabolic, antenna ranging from 1 to 3 square feet, many of which can be attached to a window. It is an ideal system for developing nations because there is no need for a high-cost infrastructure.

First-generation DBS systems are already operational in India, England, Japan and most recently, the United States, and they reach national and regional audiences. Satellite Television Asia Region, bought by Rupert Murdoch's Newscorp, has a potential viewership of about *3.3 billion people*. While such systems will prove to be a boon to global advertisers because the cost of reaching viewers will be extremely low, so too could it be effective for a dictator to use with a concerted, sophisticated propaganda effort to cause global upheavals overnight.

High-Definition Television (HDTV).

HDTV is a new, broader bandwidth television format that produces a higher-quality image resolution that promises to replace all the diverse broadcast standards with a single system. While Japan has had an HDTV system in limited operation for several years, FCC/NIST[12] approval for a U.S. digital system ended further Japanese efforts. Once a U.S. standard is approved, however, Japan's Ministry of International Trade and Industry could drive a marketing thrust to corner the global hardware manufacturing and distribution business, much as it has already done in current TV-related hardware. A monopoly could be dangerous in that it could regulate distribution of hardware by fixing prices.

Digital Video Manipulation.

The hybridizing of computers and television has led to techniques generally lumped into the category known as EFX (electronic effects), morphing, or toasting. Simply put, it is the ability to drive video into any form that is desired, whether an event actually occurred or not. Mixed with digital audio techniques, it is possible to make the image of *anybody* doing *anything*.

In the movie "Forrest Gump," the image of actor Tom Hanks digitally interacted with several U.S. Presidents in a very realistic manner, as did Woody Allen years before in "Zelig." While these effects were manpower- and time-intensive, industry experts estimate a two-generation improvement in processing speed and software will allow near-real-time manipulation. Thus, any well-funded group could stage a political event without it ever occurring. Want Saddam to tap dance with Ginger Rogers? Can do. How about Yeltsin rapping with Hammer? Yep. How about Rafsanjani bungee-jumping with Rushdi? There are very interesting possibilities!

Microsats.

Microsats are small single-purpose communications or reconnaissance satellites launched in time of need. Such satellites allow a video or data communications net to be erected quickly, or allow rapid viewing or targeting of the battlefield. In the hands of an adversary, comsats could complicate our C^2W efforts because of the redundancy of targets and resilience of the network. Small recon satellites can provide information on a just-in-time basis and could retard U.S. actions.

Superconducting Supercomputers.

SCSCs will provide orders-of-magnitude increases in information gathering, encryption and dissemination. UAVs with on-board SCSCs will be able to produce finished intelligence products in near-real-time from the point of action. Such products will include military and police intelligence. In the hands of an adversary, they could create domestic political turmoil by gathering and disseminating select, sensitive military-political information which could adversely affect a friendly nation's political focus.

KA-Band Uplinks.

Satellite uplinks in the frequency range above Ku will provide man-portable video communications links from anywhere to anywhere. Integrated with phased-array micro electro-mechanical systems antennas, they will provide small, hard-to-recognize devices that can pour sensitive information into the system. In the hands of an adversary, they provide cheap multiple redundancy that will made C^2W efforts difficult.

Computer/RF Communicators.

Hybrids of computers and advanced RF transmitters will allow portable information gathering and dissemination to large numbers of people. In the hands of an adversary, sheer numbers will complicate the ability to conduct C^2W against individual transmitters and make transponders the most important targets.

Current U.S. SOFTWAR Liabilities

America's antiquated ideological dissemination structure is made moribund by accretions of useless, overlapping bureaucracies that evolve with glacial slowness. The U.S. lags far behind the rest of the world, which has embraced revolutionary, Third-Wave changes in televised information projection. So viscous is the quagmire of U.S. information projection (still called by its World War II-era misnomer of Psychological Operations—or PSYOP) that not one unilateral effort has ever been made to reach a target television audience and attempt to affect the body politic as a whole, even though effective TV communication could prevent the start of a war, cause mass protests and create major morale problems, and possibly even topple a hostile government from power.

No unilateral attempt was made to reach the total Iraqi television audience prior to or during Desert Shield or Desert Storm, and to date no attempt has been made to try to affect the viewing population in the Balkans, despite recommendations from numerous advisory bodies.

An airborne/airmobile TV broadcast system is the best method for transmission, because it has the advantages of rapid mobility to the target area and mission flexibility over ground- or sea-based TV systems. The existing U.S. system called COMMANDO SOLO-II is at best obsolete for most SOFTWAR missions for several reasons.

No Clear Plan for Strategic PSYOP

The current command and control of strategic TV psychological operations, here identified as SOFTWAR, is detached from the business-end dissemination units such as COMMAND SOLO-II. Regional military commanders have staffs that are not literate in video and thus must rely on obsolete doctrines and technologies. Even U.S. Special Operations Command has downgraded the visibility of its Psychological Operations staff proponent. Therefore, in the global TV environment where speed is everything, little can be accomplished with the current antiquated PSYOP system. In the past, the PSYOP command and control muddle has been further worsened at the theater and strategic levels by a finger-pointing, shoulder-shrugging, bureaucratic mire created by conflicting interests and turf fights among the State Department, the U.S. Information Agency, the Central Intelligence Agency and Department of Defense (DoD). While there is still no NSC-based global oversight on an ongoing basis, reasonable coordination and deconfliction have been accomplished on a theater basis for operations in Haiti and now for the Balkans.

What is needed is clear leadership that designates the defense department as the lead agency in strategic TV PSYOP, because DoD alone has the aircraft, hardware, logistics, and (most importantly), access to world-class reservist personnel to effectively perform the SOFTWAR mission. A joint military unit should be established using the approach of the World War II British Political Warfare Executive under Mr. Sefton Delmer: a small, highly knowledgeable, technically-advanced group, administratively controlled by the Secretary of Defense and under the operational control to the relevant theater commander during a crisis. This SOFTWAR unit should be composed *entirely of hand-picked reservists with full-time, real-world jobs throughout the television industry.*

No PSYOP Flag Billet

There are currently no billets for flag officers in either PSYOP or Information Warfare (much less SOFTWAR); therefore, these war forms are not represented adequately at the theater level. A SOFTWAR/INFO WAR unit should be commanded by a full-time, reserve flag officer with world-class experience in the TV medium. This general officer must conduct a continuing liaison with the various theater commands, informing and educating them as to the potential of SOFTWAR operations in their areas of responsibility.

This citizen expert-as-soldier approach is not new: During World War II, RCA President David Sarnoff was appointed as a brigadier general in improve SHAEF communications; film director Frank Capra was commissioned as a major and produced the *Why We Fight* and *Know Your Enemy* movies; reservist William Donovon was appointed major general to build and operate the Office of Strategic Services (OSS), and he in turn commissioned film director John Ford to run the OSS film unit.

The SOFTWAR unit should not work as a CIA operation, because those civilians with real television credentials would be instantly fired from their civilian media jobs should the CIA connection be discovered. Guardsmen and Reservists, because of their overt and time-honored citizen-soldier status, would not suffer from an association with DoD.

Ignorance of Real-World TV in Joint Planning

U.S. Special Operations Command continues to update the PSYOP doctrine, to include use of the television medium, with little true understanding of the current state-of-the-art or the day-to-day realities of the global television business. There is no one at the command or Joint Staff level in a decision-making position with career credentials in global or even network broadcasting. How can the U.S. expect to produce effective TV counter-propaganda with video illiterates leading video neophytes?

In current doctrine, there are no provisions for carrying a C-band and/or K-band commercial satellite uplink or for integrating an uplink into the system. An uplink would provide access to commercial capacity during operations, as well as provide the ability to soft-jam or spoof enemy use of satellite transponders in a given footprint.

There also are no current provisions for dealing with Direct Broadcast Satellite transmissions which can cover entire regions of continents. This makes COMMANDO SOLO-II TV functions obsolete. A DBS footprint is about 2,000 miles in diameter, while COMMANDO SOLO-II is about 100 miles. DBS also operates in a completely different frequency range from COMMANDO SOLO-II, and advanced DBS models will most likely use an HDTV format.

There are no provisions or plans for HDTV broadcasts from COMMANDO SOLO-II. Now emerging from development, American HDTV may well provide a single world broadcast format, rendering most COMMANDO SOLO-II TV functions obsolete. Similarly, there are no provisions or plans for completely digitizing what is a mostly analog COMMANDO SOLO-II system. Using digitally-based machines provides a tremendous amount of flexibility in reception, processing, and dissemination of the video. Nor are there plans for using existing Digital Audio Tape and off-the-shelf computer capacity for real-time video or audio deception mimicry, which would be extraordinarily useful in both conventional and special operations.

Lack of Organic Unmanned Aerial Vehicles

There are no provisions for either ground or air launching of organic UAVs to transmit TV pictures to an enemy population. Such cheap, off-the-shelf, semi-expendable drones are not only force multipliers, but they also preclude the loss of a COMMANDO SOLO-II (of which there are only four, with two follow-on aircraft) and its highly skilled, hard-to-replace crew of 12 or more.

Obsolete Doctrine and Personnel Policy

The Army's doctrine calls for the PSYOP battalions to form the PSYOP campaign and then give the ideas to the PSYOP Dissemination Battalion for production and dissemination. This works fine for radio, leaflets and loudspeakers, but it flies in the face of what television professionals have known since Marshall McLuhan defined the phrase "the medium is the message." Television is different in that it is a "cool medium," where perception of images outweighs reality. In order to maximize the effect on a target country's TV system, the PSYOP originators and TV producer/disseminators must be one and the same. Otherwise, the cultural earmarks of the enemy's TV system will not be accurately mimicked, and therefore counter-propaganda will not have the desired impact on the target audience.

Although the 4th POG is a USSOCOM asset, Army personnel policies still apply. Army personnel policy is so myopic that it rotates 4th Psychological Operations Group's (POG) TV dissemination personnel every two or three years; thus, the highest quality video product that can be expected is at the community college level. This is not good enough to engage in real-time or near-real-time global TV counter-propaganda, where adversaries are highly skilled in the use of TV as a propaganda medium.

The Army's personnel policy, on the other hand, recognizes the importance of a stable body of area studies specialists, and 4th POG has hired long-term civilian career employees who are linguistically and culturally fluent, and who have the ability to identify quickly nuances in the target culture. However, these area studies specialists are not required to have any TV skills and are thus video illiterates, unable to define or mimic traits within the target TV style and therefore useless in matters of TV counter-propaganda.

Obsolete Television Equipment

The USSOCOM budgetary policy is miserly, imprudent, and oblivious to the real-world needs of the 4th POG in many areas. For example, 4th POG's recently improved production studio is a leap forward for the military, but it is still primitive by network standards and comparable to facilities in the poorest of developing countries. The facility currently has very little advanced video equipment such as state-of-the-art computer-driven video manipulators, digital audio tape machines, mass high-speed dubbing equipment, network-class video tape machines, and uplinks. Setting aside for a moment sub-optimal personnel policy, a mere $10 million dollars and a smart leasing policy would solve most of these problems.

Ineffective Inter-Service Interface

The lack of effective interface between the 4th POG and the 193d Special Operations Group is a serious problem. It appears that the technology and depth of capabilities of COMMANDO SOLO-II are grossly under-utilized by the Army PSYOP community, something on the order of playing Nintendo on a Cray. This gap in understanding and use, however, amounts to a serious degradation of a theater commander's ability to use TV to affect the morale and operations of the enemy.

This is not a slight of Army PSYOP personnel; it is simply that there is so much technology and so many methodologies of operation aboard COMMANDO SOLO-II that by the time a 4th POG disseminator could become proficient with the equipment, he would have been rotated out of the unit. The only people who are truly knowledgeable are the 193d's senior electronics NCOs, who have been working with the planes for 20 years. They are, however, doctrinally restrained from producing PSYOP materials.

The situation has been exacerbated by the lack of adequate interface. The 4th POG is an active Army unit located at Fort Bragg, North Carolina, while the 193d SOG is an Air National Guard unit located some 500 miles away at Harrisburg, Pennsylvania. The two units thus are precluded from operating together on a daily basis. Day-to-day familiarity and practice of highly perishable video skills are absolutely critical to effective TV counter-propaganda. Proximity is no longer the real issue, but what is needed is fiber optic connectivity.

During Desert Storm, the 4th POG deployed in the desert, in line with its tactical doctrine; while the 193d's electronics-packed EC-130s were tied to air bases with hard surfaced runways. The two supposedly symbiotic units were separated by many miles. As a result, they were forced to use such primitive measures as playing a PSYOP tape through a telephone line and re-recording it at the COMMANDO SOLO end.

Even if the 4th POG had a quadriplex data link, transmitting from its base to the COMMANDO SOLO aircraft, the optimum effect of near-real-time counter-broadcasting would not be achieved because of turnaround times, vagaries in transmission quality and the multiple generational degradation of video and audio productions. What is needed is more "jointness:" an integration of collection, production and dissemination functions aboard the COMMANDO SOLO aircraft by a joint-service crew.

Lack of Rapid Airlift and Logistics Support

Getting the 4th POG into theater in force with all the gear needed to do TV operations is retarded by lack of direct airlift support. The Army does not recognize the predominant importance of TV counter-propaganda and therefore treats the 4th POG's TV assets as just another bunch of grunts with junk to haul. The 4th POG was not fully operational in Desert Storm for many weeks.

The Air Guard's 193d SOG, by contrast, deployed, activated and was largely self-supporting during Desert Shield and Desert Storm, because its assigned "slick" C-130s (which had electronic support duties) were not needed during the operation. Had it not been for that special circumstance, the 193d would have been dependent on standard airlift priorities and could not have deployed as rapidly or been able to sustain its tempo of operations. This points again to a need for a joint-service, autonomous organization.

Inappropriate and Obsolete Aircraft

COMMANDO SOLOs are so heavy, slow and altitude-limited that in anything but a permissive battlespace, they are nothing more than huge and expensive targets for man-portable surface-to-air missiles. The C-130 airframe in the COMMANDO SOLO configuration has reached its maximum available payload, fuel, and electrical capacity; and it is restricted to landing on hard-surface runways, making it difficult to interface with the 4th POG's TV unit. The aircraft sits very low to the ground, necessitating expensive custom antenna to be hung from the wings, further reducing its already marginal cruising speed and limiting its crosswind take-off and landing capabilities. Further, the high empty weight of COMMANDO SOLO precludes the aircraft from reaching high enough altitude to radiate an optimum TV pattern and leaves only 4-5 hours of fuel. This means that every time it flies outside the local area it needs tanker support or it must land to refuel. Though the new COMMANDO SOLO has more directional TV radiating capability, enabling it to propagate in a non-circular manner, but its service ceiling limitation precludes effective TV transmission beyond about 50 miles, making this very expensive aircraft a sitting duck to the simplest handheld SAMs.

Military Prejudice Against PSYOP

The terms Psychological Operations or Psychological Warfare cause instant reticence on the part of conventional commanders. Broadly speaking, most commanders simply don't and don't want to understand PSYOP. The whole concept needs to be recast in terms more acceptable to conventional soldiers and re-emphasized as a force multiplier.

SOFTWAR: The Key to Future Conflict

The United States must adapt to the changes of the Information Age and organize for dealing with these realities. Global TV (GTV) provides potential adversaries with a cheap, accurate, real-time, politico-military intelligence service that simultaneously acts as an extremely potent instrument to affect adversely and directly the U.S. domestic body politic. The use of both GTV intelligence as a political instrumentality by unsophisticated adversaries (such as the Somalis, Haitians, and Bosnian Serbs) has led to rapid and dramatic U.S. policy reversals.

Current U.S. thinking on Information Warfare is erroneously trying to fit this Third Wave war-form into an obsolete Second Wave pyramidal organization, fed by the need to maintain turf in a declining budget environment, rather than a need to reshape the whole U.S. politico-military system to deal with most probable future threats. This situation is worsened by the culture of a military whose selection process is geared to Industrial Age standards and is biased against right-brain non-linear thinkers, thus further slowing the speed with which a pyramidal organization can act against IW threats.

A rich, sophisticated niche-competitor, with a charismatic, TV-capable, multi-lingual leader, using direct broadcast satellites could unify other nation-states, virtual nations (both criminal and corporate) and sub-national political or religious groups very quickly to form short-term, goal-oriented alliances. Such an unconventional alliance could easily overwhelm U.S. interests in a series of brief, swift, politico-military actions. The U.S., in turn, with its ungainly military structure and vulnerable domestic body politic (and thus vulnerable national leadership) would not have time to react before the adversary would have accomplished its purposes.

As an adjunct, this hostile amalgam and its charismatic leader could challenge U.S. dominance of space, because all U.S. thinking is based on countering a power with space-faring assets, when in fact a well-financed adversary could simply buy or lease them from existing resources. The simple C^{3}I expedient of using commercial communications, sensor satellites, and comsat-linked recce extensors with commercial encryption could make such an adversary relatively invulnerable to U.S. countermeasures by hiding within the global commercial system. This setup, much like the "hugging tactics" practiced by the Viet Cong against airstrikes, would leave the U.S. with the no-win option of having to take out the entire commercial system.

SOFTWAR is warfare by new means, but the objective is the same. Therefore, it is within the DoD mission of protecting the national security of the U.S. What is needed is a very small, transparent, largely civilian SOFTWAR planning and operations cell in the Office of the Secretary of Defense, whose members are reservists with career-long skills in TV production, advertising and dissemination and who can perform operationally. Their mission should be to study the effects of GTV on belligerent conflict, operations-other-than-war (including peacekeeping and peace enforcement), and war forms resulting from alliances between virtual nations and niche-competitors. Moreover, this SOFTWAR cell should develop doctrine for SOFTWAR politico-military operations.

This doctrine should include both active and passive counter-measures to the effects of GTV, integration of Cyberwar tactics, TO&E for a strategic U.S. IW/SOFTWAR unit, including unmanned aerial vehicles designed for real-time information gathering, processing, and dissemination. In short, their mission should be to develop methods to see through the ambiguities in warning of a SOFTWAR campaign, to devise counter-measures, and to implement them.

Is SOFTWAR real? Many conventional thinkers may not believe so. The issues are arguable. But as General Giulio Douhet, the prophet of air power, said some 70 years ago:"Victory smiles upon those who anticipate the changes in the character of war, not upon those who wait to adapt themselves after the changes occur."[13]

Endnotes

1 Sun Tzu, *The Art of War,* (edited by Samual B. Griffith), Oxford: Clarendon Press, 1963, p. 77.
2 Robert Kupperman interview with the author, January 1992.
3 ABC News, *20/20*, 17 January 1992.
4 Jeff Kamen, "CNN's Breakthrough in Baghdad, Live by Satellite (Censored)," *Washington Journalism Review*, March 1991, p. 27.
5 Barbara Matusow, " Wired!" , *Washingtonian*, March 1991, p. 159.
6 Ibid., p. 74..
7 Howard Kurtz, " Media Notes," *Washington Post*, March 17, 1991.
8 "...talking with David Frost." Interview with R. E. "Ted" Turner, Public Broadcast System, October 25, 1991.
9 Kamen, *op. cit.*
10 *Washington Post*, September 5, 1993, p. A-41. Emphasis added.
11 *New Yorker Magazine*, Comment Section, March 15, 1993, pp. 5-6.
12 Federal Communications Commission, National Institute of Standards and Technology.
13 Guilio Douhet, *The Command of the Air*, New York: Coward-McCann, 1942, Book I, p. 30. See also: Basil H. Liddell Hart, *The British Way in Warfare*, London: Faber and Faber, 1932, p. 11; and I. B. Holley, Jr., *Ideas and Weapons*, Hamden, CT: Archon Books, 1953, pp. 3-22.

Information Warfare: The Future

John L. Petersen ©

During the twenty years that bracket the last decade of the twentieth century and first one of the twenty-first, humankind will experience a period of change unequaled in the history of the world. Never before have fundamental shifts in science, technology, social values, global population, and environmental pollution even happened, let alone converged together in such a short period of time. These two decades constitute nothing less than a paradigm shift. We are moving, at rates that will increasingly appear to be almost instantaneous, into a new era of human history that will not be familiar to those baby-boomers who now predominate American society.

Although the specific details of the future that will come from this convergence are impossible to predict, there nevertheless are some broad notions that are likely to spill from this transition to a new era. First of all, it is a paradigm shift—the whole framework that is used for describing reality is being redesigned. The underlying science that explains the behavior of our physical surroundings, and in turn the companion notions of philosophy, psychology, economy and social values are being assaulted on almost a weekly basis with new and different findings and ideas that seem to be more accurate than those notions which we took for gospel only last year or last month.

Secondly, when the underpinnings of the industrial social system start shaking, then the whole system shakes. It is almost certain, then, that every significant area of human life will have to deal with major change in the coming years—and that includes our notion of security. In a very uneven world populated by whole civilizations living at the same time in pre-industrial, industrial, and post-industrial conditions, what contributes to our security and what, if anything, we can do about it, will quickly shape our priorities, the role of the military, and the way we attempt to influence others.

Although change is advancing on many fronts simultaneously, it is obvious that one of the major drivers and definers of the new era is technology in general and information technology in particular. In much the same way that the printing press five hundred years ago revolutionized how humans displayed and manipulated knowledge (and in so doing catapulted Europe into the Industrial Age) so the microprocessor is similarly providing the ability to generate and distribute information orders-of-magnitude faster and more efficiently than the speediest high-speed web lithography press that exists.

These quantitative advances are also producing qualitative change. We are redefining what we value. It comes from common aspects of quantum mechanics, biology, management theory and computer science that all point to every important human problem being a systems problem. Everything is connected to everything else in a web of immense complexity and interdependency.

The level of complexity is such that these systems are all "out of control"—at least in human terms. As is obvious from rather vain attempts to manipulate the economy, it is impossible to anticipate what will result from the use of a force designed to effect certain behavior change in a large, complex system. There always appear to be second-, third-

and fourth-order implications that were never part of the original plan. Complex systems adjust and adapt to their conditions in very sophisticated and surprising ways, even though component parts are often driven by a set of very simple principles. It should be obvious: there is no central controller who dictates how families, economies, governments, educational systems, and even Pentagons work.

Requirements for Healthy Systems

What contributes to the health and well-being of systems? First of all, it revolves around *cooperation*. Because the components of a system are inter-dependent, when a part does not work well, in some ways it negatively effects the efficiency and effectiveness of every other part. This notion is slowly becoming clear to developed societies: the welfare of the individual/ company/state/nation is directly and ultimately tied to the health of the larger system(s) in which we all operate. Wars and other conflicts always seem to produce as many problems as they solve, with a host of unanticipated negative side effects. Injuring other parts of the system always turns out to have an element of self-injury. So even at high levels in the Pentagon, military leaders are coming to believe that the age of large Napoleonic wars is over, and the use of militaries in the future may well be quite different than in the past. As in the rest of nature, the objective is to get all of the parts working well together.

That only happens if there is also effective *communication*—cooperation with information. Knowledge must be shared so that each part of the system can effectively evolve and adapt to changes in the larger operating environment. This puts a premium on timely and accurate knowledge. Conveniently, the evolution of global communications networks like the Internet and the World Wide Web are putting in place the architecture that truly allows money, ideas and other information to almost instantly transit the globe with little or no thought for cultural or political boundaries.

And so, in part because new technology allows it, and partly because we know that healthy systems require it, the relative importance of information is changing. Information—in many different forms—seems certain to be the capital commodity of the future, replacing the historical role of money and physical force.

A New World, A New Security

This all is another way of saying that we are participating in an accelerating shift to a new era that is producing a *redefinition of the notion of security*. We have new sets of global problems that discount traditional narrowly-focused national interests; we are finding that the Newtonian notion of using brute force to effect behavior change is crude, inefficient and usually adds to our problems; we are coming to understand that nurturing systems requires new mind-sets and tools; and, at the same time, we are trying to cope with the shift of the underlying metric used by humans to establish value.

These combinations of trends assure that some aspects of war and conflict in the future will be quite different from what they have been in the past. But these changes will not be either instantaneous or uniform. The planet's peoples do not march ahead in lock-step into the new age. Reality is messy. Most humans are not participants in the information age. Huge numbers are working hard just to become industrially adept.

Equally large groups are struggling with subsistence. Different people see reality through different lenses and naturally reach for different tools to resolve problems. So, as the Tofflers have suggested, we will pursue our interests in the future on three fronts: with those groups having an industrial mind set, those with an agrarian outlook, and also with those on fast-moving post-industrial leading edge.

By definition, a post-industrial world will be fundamentally different than the familiar industrial era. But as we attempt to understand and respond to the new reality, one important thing must be kept in mind: our industrial-age experiences and tools will not be effective in this new context which has different values and operates from new structures. Nevertheless, our natural inclination is to try to understand the future by overlaying the past on top of it.

Adapting Infotech to Old Ideas

At the present time, for example, much of the thinking about future information warfare looks suspiciously familiar—new versions of old ideas. The traditional uses of militaries have simply been embellished with new information technology. What have militaries always done? Break things and kill people, many would say. So in the same way that in the commercial world a new generation of technology is used to do old things better—word processors replacing typewriters—the military is looking at future warfare with a perspective that presumes that the extraordinary characteristics of information technology will essentially be used to break things better and therefore kill people more efficiently.

The imagery is everywhere. Information warfare planners presume that we can use new technologies to take out electrical grids, degrade enemy sensor systems, foul-up computers, and disrupt lines of communication. Rather familiar military objectives are targeted using new technology. This kind of thinking is built around the assumption that valuable things are tangible and physical and that IW technology is best used as a sledge hammer to overpower the opponent. It presumes a zero-sum game, where if I damage your "thing" and keep mine intact, then you won't be able to use yours. I will, and therefore I will "win."

In the same way that new uses for PCs originally revolved around manipulating spreadsheets of numbers faster and better, almost certainly some aspects of future IW will also include these traditional electronic warfare missions. But, if information is becoming the capital commodity of the future, then human activities will inevitably take on some of the intrinsic characteristics of information—and that is a really new world.

The Unique Qualities of Information

Information, for example, is not zero-sum. It can be given away and still retained. It can be impossible to determine that it has been stolen (from off of a hard drive, for example). It is not obvious who is carrying what, if any, information, and it is not possible to simply empty one's mental safe to determine what one knows. With the global networks that are now in place, information can be distributed almost instantaneously world-wide at very little cost. Unlike something that is tangible and can be sensed and measured, it is becoming increasingly harder to determine if some kinds of information (like photographs) represent reality or not.

Our whole industrial, economic and governmental systems, and in fact our military, are built around the notion of tangible, measurable things being valuable. But that is changing. As we move into the coming decades, in the same way that desktop computers are now beginning to be used for any number of new applications that weren't invented or possible ten years ago, so IW will evolve to both become more congruent with the thinking of the times and also to use new capabilities which don't yet exist.

The transition will be interesting, for new infowar thinking does not easily extricate itself from a social and industrial system that is philosophically derived from a physically-based world. It is hard to conger up a whole new logic—a whole new framework for thinking—for how people might bring this new technology to bear to accomplish their goals. The discontinuities are not trivial. Infowar requires no literal battlefield, for example. An individual (who may or may not be associated with a particular group or nation-state) may be as powerful as many thousands or millions of conventionally outfitted people. And then, as we will see, one may not even know that they have been targeted. In fact, the most sophisticated and important IW "battles" of the future may be waged with adversaries who never know they were "defeated."

The evolution is likely to be quite rapid. Although sophisticated thinking about IW did not much exist five years ago, now more than thirty countries are working on developing the technologies. If the maturation of this area grows as quickly as the information technology industry in general, then it will probably see twenty percent annual growth rates in capabilities for the foreseeable future. The transistor was invented about forty-five years ago, and the semiconductor industry saw regular compounded increases year after year. That exponential acceleration only recently translated into the global explosion that we are now experiencing.

Because the equipment is intrinsically dual use, and there is now a rapidly growing universe of accumulated understanding of what the technology might be able to do being generated by an exponentially growing group of people who are involved in it, it is quite possible that the development of IW will be more rapid than has been information technology in general. Every year there are many more people across the world thinking about the subject, and that almost guarantees regular breakthroughs.

Unlike most traditional military subjects, the commercial world also has an interest in many IW-associated areas. Information security, for example, is a huge problem for financial and research institutions. Also unlike most other areas of military activity, a group or individual interested "getting into the business" of IW can set up an entry-level operation with little more than a PC, a modem and some readily-available software. There are a lot of reasons to suspect that IW will be a growth industry in the coming years.

As suggested earlier, the first generation of a technology is almost always used to do a familiar task more efficiently. The first "horse-less carriages" really did look like carriages, with the driver sitting outside in the rain and snow. Similarly, it's likely that more people currently use computers for typing documents—like a typewriter—than anything else. It takes time for designers to become familiar enough with the unique character and strengths of a technology that it evolves into a second generation that produces applications that never could have existed before.

Advanced First-Generation Infowar

The early indicators of advanced first-generation infowar already are emerging. They seem to be informed by a number of broad trends. One trend appears to be *customization* or *discrimination*. In the commercial world, the industrial approach of *mass* production of large numbers of common things is giving way to customization. As it becomes possible to more completely describe items in digital terms, control processes with speed-of-light information technology, and communicate instantaneously between the important nodes of systems, it becomes easier and easier to produce single products and events that are unique and cost less than mass-produced ones.

Increasing memory and computing capabilities also produce *more definition*—more bits describing a given thing. This allows better discrimination—the ability to focus on smaller and smaller components of systems. Instead of looking at a whole bridge, for example, increased discrimination begins to allow one in time to consider one span, then one beam and, perhaps ultimately, one critical rivet or bolt.

As the capability to describe things in more detail expands, one gains a greater understanding of the inner workings of systems—*better analysis*. With more and more definition, it becomes increasingly obvious how relatively important a subcomponent is to the overall operation of the system. A very few high-priority nodes on which all of the rest of the system depend can then be targeted. Think of the *Starwars* film where the computer in the commandship has identified the single valve in the death star which Luke Skywalker targets to cause the whole system to collapse.

This kind of analysis, of course, can take place at a variety of levels: mechanical, economic, military, political, and even in social and psychological terms. It seems likely, for example, that with enough information of appropriate granularity we will be able to construct models of the psychological support systems that personally sustains certain oppressive leaders. Should the need arise, we could ultimately target our efforts exclusively on the very small number of keystone vulnerabilities that could quickly erode the foundations of the system that support them.

Advances in technology now allow the development of whole new classes of information weapons—*Infobombs*. Although eschewing kinetic principles, they nevertheless are quite destructive. "Knowbot" (knowledge robot) bombs are specialized versions of computer viruses that, navigating through cyberspace, target a specific chip or component in a particular computer and render it useless. In time they will become autonomous, searching on their own for the critical node in the specific location that they have been assigned, acting, perhaps, much like white blood cells cruising around always looking for a wound that needs stanching.

Winn Schwartau, in his book, *Information Warfare*, talks of high energy radio frequency (HERF) guns that from perhaps a quarter-mile away can focus a narrow beam of energy through walls onto a specific computer. The intensity of the energy would overwhelm the electronics of the computer and "fry" it, operating much like a localized version of a nuclear electromagnetic pulse.

What this all means is that in the field of information warfare we seem to be moving toward a time in the not-too-distant future when highly customized tools can be used against very specifically identified small, but very important, system subcomponents. We are moving from sledge hammers to tweezers.

Second-Generation Infowar

This all presumes that we want to continue to break something, or render it inoperative. In the end, as the ancient Chinese strategist Sun Tzu made clear, warfare is not about equipment or armies. It is about influencing peoples minds. *Warfare is about achieving behavior change*, and the highest art is to accomplish that change without a single shot being fired. That is, of course, how we try to operate within our families, companies and country. It seems fair, therefore, considering the global trends that are in place, that this philosophy will expand to involve more of our international relationships.

This old advice sounds suspiciously like the new understanding we have about systems dynamics. It is much better to influence the behavior of a system without damaging it than to break something that later must be repaired. In the broad sweep of history, it seems that humanity is clearly heading in this philosophical direction. As societies have evolved, there clearly has been a movement away from using force to solve problems toward other more benign forms of conflict resolution. If this trend continues, then one can foresee the day when much of the large-scale conflict for a country like the U.S. revolves around manipulating information.

Infowar is Like Advertising

If the advanced first-generation of this discipline uses IW in tweezer-like ways in zero-sum strategies against physical targets, then what might follow that? What will the second-generation of Infowar look like?

Well, it probably looks much like advertising—only running the gamut from blatancy to new levels of sophistication and subtlety. All of human communications involves the manipulation of information. There are many different ways to say essentially the same thing, but the results will vary widely, depending upon the situation and the approach selected. We therefore modulate our messages throughout each day—conversation after conversation—always with the objective of achieving particular ends.

Advertising is the same idea prosecuted on a more formal basis. Advertising anticipates a certain kind of person (income, interests, beliefs), being in a particular "place" (driving, reading a magazine, watching TV), at a given time. Given those demographics and psychographics, the design professional attempts to invent messages, forms, ideas, colors and styles that will get the attention of the reader/listener/viewer and convince him or her to behave in a way that will accomplish the objectives of the advertiser—usually to trade money for a particular product or service. Of course, the same process works in intangible areas like politics, religion, education and charitable work.

Away from Hardware Toward Ideas and Perceptions

There are a number of basic concepts and new technological capabilities that seem to be pushing in this direction. First, we appear to be at the beginning of a change in focus away from hardware toward ideas and perceptions. If, in general, information is becoming humanity's capital commodity and technology is becoming increasingly ephemeralized—more transparent, then it is likely that these trends will manifest themselves in the IW arena. The fact that there are few, if any, things more powerful than ideas for changing the behavior of people, and the technology is already in place that could be used to change societies by manipulating the ideas and images that they receive. This only lends fuel to this trend.

How does one decide what is really happening in this country and the world? Newspapers, magazines, radio, TV, and now, the Internet, are the conduits that extend our awareness out further than the line-of-sight. We are almost exclusively dependent upon this global network to make us aware of most of what is happening on the planet, so we therefore put a great amount of trust in the credibility and integrity of the print and electronic media. Because people have this fundamental dependency upon the global information system, it presents an interesting "opportunity" for manipulating the information that flows through it—as every advertiser and politician knows.

A variation on this theme is the potential to manipulate "memes"—big, powerful ideas that move people to action. There are images and concepts—like the current problems with environmental pollution, nuclear war, and abortion—that are so important to some people that they initiate significant behavior in response to them. For the first time in history, the global information system provides the potential to orchestrate and also manipulate memes. Sophisticated "big ideas" can be launched into multiple levels of cyberspace with the confidence that within a matter of days almost all of the targeted citizens will have become exposed to them. A campaign could be initiated that would, using the creative output of a team of undercover news directors, film producers, commentators and other professionals, roll out a number of programs to establish the importance of a particular idea and then systematically reinforce it over time with follow-up material.

One would make a mistake to think of such an assault in terms of the obvious and rough-edged process of present political campaigns or the in-your-face attempts of 30-second TV spots to acquire your money. We are talking here about a sophisticated, clandestine, very well-orchestrated campaign executed with a level of effectiveness that will be available only a couple of decades from now.

Furthermore, it may not be obvious that a message of any kind is being communicated. New findings in science and growing understanding of the physical effects of the electronic media suggest that more powerful forms of subliminal communication will become available in the future. Invisible messages could be broadly inserted within the news and entertainment media targeted on an unwitting public. Although this might be hard to do in this country, there clearly are other places where such things could probably be accomplished easily.

Changing "Reality"

What if the word that you heard from the mouth of a high official on television was not the word that the person said? What if somewhere between the source and your set could, on-the-fly, selectively change certain words? It would be very hard for the official to offset the damage after the fact. The same could be done with the print media—modifying a story, perhaps only slightly, somewhere between the editor and the press. Technology is coming that will allow this kind of manipulation, and around that potential capability will almost certainly grow the ability to accomplish such legerdemain.

With the digitization of most data, it is becoming essentially impossible to know what is "real." It used to be that one could generally have confidence in the legitimacy of a photograph, particularly if the negative was available. Now images, sounds, and even tactile impressions can be designed in a computer and output with no discernable difference from "reality." No longer is there any intrinsic integrity in any medium—if there ever was so. The technology is only a neutral tool, but now it allows, in ways never before possible, the toying with reality—developing images and sounds that are most convincing.

This ability to manipulate reality is advancing on a number of fronts. One fast approaching capability is projection holography. Within 20 years it should be possible to project light sculptures of very high fidelity into mid-air. People and things will look like they are there—but they really aren't. One immediately thinks about using this for camouflage, but that is adapting the technology to traditional ends. Better to envision it as seeing someone across the street and not knowing if the image was a person or not. Or swearing in court that a certain thing happened because you "saw" it, never knowing that what you saw didn't, in fact, occur as you observed it.

One could speculate endlessly about the nexus—the endpoint—of all of this technology and shifts in values—and probably be wrong, for it is impossible to predict. But we can probably get a flavor of what might happen, or at least what might be possible. That picture is a world of warfare that is almost unrecognizable today. It is a world where knowledgeable people seriously question the validity of all that they see and hear—and at the same time are increasingly dependent upon the same network and sources for informing their life.

It is a world where ideas, messages, and admonitions are focused on individuals and groups who never figure out that they have been soldiers in a battle. The most successful campaigns, by definition, are never public. The adversary never knows that he or she was in a skirmish. This does not presuppose that the targeted person "loses" or thinks that he is worse off. They may not even be unhappy with their new behavior. Remember, the whole notion works only if the whole system works well. Therefore, it is likely that more and more, Infotech and Infowar will be drawn into proactive, preventative roles and missions, designed to assure that some failing or weak part of the system is "tuned," resulting in a larger system that is healthier.

These notions are far enough removed from the present understanding of how humanity and warfare works that some readers will scoff at them and question even the plausibility of such a world. But one need only look back twenty years at how business had no desk top computers, and manufacturing carbon paper was a profitable business. There was no e-mail, no local area networks, and certainly no Internet. One could not have imagined "virtual corporations" or any other of the multitude of new ideas that now drive our lives. Take that amount of change, double it because of the maturity of the technology, and then lay it out toward the horizon. In a rather easy-to-understand way, we can see that it will be quite different then.

But the rate of this change is accelerating. If present trends continue, in 2015 there will be more than 5,000 times more information in the world than there was in 1994. That is an extraordinarily different world than the one we now inhabit. And I can assure you that it will operate quite differently than the familiar one that we now experience.

Rush To Information-Based Warfare Gambles With National Security

Alan D. Campen

Converting information technology into military capability risks ceding strategic advantage to low-tech adversaries.

Information warfare, a revolutionary new strategy, can strengthen the national security apparatus by enhancing the effectiveness of existing forces and weapons. However, a precipitous rush to embrace a relatively new, poorly understood, controversial and unproved strategy is risky. Information warfare perches precariously on assumptions that, if faulty, would turn a salutary revolution in military affairs into a gamble with national security.

The U.S. military, which honed its war fighting machine to defend Central Europe against a massive Soviet juggernaut, is striving to sustain its traditional key role in national security affairs by leveraging information technology. The goal is to eliminate the gap between plunging defense budgets and unremitting demands to shoulder new missions in strange places, against unfamiliar and unpredictable foes.

Recent military expeditions, including those in Somalia, Bosnia and Haiti, have involved operations other than war, low-intensity conflict and taming the furies of tribal, ethnic or religious warfare. These conflicts have emphasized that the U.S. armed forces not only must keep the peace and manage crises around the globe, but, failing that, they also quickly and decisively must win bloodless wars against peer competitors as well as niche aggressors.

Knowledge dominance as a war winning strategy has overwhelming visceral appeal. It educes visions of an inexpensive, a decisive and relatively bloodless way to prevent or minimize armed conflict or to terminate them quickly. Creating a favorable asymmetry in the military decision-making process on the battlefield could grant instantaneous supremacy to a military force that would otherwise be inadequate to the task.

This quest for a new military strategy is impeded by the lack of historical precedent, common definitions, joint and combined doctrine, and guiding principles. Missing is a national-level policy that integrates and synchronizes military initiatives with complementary actions of non-defense activities that also would play key roles in information warfare.

Many authorities consider information warfare risky because of its many disquieting dependencies on unimpeded access to outer space, on assured dominance of the electromagnetic spectrum and on the absolute infallibility of our software-intensive military planning and decision aids. Others doubt that information warfare is relevant in conflicts dominated by regional, ethnic or religious turmoil—confrontations where sophisticated technology may prove disadvantageous to the U.S. war fighter.

Industry has had to endure downsizing to seize the illusive benefits of automation, but it is not clear if the military will make the same sacrifices to its doctrine, organization and procedures to ensure the speedy flow of information from sensor to shooter This urgent quest for relevance in contemporary warfare seems fixated on the notion that U.S. forces can wage command and control warfare (C^2W) to *outsmart* rather than to *overwhelm* opponents with massively superior forces and resources, as the United States has done so often in the past.

The Joint Chiefs of Staff define C^2W as a strategy that implements information warfare on the battlefield by integrating supporting intelligence with operations security, deception, psychological operations, electronic warfare and physical destruction. The objective is to decapitate the enemy's command structure from its body of combat forces while protecting friendly command and control capabilities against such attacks.

Information warfare is a two-sided strategy; one half of which was demonstrated convincingly during the Gulf War; the other half—the protect mode—mercifully never came into play in that idiosyncratic scenario. Experts are concerned about the uncertainties in understanding the defensive side of information warfare. These experts equate the vulnerabilities of electronic information systems to, as one says, the potential for and "electronic Pearl Harbor,"

The draft national security strategy for 1994 informs that "The remarkable leverage attainable from modern reconnaissance, intelligence collection and analysis and high speed data processing and transmission warrants special emphasis... *If properly developed and employed*, they can provide a means to dominate warfare today." [Emphasis added.]

A strategy founded on superior information presumes that the United States can absolutely dominate both outer space and the electromagnetic spectrum—the cyberspace over and around Alvin Toffler's Third Wave battleground—thereby creating a differential in knowledge, all the while shielding its control mechanisms from similar devastation. However, as the panelists at AFCEA's 1995 symposium on Information Warfare made clear, the vulnerabilities of this nation's largely unprotected communications and computer systems are many, and too little emphasis is being placed on the *protective* side of battle in cyberspace. One senior official warned of the rashness in assuming that any one side could ever dominate all aspects of cyberwar. He says that more emphasis is needed on "reducing our own vulnerabilities."

No nation is more vulnerable than the United States upon vulnerable electronic attacks, nor, apparently, more reluctant to confront this potentially disabling weakness. A sanctioned team of experts successfully penetrated over 8,000 of DOD's unclassified—but still vital—information systems. These attacks were detected by less than 5 percent of the system administrators, and fewer than 4 percent of them even reported the intrusion.

The same techniques used for these covert entries into defense systems are known to (even borrowed from) anarchistic hackers, feral crackers and seasoned espionage agents. Practices, procedures and technologies that would materially help defend against such attacks are known but largely ignored because of apathy, fear, ignorance, and arrogance. None of this augers well for a war-fighting strategy that depends so absolutely upon the integrity of information systems.

A recent conference summary from the Institute for National Strategic Studies notes, the United States no longer wields a monopoly over the technology and skills needed to "transform information technology into military advantage." The instruments of information war are now cheap, relatively simple to understand and employ, and readily available to all.

In 1994, House Speaker Newt Gingerich cautioned an AFCEA conference on information warfare that; "Cyberspace is a free flowing zone to which anyone has access, if they have a minimal level of capital...and we had better be prepared for zones of creativity in our opponents we've never dreamed of." Martin van Creveld sounded the same warning in 1991 when he wrote "The tools of information war are well-know, cheap and ubiquitous and unlikely to be monopolized by any side."

In his annual report to the President and the Congress in March 1996, defense secretary William J. Perry wrote, "IW [information warfare] is based on the need for, and use of, information in all phases of national activity—from peacetime operations through conflict...The enormous U.S. dependence on information and its supporting infrastructure simultaneously enables fielding and effective employment of the world's premier military force, and creates significant IW vulnerabilities for the United States, which DoD's IW initiatives are addressing...the vulnerabilities inherent in DoD's information systems and processes..." The secretary also reported that "DoD is studying the commercial sector's IW impact on the military and vice versa, and defining strategies to improve this relationship."

Commercialization and a growing international marketplace for space, telecommunications, computers and encryption systems has irrevocably erased any suzerainty the United States might once have wielded over the precious tools of information war. Indeed, coupling the 18-month half-life of information technology with our 15-year defense acquisition process yields the horrific prospect that our forces could easily be technologically "leap-frogged," and—once again—defeated in the first battle.

"Information-based warfare requires an understanding of the decision and thought processes of your enemy," writes one expert. But, who are these "enemies" that our warriors are the most likely to confront in the next decade? The strategy of information warfare implicitly assumes effectiveness against terrorists, ethnic groups and religious fanatics. But, that fearsome new breed of post-Cold War adversary is not stamped from the Western mold; has few if any "centers of gravity" that are prime targets for our synoptic sensors and brilliant weapons; and is not nearly as dependent as the United States on vulnerable electronic mechanisms for control.

Van Creveld writes of the impotence of Western societies in coping with emergent threats from warriors who neither appear as nor react like soldiers: "We are entering an era...of warfare between ethnic and religious groups...the inability of developed countries to protect their interests and even their citizens' lives in the face of low-level threats has been demonstrated time and time again."

To switch to a knowledge-based strategy inevitably means forsaking the proven, fault-tolerant—albeit costly and bloody—strategy of *resource-based war.* This proposed new military force will no longer derive its superior capabilities from the surge of a once-incomparable industrial base or its apparent willingness to sacrifice from a bottomless personnel pool. Instead, its effectiveness will depend solely on the agility and decisive firepower of a smaller force that has been empowered, highly leveraged, and effectively enlarged through superior knowledge. Or, as one expert cautioned, "upon a small pool of soldiers who are absolutely reliant on information." "Where," said one very senior retired military officer, "is the back-up system when this fails—as it will at some inopportune place and time?"

Agility is one of the guiding fundamentals of information warfare. But, agility now will mean much more than simply the ability to shift forces quickly about the battlefield. It now demands a proven ability to think, plan and communicate more rapidly than the opponent—to function inside the enemy's decision cycle. Each new generation of digital electronics yields dramatic reductions in the time needed to collect, process and transport information. However, lightening-fast computers and instant, global satellite communications won't solve the sensor-to-shooter problem if data must still be filtered through the labyrinth of the many-layered military organization. Detecting, fixing and striking movable targets—the military's most pressing unfulfilled need—will remain on the wish list until *functions* can be made to work as rapidly as do computers and communications. This means that organizations must shed those elements that simply filter and relay information. A rank-, protocol- and process-conscious military must make significant structural changes to its doctrine, organization and procedures and eliminate those echelons that contribute no added value to the flow of information.

A strategy of instant readiness; of rapid global deployment; and of quick, decisive victories, presupposes this nation now is willing and able to do what it has rarely done before. That is, to articulate a coherent national security policy; to predict accurately how military forces must be provisioned to underwrite that policy; and to equip and train its warriors—before the first shot is fired.

The to be supplanted *resource-based warfare* strategy made minimal demands on national intellect or foresight. It was forgiving of an apathetic public, of procrastinating political leaders, of ill-preparedness of its armed forces and of frequent ineptitude on the battlefield. The new *information-based* strategy implicitly demands that our warriors arrive on future fields of conflict prepared to fight and to win the first battle—something they have seldom been able to do in the past.

As the authors of *America's First Battles 1776-1965* concluded "The record of Americans' ability to predict the nature of the next war (not to mention its causes, location, time, adversary or adversaries, and allies) has been uniformly dismal." Professor and military historian Roger Beaumont cautions, "the time, location and conditions of war are always surprises, and these surprises will become even more frequent in a world of increasing complexities fed by rising populations and intensifying nationalism."

The nation that expects to wage and to win at information war must strike just the right balance between its offensive and defensive capabilities. If it cannot, it risks the paradox of fielding a superbly equipped offensive force that also is the most vulnerable to the tools and tactics of information warfare.

Updated from an article in the July 1995 issue of *SIGNAL*.

A Theory of Information Warfare: Preparing For 2020

Richard Szafranski

The profession of arms in a democracy is not exempt from oversight or from consideration of just conduct, even in warfare. Where the will of the people, the moral high ground, and the technological high ground are the same, the profession will remain a useful and lofty one. If, however, the moral high ground is lost, a domino effect occurs: public support is lost, the technological high ground is lost, and the armed forces are lost. It is within this framework that this article postulates a theory of information warfare[1] within the larger context of warfare and proposes ways to wage information warfare at the strategic and operational levels. The tools to wage information warfare are at hand, and because information weapons are such powerful weapons, both combatants and noncombatants need to be protected against them. The vulnerability to information warfare is universal. The decisions to pursue the development of information weapons or to prosecute information warfare are governmental decisions. These decisions need to be made consciously and deliberately and with an understanding of the moral and ethical risks of information warfare. After assessing all the risks and deciding to create information weapons or engage in information warfare, the decision makers should first have an understanding of these weapons and a weapon employment theory before such warfare starts rather than after the weapons are deployed or have already been employed.

Information

Information as used here means the "content or meaning of a message."[2] An aim of warfare always has been to affect the enemy's information systems. In the broadest sense, information systems encompass every means by which an adversary arrives at knowledge or beliefs. A narrower view maintains that information systems are the means by which an adversary exercises control over, and direction of, fielded forces. Taken together, information systems are a comprehensive set of the knowledge, beliefs, and the decision-making processes and systems of the adversary. The outcome sought by information attacks at every level is for the enemy to receive sufficient messages that convince him to stop fighting.

Why would an adversary stop fighting? There are a number of possibilities: an inability to control fielded forces, demoralization, the knowledge or belief that combat power has been annihilated, or an awareness that the prospects of not fighting are superior to the prospects of continuing the fight. These "stop-fighting" messages might be as varied in content or meaning as "Cannae has ruined you," or "Submit to the Tartar or die," or "Your counterattack has failed," or even "Your own people do not support you in warfare that kills babies." Although the methods of communicating the stop-fighting message have changed over the years, the meaning of the message itself remains fairly constant: stop fighting.

As social institutions evolved from first wave agrarian societies to second wave industrial states, information systems evolved and decision-making processes became more complex. Mercantile organizations arose within or alongside the dominant political structures, adding elements of greater complexity as the scope of their activities enlarged. Knowledge networks of knowledge workers, the newest form of institutional structure, emerged and their numbers increased in tandem with the availability of the tools of information technology. As information technology advanced, information systems allowed knowledge, or know-how, to make all the other institutional forms more effective.[3]

As societal institutions evolved, the ways in which societies fought evolved also. The terrorizing drums, banners, and gongs of Sun Tzu's warfare, aided by information technology, became the sophisticated psychological operations of modern warfare. The aim of warfare moved from, or could move from, exhaustion to annihilation to control, according to John Arquilla and David Ronfeldt.[4] Information technology may now have evolved to the point where "control" can be imposed with little physical violence or bloodshed. On the surface this appears to be a good thing. At its center, it may be a dangerous thing. Closer scrutiny should reveal which of these is the case.

What Warfare Is

Warfare is the set of all lethal and nonlethal activities undertaken to subdue the hostile will of an adversary or enemy. In this sense, warfare is not synonymous with "*war*."[5] Warfare does not require a declaration of war, nor does it require existence of a condition widely recognized as "a state of war." Warfare can be undertaken by or against state-controlled, state-sponsored, or nonstate groups. Warfare is hostile activity directed against an adversary or enemy. The aim of warfare is not necessarily to kill the enemy. The aim of warfare is to merely subdue the enemy. In fact, the "acme of skill" is to subdue an adversary without killing him.[6] The adversary is subdued when he behaves in ways that are coincident with the ways in which we—the aggressor or the defender—intend for him to behave.[7] In aiming to subdue hostile will, we must have a clear understanding of the specific nonhostile behaviors we intend to compel, or the hostile ones we want to prevent.

When the security forces of a state engage an enemy state in warfare, the government determines the specific nonhostile behaviors sought from the adversary. When other groups—guerrillas, gangs, clans—engage in warfare, the group leader decides the specific nonhostile behaviors sought. In both state and nonstate warfare forms, the decisions made by group leaders define the aims, the methods, and the desired postconflict conditions of the warfare. Even so, it is a fiction, albeit a common and convenient one, to assert that "states" or "groups" wage warfare. The decision to engage in warfare, including the decision to terminate warfare, is made by *leaders* in the state or group. Likewise, it is the hostile will of enemy leaders that must be subdued to be successful in warfare.[8] Group members, or the citizens of states, may influence the leaders' decisions, but it is the hostile will of leadership that must be subdued. If the "mandate of heaven" passes from the leader to other group members—successor leaders or the population at large—the hostile will of these new leaders must be subdued. Information warfare can help withdraw the mandate of heaven from the hands of adversary leaders.

The great discovery that launched the information age was awareness that everything in the external world could be reduced to combinations of zeroes and ones. These combinations could be transmitted electronically as data and recombined upon receipt to form the basis of information. According to the seminal work on control warfare by Arquilla and Ronfeldt, information is more than the content or meaning of a message. Rather, information is "any difference that makes a difference."[9] Information warfare is a form of conflict that attacks information systems directly as a means to attack adversary knowledge or beliefs. Information warfare can be prosecuted as a component of a larger and more comprehensive set of hostile activities—a netwar or cyberwar—or it can be undertaken as the sole form of hostile activity.[10] Most *weapons*—a word used to describe the lethal and nonlethal tools of warfare—only have high utility against external adversaries. While most often employed against external adversaries, many of the weapons of information warfare are equally well suited for employment against internal constituencies. For example, a state or group would not normally use guns and bombs against its own members; however, the weapons of information warfare can be used, have been used, and very likely will be used against both external and internal adversaries. Information warfare in the Third Reich, for example, was omnifrontal.

Information warfare is hostile activity directed against any part of the knowledge and belief systems of an adversary. The "adversary" is anyone uncooperative with the aims of the leader. Externally, this is the agreed upon "enemy," or the "not us." Internally, the adversary might be the traitor, the faint of heart, or the fellow traveler—anyone who opposes or is insufficiently cooperative with the leader who controls the means of information warfare. If the internal members of a group are insufficiently supportive of the aims of the leader during warfare, internal information warfare (including such things as propaganda, deception, character assassination, rumors, and lies) can be used in attempts to make them more supportive of the aims of leadership.

Warfare and Its Relation to What We Know or Believe

Whether directly employed against an external adversary or internal constituencies, information warfare has the ultimate aim of using information weapons to affect (influence, manipulate, attack) the knowledge and belief systems of some external adversary. It is useful in warfare, for example, for an external adversary to know, or at least believe, that the opposing state or group is united against him or her. Information warfare, simultaneously employed to make internal constituencies cooperative and external adversaries believe its enemy is a united front, is used to help seat that awareness in the knowledge and beliefs residing in the mind of adversary leadership.

The Fragility of Knowledge and Beliefs

Knowledge systems are those systems organized and operated to sense or observe verifiable phenomenological indicators or designators, translate these indicators into perceived realities, and use these perceptions to make decisions and direct actions.[11] Sensing that the plate is hot, one releases it. Observing that one's expenditures exceed income, one curbs spending. Our sensing and observing systems allow us to *know*. We decide and act based on our knowledge, but not on knowledge alone. Knowledge systems are organized according to scientific principles and sustained by the scientific method. That is, knowledge systems are organized to collect empirical data by sensing or observation to formulate hypotheses, to conduct tests that validate or invalidate the hypotheses, and to use these findings as the basis for further action. Belief systems are those implicit or explicit orientations both to empirical data in the form of verifiable perceptions and to other data or awareness (nightmares, phobias, psychoses, neuroses, and all the other creatures living in the fertile swamp of the subconscious, the collective unconscious, or Jung's "unconscious psyche"[12]) that are not verifiable or, at least, are less easily verifiable.[13] According to John Boyd, the process or act of orientation (what Boyd calls "the Big O" in the OODA [observation-orientation-decision-action] loop) also is influenced by genetic heritage and cultural traditions.[14] Thus, the orientation of American leaders is different than the orientation of, say, Japanese or Chinese leaders. The orientation of capitalists and their leaders is different than the orientation of socialists and their leaders.

Unlike knowledge systems, belief systems are highly individualized. Why? They include the stuff of the unconscious and subconscious, powerful elements of which others and even the bearer may be unaware. Even though the target of information warfare is the mind of enemy leadership, it is glib reductionism to think of the enemy as being of "one mind." The enemy is really many individual enemies, many minds. This only complicates the problem slightly. For example, if the enemy is dispersed, separate minds can be attacked separately, using the fact of isolation to the attacker's advantage. If the enemy is concentrated (and over half the people on the planet will live in metropolitan complexes by the year 2020, and will be accessible in large numbers by way of information technology), the attack can be prosecuted against large groups. Even so, the aim of warfare is to subdue the hostile will of leaders and decision makers. This can be done directly by attacks aimed at influencing or manipulating the leader's knowledge or beliefs or indirectly by attacking the knowledge or beliefs of those upon whom the leader depends for action. Leaders and decision makers usually are not difficult to identify in any organization hierarchy. When an organization applies power or force, that organization most often assumes hierarchical characteristics. Thus, the knowledge and beliefs of decision makers are the Achilles' heel of hierarchies.

Knowledge systems, because they are more scientific, are less influenced by culture and by irrational or nonverifiable factors than are belief systems, yet both knowledge systems and belief systems are components present in every human decision-making system.[15] What is known, including the methods by which it came to be known, can be tested by its relation to something else and determined to be valid or invalid, true or false, real or unreal. What is believed is not subject to all the same tests. Even so, beliefs are no less compelling than empirically derived knowledge. Both knowledge and beliefs affect human decision-making. Since the aim of warfare is to influence adversary behavior by influencing adversary decisions, information warfare actions must be directed against both the adversary's knowledge systems and belief systems. If an adversary is organized as a coalition of multiple and cooperative centers of gravity, many culturally conditioned belief systems may exist within the coalition. These may be engaged and defeated in detail. The coalition need not be separate states or groups working as an alliance. The coalition can be the constituencies within a state or within groups. Clausewitz was correct in asserting the potential liabilities associated with allies and coalitions.[16] Moreover, leaders and decision-makers of the coalition provide the most fertile targets for direct or indirect attacks.

Targeting Epistemology

The target system of information warfare can include every element in the epistemology of an adversary. *Epistemology* means the entire "organization, structure, methods, and validity of knowledge."[17] In layperson's terms, it means everything a human organism—an individual or a group—holds to be true or real, no matter whether that which is held as true or real was acquired as knowledge or as a belief. At the strategic level, the aim of a "perfect" information warfare campaign is to influence adversary choices, and hence adversary behavior, without the adversary's awareness that choices and behavior are being influenced. Even though this aim is difficult to attain, it remains the goal of a perfect information warfare campaign at the strategic level. A successful, although not necessarily perfect, information warfare campaign waged at the strategic level will result in adversary decisions (and hence actions) that consistently mismatch or fail to support the intentions or aims of the adversary leader.

A successful information warfare campaign waged at the operational level will support strategic objectives by influencing the adversary's ability to make decisions in a timely or effective manner. Said another way, the aim of information warfare activities at the operational level is to so complicate or confound the adversary's decision making process that the adversary cannot act or behave in a coordinated or effective way. In information warfare, the goal is to harmonize the activities taken at the operational level with those taken at the strategic level so that, taken altogether, the adversary makes decisions that result in actions that consistently support our aims by consistently failing to support the adversary's aims.

At the strategic level, the leaders contemplating an information warfare campaign need to know the answers to at least three questions. First, what is the relationship of the information warfare campaign to the larger aims of the campaign? Second, what is it we wish the adversary leaders to know or believe when the information warfare campaign is concluded? That is, what is the desired epistemological endstate and consequently the success criterion? Third, what are the best information warfare tools to employ in order to meet the established success criteria? That is, how will "means" be related to "ends"?

At the operational level, the leaders responsible for prosecuting the "grand tactics" also need the answers to some questions. Will there be any withheld targets or prohibited weapons in the information warfare attacks? Is the epistemological endstate to be reached all at once, everywhere, or are there interim states that need to be reached in specific geographical areas, in a specific sequence, or in specific sectors of information activity? The questions of "command and signal" also need to be addressed. Specifically, leaders at the operational level need to know when attacks will be terminated and the means by which the termination order will be communicated. These are important questions because information weapons, depending on the weapons used, may cause collateral damage to the attacker's knowledge and belief systems.[18] In the worst case, the adversary's response could include counterattacks against "friendly" information systems that are somehow indistinguishable from collateral damage caused by the information analog of "friendly fire." This thought requires some elaboration.

Warfare is a human social activity.[19] The workplace of warriors is society, the societies of those engaged in combat and the societies of active and passive spectator groups. Because it is a human activity—and one dependent on human action, reaction, and interaction—the outcomes of some warfare activities may be unpredictable. As Grant Hammond notes in "Paradoxes of War," if the outcomes of a war could be known in advance, there would be scant reasons for the loser to fight in the first place.[20] Moreover, there may be lag times between action and response; some outcomes take longer to develop than others. Thus, the notion that World War II was the outcome of World War I (or the peace treaty that terminated combat) may very well be true. The unpredictability, however, is not confined to the consequences of war termination. Specific actions in warfare can have specific and unpredictable reactions.

Information attacks—attacks aimed at the knowledge or belief systems of adversaries—can have consequences that are as unpredictable as attacks aimed at the physical destruction of property or combat equipment or those aimed at killing human beings. Suffice it to say that information attacks have stochastic effects and that unless these are considered and evaluated in advance, an information attack may not have the effect ultimately desired. Worse, it may have consequences that are so undesirable that the attacker will rue that an attack was made in the first place. The notion of stochastic effects, like the notion of collateral damage, needs to be considered at both the strategic and operational levels of information warfare.

The Target Sets of Information Warfare

The more dependent the adversary is on information systems for decision making, the more vulnerable he is to hostile manipulation of those systems. Software viruses only hurt those dependent on software. Radioelectronic combat works only against forces reliant on radios or electronics. Electromagnetic pulse generators—unless the generator is a nuclear weapon—do not affect human couriers and runners. While this suggests that only postindustrial states or groups are highly vulnerable to information warfare, the opposite may be the case for two reasons. First, preindustrial or agrarian societies still have vulnerable epistemological systems. Because information warfare can be prosecuted against the adversary's entire epistemology—both knowledge systems and belief systems—even preindustrial agrarian or primitive societies are vulnerable to information warfare. Second, industrial societies, and even some advanced industrial societies, may acquire much of their telecommunications infrastructure from more advanced or postindustrial societies or groups.

By way of analogy, consider the case of the homeowner and the architect. The homeowner may not be aware of flaws in his or her residence, but the architect is aware. Likewise, the operator or "owner" of a telecommunications system designed or built by others may be unaware of important features of which only the designer or manufacturer has knowledge. If the architect is not directly subordinate or accountable to "the owner," then the potential exists for the architect to exploit the hidden features to his own advantage. In the warfare of business competition, the architect may have the means, motive, and opportunity to exploit these features to meet the objectives of the firm, whether or not the government or the state approves of these actions.

In the case of advanced societies or groups, attacks against telecommunications systems can wreak havoc with an adversary's ability to make effective decisions in warfare. Yet, one should also appreciate that an apparition in the sky, even a natural phenomenon like a solar eclipse, can be used to attack the belief systems of a less advanced group. Totems and taboos might function equally as well as the targets or the tools of information warfare against a primitive group. Thus, vulnerability to information warfare is nearly universal, the differences being only a matter of degree.

An Illustration of Complexity

Information warfare is a complex notion. It is complex because the weapons employed are and always have been as common as words, pictures, and images, even though today these may be communicated or manipulated in uncommon ways. It is complex because the attacks are crafted by minds to affect minds. In addition, it is complex because the attacks can be direct or indirect, aimed at internal or external constituencies, the only constant being the effect sought. The desired effect of information warfare is to influence and change what the adversary believes or what the adversary knows.

The Sepoy Mutiny of 1857-58 provides an example of the complexity. The mutiny reportedly was triggered by a rumor that the British were coating rifle cartridges in animal fat.[21] Contact with this fat was taboo to the Hindu and Muslim sepoys (Indian natives in the British army). Even though the cartridge coating was *not* animal fat and could be subjected to scientific tests that would result in this *knowledge*, the sepoy *believed* the substance was animal fat. This belief was more compelling to the primitive sepoy than knowledge. Thus, it was belief, not knowledge, that influenced sepoy behavior and triggered a difficult struggle between the British and the Indians. This case is also illustrative of the fact that even though the use of this misinformation was directed against the British leadership, the attack was indirect. It was the sepoy leaders who started the rumor, and in so doing attacked the belief systems of both Hindu and Muslim sepoys to spur them to rebel against their British masters.

Thus, information warfare can be waged both internally and externally, by, against, or between societies or groups of varied technomic capability (a combination of advances in technology and the increase of economic wealth).[22] When waged against internal constituencies, its aim is to use those constituencies to meet the larger aim of warfare: subduing the hostile will of an external adversary. When information warfare is prosecuted externally, the object is to subdue the hostile will of external adversary leaders.

Vulnerable Sophisticates?

In states or groups with high technomic capability, the target set for information warfare at the strategic level is wonderfully rich: telecommunications and telephony,[23] space-based sensors, communications relay systems; automated aids to financial, banking, and commercial transactions; supporting power production and distribution systems; cultural systems of all kinds; and the whole gamut of hardware and software that constitutes how the adversary knows and what the adversary believes. Strategic information systems in states with high technomic capability oftentimes are mirrored by operational level ones of equal complexity. All are vulnerable to attack.

Information warfare need not be deferred until hostility becomes open. Adversary leadership will be less likely to fight if it believes one or more of the following: that violence is bad, or that they will be without allies, or that they will face harsh sanctions should fighting erupt, or that their industrial base will not support prolonged warfare, or that their armed forces are unready. Should actual fighting break out, attacks at the operational level can harmonize with attacks at the strategic level.

The target set at the operational level is equally lucrative when the adversary has high technomic capability and relies on automated aids to fight. Hierarchical systems are most vulnerable, but even networks have control or relay nodes that are susceptible to attack. To function effectively, networks have hierarchical elements or nodes. Often these elements are invisible—embedded software protocols, filters, sort instructions, and the like.[24] That they are more difficult to attack may not make them immune to attack.

The higher its technomic capability and the greater the number of its interactions with other groups (including internal groups) or states, the greater the state or group's potential vulnerability to information warfare. The vulnerability may increase as network size increases, dependence on the information transacted increases, or the number or volume of transactions increases. Consequently, a state or group "engaged" worldwide may be exposed or vulnerable worldwide. (If the objective of engagement is a strategic campaign aimed at affecting the knowledge or beliefs of others, then those engaged are, of course, similarly vulnerable.) Democracies are no less vulnerable than totalitarian regimes, although democratic social systems, as groups, may be somewhat more fault-tolerant. By that is meant that democracies promote diversity and diversity increases the tolerance for difference. This willingness to accept diversity (and even the bizarre), the routine coexistence of contradictory knowledge and different beliefs among individuals and groups, and the constant attempts at manipulation by marketing experts do not reduce the vulnerability of a democracy, but they do mitigate the impact of information warfare attacks. Said another way, many people in democratic nations may be immune to attacks because their knowledge may be limited, their belief systems may always be in flux, and much information registers only as noise. Thus, images of televised eroticism may have little effect on many in the United States. Yet, the same images that almost are mundane in the United States could have dramatic effects if televised in China, Iraq, or Iran.[25]

Even though the democracy's social system may be fault-tolerant, its technomic control apparatus may be less so. Banking, finance, trade, travel, and air traffic control are now and increasingly will become more dependent on information technology systems. In 1992 the United States invested over $210 billion on information technology (about half the level of worldwide investment), and the amount invested is expected to grow about 18 percent each year for the next several years.[26] As dependence on information systems grows, warfare waged by nonstate groups—terrorists, religious extremists, hostile businesses—against information systems constitutes a real threat. The bombing of the World Trade Center, whatever other general or specific objectives it might have had, apparently was designed to inflict serious damage on the trading and banking capability of the United States. The information warfare component of some future strategic warfare campaign waged by terrorists certainly will not fail to include the power production facilities and communications systems serving the principal target. Simultaneous attacks against widely dispersed nodes could have a strategic effect. That is, they could affect the knowledge, beliefs, and the will of leaders.

A cautionary note: because an information warfare campaign at the *strategic* level aims to subdue hostile will by affecting the knowledge and beliefs of the adversary, it cannot discriminate between combatants and noncombatants. Because the weapons of information warfare systematically attack the adversary's knowledge and belief systems (that which makes us different from other species), the likely outcomes of information warfare need to be evaluated consciously before information attacks are prosecuted. A successful information warfare campaign interposes a false reality on the human target. At the strategic level, these targets include both combatants and noncombatants. The interposition of a false reality ultimately may be as wrongful and inhumane as the wanton destruction of crops. To unhinge a noncombatant from reality, especially when the effects cannot be known or controlled, may be no less wrongful than to force another into starvation or cannibalism. Said another way, the principles of just war and just conduct in warfare need to be evaluated whenever *strategic* information warfare is contemplated.

Deception and disinformation, radioelectronic combat, propaganda, and the whole gamut of "psychological warfare," or command and control warfare attacks against enemy combatants at the *operational* level cannot be said to be wrongful. These aim to subdue without fighting or to reduce the amount of violence required. Becoming unhinged from reality in combat, like death or some other form of suffering, is a risk of which combatants are aware, and is a possibility that combatants must accept. Thus, as long as information warfare and weapons are restricted by norms or laws to the operational level of warfare, it would appear that they are no more or any less evil than any other weapon. The problem remains a twofold one: determining the morality of an information warfare campaign waged at the strategic level and restricting the use of information weapons to the operational level.

The decision to pursue information warfare or develop information weapons is a leadership decision. It is a strategic decision in the United States because it is the Congress, representing the entire citizenry, that links means to ends. In the United States, such a program (if done by the state) would be done with money appropriated by the Congress. The Congress, or its oversight committees, will evaluate the morality of information warfare. In the wake of this evaluation, the Congress may confine these weapons and their use to the operational level of warfare. The Congress may also establish safeguards to prevent any such weapons so developed from being used against internal constituencies. The legislative branch also may make laws preventing the use of information weapons against non-U.S. noncombatants and internal constituencies. As outsourcing and contracting out initiatives increase, the Congress also can be expected to act to prevent some commercial enterprise from developing such weapons. (Have not news stories and "exposés" produced by commercial news enterprises proven to be contrived, aimed at influencing our knowledge and beliefs? Have not subliminal messages been used in the past in attempts to influence our purchasing behavior? Have not hackers entered and affected—or infected—databases already? We need to consider that there may be only a slim difference between a hacker and a terrorist in the information age. This is especially so if the hacker can attack things like finance, credit ratings, college transcripts, or other databases upon which technomic institutions depend.) The political leaders in the United States can be expected to consider the morality of information weapons and information warfare, no matter which group develops the weapons or engages in the warfare, and to regulate their use accordingly. The Congress very likely will conclude that the employment of information weapons at the operational level is useful and necessary, but that employment against noncombatants, or their employment at the strategic level is wrong.

The United States should expect that its information systems are vulnerable to attack. It should further expect that attacks, when they come, may come in advance of any formal declaration of hostile intent by an adversary state. When they come, the attacks will be prosecuted against both knowledge systems and belief systems, aimed at influencing leadership choices. The knowledge and beliefs of leaders will be attacked both directly and indirectly. Noncombatants, those upon whom leaders depend for support and action, will be targets. This is what we have to look forward to in 2020 or sooner.

Endnotes

[1] Information warfare sometimes is erroneously referred to as command and control warfare, or C^2W. The aim of C^2W is to use physical and radioelectronic combat attacks against enemy information systems to separate enemy forces from enemy leadership. In theory, information warfare actually is a much larger set of activities aimed at the mind and will of the enemy.

[2] Chris Mader, *Information Systems: Technology, Economics, Applications* (Chicago: Science Research Associates, Inc., 1974), 3.

[3] The "waves" of societies are described by Alvin Toffler in *The Third Wave* (New York: William Morrow and Company, Inc., 1980). See also Alvin and Heidi Toffler, *War and AntiWar: Survival at the Dawn of the 21st Century* (Boston: Little, Brown and Company, 1993). A seminal work on institutional forms is forthcoming from David Ronfeldt.

[4] John Arquilla and David Ronfeldt, "Cyberwar is Coming!" *Comparative Strategy* 2 (April-June 1993): 141-65.

[5] Martin van Creveld, *The Transformation of War* (New York: Free Press, 1991), 196-205. Words like *war* and the lately contrived *warfighter* confuse the warriors in a democracy by misuse. In the United States, War (with a big W) is declared by the Congress: the people representing all the people. Executive *War Powers* are really *warfare* powers. The days of Clausewitzian, trinitarian Wars may very well be over, as van Creveld suggests. The days of warfare, however, are not over.

[6] Sun Tzu, *The Art of War*, trans. Samuel B. Griffith (New York: Oxford University Press, 1971), 77.

[7] Richard Szafranski, "Toward a Theory of Neocortical Warfare: Pursuing the Acme of Skill," *Military Review*, November 1994; and idem, "When Waves Collide: Conflict in the Next Century," *JFQ: Joint Force Quarterly*, Winter 1994-95.

[8] Joseph A. Engelbrecht, "War Termination: Why Does a State Decide to Stop Fighting?" (PhD diss., Columbia University, 1992). Colonel Engelbrecht is a colleague at the Air University's Air War College.

[9] Arquilla and Ronfeldt, note 9, 162. According to this definition, a message with no discernible "meaning" is still "information." This definition is useful when contemplating the tactics of information warfare.
[10] Ibid.
[11] *Phenomenology* can be defined as "the theory of the appearances fundamental to all empirical knowledge." Dorion Cairns, in Dagobert D. Runes, ed., *Dictionary of Philosophy* (Totowa, N.J.: Littlefield, Adams & Co., Ltd., 1962), 231-34.
[12] C. G. Jung, *The Undiscovered Self* (New York: The New American Library, Mentor Book, 1958), 102.
[13] Information warfare requires that philosophers, cultural anthropologists, area specialists, linguists, and semanticists join the "operations" staff. The days have passed when war colleges or staff colleges could neglect these other disciplines.
[14] John R. Boyd, briefing slides, subject: A Discourse On Winning and Losing, August 1987. Maxwell AFB, Alabama.
[15] Ibid.
[16] Carl von Clausewitz, *On War*, ed. and trans. Michael Howard and Peter Paret (Princeton: Princeton University Press, 1976), book 6, chapter 6, 372-76.
[17] Ledger Wood, in Runes, 94-96.
[18] The effects to which I refer are more complicated than the inability to prevent your own jamming from interfering with your own communications systems. These unconfinable, spillover effects of stray electrons can be modeled and some compensation can be made for their effects. The weapons and effects of information warfare are not so easily confinable or controllable. In warfare it is common to both demonize and ridicule the enemy. Ridicule often takes the form of jokes. If these jokes ridicule an enemy from a different ethnic group, these jokes become officially sanctioned racist jokes. If the ethnic group is part of our own citizenry, such attacks can cause collateral damage. The collateral damage to the armed forces may have effects as far-reaching as the appearance of officially condoned racism. If one accepts that weapons and attacks have stochastic effects, then some consequences are unpredictable.
[19] Van Creveld, 35.
[20] Grant T. Hammond, "Paradoxes of War," *JFQ: Joint Forces Quarterly*, Spring 1994. Dr Hammond is a colleague on Air University's Air War College faculty.
[21] George C. Kohn, *Dictionary of Wars* (New York: Facts On File Publications, 1986), 214.
[22] *Technomic* is a word coined by Col Joseph A. Engelbrecht. He defines it to mean "of or relating to progress in the development of the application of scientific principle (technology), and in the development of wealth (economics), and in the interrelationship between advances in science and the spread and increase of economic wealth. Technomic vitality. Technomic proliferation."
[23] Gerald R. Hurst, "Taking down Telecommunications" (Thesis, School of Advanced Airpower Studies, Air University, Maxwell Air Force Base, Ala., 28 May 1993).
[24] Ibid.
[25] Iran provides a good example. The Majles investigation into the Iranian department of "Voice and Vision" illuminates Iran's sensitivity to the content and meaning of pictorial messages. Consider these comments from the investigation:

> A basic criticism of the pictorial programs of the Voice and Vision is lack of attention to full veiling of women, lack of attention to the chador, and spreading of the culture of the "manteau" and scarves of the immoral kind.
> The grand leader on occasions has given opinions and directives to the Voice and Vision organization or its director. Unfortunately, the instructions and directives of his honor were not implemented. For example: . . From 1368 [21 March 198920 March 1990] to 1370 [21 March 199020 March 1991], he made reminders to the Voice and Vision on 14 occasions, the most important of which concern: A) Misinformation. B) The low level of quality of the beyond the border programs and failure to propagate and spread Islamic views in them. C) The broadcast of blasphemous sentences concerning the Sire of the Pious. . . . E) Showing actual persons in the role of the infallible imams.

See "Majles Investigates Activities of Voice and Vision," 3, 4, 15 November 1993, 5-6, in *Foreign Broadcast Information Service Report: Near East and South Asia* (FBISNES94016S), 25 January 1994, 6-8. I am grateful to Dr George Stein of the Air University's Air War College faculty for pointing out this example of what simultaneously might be internal information warfare and potential vulnerability to external information warfare. Saudi Arabia recently joined China as the most recent nation to outlaw satellite television receivers. One can easily appreciate the effects that Music Television (MTV) might have on such cultures.

26 A telecommunications executive speaking in an Air University forum under the promise of nonattribution disclosed these estimated figures.

This article is reprinted from the Spring 1995 issue of *Airpower Journal*.

Ethical Conundra of Information Warfare

Winn Schwartau

At first blush it sounds so clear. So non-violent. So intangible. Then you get to thinking about it: *Information Warfare*.

In the late 1980s, the American military began to think about a new kind of warfare. Apart from the operational considerations, there was also concern for a strategic approach which would insure American popular support for military deployments. A new and better kind of warfare; more palatable for the dinner-eating, news-watching family of four. Vietnam-era pictures on the six o'clock news graphically showed dead soldiers—ours and theirs—and children—theirs—burning from napalm strikes. These images did not fit neatly with the desired American self-image. As a country, we are not comfortable with viewing ourselves as purveyors of random violence.

The media has had a tremendous effect on how we view war, and with the advent of " anywhere, anytime" instant remote communications, our soldiers are no longer thousands of miles away, fighting for American national interests. Today, they fight in real-time, in our living rooms, where not only we, but the entire world, watch and judge their actions.

Consider the involvement of U.S. troops in Somalia. Media broadcasts of horrendous conditions, medieval chaos and civilian tragedies created a swell of support for America to "do something" to assist a helpless population. So we landed on East African shores for a peace-keeping mission; but, oddly enough, the media beat the troops to the scene. Entrenched on the hot beachheads with their cameras and boom microphones, the media filled the airwaves with live broadcasts of arriving SEALs and Marines. And then the troops went to work, attempting to bring some sort of order to a country in dire straits.

Then our exit from Somalia was as cathartic as our entry. Full-color videos of Somalian rebels dragging a dead U.S. soldier through the streets was too much for most Americans to stomach. Nearly instantly, support for U.S. intervention waned, and we pulled out.

Based upon conversations with, and getting to know, hundreds of military folks over the last five years, I believe that a new breed of soldier—a post-World War II soldier—is coming to the fore. We are being served by military leaders who are charged with defending our country, but who are also keenly aware that we do indeed live in a new world. They thoroughly understand that the typical war-fighting projection of power must be handled in ways that not only make military sense, but do not violate the political, social and ethical consciences of those who must support them.

I believe that the U.S. military genuinely wants to be a "kinder and gentler" fighting force. Inherently, we have attained what might be referred to as an "enhanced consciousness." We have a fundamental desire to whip the bad guy, but we want to do it honestly, quickly, efficiently and with a minimum of bloodshed. From what I have seen and learned as a civilian, every effort is being made to develop ways for America to fight a "clean war."

As part of the way to achieve that goal, the military has been developing an array of technologies which fit into the "non-lethal" category. Sticky-foam which, when shot out of a hand-held "cannon," binds the enemy in a spider web of inescapable gluey substances. Sonic cannons which incapacitate adversarial forces. Nerve-shattering electromagnetic emanations which effectively paralyze the enemy's ability to function. Electromagnetic Pulse Guns, EMP Bombs and HERF guns which debilitate or destroy the electronics of computers, communications, satellites or power systems. Of the "non-lethal" methods developed, none have attracted as much attention as Information Warfare.

The definition I first proposed for Information Warfare back in 1993 was a conflict in which "*information and information systems act as both the weapons and the targets*." At that time, the working military definitions of InfoWar were classified, but some versions were close to the one I offered. Today, the Pentagon's working definition of InfoWar has been expanded to include the concepts "deny, destroy or intercept adversary computer, network or communications, while protecting ones own."

The other criteria I have used when describing Information Warfare is "the total absence of bombs, bullets or other conventional tools of physical destruction." Thinking in this focused manner, concentrating exclusively within the virtual domain, or fourth dimension of warfare, hones the process of problem-solving and generates new paradigms of thought.

Within this model of (Pure) Information Warfare, many options become apparent that are not so readily available for conventional conflict. Simply put, if we (or anyone else for that matter) fly a plane into the airspace of a sovereign state and drop a load of bombs, there is a reasonable chance that such an act would be considered an "act of war." However, we must note that the U.S. has not "officially" been at war with anyone since the end of World War II, which further complicates the lines of war/no-war. (I say this with full recognition and respect for the soldiers and families who suffered during the last half century of conflict in undeclared "wars.")

Consider that in the last decade or so, several international—allegedly unprovoked—"shoot-downs" did not trigger war: the Soviet downing of KAL 007; the American missiles that destroyed a civilian Iranian jet-liner; the recent Cuban fatal interception of private aircraft in the Caribbean. Then consider that in 1986, American warplanes ravaged through downtown Tripoli, and we did not see a military response.

The bottom line we have come to accept, perhaps in too cavalier a fashion, that we are King-of-the-Hill militarily: We are the big kids on the block, and don't challenge us if you know what's good for you. Thus, one could argue, we have seen an increase in terrorist-type, State-side events by foreign elements. They can't beat us in a "fair" fight, so they resort to terrorism.

Now, with the advent of Information Warfare as an increasingly viable option to conventional armed conflict, we should inwardly examine those issues which—eventually—we must openly face, come to terms with, and if I had my say-so, clearly announce our policy and intentions to the world.

Pure Information Warfare takes many forms, and I will concern myself with only Class II and Class III InfoWar as detailed in "Information Warfare: Chaos on the Electronic Superhighway."[1]

Offensive Capabilities

Forgetting about the defensive aspects for a moment, what do we have in our arsenal that would permit the U.S. to wage InfoWar against an adversary, whether by the military or by other official, government-sanctioned organizations? Briefly, they include:

1. Offensive software: viruses, Trojan horses, embedded exported systems or other malicious software.
2. "Sniffing" the communications of foreign (domestic) civilian and military networks and communications.
3. Tempest-style eavesdropping upon electronic devices with characteristic emissions.
4. "Chipping": hardware-based malicious software embedded surreptitiously in systems.
5. Directed-energy weapons which disable or destroy electronic systems.
6. A full range of PSYOP capabilities.

Used in various combinations, deployed by a politically-willing and ably-armed force, these "weapons" have the capability potentially to enhance much of our military's conventional means of conflict.

But, should we use them, other than in times of "war," (i.e., Gulf Conflict) or as an adjunct to conventional conflict? Can the weapons of Information Warfare stand alone as means to project force? This is the ethical conundrum that we face today. Is it ethically correct for the U.S. to defend its economic national security interests by resorting to those same tactics that are used against us?

It goes without saying that the United States is a highly visible and rich target for the theft of intellectual property from the private sector, and to a lesser degree from the military sector. We have the most sophisticated spying apparatus in the world, to the tune of nearly $30 billions per year; but, to date, these immense capabilities have been relegated to Cold War tactics and military protectionism.

Should we redirect our "eyes and ears" to the industrial and economic treasures of our friends and adversaries alike, not with the prime intention of military advantage, but rather of global economic supremacy? We know full well that in less than two decades, unless radical steps are taken, the United States will become second or third in national global economic might. Should we not use the same tactics and techniques as our competition?

Do we find it ethically displeasing to "read other peoples' mail?" Why not? They do it to us. On the other hand, what choices do we have?

Is there a middle ground, perhaps, such that, while we may choose to listen to our competitors, we will do nothing overt or active to disrupt their operations or interfere with those transmission? Is that an ethical line that we should not cross? Or do we find ourselves in the position that must use clandestine and covert methods to maintain an "even playing field" of global competitiveness? Perhaps we should employ technical mercenaries, in no way officially affiliated with the U.S. government, who will remotely, invisibly and with deniability effect our will. Perhaps.

The capability distinctly exists. Some corporations allegedly are already engaged in such missions for their own interests; but, if they are caught, will the U.S. prosecute those persons and organizations that are operating—ultimately—in the best interests of our country?

How we respond to these ethical considerations and the decisions we make will set the tone for America for generations to come.

Another option we face, one which also creates an ethical dilemma, is whether we should use export controls as means of Proactive Defensive Information Warfare.

The U.S. has the capability to export technology, ostensibly for the good of the buyer and the seller. However, using advanced software and hardware techniques, we can also export goods that can effectively be used as "weapons" if indeed the need arises. In the early 1970s, according to some sources, when AT&T sold a national telephone switch to Poland (then a Warsaw Pact country), the company was asked to include "bits and pieces" that would allow the United States to remotely shut down that country's communications infrastructure. The idea was that, in the event of a Soviet attack, we would slow down and perhaps thwart hostile activities. It has been claimed by other confidential sources, that we have developed similar capabilities against North Korean 360/370 military computers.[2]

The question becomes, though, should we, as a matter of policy, exploit this capability by using "infected" or malicious software, or by installing modified silicon chips whose payload can be activated by the U.S. when deemed appropriate? In a world of global competition, and as military, national economic and civilian interests converge, how do we draw a line between those actions that should be taken, and those from which we should refrain?

Collateral Damage

I pose this hypothetical situation for your consideration: The United States is involved in an armed conflict with a recognized adversary, and we have the support of our significant allies and the majority of our population. CNN and the world's news services have access at least as open as that in the Gulf War. In order to achieve some very specific tactical goals, the field commanders are faced with a choice.

1. They can pick a sophisticated smart bomb (conventional explosive), which will almost assuredly strike the exact designated target, and will almost certainly kill a dozen innocent civilians—whose deaths will be broadcast to the world in near-real-time.

2. They can choose to use a non-lethal weapon (of whatever sort—that's immaterial here) which will have the same tactical effect as the first option. However, there will be no civilian deaths to record on video tape immediately. Instead, the planners project 100-200 collateral civilian deaths within two weeks, as a result of the non-lethal attack. What do we do?

This is the crux of the ethical conundrum that we face, for the use of non-lethal weapons in no way means that deaths will not occur, either in the short term or the long term. "Non-lethal" generally refers to the immediate casualty count of the weapon's use and to the amount of physical injuries it causes.

Further complicating the issue is the fact that Information Warfare offers additional opportunities other than in strict conflict, war or not. The techniques and offensive capabilities of InfoWar weapons can be considered part of our arsenal for:

- Operations Other Than War
- Prelude to Conflict
- Alternative to Conflict
- Sanctions
- Middle ground between diplomacy and war (conflict).

A couple of hypothetical examples should suffice:

1. Country 'A' is misbehaving, and the international community agrees that steps must be taken to bring them into line. One of the options available is to deny them access to international communications and or financial commerce. Through the use of jamming, denial-of-service attacks, or assorted other methods, Country 'A' is electronically isolated from the rest of the world. As a result, the internal economy suffers, and a range of social effects are seen and felt, perhaps including starvation, an inability to care for sick people, etc. If the only other alternative is conventional conflict, with guaranteed high-profile civilian carnage, is Information Warfare an acceptable choice for us and our allies to make? (I have had the opportunity to design for the government a range of ECO-D (Economic Deactivation) scenarios which analyze such options. The ramifications can be staggering and not obvious.)

We then have to consider if the "attacks" against Country 'A' are all conducted from outside of their physical sovereign boundaries, or are some waged from within their physical boundaries? Does this make an ethical (or legal) difference as to whether or not we take such actions?

2. Country 'A' or a non-state actor—such as a transnational terrorist organization—bombs and destroys or seriously damages a national symbol such as the Statue of Liberty. I think that it is safe bet we would retaliate strongly. If, however, a sports stadium or other less-sensitive target were bombed with little or no loss of life, our national will might not be so seriously challenged and thus our response might not be so acute. What if the attacker were somehow to electronically drain the asset base of Citibank—to the tune of some hundreds of billions of dollars, what, if anything do we do? We as a nation have to decide whether or not our economy and the civilian, wealth-producing sector are national assets worthy of protection.

If retaliation is against a nation-state perpetrator, that is one thing under international law. If, however, we attack a non-state actor within the borders of a sovereign state, the decision calculus is entirely different, particularly if our actions adversely affect the interests of that state. Physical bombings are one thing, but electronic terrorist attacks might be accomplished without the same sort of culpability of the host-nation.

Denial-of-service attacks offer a great deal of power to the Information Warfare-enabled nation-state. The targets for such attacks in today's integrated information society (given an appropriately vulnerable target) blur the lines between the military and civilian, as the increased convergence between them occurs.

Therefore, is an InfoWar attack against a power plant which services a military target acceptable, if we know that the same power source is the life-line to a civilian population as well? Or, is it politically and socially acceptable to avoid the headline-grabbing visual carnage that a military strike might cause, preferring instead to permit invisible collateral damage (although perhaps greater in terms of long-term fatalities).

Military and political planners will have to come to terms with these fundamental issues as we move into the fourth dimension of war—Cyber or Pure Information Warfare—but we must also remain acutely aware of the ramifications of such actions.

Let us say that the U.S. does initiate a sanctions-based, offensive denial-of-service assault against a target nation-state. Or, fraught with even more complexity, we launch an InfoWar offensive against a non-state entity, whose physical location happens to lie within the physical boundaries of a nation-state.

Even though the United States policy is still unclear as to what constitutes an "act of war" against us, we must consider how the target—and the international community—will view such offensive actions on our part. Perception is the name of the game; especially with a world-wide audience watching. Will the target react as though the U.S. had, in fact, declared war, absence of military action notwithstanding? Will the target in turn react offensively against U.S. interests, using conventional, unconventional or InfoWar weapons? And then what is our response?

This issue begs the question: Is Information Warfare a potential step which can lead to an escalation to a military conflict that was meant to be avoided in the first place? Or does Information Warfare present merely ethical questions, since no country with sane leadership would assault us militarily?

The definition of War in this new age of global networks, trans-national commerce, and increasing fuzziness of borders is arguable at best—and the search for a definition generates an essential debate for the future of peace. At the core of any nation-state's view of war should be a National Information Policy which clearly delineates intangible values, ethical positions, national security and the thresholds over which another nation-state must not cross. But additionally, such a policy view must include options for dealing with renegades, terrorists, corporations or individuals who provoke the international community outside of the control of their physical nation-state hosts. Can we or should we respond to a trans-national corporate attack against critical U.S. interests by taking action against that entity—even though it physically resides within a sovereign state? Or can we respond with pure InfoWar tactics, in the hope of avoiding an unpleasant international situation? Then, how do we avoid the "domino effect" that an attack upon a civilian infrastructure will likely create?

Many would maintain that an Act of War implicitly involves fatalities. I no longer believe that to be the case, and thus the ethical conundrum of exactly what is an Act of War comes to the fore. What is a measured response to an act of "cyber-aggression" against our interests? If the U.S. is hit with a non-lethal or InfoWar weapon, how should we respond? Our options are wide open today, and they will increase as our arsenals grow in sophistication and complexity. Further, as Third-World nations get "wired" to the Global Information Infrastructure, they, too, will find a demonstrable vulnerability that they currently do not have—and they will become a more viable target for U.S. response.

There are no immediate answers that are right or wrong, but the questions and conundra beget more questions and dilemmas as we look into the future of warfare. It is my sincere hope that this type of thinking and pondering will allow us all, as a nation and as a planet, to evolve our thinking past bombs and bullets, past military superiority, and find a common strength and unity amongst ourselves.

The alternative is not pleasant, for we find—each of us as we leap forward into the future—that our greatest assets are, indeed, also our greatest vulnerabilities. The ethical balance that we choose to follow in the coming decades will define us as a species.

Let's make the right choices.

Endnotes

[1] Winn Schwartau, *Information Warfare: Chaos on the Electronic Superhighway*, New York: Thunder's Mouth Press, 1994, pp. 271-311.

[2] Sources were private and confidential conversations with members of the U.S. Intelligence Community and the U.S. military, as well as a journalist from a major news organization. All spoke on condition of anonymity.

Coming to Terms With Information War

Alan D. Campen

Information war (IW) is a term on every lip, but the definitions vary, and the consequences of waging an unfamiliar form of warfare are still not widely grasped. The United States defense department is budgeting billions to enable our armies to wage "knowledge" wars. The military services have formed IW organizations, and they are busily drafting doctrine to enable the U.S. to exert its will by "outwitting" rather than "overwhelming" adversaries. But, as a commentator from the Air University wrote, "*while we don't know just what we've got here, all the services agree that information warfare is something important.*"

IW portends radical changes and challenges that have profound implications for personal and corporate as well as national security. However, only crude assessments have been made of the risks and benefits of this new mode of global competition. There is no consensus on which agency of government should lead—IW having unprecedented moral, legal and ethical, as well as military implications. Further, there are only hints of the top-level guidance that must pilot this unprecedented shift in national security policy. (see SIGNAL, July 1995).

Is IW the harbinger of the first revolution in military affairs since troops motored off to war, or, is it nothing more than a Beltway buzzword for *electronic warfare?* Perhaps IW is simply a rediscovery and reaffirmation of the 2500 year old Chinese sage Sun Tzu's pronouncement that "Supreme excellence consists of breaking the enemy's resistance *without fighting*." Or, are the experts who fuss about persistent Internet interlopers justified in their concern that we are taking a giant step down a superhighway leading to a "Digital Pearl Harbor?"

Take your pick. But, do it thoughtfully, because fundamental personal, economic and national security issues ride on what the U.S. does—or does not do—to prevail in conflict in the information age: an era when our comforting national security sanctuary of time and distance can be violated, instantly, anonymously and with impunity.

Writ very large, IW employs information to achieve national security goals by manipulating the perceptions, and altering the values and belief systems of adversaries, and thus causing a change in their behavior. In the words of professor Frederick Cohen , IW is a form of conflict "where IT [information technology] is the weapon, the target, the objective, or the method." Military author and scholar Air Force Colonel Richard Szafranski calls this war of words and wills "Epistemological Warfare," which is founded upon an intimate grasp of foreign cultures—not a U.S. long suit. Further, there may be no role for this military in this definition.

On the other hand, writ very small, IW means paying increased attention to the role that *communications* plays in every war. This simplistic definition translates into spending a few more bucks for digital networks to connect all the warriors on the battlefield; installing some firewalls to keep hackers out of the networks; and, making modest R&D investments in defensive software on the odd chance that Tom Clancy and Chris Davis might be prescient with their spine-chilling tales about villains, viruses, Trojan horses and Armageddon.

The Joint Chiefs of Staff have come down between these two extremes, and have adopted the term Command and Control Warfare (C^2W) as the legitimate "military component of IW." The JCS concept would exploit information technology to attain *dominant battlefield awareness*, so that a much smaller combat force can deliver decisive combat power more intensely, precisely and quickly. This artfully circumscribed definition of IW is a morally practical and fiscally realistic response to a nation weary of costly and bloody wars, and willing to endow its armed forces with a 1930s-slice of gross national wealth.

But while C^2W seems an eminently suitable term to describe the use of information at the tactical and operational level—that is, leveraging forces engaged on the battlefield—in a document entitled *Cornerstones of IW* , the Air Force contends that C^2W ignores the *strategic level of armed conflict*: (the forte of airpower)—as in "going downtown Baghdad"—or simultaneously striking at what Air Force Colonel John Warden calls "centers of gravity." The Air Force prefers the term "Information Age Warfare" to connote direct support of combat operations; IW being—at least by USAF definition—"a separate realm, potent weapon, and lucrative target."

The National Defense University's School of Information Warfare and Strategy proffers the term *Information-Based Warfare* to encompass the *strategic* level of conflict, and a RAND Corporation report—noting "a rapidly evolving and, as yet, imprecisely defined field of growing concern"—calls it *Strategic Information Warfare*; and concludes that IW "inevitably takes on a strategic aspect."

Whatever, these terms all refer to the military, physical, economic, political and social infrastructures that usually lie distant from the tactical battlefield: targets, that for the first time in military history, are within range of near-real-time intelligence and precision weapons.

While interpretations of IW do differ, they all share one common theme: that is, an absolute dependence upon the free flow of information to "our" side and denial to "his." But, the ability to dominate in cyberspace involves a dose of theology that is easier to expound upon than to explicate. Control of cyberspace may prove to be a phrase carelessly conceived in ignorance and arrogance.

The following analysis, employing the words *dependence*, *vulnerability* and *institutionalization.*, may help sort through the confusion.

The Past: *Information-in-War*

Information has always been an important (often vital) element in conflict. But, its role was serendipitous, and the product was untimely, unpredictable and unreliable. Accordingly, *dependence* upon information was minimal, *vulnerability* of communications systems therefore was not an issue, and, exploitation of information never was *institutionalized*—that is, no formal structure or process was established to provide for its use in planning or execution of military operations. Wars were fought with or without information. Indeed, sound military strategy assumed that an information *void* would exist. Yes, messengers were intercepted, cables tapped or cut, balloons lofted and fired upon, and radio transmissions intercepted or jammed. But there is scant evidence that any commander wagered a campaign upon the assumption of superior intelligence.

"Information-in-war" accurately describes information as an incidental *adjunct* to physical combat. The Battles of Midway and the North Atlantic are instances where the outcome of specific engagements turned on superior employment of forces: forces that became instantaneously magnified, because they were better informed through fortuitous decryption of intercepted messages.

Thus we may prudently discard analogies to the "old days and ways." Wisely or not, the U.S. is already arming itself with weapons and tactics that require—yea demand—something more than serendipitous flow and incidental exploitation of information. Indeed, as adopted by the U.S. Army—and later the Air Force—the term "Information Operations" is no longer just marketing hype and military hubris.

THE PRESENT: Command and Control Warfare

Information-based war (aka *knowledge-based war* or C^2W) arrived with the Persian Gulf War. Functioning as a vital adjunct to physical violence through attacks on information systems (radars, control centers, power grids, telecommunications, etc.), these strikes on *information systems* were to leverage the effectiveness of weapons; to augment physical conflict; and perhaps to bring Hussein to his senses short of a ground war—in short, to apply the "force-multiplier" effect.

C^2W targets are information *systems*—as distinguished from information *content*; the goal being to disrupt the flow of data within those *systems*, so that it is less useful to the opponent. *Institutionalization* has taken place in C^2W, but so far only to formally embrace the "five pillars" (time-honored tools of electronic combat, deception, operations security, intelligence and psychological operations), and couple them in a much more structured manner to physical destruction. This is achieved by cells of C^2W experts in command posts, and the formation of teams that deploy in support of joint command staffs. Yet, even this definition leaves us well short of a Revolution in Military Affairs. As Martin Libicki has written, "information warfare as a separate technique of waging way, does not exist." And so, we must look beyond C^2W and to the future.

THE FUTURE: Information Warfare (Netwar, Cyberwar)

Information Warfare, in much larger construct, merges the miracles of modern information technology to an ancient strategy of victory without violence. Here information is a *weapon* and *target* onto itself: not just a magnifier for physical forces engaged in traditional, legal wars. The targets are the opponents political, social and economic infrastructures—thus raising legal, ethical and moral issues that have not been confronted before. In this context, the target of IW is the *content* of an information system: that is, using technology to alter the *message*, not necessarily the *media*. The objective is to change the behavior of leaders by using information technology to alter the perceptions of reality, and thus the beliefs of people, and their willingness to support their leaders.

This esoteric form of IW, through "non-lethal" techniques, does not necessarily require a declaration of war—at least in the historical and legal sense of that word.

Indeed, clever implementation of IW may be undetectable, or if detected, may be anonymous. Further, it may be waged against us by individuals who operate from the sanctuary of a friendly or allied nation. Some contend IW is an on-going activity, in peace, crisis and war. In that sense it falls into a gap between diplomacy and war.

IW must be *institutionalized* and firmly and continually controlled from the very highest political authority, because there are no legal or ethical constructs to guide a nation that abhors "meddling in foreign affairs." The low cost of technology allows anybody to play; practitioners may be nations or rogue gangs, criminals, or just curious individuals. Nobody has a tactical warning systems for this kind of threat, and, more to the point, the extent of dependence upon information by the U.S. makes us particularly vulnerable to such attacks. To quote from the aforementioned USAF document: "Sophisticated, robust, multi-layered defenses for our military information functions may well be what separates us from joining the sorry league of military failures." One might easily substitute the word "nation" for "military" in that statement.

The results of an IW campaign cannot be predicted, nor is there any way of forecasting adverse reverse effects—inadvertent damage to our own systems, or harm to our objectives. Finally, IW surely will employ assets from other agencies of government, many of which have revealed—in recent (1995) national high-level exercises [1]—that they never have given much thought to becoming instruments of war.

Terminology triage

Sorting through the varying interpretations and implications of IW may be made easier if we put the various interpretations to these tests:

- Is information a *supplement* (force multiplier), or an *alternative* to armed conflict?
- How *dependent* is the enterprise (both sides) upon functions that cannot be performed without a continuing flow of accurate and precise information?
- What are the *vulnerabilities* in the organizations, systems and processes that carry, manipulate, or store that information? Do we really know—or better, do we know what we don't know—about how any (ours or theirs) information processes will function under the stresses that may be imposed upon them by skilled and resourceful opponents?
- Have the requisite defensive responses to fore- and unforeseen threats been *institutionalized*? Is there an indications and warning process in place, and somebody in *charge* ? Do *they* and *we* know what actions will be taken when stress is detected in our systems or processes?

What does the above assessment tell us?

- First. This is not your "father's C^2." The rules of engagement for IW have yet to be written; anyone can play; technology is available to, and favors none; "home court" is a disadvantage; and an information war will be a one-game contest—The American public is unlikely to countenance a rematch.
- Second. The military has quite enough on its C^2W platter. Its initiatives are on solid ground so long as they strive to bring information into better balance with the

arsenal of weapons they will be toting to war for the next 20 years. Programs to enhance C^2W—and any legitimate strategic extensions—will not be aided by public flogging of controversial *strategic* options that have no historical precedence or sound legal footing.

• Third. For the foreseeable future, the best (perhaps only) IW offense is a sound *defense*. Perhaps spending priorities ought to be changed.

Endnotes

[1] Molander, Roger C., et al, "Strategic Information Warfare: A New Face of War," RAND National Defense Research Institute, November 1995.

Information Assurance: Implications to National Security and Emergency Preparedness

James Kerr

Protecting critical U.S. infrastructures, particularly those portions dependent upon telecommunications and information technology (IT), has emerged as an important national issue. Both the public and private sector have become increasingly reliant on networks of communications systems and IT services to carry out their daily activities. This increased dependence raises unsettling questions about vulnerabilities in the nation's infrastructures. The merging of computing and telecommunications, while offering many benefits in terms of efficiency and effectiveness from a broad socio-economic perspective, has made information technologies attractive targets for potential adversaries. Private industry, including telecommunications companies, computer manufacturers, information systems designers and a growing host of IT service providers, have made great strides in building a safe, robust and reliable information infrastructure to serve the increasing demands of the American public, business, and government. But along with this increasingly complex network come increasing security risks, potentially affecting the national and economic security and emergency preparedness posture of the U.S. For this reason, government must maintain a strong partnership with the private sector to assist in ensuring that national security and emergency preparedness (NS/EP) requirements are engineered into this vast network, as new technologies and services are made available to its customers. It is with this Information Assurance philosophy that the National Communications System (NCS) is approaching the 21st century.

NCS Background

The NCS was established in 1963 by President Kennedy in the aftermath of the Cuban Missile Crisis, during which the President and his key officials were unable to communicate adequately and reliably. Formed in an effort to resolve perceived interagency telecommunications problems, the NCS has evolved substantially to meet new challenges posed by changes in domestic telecommunications regulatory policy, the perceived nuclear threat to the United States, and the dynamic and profound changes in information technologies. In particular, the evolution of the NCS was significantly affected by two specific events during the 1980's: (1) the divestiture of AT&T, and (2) the realization that the nation's telecommunications infrastructure is an essential component of deterrence and recovery in the face of a major attack. Consequently, in 1984, the role of the NCS was revisited in Executive Order (E.O.) 12472, *Assignment of*

National Security and Emergency Preparedness Telecommunications Functions, which led to the expansion of NCS membership to include 23 Federal departments and agencies with critical telecommunications roles and requirements, and a new NCS administrative structure.

The prospect of AT&T's divestiture in 1984 not only promised to introduce a whole new set of companies into the marketplace, but was perceived as rendering the notion of a single point of contact for NS/EP telecommunications a thing of the past. To address this concern, and to provide a mechanism to address NS/EP telecommunications needs, a set of policy and organizational constructs was implemented in the 1980s. Those constructs included the realization that there was an urgent need to emphasize the importance of joint industry-Government cooperation in addressing NS/EP telecommunications matters, especially considering the Government's pervasive and growing reliance on the Public Network (PN). As a result, E.O. 12382 established the President's National Security Telecommunications Advisory Committee (NSTAC) in 1982 to advise the President on NS/EP telecommunications policy issues as needed in the changing world environment. This unique industry advisory committee includes among its 30 members the leaders of the nation's largest telecommunications and information technology companies. The Manager, NCS, acts as the designated Federal official in the deliberations of this body.

One notable joint NCS-NSTAC activity is the National Coordinating Center (NCC) for Telecommunications. The NCC was formed as an authoritative entity to coordinate initiation and restoration of NS/EP telecommunications services and provides an operational framework for the working relationship between the telecommunications industry and the federal government for assuring NS/EP telecommunications exist during times of crisis. The NCC monitors the status of the PN, provides for the rapid exchange of information among Government and industry representatives, and expedites NS/EP telecommunications responses. Under the Federal Response Plan, the NCC operates in an all-hazards environment, supporting NS/EP telecommunications for emergency planning and response personnel throughout a broad spectrum of emergency or crisis situations.

An additional responsibility was assigned to the NCS in an April 1990 memorandum from the Chairman of the National Security Council (NSC) Policy Coordinating Committee for National Security Telecommunications and Information Systems to the Manager, NCS. This memorandum tasked the Manager to determine what actions are needed from the government and industry to protect critical national security telecommunications from the threat of computer intruders. In response to this tasking, the Manager, NCS, requested the NSTAC work with the Government to provide industry's perspective. The NCS and NSTAC identified several areas in which action was needed. In 1991, the Manager, NCS, and NSTAC established separate but closely coordinated Network Security Information Exchanges (NSIEs) to identify issues and share information about penetration and/or manipulation of software and databases affecting NS/EP telecommunications. The NSIE process has been extremely successful as a joint government-industry forum to exchange information on electronic intrusion threats to and vulnerabilities of the PN. Also in 1992, the NSTAC established the Network Security Standards Oversight Group to examine security-related telecommunications standards.

Both the NCC and NSIE demonstrate that the NCS has evolved to become a model for industry-government cooperation. Born of the government's reliance on commercial telecommunications, the NSTAC, the NCC, and the NSIE have consistently proven their value as mechanisms to facilitate the joint industry-government process. In analyzing telecommunications requirements and vulnerabilities in the PN, these structures have served the nation well as the telecommunications industry diversified and matured, information technology evolved, and the threat environment changed as the bipolar world order was replaced by a less predictable, geopolitical climate.

In today's environment, however, the NCS is confronted by a markedly different landscape than in the past, as characterized by the following facets:

• Shift from purely telecommunications to information services

• Changing definition of NS/EP and the need to respond to more diverse emergencies (e.g., electronic intrusion, terrorist incidents, and nuclear, biological, and chemical contingencies)

• Increased public and private reliance on information technology, including the Internet and on-line services

• Continuing deregulation of the telecommunications industry

• Increased demands for network security and information assurance

• Movement to high bandwidth, video and wireless services

• Constrained fiscal resources in government and corporate/government "reengineering."

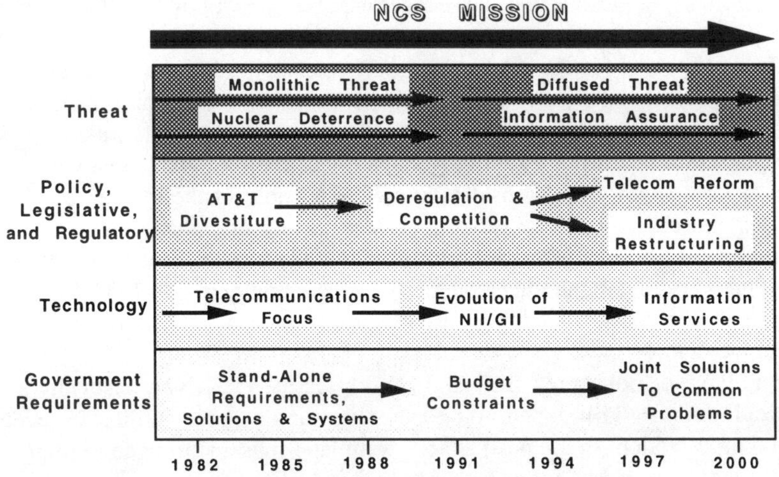

Figure 1. Evolving NCS Mission

The U.S. Government, in such areas as defense, diplomacy, emergency response, public welfare, health care and finance, is seeking to leverage the capabilities of IT to an increasing degree, balancing its fiscal and resource constraints with a heavier reliance on the Internet, on-line services, and other advanced IT applications. In most instances, the primary focus of acquisition programs is to obtain the most sophisticated IT service or product possible. NS/EP and security requirements are often secondary considerations in this process. The NCS, with assistance from the NSTAC and through its distinctive interagency process, examines the Nation's NS/EP telecommunications requirements and helps individual member departments and agencies to focus on their specific NS/EP needs. Most recently, attention has been focussed on the risk to the security of the public network from those who would seek to harm the national and economic security by exploiting weaknesses (physical or electronic) in the U.S. information infrastructure. This risk encompasses elements of threats posed, known or unknown vulnerabilities, deterrents to malicious intentions, and counteractive protective measures. In general, threats are mitigated by deterrents, and vulnerabilities are mitigated by protective measures. Under this framework, the government and NSTAC NSIEs performed a risk assessment of public networks, and documented their findings in An Assessment of the Risk to the Security of Public Networks (December 1995). Their findings are summarized in the following two sections of this article.

The Nature of the Threat to Public Networks

In general, the PN is an attractive target for computer intruders because the cost and risk of getting caught are low and the return is potentially high. Traditionally, computer intruders have been viewed as young, amateur computer enthusiasts, motivated primarily by curiosity and technical challenge. Analysis of computer intrusions in recent years, however, indicates that there is now an older generation of computer intruders for which financial gain is a more prominent motivator. In addition to accessing telecommunications and other IT systems for personal use, these older intruders are willing to sell their skills for industrial espionage, and law enforcement has seen troubling indications of their collusion with organized crime and foreign intelligence services. The days of the computer intruder being viewed as a minor annoyance are gone. Evidence is mounting that in many cases of computer break-ins, the network itself may be the target. In the case of corporate insiders, the motives appear to be financial gain or revenge. Since they are granted varying degrees of physical and electronic access, insiders know the security of the system and raise no alarm by their presence. For these reasons, insiders acting in collusion with an outside threat (such as a foreign intelligence service) could provide targeted access to software and databases to meet specific requirements of their outside accomplices. In 1994, for instance, an insider provided thousands of calling card numbers to an outsider who then sold them to foreign computer intruders.

Intruders have demonstrated their ability to effectively and systematically exploit PN software. Intruders' skills appear to be increasing, and the most skillful intruders are adept at eluding detection. In the past, attacks were laborious and time consuming, often using social engineering and other techniques that took advantage of poor password management and other security weaknesses. Although computer intruders continue to exploit these vulnerabilities, they now also use increasingly advanced software tools and networking techniques. They use customized software programs to target specific types of computers, networks, or network elements, such as malicious code designed to attack a specific software vendor's product, or viruses to target anti-virus software. Powerful, user-friendly network scanning software tools such as SATAN (System Administration Tool for Analyzing Networks) are shared among intruders and are easily available to download over the Internet. Unfortunately, system and software vendors usually cannot respond with fixes in a timely manner to prevent break-ins. In addition, because some of these tools can attack a system at multiple levels or attack more than one network element at a time, it is often difficult for system administrators to determine if their network is the target of a coordinated attack before it is too late to prevent it. The use of these tools has two consequences: (1) the number of individuals capable of attacking the PN *increases* as the required level of skill *decreases*, and (2) the less-skilled individuals can gain access to systems about which they know very little, increasing the likelihood that they could damage them, even accidentally.

The determination of the intruders, the growing ease with which they can attack the PN, the difficulty in detecting their activities, and the increasing complexity of recovering systems, are all reasons for serious concern. Further, intruders have the skills to access and damage the PN, and can cause significant denial and degradation of service. The government and NSTAC NSIEs' risk assessment concludes that the electronic intrusion threat to the PN has grown since the last risk assessment in 1993, primarily because of the increasing sophistication of the intruders and the more advanced methods of attack.

As noted earlier, the threat can be mitigated by deterrents. One important agent of deterrence is law enforcement. Equipment and software vendors, service providers, and their customers must work in partnership with law enforcement to report intrusions, help identify intruders, cooperate in investigations, and help prosecute computer intruders who attack PN elements. A positive sign that this partnership has been strengthened in recent years is that the number of computer intrusions reported to law enforcement has increased. However, whether this increased reporting is being outpaced by an increasing number of intrusions is difficult to determine with certainty. Law enforcement and the private sector also need to continue cooperating in activities such as joint investigations, training, education and awareness, and exchanging technical information. In addition to law enforcement, the Department of Justice (DOJ) is proposing improvements to Federal computer crime laws to: (1) upgrade a class of intrusion from misdemeanors to felonies, (2) revise the definition of "Federal interest computers" to include those used in interstate commerce and communications, and (3) expand the definition of "damage" to include any impairment of data integrity or availability that threatens public health and safety. DOJ is also proposing changes to sentencing guidelines to encourage judges to consider factors beyond economic loss to the victim in sentence determination. A final deterrent is education and awareness programs. These can help deter young people from getting involved in computer crime by making them aware of the consequences of these intrusions, both for the individual and for society. In their 1995 PN risk assessment, the government and NSTAC NSIEs state "The effectiveness of deterrents may be limited, but deterrent capabilities within the U.S. are among the best in the world, and are improving..."

Robustness of the PN

Vulnerabilities are flaws in the PN's fabric, either known or unknown to the system administrator, that allow intruders to enter the network's computerized elements. In recent years, PN service providers and equipment vendors have become more aware of the vulnerabilities that affect their systems. Security audits, information sharing activities (e.g., NSIEs), and incident response teams (e.g., Computer Emergency Response Team [CERT]) have revealed many vulnerabilities. Many computer owners have taken steps to mitigate these vulnerabilities; others have not. The potential impact of these known vulnerabilities on the PN has increased because the size and functionality of modern switching elements and support systems have grown over the years. The compromise of certain switching elements or operations support systems can have much more widespread consequences than in the past. Some of these known vulnerabilities, such as dial-up modems or failure to change default passwords, are easily fixed; however, because of time and resource constraints, they are frequently overlooked and leave the system vulnerable to intrusion.

Other types of vulnerabilities are less apparent. Connections to the Internet are increasing, and while many service providers have exercised due care in isolating critical network systems and components from more open-enterprise data networks—such as the Internet—there may still be potentially exploitable connectivity, such as through a restrictive router or firewall. As such, firewalls should be viewed as one component of a comprehensive security program—not as a panacea. The false sense of security provided by firewalls has caused many systems administrators to decrease their reliance on traditional systems security methods. As a result, many systems have become more vulnerable to intrusion attacks. For example, a firewall that recognizes trust relationships between nodes within a network, but does not restrict internal network addresses originating from outside the protected network, may be susceptible to an attack by an intruder outside the network, impersonating one of the trusted sites. This is commonly called "spoofing." Centralization of operations, administration, maintenance and provisioning functions at a single location can also increase the network's vulnerability. While there are security advantages to this, a compromise of a system serving one of these centralized centers would affect communications over a wider area than 5 or 10 years ago. In addition to these known vulnerabilities of mature, well-established systems, there is rising concern about the lack of security in emerging and future technologies, which may not always include adequate security features. Often these products are brought to market before security problems are known or can be resolved. Or, in some cases, security solutions in older technologies may not be carried forward to the new products. Examples of new technologies in various stages of implementation throughout the PN are Intelligent Networks, Common Channel Signaling, Asynchronous Transfer Mode switching, Synchronous Optical Networks, and Integrated Services Digital Networks.

The telecommunications and information technology industry is changing rapidly, especially with the recent passage of the Telecommunications Act of 1996. New service providers (e.g., cable TV providers, electric utilities, Internet connection services) are entering the communications market, requiring interconnection with more traditional providers. Likewise, the distinction between local exchange common carriers and long-distance interexchange carriers is rapidly disappearing. The dynamic nature of the industry, and its importance to national security, will require a continuing emphasis on information and network security. Also, because it involves increased access to communications networks by external service providers, security concerns have arisen from the Federal Communications Commission's Open Network Architecture regulatory framework.

Over the past few years, the telecommunications industry has responded to perceived risks from electronic intrusions by implementing network security plans and programs. Examples of these include properly configured firewalls, internal network partitioning, strong authentication techniques (e.g., one-time passwords), strong corporate security policies, and security training and awareness. In addition, government and industry are engaging in security research and development. The National Security Agency and the National Institute of Standards and Technology have programs to make the results of their R&D available to industry. As the public becomes more aware of the security issues associated with IT, demand for security products is likely to foster even more security R&D.

In making security decisions, government and industry are applying the principles of risk management. Although it is not feasible for organizations to prevent all intrusions from both internal and external sources, they can operate within acceptable levels of risk. Risk management principles suggest that organizations focus on spending resources to deploy safeguards to protect themselves against intrusions that could cause the greatest amount of damage, but be prepared to react to other intrusions as needed. This requires that organizations must be able to detect intrusions. Many companies are slow to adopt adequate security tools and provide sufficient numbers of trained system security administrators to do an effective security job, often because the perceived risks are low. Awareness of risks to the network and implementation of prudent actions are critical steps enabling cost effective and sound security programs. Exchanging information on threats, vulnerabilities and remedies, as done by the government and NSTAC NSIEs, helps improve understanding and increase security awareness, thus facilitating increased reporting, elevating management awareness of risk, and resulting in more support for security activities.

Importance of IT to U.S. Domestic Infrastructure

The realm of Information Assurance and IT ramifications reaches far beyond simply the ability to communicate. The electronic web of computers and information technology touches virtually every element of U.S. domestic infrastructures. Besides telecommunications, the nation's financial systems, stock and commodity exchanges, air traffic control systems, electric power generation and distribution systems, and transportation networks all increasingly depend on IT networks for their operation and health. While this has obvious implications to Information Assurance for day-to-day normal business operations, the magnitude of its impact is magnified in situations of national crisis and disaster response. The risk of infrastructure service denial also extends into destructive threats, such as terrorism. The U.S. can no longer assume that it is a "sanctuary;" terrorists can strike anywhere at anytime. The vulnerability of the IT thread that ties together the fabric of the U.S. infrastructure makes this threat all the more menacing. Domestic and foreign terrorism, natural disasters, accidents, and acts of war are broad examples of potential infrastructure service interruptions. Specific examples of malicious actions include the bombings of the Murrah Federal Building in Oklahoma

City and the World Trade Center in New York City, and the use of lethal chemical agents in Japan. Other less foreseeable events, like the signaling software failures that resulted in widespread telephone outages in 1991, and natural disasters such as Hurricane Andrew, can have a significant detrimental impact on information technologies that serve communications as well as other vital infrastructure services.

Current Focus on Information Assurance

In response to the growing importance of IT security, in November 1995 the Office of the Manager, NCS (OMNCCS), established a branch office under the newly reorganized Plans, Customer Service, and Information Assurance Division (N5) to address security issues regarding the broader spectrum of telecommunications and information systems and to improve awareness within Government and industry of the need to protect the critical information systems that support NS/EP requirements. The N5 Information Assurance (IA) Branch was established to combine the network and information security initiatives of the OMNCS under a common program to increase their efficiency and effectiveness, apply a coordinated direction, and increase the general awareness of the importance of network security and information assurance to the NCS, government and industry community. The IA Branch also provides technical support to the NSTAC on IA-related issues. As part of its mission, the Branch participates in, administers and provides technical support to the NSIE process. The joint efforts of the government and NSTAC NSIEs to address network security in the telecommunications industry have provided a model for government-industry interaction and have yielded findings that may be useful in addressing information assurance issues within other domestic infrastructures.

May 1995, the NSTAC formed an Information Assurance Task Force (IATF) to serve as the focal point for NSTAC IA activities, work with the U.S. Government on issues concerning IA, and propose high-level IA policy recommendations to the NSTAC for presentation to the President. As part of its mission, the IATF recognizes the dependence of the energy, finance and transportation infrastructures on telecommunications and information technologies and their importance to the national and economic security of the Nation. In that context, the IATF is conducting risk assessments in these sectors to ascertain:

- IT systems that support various infrastructure functions (e.g. power generation and distribution; electronic funds transfer; air and rail transportation control);
- The extent to which these systems depend upon information technology, and the impact to those systems if the information infrastructure were disrupted;
- The maturation of industry migration efforts (e.g., impacts of deregulation in the energy industry, threat of liability, emerging business markets and competition);
- The state of awareness within each industry of risks and vulnerabilities in their IT support systems;
- The extent of mitigation and protection measures to these risks and vulnerabilities; and
- How NSTAC can assist in identifying and mitigating risks.

This assessment of risks will include a review of areas such as policies and procedures, threats, electronic intrusion incidents, vulnerabilities, detection and monitoring schemes, auditing, system integrity, access controls and protective measures. In particular, the assessment will focus on each industry's IT system architecture, including:

- Industry organization (nation, region, and local);
- System control links and control management systems;
- Degree of dependence on private/commercial systems;
- Interconnection between private and public data networks; and
- Degree of reliance on public networks.

The first infrastructure the IATF is assessing is electric power generation and distribution. An available, highly reliable supply of electric power is essential to all domestic infrastructures. Electric power is of particular interest because the telecommunications and electric power infrastructures are highly dependent on each other. Electric utilities devote a large amount of resources to applying centralized automation technology involving extensive use of high-speed digital computers, supervisory and control systems, communications and telemetering systems. In addition, there are growing similarities between the electric power grid and telecommunications in terms of their dependence on information systems.These similarities and interdependencies will be intensified as a result of the Telecommunications Act of 1996, which allows the power industry to provide telecommunications and information services, and the deregulation of the power industry, which will stimulate the industry to use telecommunications networks to facilitate electrical power distribution. These factors will combine to increase the degree of interconnection between telecommunications networks and electric power companies' networks. Consequently, there is the expectation that great benefit can be derived from a collaborative effort between these two critical industries to share their perspectives on the risks to national information systems. The IATF plans to complete the energy sector risk assessment in Fall 1996. The financial and transportation risk assessments will be conducted in late 1996 and 1997.

Other government agencies are recognizing the critical importance of IT to their operations, particularly during times of national crisis. The Department of Defense (DoD) has begun a number of initiatives to protect its information resources from attack. For example, the Defense Information Systems Agency (DISA) operates the Automated Systems Security Incident Support Team (ASSIST). ASSIST responds to Defense intrusion incidents worldwide, providing alert bulletins and technical assistance on a client-confidential basis to any member of the Department of Defense and its contractors. Additionally, as part of DISA's effort to assess DoD IT security, the Center for Information Systems Security (CISS) has launched test attacks on thousands of DoD computers to emphasize to DoD leaders the critical importance of computer security and intrusion reporting. Defense and military leaders are also recognizing the increasing reliance upon U.S. domestic commercial infrastructures for the timely movement of DoD resources, military force projection, and the ability to mobilize, deploy and sustain forces and execute tasks of the National Command Authorities.

IT security is being aggressively studied and managed on the civil side of government as well. Several agencies, including the Department of Energy, Veterans Health

Administration and the National Aeronautics and Space Administration, are operating computer intrusion response teams and capabilities to improve their ability to detect and react to attacks on IT systems. In February 1996, the Office of Management and Budget released a revised Circular A-130, which provides uniform government-wide information resources management policies and contains updated guidance on the security of Federal automated information systems. In particular, OMB Circular A-130 tasks the National Institute of Standards and Technology to develop and issue security standards and guidance for Federal agencies and to coordinate Federal incident response activities.

On February 10, 1996, the President signed into law The National Defense Authorization Act for Fiscal Year 1996. Section 1053 of the act calls for, "a description of the national policy and architecture...governing the plans for establishing procedures...necessary to perform indications, warning, and assessment functions regarding strategic attacks by foreign nations...or any other entity against the national information infrastructure." Indications, warning, and attack assessment functions and capabilities (e.g., intrusion detection tools) are key elements of any government or industry Information Assurance or defensive information warfare capability. The act also calls for "an assessment of the future of the National Communications System (NCS)...whether there is a federal interest in expanding or modernizing the NCS in light of the changing strategic national security environment and the revolution in information technologies...and the best use of the NCS...as an integral part of a larger national strategy to protect the United States against a strategic attack on the national information infrastructure." According to Senator John Kyl (R-AZ), who originally offered this section as an amendment to the defense bill, "There is currently no defense against attacks on our Nation's information systems, which include our defense, telephone, public utility, and banking systems. Military officials have no ability to protect our country from cyberspace attacks, and no legal or political authority to protect our information systems against another country's offensive...We must begin now to elevate our efforts to protect the national security interest of this country." The Administration is currently formulating a strategy to respond to the act.

Conclusion

The security of information technologies is of paramount importance to maintaining U.S. national security, supporting emergency preparedness activities, and effectively competing in a global market place. The ability to protect, detect and react to computer attacks is vital in this regard. Crucial segments of the federal government and the national economy rely on IT; the inherent risk of that dependence, however, continues to grow. Critical U.S. infrastructures, such as energy, finance and transportation, have built and rely on a high level of public trust. Protecting these infrastructures from the probings and attacks of electronic intruders and others with malicious intentions is critical to the U.S. maintaining that trust and assuring a reliable and secure NS/EP response capability. A strong relationship between government and industry built on mutual trust is essential in continuing to improve and build upon the nation's information infrastructure.

Epilogue

Douglas H. Dearth and R. Thomas Goodden

What Is Information Warfare?

The attempt to answer this question is rather more complex than the asking of it. Tom Rona, the original coiner of the term, essentially would describe Information Warfare as a "battle of decision systems." While something of a ground-breaking concept, this is essentially a technical approach. Looked at in one way, warfare has always been a struggle between decision systems. George Stein holds that "Information warfare, in its broader sense, is simply the use of information to achieve our national objectives." Further, he says that: "Information warfare, in its essence, is about...the way humans think and, more important, the way humans make decisions."[1]

The Tofflers would describe IW in broader terms: as "a new 'war-form.'"[2] Their concept, and that of many more recent commentators, *is that Information Warfare is a way of thinking about war, warfare, and conflict.* It is a different way of applying military power.

Part of the mystique—and promise—of Information Warfare is that it may be broadly applied as part of a national policy designed to obviate the need for traditional military involvement. It is in some ways Political War beyond the bounds of diplomacy in which weapons are intangible in appearance and very tangible in result. This is a new breed of weapon which leaves neither "smoking gun" nor plausible trace. It is a weapon—and a campaign—which may be launched by a Head of State, with or without the involvement of his military force options.

Information Warfare also constitutes an operating or conflict environment. The attempt to "digitize the battlefield" that is currently underway in the U.S. Army, on its face, seems to be a limited technical approach to the broader issue. It is not inappropriate; in fact, it is necessary; and it tacitly acknowledges that something is significantly different in the arena of armed conflict. Others would describe Information Warfare as simply "C^{2}W by another name." But, as Campen argues in his essay, [3] it is not.

Command-and-Control Warfare (C^{2}W) is the tactical application of the much broader phenomenon of Information Warfare, but this approach is not inappropriate for the U.S. Marine Corps, which essentially is a tactical-level force. It must be acknowledged, too, that Information Warfare is something of a fad today; used by many military establishments to defend existing organizational turf and to acquire more—often at the expense of other organizations and efforts.

The defense department defines Information Warfare as: "actions taken to achieve information superiority by affecting adversary information, information-based processes, information systems and computer-based networks, while defending one's own information, information-based processes, information systems, and computer-based networks."[4]

Confusion about these concepts is further exacerbated by other new terms: *Cyberwar*, *Netwar*, and *Knowledge War*. For Arquilla and Ronfeldt, the distinction is presented thusly: Netwar is "societal level 'ideational conflicts' waged through internetted modes of communication," whereas Cyberwar applies "at the purely military level."[5] Hence, "[N]etwar refers to information-related conflict at the grand level between nations and societies." Further, "netwar represents a new entry on the spectrum of conflict that spans economic, political, and societal as well as military forms of 'war.'[6] In contrast, "[C]yberwar refers to conducting, and preparing to conduct, military operations according to information-related principles."[7] For the Philippe Baumard, *Knowledge War* is the follow-on to Information War, and is distinguishable by the fact that it necessitates growth beyond the systematizing of *information* and into the systematizing of *thought* and *analytic process*. His is a world of anticipation of threat activity and immediate, measured, flexible response. *It is Information Warfare to the next level.*[8]

All of these concepts are valid, but it is the intent of the authors, and many of the contributors to this book, that the widest possible definition be applied to the phenomenon of Information Warfare. Some would criticize such an overly broad interpretation, but our fundamental approach to the issue is that there is something qualitatively different about Warfare in the Information Age.

Major Themes

We wish to leave the reader with a number of broad major themes concerning Information Warfare. We address these serially in this epilogue to focus upon them individually and severally. The goal is to draw common threads from the varied perspectives of the contributors, from which the reader may form conclusions and models for further analysis. These themes cut across both cultures and societal domains, as well as professional disciplines, some with unique frames of reference. One of the hardest concepts we have found in grappling—and observing others grapple—with the scope and bounds of Information Warfare, is that it is so catholic, so flexible, and appears to show such promise.

Paradigm Shift

This term may be hackneyed and over-used, but it is apt nonetheless. Historically, we are experiencing a set of highly significant changes in virtually every aspect of life, and those changes are being driven or facilitated largely by innovations in information technology. In some respects, the shift is rather subtle and barely noticeable, especially in short-term perspective. In other respects, changes are clearly visible and nearly volcanic in their impact and influence. Many—particularly in military establishments—prefer evolution to revolution; but it would seem difficult to portray the large changes wrought in so short a time by the micro-processor as merely marginal change of an evolutionary nature. Rather, we are witnessing a significant historical "step-change." Bias and perspective determine how we see the world. If one does not look for change, one will not likely find it; and, with conservative biases and perspectives, one is apt frequently to be surprised.

The Need for Policy

Information Warfare is not clearly defined, nor is it universally understood, for two reasons. First, it is a new and still evolving concept. Second, it has not been harnessed within a national policy context. Therefore, the frame of reference for defining it is essentially still within the eye of the beholder. No one is more aware of that than the Director of Central Intelligence, Dr. John Deutch. We asked him recently to comment on the "stakeholders" who have emerged to debate national IW policy, and their respective positions. He responded that, except for the DoD, which has thought long and deep on the topic, the numerous other cabinet and agency-level policy-makers have only begun to consider what it is and what its potential may be. For that reason, Deutch believes that it is too early to formulate policy.[9]

We see a microcosm of the DCI's concern in just comparing the approaches of the authors in this volume. Petersen sees IW in terms of the physical metaphor of "tweezer" precision.[10] Brown sees it in terms of the larger context of an aperiodic revolution in military affairs.[11] These and other authors shape their visions of the utility and the prognosis for IW based on their own unique frames of reference. The practice of IW will follow from the definition of policy. The scope of possible and allowable actions will narrow the breadth and increase the depth of the use of this new war-form.

Role of Intelligence

On the face of it, one might expect that the Intelligence Community—as a "knowledge" industry—might be best suited in the national security structure to cope with the unsettling aspects of organizing for Information Warfare. Yet, it is likely that this community will suffer every bit as much as other functions in adapting to post-Modern forms of organizing work and warfare.

When IW eventually is defined in the context of a national policy, intelligence will play an intuitively important role. Brown sees the value of isolating a specific type (Type III) of IW which exploits information systems for intelligence, while other types of IW actions manage perceptions or deny, distort, destroy or degrade the adversary's decision systems.[12] Steele sees the breadth and depth of intelligence effort needed to quantify IW threats and coordinate IW actions. He calls for a *virtual* community with sufficient reserves to mobilize in the face of an anticipated surge in supporting intelligence requirements.[13]

Clearly, intelligence will play a significant role in recognizing a "red" attack as well as a "blue" opportunity. Intelligence will identify "red" vectors as well as "blue" methods of inoculation for defense. Intelligence will quietly surveil "red" decision cycles and reaction to "blue" initiatives. It will also assess the impact on "red" of "blue" methods of attack, providing feedback that forms the basis of dynamic change in methods as well as symmetry and sufficiency in levels and durations of "blue" IW attack.

At issue is whether the IW "sensor-to-shooter" connectivity can function efficiently in an operational environment where intelligence collection, analysis and management is functionally separate from the IW operator. One could make the analogy to playing the piano with the right hand of one artist and the left hand of a second artist. Beautiful music cannot be produced the first time they read the music together. They must operate as one entity.[14]

Levels of War

The levels of war—tactical, operational, and strategic—are being blurred by information technology. As military practitioners and observers know: Efforts at the tactical level of war—at which engagements and battles are fought for limited objectives—are aggregated at the operational level of war in the form of campaigns. This is a process to muster broader efforts over wider terrain, space and time, in a theater-of-operations—which are directed toward achievement of national war goals at the strategic level in theaters of war. These three levels of war historically have been distinguished by the size of forces and volume of resources employed, the breadth of terrain and space over which forces are deployed, and the time expended in the prosecution of operations. These levels overlap somewhat: there are instances in which the tactical and operational levels and the operational and strategic levels blend—but on the margin.

Since at least the Napoleonic Era at the dawn of the Industrial Age, the distinct trends have been larger and more varied kinds of forces deployed over increasingly broader terrain and space and distance, often with the decision cycles of operations consuming decreasing periods of time at each level of war.

Various aspects of information technology and Information Warfare provide the prospects for significant change in certain of these trends: Mechanisms of force continue to proliferate, but the size of forces can decrease. Breadth of terrain and space and distance can continue to grow to the physical limits of the planet and into space. Time will shrink, with the increase of the speed with which—and the distance over which—force can be employed. Hence, the discernible distinctions among the levels of war will be increasingly blurred; and this will complicate the nature of political and military planning and decision-making.

DeCaro,[15] Petersen and Brown, among others, sense that the "packaging" of Information Warfare into a division of labor that fits convenient military doctrine and organization may be passé. The smallest team of specialists, operating covertly under direct civilian control and tasking, could apply strategic, operational, or tactical IW tools against any level of an adversary's decision system. Military knowledge, let alone supervision, may have never been a consideration in the planning, but may be significantly influenced by the results.

Civil-Military Divisions

In a similar fashion and for the same reasons, the distinctions between the civilian and military realms are being blurred. The idealistic distinctions between these realms—to the extent that they were ever really applicable—no longer hold. The Clauswitzian concept of the trinity of "Army" (really "Forces"), the "State," and the "People" is more valid than ever on one level; but, in the Information Age, the State and the Forces will no longer necessarily possess a monopoly over the means of violence—especially "information violence." Further, national centers-of-gravity increasingly will reside in the civil sector, e.g., the national banking and finance industries and power generation and distribution systems. The civil sector—in terms of production and morale—have long been important to warfare. In an age, however, when production is measured more in terms of intangible knowledge than tangible goods, and when the value of knowledge applies equally in both civil and military sectors, the distinction between the two realms will blur even more. The further implications are that the future civilian infrastructure will be an even more prominent target of attack than was the case in the Industrial Era. And, they may not be defendable by military forces.

Principal Domains

The Information Age will influence virtually every facet of human enterprise. Given that different analysts and observers view human enterprise from varying frames of reference, it is useful to place the concept of Information Warfare into the context of some of these major domains. Certain of the major themes discussed above—particularly paradigm shift—can be discerned in each of the following domains.

Political/Cultural/Social

In the broad context of history, at each stage of human development dominant forms of political, cultural and social organization have influenced and shaped the nature of warfare. While the relationship has been interactive and reciprocal, political, cultural and social forms have determined war-forms. Consider just the period since the Fall of the Roman Empire.

In the pre-Modern period (roughly from the 5th Century until the Enlightenment), the controlling paradigm was faith. The dominant institution in Europe was the Roman Church, and the source of human salvation was sought through scripture. The nature of analysis was essentially mystical. Governance was generally autocratic. Information was controlled, additive, and generally inaccessible to all but the Church hierarchy.

By contrast, in the Modern period (from the Enlightenment until the late 20th Century), the controlling paradigm was reason, rather than faith. The dominant institution became the nation-state. Hope was expressed more through science than through scripture. The nature of analysis became more linear and predictive, and governance became more democratic. Information—because of the printing press and successor information technologies—was less controlled, yet until comparatively recent times was still largely the province of learned—but expanding numbers of—elites.

In the post-Modern period (roughly the past 30 years), the controlling paradigm of society, culture and politics has become more that of intuition. There is no longer a single dominant institution equating to the Church or the State. Rather, transnational and non-state institutions increasingly predominate. Hope for human betterment is expressed more through the marketplace—of ideas as well as goods. The nature of analysis is no longer linear and predictive; it is more complex, chaotic, and non-linear. Governance is becoming more confederal and anarchistic, as old forms and concepts of control prove to be inefficient or are simply ignored. Information is increasingly accessible, portable, voluminous; it is growing exponentially.

As Arquilla and Ronfeldt have observed: "[T]he information revolution, in both its technological and non-technological aspects, sets in motion forces that challenge the design of many institutions. It disrupts and erodes the hierarchies around which institutions are normally designed."[16]

Thus, the current Information Revolution—as its historical predecessors have done—will diffuse and redistribute power, alter and strain relationships among people and organizations, and cause those entities to change—often quite dramatically. In the process, the nature of organizations will change: Networks will become more prominent than hierarchies.

Legal/Ethical

The legal domain comprises a cumulative construct of foundation law and common practice upon which has been overlaid the opinions of courts and legislatures. The modern result is a code. The role of ethics in the process has been that of forming the outer bounds within which law, and decisions may be added to code without violating basic human values.

Law and ethics protect the equities of social man. Property, chattels and basic interpersonal relationships, like marriage, are carefully prescribed and protected. Information Warfare provides the capability to alter and disturb the systems through which we account for property and possessions, as well as our legal identities (as recorded in licenses, tax data bases, DNA pools, medical records, insurance policies), and even our basic rights (such as access to credit, to information held on us by government, and our freedom to express ourselves via the media).

Because common law is built on precedence, the remedy for information attack may come long after the attack. As Baumard suggests, it may be crafted to the purposes of giant information systems rather than to the advantage of individuals. We see such struggles today in legal battles against large corporations (e.g., the tobacco industry). The legal talent and tools of perception management—a form of information warfare—available to these industry giants dwarfs that of the plaintiffs, local prosecutors, witnesses and friends of the court, against which they are arrayed.

At issue in the formulation of national policy for information warfare is the adequacy of extant law and the appropriateness of proffered changes. The issue is a fundamental Constitutional one. On one side are arrayed the several agencies of DoD who believe their charters give them the responsibility to protect the Defense Information Infrastructure (DII), and the National Information Infrastructure (NII) upon which it rides. On the other side are arrayed the private carriers and citizens who are the owners of much of the NII, as well as the majority of users.

Despite statistics which show that DoD traffic on the NII accounts for about 15% of total loading, NSA and DISA, worried about the security of the DII, would impose network security standards that some regard as onerous. They cite the possibility of network disruption or loss if security is not tightened. Each points to the Communications Act of 1934 as justification for taking over the NII in time of war. "War" in the Information Age remains to be defined.

The key question is: How much government control of the NII is permissible in a free society, regardless of threat? The question has both legal and ethical aspects. As we struggle to establish an Information Warfare policy upon which there is sufficient agreement, we are making surprisingly robust progress under existing law. The recent first-time use of a court-ordered monitoring of electronic communications is a model for investigations. This case of an Argentine citizen involving months of careful screening of Internet nodes, with American authorities manifesting a clear understanding of the need to protect the privacy rights of thousands of other users. This incident highlights the permeability of international borders in the Information Age. The U.S. Attorney in the case termed this "...a glimpse of what computer crime-fighting will look like in the coming years."[17]

Technical

The technical domain is the "tactical battleground" upon which one first sees the incremental escalation of the digital tools and weapons of Information Warfare, if not the methods of application. Here is where the IW devices—viruses, morphing software, corrupted chip-sets, firewalls, encryption schemes, etc.—are created by technologists. They will be later used by operational specialists whose creativity is measured in net effects, not in engineering prowess. The technical domain is so carefully constructed of Newtonian science, mathematics and mechanics that to say it is neutral in the policy and practice of Information War may be to state the obvious. Few technologists have the acumen to foresee the eventual uses of their contributions.

It could be argued that the "technologists" are as manipulated as are the victims of Information War. It may have always been thus. Nobel, the inventor of dynamite, stands out as an early example of technologist-cum-victim of the unintended military use of his invention. More recent history recounts the latent misgivings of some of the scientists involved in the Manhattan Project of World War II. In the end, their argument fails. Naiveté among scientists and technologists, if it ever existed, is quite rare.

In the Information Age, few scientists will miss or understate the intended use of their creations. The more likely failing is that they may understate the collateral effects. Witness, for example, the effects of the "Internet Worm" loosed by young Mr. Morse in 1988. It is the potential for hidden "rebound-effect'" in offensive IW measures that most worries the carriers. Similarly, it is the unending episodes of 'holes' in firewalls and encryption software that worry the ultimate consumers.

Commercial

In the private sector we all share three fundamental expectations regarding information: availability, integrity, and confidentiality. Baumard sketches the alternative future of the commercial domain in the Information Age—one in which the commercial information infrastructure cannot be defended. Thus, his assertion of the need for offensive IW capabilities by commercial entities. Goodden, on the other hand, sketches the strategic means of stanching the drift into this alternative. Clearly, the challenge to businessmen is more than the mere application of good information management policy, and practice straight from the MBA texts. Libicki makes the point that this is not business as usual. If the same flaw in UNIX 'Sendmail' were used to attack Rome Labs—six years after it was used to spread the 'Morse Worm'—then corporate managers have not grasped the obvious. Loescher asserts the need for private sector management to "lead or get out of the way."[18]

Management must be prepared to react dynamically to the more subtle aspects of hostilities Information War. Moreover, business managers may have to operate out in front of legal systems for redress of wrongs. This is not a call for vigilantism. It is an acknowledgment that legal redress for future information attacks, if ever fully available, will be very late in coming. It falls to management to anticipate the capital needed to restore commercial operations in the aftermath of attack, while they await the findings of a ponderous legal system. Information surety may eventually become an insurable commodity if and when the standards and means of risk sharing among underwriters can be worked out.

Military

Just as the form of militaries and the form of war derive from the nature of culture, society, and politics, they also derive from the nature of dominant economic systems. As the Tofflers remind us, "...the way we make wealth and the way make war are inextricably connected."[19] Thus, the pre-Modern militaries concentrated on sheer force as the principal means of coercion; whereas, in the Modern period, the controlling military paradigm was the technology of weaponry. Forces became larger, but the nature of force changed through technology.

In contrast, in post-Modern period, *the principal military paradigm is information superiority, just as it is in the commercial domain.* The emphasis is more upon subtlety, finesse and agility than upon brute force. Technology is more important than ever; but the technology has radically changed. Hierarchical structure has been a hallmark of military organization. In the future, these hierarchical arrangements—and mindsets—will be challenged and to some extent replaced by arrangements that more resemble networks.

Key Issues

Here are several issues that seem most germane to the discussions of Information Warfare, as they derive from the themes and domains above. While we believe that virtually all of these issues are interrelated, they need to be isolated for discussion.

Time, Distance, and Speed

Since the early days of the Industrial Age, time increasingly has been compressed; yet it has become more important. For instance, visit a museum or Colonial plantation and observe the clocks of the 18th Century. They had only an hour hand. Today, by contrast, many endeavors are time-measured in hundredths of seconds. Initially, it was transportation technology that drove this compression. The steam engine was applied to ground and then marine transport. Later the telegraph—and then wireless telegraphy—enabled *information* to be passed over greater distances with amazing speed.[20] There followed the telephone and its adjunct—actually a technology that pre-dated the telephone—the facsimile machine. Then it was television, which introduced the added dimension of more vivid graphical—and life-like—images. More recently, it has been the computer—and particularly the microprocessor—linked via local- and wide-area networks. Thus, speed has increased ever more dramatically as a function of distance. The result is that *distance means less—and, hence, time is compressed.*

These changes apply to all domains. The instant feedback provided by modern electronic communications affects the political, cultural and social spheres as readily as it does the commercial and military arenas. When President Bush was challenged on global television to a debate on the Kuwait issue in 1990, it was recognized that a response—in the negative—was required via the same medium within an hour. By the same token, cultural and social trends proliferate very quickly among the Third-Wave countries and to the rest of the world. The global currency market now operates 24 hours a day, and stock and commodity positions are calculated instantaneously. The U.S. Air Force's Air Tasking Order procedure now demands a 24-hour turn-around against military targets.

Expectations

The result is not just efficiency—the saving of time and labor. It is that, but it is far more. It changes peoples' expectations. They understand they can know more about more with less expenditure of effort, and in less time. The more they *can* know with less time and effort, the more they *want* to know with even less expenditure of time and effort; and soon they *demand* it.

People's expectations also have changed by virtue of what they know. Reading about events—seeing and interpreting symbols on a page—is different than viewing vastly more life-like images on a screen. It is much more realistic, because interpretation is easier. It requires less imagination, and the same time it fires the imagination. While people are drawn to the vividness of the images, they can be repulsed by those same images. The interpretation is more intense.

The change in expectations applies to all the domains. Politically, the potent images of starving Somali children, butchered Rwandans, or a bludgeoned Los Angeles motorist, virtually demand a political response—now. Reports of defective commercial products will very quickly drive a company to bankruptcy. The latest rock music craze will sweep the world in days—and be replaced by something else in a week. Generations of computer technology will progress within 18-24 months, rendering corporate and government management and procurement policies laughable.

For the military—and government generally, the omnipresent and seemingly omniscient global media mean that every decision and action is immediately transparent to national and international scrutiny. The butcher's bill of the Somme, Vimy Ridge and Passchendaele will never again be paid by a democratic power. Even a single military casualty will be the subject of immediate coverage and public scrutiny. The risks will be: hyper-sensitive decision-making and timid military leadership in the face of fickle public emotions.

Public Diplomacy [21]

Public diplomacy is a term that refers generally to those government activities designed to inform and influence foreign publics. If traditional diplomacy is state-to-state, public diplomacy is state-to-foreign populace. Although not a new concept, it has taken on new importance as a result of the global communication explosion. At the core of this policy is the belief that democratic countries are less likely to war on each other than non-democratic ones. Further, the ability of the American government to communicate effectively and persuasively should result in other governments' policies and behaviors that are generally supportive of American foreign trade and security policy interests. As the current National Security Strategy asserts: "We now have a truly global economy linked by an instantaneous communications network, which offers increasing opportunities for American jobs and American investment. The community of democratic nations is growing, enhancing the prospects for political stability, peaceful conflict resolution, and greater dignity and hope for the people of the world."[22] Further, the Director of the U.S. Information Agency has stated recently: "In an increasingly interdependent world, with a fresh constellation of domestic and international forces at work to determine how nations act and react to the world around them, the use of public diplomacy represents a necessary and forward looking component of our foreign policy."[23]

In addition to traditional U.S. Government use of short-wave transmissions by Voice of America, Radio Free Europe and Radio Liberty, and more recently broadcasts by Radio and TV Marti, USIA now offers high-quality program material via satellite to anyone who wishes to download the signal. Its WORLDNET television service provides programming via satellite to U.S. Embassies worldwide for release to local media.

Public diplomacy does not depend solely upon government media capabilities. Rather, policy-makers can rely upon the fact that public statements will be picked up and relayed as part of private media broadcasts. This does not mean that there is a huge, government-controlled effort to manage the information that is fed to the domestic and foreign media. To the extent that the Administration believes that clear articulation of policy to the media will foster support for policy, it intends to ride the information highway for maximum benefit, thus bypassing—or augmenting normal state-to-state channels. Again to quote Dr. Duffy: "By expanding our reach beyond traditional government-to-government channels of communication, to overseas publics, we can communicate directly to their publics American interests and ideals, and in so doing lay the groundwork for the next American century."[24] Thus, we can see in this "legitimate" foreign policy function of government the paradox of purposeful erosion of a traditional criteria of national sovereignty.

Global Information

The overarching concept that drives the analysis of IW policy and practice must be that of the *global information infrastructure*. National control of information is tenuous—if possible at all. The same is true for Information Warfare.

Moreover, the global information infrastructure is becoming more ubiquitous. With the multiplicity of media, access, and service-providers comes a redundancy and survivability that challenge the notion of denial and disruption of service. The threshold of the Information Age saw the successful severing of Panamanian and later Iraqi C^3 and telecommunications, but the world has learned from these experiences. Aiding the learning process has been a steady erosion in the acquisition and operating costs of digital communications. Whether the threat is fire, flood, or Information Warfare, systems developers continually add new tools to their capabilities for assuring service via alternate routes and standby systems.

Sovereignty

Traditional Concepts. The nation-state—a derivative of an earlier great Information Revolution—combines the intangible *idea* of a people (a nation) with the tangible construct of a political and economic entity (a state). A state, under international law, possesses sovereignty. That means that the state is the final arbiter of order within its geographic confines; and the state is required, as a basic and fundamental attribute, to defend its physical integrity. Both requirements depend upon force: internally, the ability to compel minimal order and obedience to laws; externally, the ability to deter or defeat foreign threats to the interests and existence of the state. Further, the state traditionally has the sole responsibility for dealing with other states.

Erosion of Traditional Concepts. Increasingly, the traditional attributes of the nation-state are being eroded, and much of this erosion is a result of information technology. The state will not be able—in the age of information violence—to dominate the means of force, nor will any state be able to deter or defend against information attack. States also are no longer the only—or necessarily the most important—actors in the international arena. Increasingly, non-state actors deal across state boundaries with each other and with states on a nearly independent footing. There is a general erosion of the concept of sovereignty. While some nation-states are "failing" because they cannot fulfill the basic traditional criteria of sovereignty, mature and successful states also are witnessing a similar erosion of traditional controls, largely as a result of the effects of information technology. The state will not fade away. States will remain as primary and important actors in the international arena, but they will represent only one of many forms of political organization, power, and interaction.[25]

Virtual Community

There is developing today a concept of virtual communities.[26] These are associations of people who communicate with each other in cyberspace because they have common interests, irrespective of "national" identification. There has long been this sort of transnational communication between people with common professional and avocational interests. Today, however, the capability afforded by the Internet enables literally anyone to form such associations—really networks—and relationships. Such communications may foster human understanding. But, because their fundamental attribute is ability to bypass traditional hierarchies, they could complicate nation-state policies—or render state barriers increasingly irrelevant to growing numbers of people. On the other hand, the Internet provides a fine mechanism for the expression and organization of political and social discontent and opposition.

In a symposium on the Internet held at the ITU Telecom 95 quadrennial, global telecommunications conference, it was suggested from the audience that the International Telecommunications Union, a function of the United Nations, grant the privilege of individual membership, including a subscription to the Internet. It was seen as part of a grass-roots, global village effort to *connect* the world (theme of Telecom 95) and extend the Internet into true global ubiquity.

Crime/Rules of Evidence

Since the first wave of hacker break-ins against U.S. telephone companies, the country's law enforcement and judicial systems have struggled to define the crime, show evidence of loss to the victim, and show a convincing path back to the accused perpetrator. The process has only recently gained enough statutory authority, appropriate investigative techniques, and prosecutorial (and judicial) savvy, to make headway. Juries still have great difficulty determining whether alleged losses are serious enough to warrant criminal sanction, and whether victims are culpable for failure to adequately defend their property.

1996 marks the first use of a wiretap to document the actions of a criminal using a computer to illegally enter privately-owned networks for theft and malicious destruction. New legislation has created additional statutory authority for combating computer crime in each of the last three Congresses. At issue now is whether the new authority is enough, or too much.

Investigative Techniques

In The Cuckoo's Egg, Clifford Stoll recounts the techniques he and neophyte law enforcement authorities used to track the people who broke into his computer network.[27] There is now a major computer crime division in the Department of Justice. At least one prosecutor in the Chicago area has parlayed his hard-won experience at tracking computer crime in the late 1980s to garner national repute as an instructor in investigational and judicial preparation of computer crime cases. There are now private investigators who conduct their business solely on computers, and the U.S. Army has begun training its counter-intelligence and counter-espionage agents in "digital tradecraft."

Technology must further assist this process. More fidelity is needed in the development of pattern recognition and correlation systems by network analysts and managers, so that unambiguous pointers may be made to the fact and source of electronic attack. There also is need for law enforcement agencies and the courts to develop guidelines and procedures to insure privacy of individual and corporate electronic data and communications.

Intellectual Property

Two efforts define the issues of intellectual property in the age of digital telecommunications and Information Warfare. They are: the struggle of the Intelligence Community to adapt to the Internet as a source of intelligence information, and the attempts of the legal establishment to prosecute theft of intellectual property when the theft leaves no evidence of crime. In the former case, a community of analysts which requires broad access to published works, has come up against legions of information collectors and brokers who want to be paid for their value-added services.

Often these services are the mere writing of an article based on an interview with one or more public officials. The gathering of data to support just one position paper for a policy maker may touch one hundred or more such copyrighted sources. Fees for the use of a photo, passage or even an idea may be as high as the market will bear. The cheaper alternative may be limited to re-interviewing where possible.

For many of the original writers, the article in question is their only source of income—an increasingly common occurrence—as free-lance telecommuting journalists, working from home, ply their craft. The challenge is to compensate authors without either ballooning the cost of policy analysis, or dragging out the derivative publishing process by intermediate bargaining of permissions and fees.

In the latter case of legally sifting through the ownership of intangible ideas, the courts are faced with an avalanche of data. Much of it is parsed electronically with neither threads to the originator, nor clear distinctions that support unitary authorship. The problem is less in the novelty of the crime than in the magnitude of the purported losses. Historically, every publisher has routinely dealt with frustrated authors who see their original work from an obscure, unsolicited manuscript in the latest box-office smash, or on the best-seller list. Today, the problem is global and is magnified a thousand-fold. The answer will be in the necessity to broker rapid compromise in order to preclude a collapse of the judicial system from shear weight of cases.

Innovation

The future of Information Warfare will see a dizzying pace of innovation which escalates the art and practice of this form of belligerency. *Innovation* here is used to mean the creation of a prototype new tool or process of IW, either offensive or defensive. In this context, it differs from *development,* which focuses more on the bringing of the prototype to multiple users. The difference is that the development process allows serial looks at the prototype from several perspectives to enhance its value, improve its shortcomings, and prepare it for use in a systems context.

The process of moving from innovation to development has a cost in time which may significantly impact on escalating IW practice. Moreover, the movement to development is an artifact of organized government and industry. It is a process to limit collateral damage from unforeseen side-effects. As such, innovation by the attacker—who worries little about such things—is inherently a faster, less documented process.

If the process of innovation accrues more to the attacker than to organized resistance, what can the victim do to overcome his disadvantage? The answer must lie in analyzing whatever evidence remains of a new attack for pointers toward sloppy design or unintended side-effects that may assist in tracking, remediation or countermeasure development. The idea is to turn rapid prototyping against the designer-attacker.

Development

In the world of 2010, the art and practice of Information Warfare will have evolved to a point where many of the present issues will be overcome by events. The key needs—recognizing, responding and tracing an information attack—will have been developed. The specter of an alternative chaos will drive these developments out of necessity.

Like the strategic weapons of the Cold War Era, these developments will be overshadowed by new devices, techniques, countermeasures and challenges in unending rounds of escalation. Just as we tend to minimize the damage done by a single bullet, having been inured to the frequency of such attacks, we will minimize the effect of the low-rate digital attack. In 2010, the focus of IW will be the aggregation and loosing of mega-data to confuse entire information fusion systems. Summations of minuscule stratagems and partially-fused mega-files will unite with false-images and faked reactions to drive correlation and fusion engines toward false results.

These attacks will exploit weaknesses in the algorithms of artificial analysis. The shear volume of data will militate against a man-in-the-loop. Avoidance of surprise or mis-calculation will be the function of continually bringing on innovative, closely-guarded, short half-life improvements to pattern recognition subsystems and decision engines.

Security

Security becomes a transient state in digital warfare. In the past, information security was thought to be achievable by adherence to time-honored procedures and physical barriers—locking, unlocking, double-checking and double-wrapping. Now security begins with use of the latest software known to withstand contemporary digital attack, and ends with perfection of the newest escalation in attack mechanisms. The timelines for this cycle may soon be a matter of only hours or days.

Methods must be perfected which enable pattern recognition and surveillance of networks and computer servers for signs of failed security conditions. The problem is complex. It is compounded by successful methods of attack at all levels of commercial computer and network security. Ten years ago, NSA security experts preached that the only secure computer was a stand-alone unit. Today, following several rounds of firewalls, spoofers, packet sniffers, and failed key systems, one wonders if the statement is still valid.

While computer attack methods drive a spiraling round of measure and counter-measure, the Information Warfare community moves inexorably closer to adoption of the very "stovepiped" organizations and practices which it was designed to eliminate. Colonel Mike Tanksley, an Army pioneer in IW, served in the Desert Storm. He frequently lectured after the war on General Schwartzkopf's efforts to break the many stovepiped organizations under his command, in order to attain the level of lateral coordination he needed to pursue synchronized warfare. His was a success story which hinged largely upon force of personality. We cannot take such forcefulness for granted in the leadership of the next Information War.

Psychologists like Orin Clapp have been warning us for decades that the more compartmentation we bring to operations in which time is compressing, the more entropy we accrue. Entropy is a familiar term to the science of thermodynamics and to complexity theorists, who together recognize the opportunity cost of allowing energy to dissipate. It is an appropriate metaphor for the loss of combat energy which accrues from compartmentation of effort at the cost of synchronization. When measured objectively, the cost of compartmented security is most often found to be in excess of that needed to do the job. Compartmenting IW initiatives and tools is a sure way of guaranteeing that civilian industry is incapable of inoculating its networks against state-of-the-art attack mechanisms.

Nature of War, Conflict, and Force

The *purpose* of war will remain that of imposing one's will on one's opponents. The *nature* of war, however, *will change considerably*. For forces configured for Information Warfare, the preference will be for conflict that is dominated by the advanced nature of decision systems, and by more subtle means of waging war. Niche competitors will be able to operate in this environment. Forces configured for IW will have at their disposal a wider array of the means of destruction, but the nature of those mechanisms will result in a proliferating means of conflict. The traditional means of firepower and maneuver will be augmented—and perhaps in the long run will be replaced—by methods of attacking one's opponents with electronic technological methods. As Winn Schwartau points out, however, the ultimate outcome of applying those methods will not necessarily be free of lethal outcomes.[28]

Asymmetrical War: Hierarchy and Intensity

Throughout the Industrial Age, advanced military powers were beset by the difficulties attendant to combating inferior powers. Often, the inferior power either prevailed against the odds or made the cost—material, moral and political—of continuing the fight prohibitively high for the great power. In the information age, the superior power need not be hampered by such difficulties. The injunction is: "Don't fight a lower-level enemy with a lower level of warfare.[29] The impulse is understandable; but if the inferior power does not manifest the Third-Wave vulnerabilities associated with the Information Age, it is difficult to see how this injunction will be universally applicable.

Another proposition frequently offered is that: "If you are going to make war, then make it.[30] The argument is for all-out war, once the issue is joined. This proposition will be even more difficult for the great power to honor in the Information Age. Again the problem is that of asymmetrical warfare. The now-discarded term "low-intensity conflict" was apt, and the conundrum remains for the great power. There will be instances when, for the great power, the issue at the heart of the conflict is not a "survival" issue. For the lesser power, it frequently will be. While one may always caution the great power against engagement in such follies, the fact will remain that great powers will always face issues of a "world order" sort that will tempt them to apply muscle and prestige to its solution; but a fight to the death will not be reasonable. Judicious application of certain IW methods, however—such as global information campaigns, might provide an added edge to the effort.

Laws of War and Rules of Engagement

The laws of war are intended, *inter alia*, to preclude military action against non-combatants, refugees and displaced persons, and those who have laid down their arms. Under the Geneva Conventions, field commanders assume legal responsibilities for the care of such individuals within areas under military control. How does one define such an area in the intangible arena of Information War?

How does a commander segment his IW attack to preclude collateral damage to hospital patient care, or civil air traffic control systems? How is culpability assigned for errors of commission or omission? How is the soldier who mistakes an Airbus for a MIG shielded from the justice (or retribution) of a foreign nation or an international court?

Nations must develop their own policies, legal precepts, operational concepts, and rules of engagement for Information Warfare. It will then be necessary for nations to negotiate international Laws of War to account for this new war-form. Of course, this process will not account for the actions of non-state actors and cyber-terrorists, just as laws governing conventional conflict do not do so adequately.

Lethality, Effectiveness, and the Ends of War

Electronic means of combat in Information Warfare potentially will enable a sophisticated power to effectively neutralize an opponent without necessarily inflicting physical destruction upon the opponent's forces, infrastructure, and population. Increasingly, *the purpose of war can be separated from the means of war.* A nation's will can be inflicted upon the opponent without necessarily affecting widespread havoc. The force commander can accomplish *effectiveness* in combat, without necessarily being lethal about it. These proliferating means of conflict hold the prospect of devaluing the traditional ends of war. Theoretically, the crushing of front-line forces, destruction of national infrastructure, and occupation of territory might not be necessary to inflict one's will upon the opponent. The difficulty will arise in asymmetrical conflict. A second-wave opponent might not be convinced that he is beaten until his capital is occupied. IW theory and doctrine have not yet addressed this problem.

OODA-Loop/Decision Models

A decision model lies at the heart of the concept of Information Warfare. A derivation of Shannon's communications model that emerged at about the time of the development of the transistor in the late 1940s, decision science and cybernetics have grown markedly in the post-World War II "Age of Computers." In the 1970s, the principle was restated by Colonel John R. Boyd as the Orient-Operate-Decide-Action (OODA) Loop. The contributors here are agreed that IW is fundamentally an effort to influence or manipulate the flow of information from sensors or feedback mechanisms to the point of decision in an adversary's decision cycle.

If influence or manipulation by technical means is the *science* of Information Warfare, the *art* is in doing it in a predictable, timely, and consistent way. Without such attributes, IW may be only a support function of strategy. With such attributes, it could well be a strategy unto itself.

Peer and Niche Competitors

During the Cold War, America's strategic attention was riveted upon the Soviet Union, its only peer competitor. Much less attention was paid to China. Other policy challenges were largely subsumed within this construct. Regional and transnational issues (e.g., the Middle East and terrorism) were sorted out largely in terms of their relationship to the overarching Soviet threat. Since 1989-1991, the United States has had no peer competitor. This situation is traumatic for the garrison-state mechanisms such as the Defense Establishment and the Intelligence Community. In fact, it took both establishments some time to digest the fact that their reason for being had been severely challenged.

It is interesting to speculate about the prospects for a cutting-edge concept such as Information Warfare in light of the observations of Elin Whitney-Smith that, in the broad sweep of history, only peer competition seems to have fostered significant advancements in technology, tactics, strategy and organization for military establishments.[31] Perhaps what is different today is that technology has taken on a life of its own. Perhaps in the coming age, it will be commercial advances that will drive military innovation. If so, this situation would re-establish the dominant trend before the post-World War II garrison state period. Since the United States has numerous proximate and potential commercial peer competitors in information technology, perhaps this will drive continued military innovation in the Information Age.

There are robust indications that the American military—despite its inherent conserving and conservative tendencies—will not repeat its experiences of the inter-war period when it was seized with the design of the cavalry saber, when equestrian subjects predominated at the Army Command and Staff College, and Henry Arnold was discouraged from flying aeroplanes—and all of this in the face of the experience of Cambrai and German experiments in Spain.

Expectations

Where do we go from here?The practice of Information Warfare is being escalated and refined on a daily basis. Witness the numerous Internet bulletin boards which talk of computer attacks and vulnerabilities. Not so, however, the policy community.

If we are to pursue IW in terms of manageable strategy and tactics development, we must proceed from an early understanding of policy bounds. The analogy is to development of a laser that turns the quartz crystal of a tank range-finder opaque, while blinding the gunner in the process. The project was abandoned by the originating contractor when it was shown that the company culture did not permit develpment. Current developments in the realm of IW progress within the larger context of the latest Revolution in Military Affairs. The criteria for a complete RMA are threefold: development of an enabling technology (the what), development of a rationalizing doctrine for employing the technology (the why), and the design of new organizations for employing the technology in accordance with the doctrine (the how).

It is reasonable to assume that the fulfillment of the RMA will be even more chaotic than has been the case previously. Technology is developing very quickly. Doctrine is lagging, in part because of the speed of technological progress, and partly because of a paucity of policy guidance. Hence, sensible organizational reform is not in place. Comprehensive education and training is even more of a chimera.

Linear thinkers would ask that the process progress in an orderly manner from authoritative policy to doctrine to organizational innovation to operational employment. In the coming age, however, the process likely will develop in a more non-linear fashion.

In a system devoted to stability and continuity, there are few politicians and decision-makers who will readily grasp and support revolutionary change. Therefore, comprehensive and visionary policy will not likely to be proffered soon. An attempt to craft doctrine without policy guidance is a prescription for disaster—or at best embarrassment. Management in a vacuum is not acceptable in Information Warfare. Meanwhile, within the bounds of proper civil-military relations, policy and strategic guidance can be nudged and guided by information specialists, defense intellectuals, and military professionals.

Nonetheless, experimental doctrinal work must progress with evolving policy guidelines, and some organizational innovation can also proceed. The kinds of provocative articles that have appeared in professional publications over the past several years are appropriate in this regard, and they should continue. Certainly, widespread professional education must be conducted at all levels throughout the Defense Establishment and the Intelligence Community, with the purpose of encouraging widespread familiarity with concepts and issues. Within the limits of evolving policy and doctrine, there is a need for appropriate skill-producing training in all services and combat support agencies.

The authors and the contributors to this book hope that their efforts will go some way toward fostering the development of coherent policy, and will contribute to meaningful education in the developing art of Information Warfare.

Endnotes

1 See George J. Stein, "Information Warfare," in this volume.

2 See Alvin and Heidi Toffler, *War and Anti-War: Survival at the Dawn of the 21st Century,* Boston: Little, Brown and Company, 1993, particularly pp. 81-85.

3 See Alan D. Campen, "Coming to Terms With Information Warfare," in this volume.

4 Chairman of the Joint Chiefs of Staff Instruction 3210.01, 2 January 1996, p. 6. This rather labored definition has replaced the more common-sense 1994 definition: "actions taken to achieve information superiority in support of national military strategy by affecting adversary information and information systems while leveraging and protecting our information and information systems." This definition is much closer to that employed by, for instance, the Australian Defense Forces.

5 John Arquilla and David Ronfeldt, "Cyberwar Is Coming!" RAND P-7791, 1992, p. 2.

6 Ibid., p. 5.

7 Ibid., p. 6. It appears that the U.S. military establishment is having sufficient difficulty coping with the basic concept of Information Warfare that the terms cyberwar and netwar do not appear in doctrinal material.

8 See Philippe Baumard, "From InfoWar to Knowledge Warfare: Preparing for the Paradigm Shift," in this volume.

9 Response to a public question following his keynote address to the AFCEA Spring Symposium on Intelligence, 4 April 1996. Interestingly, Dr. Deutch did comment that he thought that the Defense and Justice Departments currently are the biggest "stakeholders" in the IW issue.

10 See John Petersen, "Information Warfare: The Future," in this volume.

11 See Michael L. Brown, "The Revolution in Military Affairs: The Information Dimension," in this volume.

12 See Brown, ibid.

13 See Robert David Steele, "Creating a Smart Nation: Information Strategy, Virtual Intelligence, and Information Warfare," in this volume.

14 Current proposals circulating in the House Permanent Select Committee on Intelligence to separate the "I" from "C^3I" at the Defense Department might prove to be a step backward. Whereas, the Navy and Marine Corps have completely integrated the C^4 and Intelligence functions at the service level.

15 See Chuck deCaro, "SOFTWAR," and Petersen and Brown, op.cit., in this volume.

16 Arquilla and Ronfeldt, op.cit., p. 3.

17 Pierre Thomas and Elizabeth Corcoran, "Argentine, 22, Charged With Hacking Computer Networks," *The Washington Post*, March 30, 1996, p. A-4.

18 See contributions by Baumard, Goodden, and Loescher, in this volume.

19 Tofflers, op. cit., p. 64.

20 It is interesting and significant that the steam railroad did not become an effective—much less efficient—means of transport until the application of the telegraph—an information technology—enabled the deconfliction of train schedules.

21 The authors wish to acknowledge the contributions of Mr. Charles A. Williamson regarding this issue.

22 A National Security Strategy of Engagement and Enlargement, The White House, February 1996, Preface, p. i.

23 Statement of the Director Dr. Joseph Duffy, U.S. Information Agency, Office of Public Liaison, 12 April 1996.

24 USIA, ibid.

25 The literature concerning this phenomenon is voluminous. For one of the best discussions, see: Walter B. Wriston, *The Twilight of Sovereignty: How the Information Revolution is Transforming Our World*, New York: Charles Scribner's Sons, 1992.

26 See, for example, Howard Rheingold, *The Virtual Community: Homesteading on the Electronic Frontier*, New York: Harper-Collins, 1993.

27 Cliff Stoll, *The Cuckoo's Egg: Tracking a Spy Through the Maze of Computer Espionage*, New York: Doubleday, 1989.

28 See Winn Schwartau, "Ethical Conundra of Information Warfare," in this volume.

29 Owen E. Jensen, "Information Warfare: Principles of Third-Wave War," *Airpower Journal* (Winter) 1994, p.41.

30 Jensen, ibid.

31 See Elin Whitney-Smith, "War, Information and History: Changing Paradigms," in this volume.

SELECTED READINGS ON INFORMATION WARFARE

Adam, John A., "Warfare in the Information Age," *IEEE Spectrum*, September 1991.

Andrews, Duane P., and Knecht, Ronald J., "Improving the Security of Information in DoD," 1994. Report prepared for the ASD C3I, DoD.

Arnett, Eric H., "Welcome to Hyperwar," *The Bulletin of the Atomic Scientists*, September 1992.

Arnold, H. D., et al, "Targeting Financial Systems as Centers of Gravity: 'Low Intensity to No Intensity' Conflict, Dept. of the Air Force, National Security Affairs, Maxwell AFB, Alabama, 1994.

Arquilla, John and Ronfeldt, David, "Cyberwar is Coming!" *Journal of Comparative Strategy, Volume 12, no. 2.*

Arquilla, John, "Strategic implications of information dominance," *Strategic Review, Summer 1994.*

Bankes, Steve, and Carl Builder, "Seizing the Moment: Harnessing the Information Technologies," *The Information Society*, Vol. 8, No. 1, 1992.

Beniger, James, *The Control Revolution*, Cambridge, MA: Harvard University Press, 1986.

Benedickt, Michael Ed., *Cyberspace—First steps*, MIT Press, Cambridge, 1991.

Berkowitz, Bruce D., "Warfare in the Information Age," Issues in Science and Technology, Fall 1995, National Academy of Sciences

Berry, F. Clifton, Jr., *Inventing the future: How science and technology transform our world*, Brassey's Inc., McLean, VA, 1993.

Biscone, Gregory A., Hawkins, James R. & Mauer, Anthony M.,"Campaigning for Information Dominance," Air Command and Staff College course materials, Maxwell AFB, AL.

Branscomb, Anne Wells, *Who Owns Information?*, Basic Books, Harper Collins, 1994.

Brodie, Bernard, From Crossbow to H-Bomb, Indiana University Press, 1973.

Bunker, Robert J., "Transition to Fourth Epoch War," *Marine Corps Gazette*, Sep '94.

Burnette, LCDR Gerald, "Information, The Battlefield of the Future," *Surface Warfare*, July/August 1995.

Canavan, Gregory, *Simulation, Computing, Information and Future Warfare,* Los Alamos National Laboratory, LA-12490-MS.

Campen, Alan D., ed., *The First Information War*, AFCEA International Press, Fairfax, VA, USA, October 1992.

---------"Information Warfare is Rife With Promise, Peril," *Signal,* November 1993.

---------"Technology Trumps Policy in Information," *Signal*, February 1994.

---------"Competition, Consumers Are Shaping Information Highway," *Signal*, March 1994.

----------"National and Private Interests Clash Over Information Security Policy," *Signal*, May 1994.

----------"The Change From Firepower to Knowledge Power," Chapter 18 in *The Science of Command and Control, Volume III: Coping With Change*, AFCEA International Press, Fairfax, Virginia, 1994.

Campen, Alan D. "Rush to Information-Based Warfare Gambles with National Security," *Signal*, July 1995.
----------"Vulnerability of Info Systems Demands Immediate Action," *National Defense*, November 1995.
---------"Personal Information Watchman and Things That Go Bump in the Night," *Signal*, February 1996.
Chairman of the Joint Chiefs of Staff (CJCS) Memorandum of Policy (MOP) 30, Command and Control Warfare, 8 March 1993.
Clapper, James R. and Trevino, Eben H. Jr. "Critical Security Dominates Information Warfare Moves," *Signal* March 1995).
Cohen, Eliot A., "A Revolution in Warfare," *Foreign Affairs*, March/April 1996.
Cohen, Frederick B., "Protection and Security on the Information Superhighway."
Cook, W. C., *Information Warfare: A New Dimension in the Application of Air and Space Power,* Air War College, April 1993.
Cooper, Pat & Oliveri, Frank, "Air Force Carves Operational Edge in Info Warfare," *Defense News*, 21-27 August 1995.
Cooper, Jeffrey R. "The Coherent Battlefield: Removing the 'Fog of War': A Framework for Understanding an MTR of the 'Information Age.'" SRS Technologies, June 1993.
"Computer System Intrusion Threat Fuels Information Security Debate." *National Defense* October 1995.
"Cornerstones of Information Warfare," United States Air Force White Paper. (undated, but 1995)
"Data Security, Special Report," *IEEE Spectrum*, August 1992.
Dearth, Douglas H., and Goodden, R. Thomas, eds. *Strategic Intelligence: Theory and Application*, U.S. Army War College, Second ed 1995.
Defense Science Board. Report of the Defense Science Board Summer Study Task Force on Information Architecture for the Battlefield. Defense Technical Information Center, AD-A285745, October 1994.
DeLanda, Manuel, *War in the Age of the Intellligent Machines*, New York: Zone Books, 1991.
Der Derian, James, "Cyber-deterrence," *Wired* 2.09, 1994.
DiNardo, R. L. and Hughes, Daniel J., "Some Cautionary Thoughts on Information Warfare," *Airpower*. 1995.
Dishong, D. J., *Studying the Effect of Information Warfare on C2 Decision Making*, Naval Postgraduate School, June 1994.
Dretske, Fred., *Knowledge and the Flow of Information*, MIT Press, Cambridge Massachusets. 1981.
Dunlap, Charles J., Jr., "How We Lost The High-Tech War of 2007," *The Weekly Standard*, January 29, 1996.
Elam, Donald, LT USN, et al, "*Information Warfare: A Revolution in Modern Warfighting Concepts*," unpublished paper prepared for EO 3802, Electronic Warfare Computer Applications, Naval Postgraduate School, June 5, 1995.

Elliot, Ronald D. & Bradley, Scott, *Effective Command and Control: Affordable Revolutionary Opportunities to Improve Modern Defense Capabilities*, undated.
Emmett, Peter C., SqdLdr, "Software warfare: The militarization of logic," *Joint Force Quarterly*, Summer 1994.
Felker, Ed. "Information Warfare: A View of the Future." A Common Perspective: *Joint Warfighting Center Newsletter*, September 1995).
FitzGerald, Mary C., "Russian Views on Information Warfare," Army, May 1994.
FM 100-6 (draft), "Information Operations," Department of the Army, July 1995.
Fogleman, General Ronald R., "Fundamentals of Information Warfare— An Airman's View," Air Force Update 95-09.
Fogleman, General Ronald R., "Information Operations: The Fifth Dimension of War," *Defense Issues*, Volume 10, Number 47.
Forester, Tom, The Information Technology Revolution, The MIT Press, Cambridge, Mass., 1985.
Garigue, Robert., "Information Warfare Concepts," Draft 2.0, DSIS DND Government of Canada, 1995. (Recommended and available on the Internet)
Gelernter, David, *Mirror Worlds, or the Day Software Puts the Universe in a Shoebox...How It Will Happen and What It Will Mean*, New York: Oxford University Press, 1991.
Geyelin, Milo. "Why Many Businesses Can't Keep Their Secrets." *The Wall Street Journal*, 17 November 1995.
Grier, Peter, "Information Warfare," *Air Force*, March 1995.
Griffith, Thomas E., Jr., Strategic Attack of National Electrical Systems, Air University.
Hammes, Thomas X., "Evolution of war: The fourth generation," *Marine Corps Gazette,* September 1994.
Hasslinger, Karl M., Commander USN, "Information Warfare: What is the Threat?" November, 1995. Paper submitted as elective requirement to U.S. Naval War College.
Hughes, Wayne P., "*Command and Control Within the Framework of a Theory of Combat,*" Naval Postgraduate School.
Hunter, Roger C., "Disabling Systems and the Air Force," *Airpower Journal*, Fall 1994.
Hurska, Jan., *Computer Viruses and Anti-Virus Warfare*, Ellis Horwood Publishers. New York 1990.
Hust, Gerald R., "Taking Down Telecommunications," Air University.
Hutcherson, N. B., *Command and Control Warfare: Putting Another Tool in the War-Fighter's Data Base,* Air University, September 1994.
"The Information Advantage," *Economist,* 10 June 1995.
"Information Architecture for the Battlefield," Defense Science Board Summer Study Task Force, October 1994.
"Information Warfare: Pouring the Foundation," United States Air Force White Paper (draft), 19 December 1994.
"Information Warfare: Legal, Regulatory, Policy and Organizational Considerations for Assurance, July 1995. Research report for the Joint Chiefs of Staff.
Jensen, Owen E., "Information warfare: Principles of third-wave war," *Airpower Journal,* Winter 1994.

Joint Publication 3-13 (draft), *Joint Doctrine for Command and Control Warfare (C2W): Battlefield Application of Information Warfare*, March 1995.
Kabay, M. E. "Prepare Yourself For Information Warfare." *Computer World* March 1995.
Kelly, Kevin, *Out of Control: The rise of neo-biological civilization*, Addison-Wesley, 1994.
Kraus, George F. Jr., *"Information Warfare in 2015," Proceedings*, August 1995.
Krepinevich, Andrew F., "Keeping pace with the Military-Technological Revolution,*" Issues in Science & Technology*, Summer 1994.
------------- "Cavalry to Computer: The pattern of military revolutions," *The National Interest*, Fall 1994.
"Leveraging the Infosphere: Surveillance and Reconnaissance in 2020," *Airpower Journal*, Summer 1995.
Lewonowski, M. C., "Information War," Air War College, 1991.
Libicki, Martin C., *The Mesh and the Net: Speculations on Armed Conflict in a time of free silicon*, National Defense University, 1994.
---------, "What is Information Warfare?" National Defense University, August 1995.
Libicki, Martin C. & James A Hazlett, "Do We Need an Information Corps?" *JFQ*, Autumn 1993.
-------- "The Revolution in Military Affairs" *Strategic Forum,* November 1994.
Luoma, William M., "Netwar: The Other Side of Information Warfare," Naval War College, 8 February 1994.
Mann, Edward, "Desert Storm: The first information war?," *Airpower Journal* Winter 1994.
Marshall, Andrew W., "Some Thoughts on Military Revolutions - Second Version," Office of Net Assessment Memorandum for the Record, 23 August 1993.
Mazarr, Michael, et al, The Military Technical Revolution: a structural framework, Centre for Strategic and International Studies, 1993.
Minihan, Kenneth A., "Information Dominance: Meeting the Intelligence Needs of the 21st Century," *American Intelligence Journal*, Spring/Summer 1994.
Molander, Roger C., et al, "*Strategic Information Warfare: A New Face of War*," RAND National Defense Research Institute, November 1995.
Munro, Neil. "The Pentagon's New Nightmare: An Electronic Pearl Harbor," *Washington Post*, 16 July 1995.
National Computer Security Association, Information Security Catalog, Spring 1996. (Lists 40 new books, conference proceedings and periodicals on computer and information security.) e-mail contact<wharper@ncsa.com.
Nye, Joseph S., Jr., and Owens, William A., "America's Information Edge," *Foreign Affairs*, March/April 1996.
OPNAVINST 3430.26, Implementing Instruction for Information Warfare/Command and Control Warfare (IW/C2W), 18 January 1995.
Peterson, John, *The Road to 2015: Profiles of the Future*, Waite Group Press, 1994.

Peterson, Major M. J., "Diving in Headfirst: The Air Force and Information Warfare," *Air Chronicles.*
"Policing Cyberspace," *U.S. News & World Report*, January 23, 1995.
Power, Richard. "CSI Special Report on Information Warfare." *Computer Security Journal 11, No 2* (October 1995).
The President's National Security Telecommunications Advisory Committee (NSTAC). Fact Sheet (26 February 1996).
Probst, David K., "Now HPCC, and Their Impact on a Unified Strategic Military Doctrine for U.S. National Defense Through the Year 2015," 1995.
Rona, Thomas, "Weapon Systems and Information War," July 1976, Boeing Aerospace Company. (possibly the first use of term Information Warfare.)
Ronfeldt, David, "*Cyberocracy Is Coming,*" *The Information Society*, Vol. 8, #4, 1992.
Rosen, Stephen, Winning the Next War—Innovation and the Modern Military, Cornell University Press, 1991.
Rothrock, John, "Information Warfare: Time for Some Constructive Skepticism?," *American Intelligence Journal*, Spring/Summer 1994.
Ryan, Donald E., Jr., "Implications of information-Based warfare," *Joint Force Quarterly,* Autumn-Winter 1994-1995.
Schwartau, Winn. *Information Warfare: Chaos on the Electronic Superhighway.* New York: Thunder Mouth Press, 1994.
Science Application International Corporation (SAIC), "Planning Considerations for Defensive Information Warfare—Information Assurance ," 16 December 1993.
Scott, William B., "Information Warfare Demands New Approach," *Aviation Week & Space Technology*, 13 March 1995.
Skukman, David, *The Sorcerer's Challenge: Fears and Hopes for the Weapons of the next Millennium,* Hodder & Stoughton, 1995.
Smith, K. B., "Crisis and Opportunity of Information War," Army Command and General Staff College, 6 May 1994.
"The Softwar Revolution: The Ties that Bind," *Economist*, 10 June 1995.
"Special Report on Information Warfare," *Computer Security Journal*, Fall 1995.
Steele, Robert D., "*The Military Perspective on Information Warfare: Apocalypse Now*", Keynote Speech to Second International Conference on Information Warfare, 19 January 1995.
--------- "*The Transformation of War and the Future of the Corps,*" 28 April 1992.
--------- "*War and Peace in the Age of Information (*Text)," Superintendent's Guest Lecture, Naval Postgraduate School, 17 August 1993.
Stein, George J., *Information War—Cyberwar—Netwar*, Air University.
-------- "Information Warfare," *Airpower Journal,* Spring 1995.
Sullivan, Gordon, and Coralles, Anthony M. "The Army in the Information Age." Carlisle Barracks: Strategic Studies Institute, 1995.
Sullivan, Gordon, and Dubik, James M. "War in the Information Age." Landpower Essay Series 94-4, Arlington, Va: AUSAInstitute of Land Warfare, 1994.
Thompson, Mark, "If War Comes Home," *Time*, 21 August 1995.

Toffler, Alvin & Heidi, *War and Anti-War: Survival at the dawn of the 21st Century,* Little, Brown, 1993.
Vickers, Michael G, "*A concept for theater warfare in 2020,*" Office of Net Assessment, 1993.
Waller, Douglas, "America's Persuader in the Sky," *Time*, 21 August 1995.
--------- "Onward Cyber Soldiers," *Time*, 21 August 1995.
"White Paper on Information Infrastructure Assurance." Prepared by the staff of the Security Policy Board, December, 1995),.

This reading list was drawn from the resources of the School of Information Warfare and Strategy, at The National Defense University; the Naval Postgraduate School: and, postings on the C4I-Pro list on the Internet.

About the Authors

Adams, James, is Washington Bureau Chief of *The Sunday Times of London*, reporting on American politics, terrorism, international relations, and intelligence matters. He previously served as Managing Editor of *The Sunday Times* and as its defense correspondent. He is the author of 12 books of non-fiction and has recently completed the first of a series of post-Cold War espionage novels, and the first of a series of screenplays for Interactive CD-ROM. He can be reached at <72360.3524@compuserve.com

Baumard, Philippe, is the former Secretary of the Commission of Economic Intelligence and Corporate Strategies, 1993-1994. He co-authored the Committee Report that led to the creation of the Committee of Economic Security and Competitiveness (CCSE). Dr. Baumard authored 4 books on organization and strategic management of knowledge, including *Puzzled Organizations*, forthcoming by SAGE Publications (London, New York) in 1997. He is former Visiting Scholar of New York University, the University of Technology, Sydney and Oxford University. He can be reached at <pbaumard@paris9.dauphine.fr

Brown, Michael L., is a retired Army officer at the Strategic Assessments Center of Science Applications International Corporation in McLean, Virginia. He has served as Military Assistant to the Director of Net Assessments in the Office of the Secretary of Defense, as well as Special Assistant to the Supreme Allied Commander in Europe, and the Secretary of the Army. He holds a PhD from Harvard. He can be reached at <mike_brown@cpqm.saic.com

Campen, Alan D. is Manager of AFCEA International Press and adjunct professor at the School of Information Warfare and Strategy, National Defense University. He was contributing editor of *The First Information War* and writes for *SIGNAL* magazine. He was Director C^2 Policy, office of the undersecretary of defense, policy. He can be reached at <AlanC3398@aol.com

de Caro, Charles, is the founding President and CEO of Aerobureau Corporation in McLean, Virginia and a former Special Assignments Correspondent for Cable News Network. He has worked for regional news organizations and is a former member of the U.S. Army Special Forces and is a graduate of the University of Rhode Island.

Dearth, Douglas H., teaches at the Joint Military Intelligence Training Center in Washington, D.C. A veteran of 25 years in the intelligence business, he has served on the faculty of the U.S. Army War College, as advisor to the Commander-in-Chief of U.S. Special Operations Command, and as Special Assistant to the Executive Director of the Defense Intelligence Agency. He is the co-editor of *Strategic Intelligence: Theory and Application* and lectures widely in the U.S. and Canada on military and intelligence matters and issues of world change. Mr. Dearth served in both military and civilian capacities in the Republic of Viet Nam and holds degrees in Political Science and International Relations from The Ohio State University. He is also a graduate of the Army War College. He can be reached at <dhdearth@aol.com.

Denning, Dorothy E., is Professor of Computer Science at Georgetown University, Washington, DC. She received the Ph.D. degree in Computer Science from Purdue, was a member of the research staff at Digital Equipment Corporation Systems Research Center, a Senior Staff Scientist at SRI, and an Associate Professor of Computer Science at Purdue University. She is past President of the International Association for Cryptologic Research; the author of *Cryptography and Data Security,* and numerous papers on information security. She can be reached at <denning@cs.georgetown,edu.

Goodden, Royal Thomas, is Principle Member of the Technical Staff at The Analytic Sciences Corporation and Visiting Professor in Strategic Intelligence at the Joint Military Intelligence College. His PhD in Public Administration is from George Mason University. He specializes in market research and analysis for the telecommunications industry. He has worked on national security issues in both government and private industry. A former faculty member at the U.S. Army War College, he is co-editor of *Strategic Intelligence: Theory and Application* He can be reached at <goodden@adams.patriot.net

Kerr, James, is an Electronics Engineer assigned to the Information Assurance Branch, Office of the Manager, National Communications System, and has worked on National Communications Security and Emergency Preparedness telecommunications matters since 1988. He has a Bachelor of Science Degree in Electrical Engineering from Pennsylvania State University and is pursuing a Master's Degree in Information Systems at George Mason University.

Knecht, Ronald, is with Science Applications International Corporation, in McLean, Virginia. He was special assistant to the Assistant Secretary of Defense C^{3}I in 1993-95. He can be reached at <RON_KNECHT@cpqm.saic.com

Kuehl, Daniel, is a professor at the School of Information Warfare and Strategy at the National Defense University, in Washington, D.C. He is a retired Air Force officer with wide experience in nuclear planning and airpower doctrine. He holds a PhD in history from Duke University, and can be reached at <kuehld@ndu.edu.

Libicki, Martin, is a Senior Fellow in the Institute for National Strategic Studies at the National Defense University, in Washington, D.C. He is the author of several books and articles on information warfare. His recent works include: *What Makes Industries Strategic* (McNair Paper 5, November 1989), on technology development and vulnerability; *The Common Byte*, on information technology standards; and *The Mesh and the Net* (McNair Paper 28, March 1994), on the impact of new information technology on war and national security; and *What is Information Warfare?* (1995). He can be reached at <libickim@ndu.edu.

Loescher, Michael, Commander USN, is Director of Strategic Planning, Office of the Deputy Assistant Secretary of the Navy (C^4I). He is the author of Navy's Copernicus Architecture, which in 1989 provided both the underpinnings for modern naval command and control, and became the functional basis for C^4I for the Warrior. He is the author, with VADM A. K. Cebrowski, of Navy's Information Warfare doctrine. He has been repeatedly honored for his writings, including AFCEA Author of the Year and twice selected by Federal Computer Week as one of the top 100 Federal Employees for his contributions to government information systems. He can be reached at <loescherms.nimitz@NAVAIR.NAVY.MIL

MacDoran, Peter F., is associated with International Series Research, Inc., Boulder, Colorado. He can be reached at <pmacdorn@isrinc.com.

Petersen, John L., is President and founder of The Arlington Institute in Arlington, Virginia, a research and policy institution specializing in the changing nature of security. He is a veteran of naval service in Viet Nam and the Persian Gulf. He has worked in presidential campaigns and has served on the National Security Council staff and in the Office of the Secretary of Defense. He is the author of *The Road to 2015*. He can be reached at <71650.144@compuserve.com.

Rona, Thomas, is adjunct professor at the School of Information Warfare and Strategy, National Defense University. He was a physics professor at MIT and served on the staff of the undersecretary of defense for policy, Department of Defense, and in the White House Office of Science and Technology.

Schwartau, Winn, is Executive Director of Interpact, Inc., in Seminole, Florida and often referred to as the civilian architect of Information Warfare. He is a lecturer and author of *Information Warfare: Chaos on the Information Highway*, *Terminal Compromise*, *The Complete Internet Business Toolkit*, and the forthcoming update to *Information Warfare.* He is co-organizer of the annual InfoWarCon symposium. He can be reached at <winn@infowar.com.

Steele, Robert D. is founding Chairman and CEO of Open Source Solutions Group in Oakton, Virginia. He is a former Marine Corps officer and clandestine services officer. He is the author of numerous articles promoting change in the intelligence profession, improving exploitation of open-source information, and the creation of a national information policy. He holds graduate degrees in International Relations and Public Administration, and is a graduate of the Naval War College. He can be reached at <ceo@oss.net.

Stein, George J., PhD Indiana University, is Chairman of the Department of Conflict & Change, and Professor of European Studies at the Air War College, Maxwell AFB, Alabama. He taught in the School of Interdisciplinary Studies, Miami University, Oxford, Ohio. His most recent publication is "Information Warfare - Netwar - Cyberwar," in: B.R. Schneider & L.E. Grinter (eds.), *Battlefield of the Future: 21st Century Warfare Issues,* (Air University. Press, 1995) He can be reached at <gstein@max1.au.af.mil.

Szafranski, Richard, Colonel USAF, is the first National Military Strategy Chair of the Air War College. He has served as a commander and staff officer in Strategic Air Command, North American Space Command, U.S. Space Command, and Air Force Space Command. He commanded B-52 units at the squadron and wing level, most recently as commander of the 7th Bomb Wing. He can be reached at <rszafranski@max1.au.af.mil

Whitney-Smith, Elin, is currently affiliated with the Institute for Social and Organizational Learning at George Washington University. She has taught at San Jose State, George Washington, and Old Dominion Universities; and has been a consultant to several federal domestic and military organizations. Her doctorate in Engineering Management was taken at Old Dominion. She can be reached at <elin@tmn.com and at http://www.well.com/user/elin.

Williamson, Charles A. is responsible for public diplomacy policy in the Office of the Secretary of Defense in Washington, D.C. He is a retired career Air Force officer, with 28 years service in Viet Nam, Japan, and the United States, dealing with intelligence and psychological operations. He formerly served as Deputy J-2 and as J-9 at U.S. Special Operations Command. Mr. Williamson holds degrees from Miami University of Ohio and Michigan State University, and is a graduate of the NATO Defense College and the DIA Post-Graduate Intelligence program.